T0367309

American Justice in the Age of Innocence

Understanding the Causes of Wrongful Convictions and How to Prevent Them

Sandra Guerra Thompson,
Jennifer L. Hopgood
&
Hillary K. Valderrama, Editors

2011

A Project of the
Criminal Justice Institute
University of Houston Law Center
Sandra Guerra Thompson,
Director.

iUniverse, Inc.
Bloomington

American Justice in the Age of Innocence

Understanding the Causes of Wrongful Convictions and How to Prevent Them

iUniverse books may be ordered through booksellers or by contacting:
iUniverse
1663 Liberty Drive
Bloomington, IN 47403
www.iuniverse.com
1-800-Authors (1-800-288-4677)

ISBN: 978-1-4620-1410-1 (sc)
ISBN: 978-1-4620-1411-8 (hc)
ISBN: 978-1-4620-1409-5 (ebk)

Library of Congress Control Number: 2011909628

Printed in the United States of America

iUniverse rev. date: 06/14/2011

CONTENTS

I. Introduction

The American criminal justice system is a delicate and intricate system that balances the needs of communities across the nation with the rights of criminal suspects. Understandably, for many years the system's focus has been on guilt: what standard of proof must be met to prove guilt, what may or may not be used to prove guilt, or whether guilt of other crimes may be used to prove guilt in the instant case. But, due in large part to the exoneration of over two hundred wrongfully convicted individuals across the United States, the focus is increasingly shifting to innocence. In the face of the disturbing realization that the system has failed so many, there is a renewed interest in making sure that the innocent are protected from wrongful conviction and recognition that existing safeguards are insufficient to meet this goal.

With this renewed interest in innocence growing in courtrooms and legislatures across the nation, difficult questions emerge. What does American justice in the age of innocence look like? What procedural mechanisms can be adopted to ensure the integrity of the system while preserving its effectiveness in protecting the community it serves? What factors lead to wrongful convictions, and how can they be avoided? What procedures could be adopted to provide effective relief to those who have been wrongfully convicted? Though there are no easy answers to these questions, the authors in this collection provide insightful articles collecting research and making suggestions for improvement to the criminal justice system. This anthology provides information about what factors cause wrongful convictions, how the adversary system can be improved through increased discovery,* and why creating avenues to uncover actual innocence is a vital part of this new focus. It is dedicated to providing policymakers with the information needed to make informed decisions about what American justice in the age of innocence should look like.

Though there are multiple causes of wrongful convictions, several culprits stand out. Eyewitness identifications, custodial interrogations and confessions, jailhouse informants, and the use of questionable forensic science have all been linked to wrongful convictions. Erroneous eyewitness identifications are linked to approximately three-quarters of all DNA exonerations. Authors Brian Harrison and Christina M. Griffin describe the dangers of current identification techniques and suggest changes to minimize those dangers in the future. Harrison suggests such changes as increasing the use of reliable identification procedures (such as double-blind and sequential line-ups), requiring authorities to obtain a confidence statement from the eyewitness at the time of the identification, and ensuring that all non-suspects in any line-up bear some resemblance to the eyewitness's previous description of the culprit (rather than resembling the suspect). As a final measure, he recommends that any identification that does not follow these guidelines should be excluded from court. Griffin further addresses the "best practices" recommended for reducing erroneous identifications. She addresses the implementation of these changes at the state level by comparing the different legislative approaches and policy standards used by states. She analyzes the different approaches and suggests what would work best in Texas, thus tailoring a path for reform in Texas, as well as other states considering procedural reforms.

Next, Tanya Broholm and Hillary Valderrama discuss custodial interrogations and confessions. Custodial interrogations are intended to produce a true and accurate account of events from suspects, but there is ample evidence that many of the interrogation procedures currently employed create a danger of false confessions. Once considered a rare occurrence, the work of innocence projects around the country has conclusively demonstrated that false confessions happen with some

* In criminal cases, discovery refers to the efforts of each side to obtain information before trial through demands for production of documents such as police reports, photographs, the results of forensic testing, statements attributed to the defendant, and potential witnesses.

frequency and are also linked to wrongful convictions. More problematic still is the fact that jurors accord confession evidence disproportionate weight in delivering their verdicts. Broholm describes several cases involving false confessions and concludes that videotaping interrogations in their entirety is necessary to safeguard the rights of the accused and the integrity of the criminal justice system. It also gives the judiciary more reliable evidence to evaluate motions to suppress confessions. Valderrama details various risk factors linked to false confessions. She proposes the elimination of several popular interrogation practices (such as minimization, maximization, and the use of falsified evidence), videotaping interrogations in their entirety, and creating procedural mechanisms to ensure that only reliable confessions are presented to jurors.

The use of jailhouse informants or "snitches" presents yet another opportunity for reform. As Matthew Gilliam discusses, due to the fact that such informants are frequently offered substantial reductions in their sentences in return for their testimony, they have strong incentives to fabricate confessions. As a result, jailhouse informants are among the leading causes of wrongful convictions in the United States. Gilliam advances Illinois' legislation regarding the use of jailhouse informants as a model for other states. He also concludes that rigorous compliance with the letter and spirit of the mandates of *Brady v. Maryland* requires that prosecutors diligently provide defendants with exculpatory* evidence regarding jailhouse informants. Such information could include the informant's criminal history, any other statements made by the informant, and whether the informant has ever testified for the prosecution before in another criminal trial. Establishing clear boundaries for the use of jailhouse informants and giving defense counsel impeachment evidence regarding the informant ensures that only sufficiently reliable testimony is presented to the jury and that the jury has adequate information to evaluate the credibility of that testimony.

After addressing the causes of wrongful convictions, this anthology shifts its focus to methods for improving the adversary system through discovery. Adequate information regarding the opposing party's case is

* Refers to evidence which has a tendency to justify or excuse an accused defendant's actions and which will tend to show the defendant is not guilty or has no criminal intent.

essential in any litigation, and criminal cases are no exception. Recently, there has been a growing movement to statutorily require prosecutors to maintain "open file" policies under which they provide the contents of their files to the defense counsel. However, less attention has been paid to defense disclosure and under what circumstances defense attorneys should be required to open their file to the prosecution. Ryan King discusses the merits of reciprocal discovery and provides recommendations for the implementation of such a system. Specifically, King addresses the Texas Senate Bill 560 proposed in 2005, which would have created disclosure obligations for both the prosecution and defense attorneys that far surpass current requirements. But it did not pass. He argues that this law deserves further consideration. By requiring disclosure of these types of information for both the defense and prosecution, courts will be able to better fulfill their role in "seeking the truth" and discourage "trial by surprise" for either side.

The final section of this anthology is dedicated to providing relief to those the system has failed by creating avenues to discover actual innocence. In the absence of a state's affirmative commitment to seek out wrongful convictions, wrongfully convicted individuals may never be identified or successful in seeking relief. Jennifer Hopgood discusses the difficulties inherent in seeking relief for wrongful convictions, even where DNA evidence is available to a defendant. Despite the availability of a state statute ostensibly providing for access to DNA evidence, Hopgood finds that individuals pursuing claims of wrongful convictions in Texas experience great difficulty in obtaining access to the DNA evidence that could exonerate them. Her research suggests that even a mechanism providing access to DNA evidence may only nominally increase an individual's ability to obtain relief for a wrongful conviction. Additional measures are needed, and statutes providing for such access are not adequate substitutes for concerted, systematic efforts to identify and resolve claims of actual innocence.

Finally, Yesoro Olowo-Okello and Emily Earthman Ziemba make convincing arguments in favor of state innocence commissions that affirmatively seek to identify and rectify wrongful convictions. Olowo-Okello takes a closer look at the habeas appeals system as contrasted with the creation of an "innocence commission," which is specifically tasked with uncovering wrongful convictions. Habeas appeals are highly technical and subject to a myriad of rules as to what claims can be pursued, the timeline for pursuing such claims, and whether later-discovered claims may be raised after an initial habeas appeal is filed. Procedural requirements inherent in the habeas process often preclude effective relief if evidence of innocence is discovered late in the process. Olowo-Okello concludes that habeas petitions are insufficient to address the problem of wrongful convictions and argues for the creation of an innocence commission in the style of North Carolina's, the only one of its kind.

Ziemba concludes this anthology with a comparative discussion of innocence commissions in the United Kingdom and Canada. She argues that the rising number of exonerees clearly points to the need for a systematic reform in the criminal justice system, and that innocence commissions are a vital component of such systems. She examines the different structures and rules that operate within the Canadian and British models and makes the case for certain aspects of each to be adopted in the development of innocence commissions in this country.

Readers will notice that a number of the articles in this anthology address Texas law to a greater or lesser degree. This project originated as a class exercise at the University of Houston Law Center. The articles were intended to be offered as a resource tool for the Timothy Cole Advisory Panel on Wrongful Convictions (TCAP). The TCAP was created by the Texas legislature in 2009 to study the causes of wrongful convictions and to make suggestions for legislative reform. The panel plans to release its findings and recommendations before the session of the Texas Legislature beginning in January 2011. The lessons in this collection of articles, while providing invaluable insights for the TCAP, also have much to offer policymakers in other states as well. The research in Jennifer Hopgood's article on access to DNA testing, for example, while directly applicable only to Texas, serves as an important cautionary tale for other jurisdictions. It is simply not safe to assume that any prisoner who requests DNA testing of evidence in his or her case will obtain such testing. Do state statutes give an appropriate level of access to DNA testing? Are courts properly interpreting those statutes? These are important questions, and researchers should consider replicating Hopgood's work for other states.

While the prospect of reforming the criminal justice system in order to prevent wrongful convictions may be daunting, it is both a necessary and attainable goal. Several of the reforms proposed by the authors have already been implemented in domestic or international jurisdictions and may cost relatively little. Others may require more thorough intervention from state legislatures. However, given the incredibly high cost of wrongful convictions as described in this anthology, these investments are worthwhile and will pay dividends by restoring the public's confidence in the justice system. Whatever measures are ultimately adopted, accuracy and fairness should be hallmarks of American justice in the age of innocence.

II. ACKNOWLEDGMENTS

This book is the product of the hard work of many people. The editors owe a debt of gratitude to two people without whom the project would not have been possible. To Brooke Sizer (University of Houston, J.D. 2012), we are grateful for her excellent assistance in reviewing earlier drafts of this manuscript. Her dedication, good sense, and courageous pursuit of the truth greatly improved the quality of the book. The other person whose talents must be mentioned is Amanda Parker (University of Houston, B.A. 2010). Amanda is wholly responsible for bringing the work of many together and creating one, cohesive document. We are grateful to her for her outstanding computer skills and editing talents.

Finally, we could not have produced this book without the support of the Criminal Justice Institute (CJI) at the University of Houston Law Center, and, in particular, Dean Raymond T. Nimmer, as well as the many individuals who support CJI's activities. Finally, Professor Thompson would like to extend special thanks to her colleague and friend, David R. Dow, who is responsible for her appointment to the Timothy Cole Advisory Panel on Wrongful Convictions. Her involvement with the advisory panel inspired her to teach the course that produced the essays in this book.

III. Causes of Wrongful Convictions: Unreliable Evidence

A. Eyewitness Identification

Eyewitness Identification: The Science and Need for Reform

Brian M. Harrison*

I. Introduction

With over 253 exonerations nationwide, wrongful conviction has become the most visible criminal justice issue of our time.[1] With each exoneration a small part of justice is restored, but a larger portion of the public's trust in the court system is lost. And, there are indications that these exonerations may represent the tip of an iceberg. The vast majority of exonerations are possible only because biological material exists for DNA testing. Unfortunately testable evidence exists in only a small fraction of total crimes. Faced with a crisis, the full dimensions of which we may never grasp, many states are reforming their trial practices to prevent further miscarriages of justice.

Involved in 75% of all exonerations, eyewitness misidentification is by far the largest cause of wrongful conviction.[2] Reform is desperately needed, and this article outlines some of the proposed changes. Part II surveys the extensive scientific findings of researchers in the field

* Brian Harrison is a 2011 J.D. candidate for graduation of the University of Houston Law Center.

and addresses the factors that affect an eyewitness's ability to identify a suspect. By understanding the various factors the police can develop new and more accurate techniques to avoid false identifications. Part III makes specific recommendations for jurisdictions by surveying the research into best practices as well as the reforms of selected states. These recommendations include: give cautionary instructions to the witnesses, be deliberate and careful in the crafting of the lineup, avoid bias by using a blind administrator, use a sequential presentation of the lineup, record the witness' statements at that time, and exclude improper eyewitness identifications. By implementing these various reforms mistakes in eyewitness identifications can be reduced, helping prevent wrongful convictions.

II. An Introduction to the Forensic Science of Eyewitness Identification

An identification lineup can be usefully seen as a type of experiment.[3] The central purpose of an experiment is to test the investigator's hypothesis, the belief or assumption about the world and its workings. In an academic setting, this may look like anything from tests measuring human heart rate following a sudden noise to tracking the movements of subatomic particles in a super-collider. In these scenarios, the hypothesis or test question will be the intensity and duration of an elevated heart rate, or the precise speed and direction of the particles.

In the law enforcement setting, experiments will chart DNA structure and compare fingerprints. Here, the unknown variable is the identity of the culprit, and the investigator's hypothesis will be that the suspect in custody is the perpetrator of the crime. Instead of making educated predictions and testing those predictions with real-life experience, the police investigator will test her hypothesis by comparing the suspect's DNA or fingerprints with material found at the crime scene.

Eyewitness identification procedures are no different.[4] The police have a hypothesis: the suspect is in fact guilty. Officers construct a test, assembling photos of the suspect and those of known innocents. The police conduct a procedure by presenting the lineup to witnesses.

Officers record the data, which comes in the form of an identification of varying certainty or no identification at all. Detectives then use this new evidence to re-examine their hypothesis, the culpability of the suspect.[5]

There are two differences, however, between super-colliders and DNA on one hand, and eyewitness identification on the other. The first is that where physics and DNA have a material *thing* that can be seen and measured, eyewitness evidence is a memory trace with no physical being independent of its expression by the witness. The other key difference is that while police have fairly strict, accepted protocols designed to prevent contamination and ensure reliability when collecting DNA, law enforcement use almost haphazard, "common-sense" methods for collecting eyewitness identification. These methods do little to minimize the risk of contaminating the memory evidence.

Scientists have devoted extensive study to these identification collection systems.[6] Researchers have identified a number of variables that contribute to and affect both the witness and the recording of the identification. Those seeking to improve these practices must have a working knowledge of this science.

A. Estimator Variables

Variables weighing on eyewitness accuracy but not under the control of police investigators are called *estimator variables*.[7] The term originated from the idea that psychologists can, at best, only "estimate" the effects of such variables or factors in a given situation. [8] No witness will have an ideal opportunity to gather a perfect memory of the perpetrator's appearance, so it is important to know what factors make an error more likely.[9] While there is little law enforcement can do to limit estimator variables, understanding how they affect witnesses drives home the importance of proper evidence-gathering techniques. The variables include exposure duration, weapon focus, cross-race identification, and delay.

Some Estimator Variables That Affect Identification Accuracy

- Exposure Duration
- Weapon Focus
- Cross-Race Identification
- Time between Crime and Confrontation

1. Exposure Duration

How long a witness views a perpetrator may seem like such an obvious factor in determining identification accuracy that it could go unmentioned. But, as a critically important factor in accuracy, exposure duration bears discussion.[10] Like many aspects of eyewitness identification, its intuitive appearance belies a complex undergrowth of issues and concerns.

In *Manson v. Brathwaite*, the Supreme Court has declared "the opportunity to view", or exposure duration, as one of five critical factors in determining the reliability of an identification.[11] This *Manson* test spurred a significant body of research, and exposure duration was an early focus. A meta-analysis, or compilation of results from many experiments, indicates that witnesses with "long" exposure times correctly identify the culprit 69% of the time, while those permitted only a "short" viewing of the culprit are only successful at a rate of 57%.[12] The edge that a greater exposure time might have seems less than what one might expect, a fact noted by several observers.[13] In fact, the rate of misidentification is statistically constant, with witnesses picking the wrong individual at a rate of 34% and 38% with long and short exposure times, respectively.[14]

Complicating matters is the tendency of witnesses to overestimate their exposure, especially if other estimator variables like stress or a weapon are involved.[15] This leads investigators and courts following the *Manson* test to give the identifications more credence even as the science shows little benefit. If we assume that the majority of actual witnesses only see the perpetrator for a short time and that those occasions with a longer exposure give only a limited benefit, eyewitness accuracy starts at a fairly low baseline.

2. Weapon Focus

Researchers have long suspected that the presence of a weapon in an eyewitness scenario would result in a less accurate identification, an effect called "weapon focus."[16] It is thought that an eyewitness gives more attention to a weapon, leaving less time to spend on the culprit's face.[17] A meta-analysis, in which researchers compiled much of the research conducted on the topic, detailed adequate evidence to support the theory.[18] The research specifically found the effect most acute when witnesses described specific features of the culprits, known as "feature accuracy."[19] The effect on identification accuracy, picking the true target out of a lineup, was less pronounced but still strong enough to support the theory.[20]

Archival studies and statistical analyses of actual identification figures from select police departments have come to mixed conclusions on weapon focus. One study, taken from figures for a jurisdiction outside of Vancouver, Canada, roughly supported the laboratory results.[21] Once again, there was a lesser effect on the ability of the witness to provide a description and a "relatively robust" negative effect on identification attempts.[22] Witnesses to weaponless crimes identified the police suspect in 73.33% of cases, whereas only 30.61% of witnesses to crimes involving a weapon could do the same.[23] But the report pointed out that weapon-crime witnesses were run through lineups after much longer periods from the crime than weaponless witnesses. Such long delays, the negative effects of which are better documented than weapon focus, might have been responsible for the difference in identification accuracy.[24] A later meta-analysis, taking data from the Sacramento Police Department, stated that "support for the weapon focus effect was not evident" in their study, and further found that witnesses to weapon crimes identified suspects with *greater* accuracy when there was at least some other probative* evidence.[25]

Recent commentary on weapon focus has tried to rehabilitate its image, pointing out that witnesses truly affected by the presence of a weapon might acknowledge their faulty memory by declining a lineup.[26] What conclusion can be drawn is that any weapon effect is somewhat

---

* Having the tendency to prove.

small, limited to identification accuracy, and felt to be only somewhat reliable by psychologists in the field.[27]

3. Cross-Race Identification

While research shows that the race of either the witness or the perpetrator makes little difference in accuracy, the studies do conclude that cross-race identification is inherently less reliable.[28] The leading analysis of the issue, combining studies over a thirty-year span, determined that witnesses were 1.4 times more likely to correctly identify a same-race perpetrator than one of another race.[29] These experimental results are supported by real-world archival data, which show intra-race identifications are 1.3 times more accurate.[30] Self-reported racial attitudes made no impact on this difference, though the group reporting more interracial contact did show a small advantage in identification.[31] While this negative cross-race effect appears across all races, studies agree that it negatively affects whites more strongly than other groups.[32]

Cross-race bias is well accepted in the psychological community, with almost 75% of psychologists polled believing the science is at least "generally reliable" and with none questioning its validity.[33] It is accepted that cross-race bias reliably weakens the ability of a witness to accurately identify a perpetrator, a huge problem in our pluralistic society.

4. Time Between Crime and Confrontation

Common sense and experience tells us that memory decays over time. Psychology has been able to prove this notion for over a century, and recent research has shown that a stranger's name is little easier to remember than a stranger's face.[34]

While experimental science shows a great decline in accuracy proportional to the delay before identification, police statistics show a precipitous decline in real witness' abilities to finger the culprit.[35] In one study, seven out of ten robbery witnesses identified the police suspect when interviewed less than a day after the crime. This number dropped to slightly less than half when the timeframe was less than five days, and down to only a third of positive identifications when interviewed within a month. When the timeframe was over a month, accuracy dropped to slightly less than mere chance, or only 14% in a six-person lineup.[36] Another study found that witnesses interviewed within a week of the crime picked the police suspect 10% more often than those after a greater delay.[37] While both archival and experimental studies often disagree on the exact rate of decay, a substantial majority of psychologists agree that the forgetting curve negatively affects the ability of witnesses to make reliable identifications.[38]

While it might surprise few to learn that the passage of time degrades memory, the degree to which police practices can influence this decayed memory is especially troubling.[39] While a more complete discussion of police practices will follow, it is important to note that memories removed even by only a short time from the events are quite fragile.[40] In the two archival studies cited here, over two-thirds of identifications were made after a week, a period of time widely regarded as the precipice for memory loss.[41] This emphasizes the need for great care in collecting a witness' identification evidence.

B. System Variables

System variables represent the effect that the method of collection has on the accuracy of the identification.[42] The way police construct and present the lineup has a profound effect on the witness' reliability. The "system" in this term of art refers to the criminal justice system.[43] Since the system can control and theoretically eliminate such variables, they have attracted quite a lot of research attention. Many variables are somewhat counter-intuitive, and so require an in-depth explanation. This section will first describe the eyewitness interview procedures of many police departments in Texas and will then explain the effects of five main variables: presentation of suspects, lineup instructions, lineup composition, administrator suggestiveness, and witness confidence.

Regarding current eyewitness procedures, only approximately 12% of police departments in Texas have written eyewitness policies; however, determining the policies of many is relatively easy given recent survey results and what is known about standard practices across the country.[44] Police obtain from the witness a description of the culprit. Based on this description and sometimes other evidence, police detain a suspect. An officer, usually the investigator of the case, constructs a photo lineup (more rarely a live one), comprised of the suspect and five fillers, or foils, chosen based on their similarity to the suspect. This investigator then simultaneously presents to the witness the images of the five fillers and the suspect, known as a "six-pack," referencing the six individuals in the lineup. More often than not the witness is unable to quickly identify anyone, and the witness and the investigator have a conversation about what features of the photographs bear a resemblance to the memory. The interview will end with the witness making no positive identification, picking a foil, or choosing the police suspect. This process may be repeated, depending on the needs of investigators.

As we shall see, memory is every bit as fragile and subject to ruin as DNA and blood evidence. These sorts of practices, highly unscientific and "unhygienic," carry great risk of contaminating the witness' memory evidence.

1. Presentation of Suspects

There are two dominant methods of administering a lineup. The procedure in use throughout Texas and much of the country is a *simultaneous lineup*, where the photos of the fillers and the suspect are shown to the witness at the same time.[45] A newer procedure in use in a minority of state and local jurisdictions is the *sequential lineup*, where the witness is shown the photos one at a time.[46] Perhaps no aspect of eyewitness science has generated more debate than the simultaneous/sequential lineup research, and it is vital to gain an understanding of the conceptual and experimental science behind the discussion.[47]

A. Relative Judgment

In many newspapers, adjacent to the crossword puzzles are a pair of cartoons or photographs. The goal of the game is to pick out a set number of differences between pictures one and two. These "spot the difference" games illustrate the concept of *relative judgment*, comparing images to each other to form an opinion. In a simultaneous eyewitness lineup, relative judgment is utilized to select the member who most closely resembles the witness' memory.[48] This makes sense at first glance, as the culprit will most resemble the witness' memory. Relative judgment fails when the culprit is not included.[49] There will always be a member of the lineup who most closely resembles the witness' memory trace; the fundamental question is whether that person is the culprit.[50]

Sequential lineups dodge this problem by requiring a witness to employ *absolute judgment*, comparing each photo with the memory of the culprit. It is only through the use of absolute judgment that the culprit, as opposed to someone merely resembling the culprit, can be identified.[51]

This analysis of relative judgment in sequential lineups has come under scrutiny.[52] Specifically, some scientists charge that sequential lineups make eyewitnesses more conservative, requiring greater confidence in their choice or that a member looks more like the culprit than in a simultaneous procedure.[53] Responding to these charges, experts advocating the relative judgment theory point to a large number of experiments documenting witnesses self-reporting their use of relative judgment.[54] These tests also concluded that those witnesses using relative judgment were more likely to make a misidentification.[55] Perhaps the most compelling evidence that relative judgment is at work in simultaneous lineups are the series of cases testing *removal without replacement*.[56] All witnesses viewed the same crime. Half were shown a "six pack" including the culprit, while the other half were shown only the five fillers. In the group shown the culprit-inclusive lineup, 54% identified the suspect and 21% made no choice.[57] One would think that the group shown only fillers would come out with a majority of witnesses declining to make identification, but this was not the case. Instead, identifications shifted to two particular fillers, with only a third of the group declined to make a choice.[58] This indicates that witnesses are not utilizing absolute judgment, but are instead choosing the lineup member most similar to their memory.

B. Results of Simultaneous/Sequential Procedure Comparisons

Whether the cause is absolute judgment or increased standards for identification, what is not in much doubt is that sequential presentation creates lower rates of misidentification.[59] In a leading meta-analysis, compiling the results of over thirty experiments, found that witnesses made false identifications in 17% of the simultaneous lineups and only 10% in sequential procedures.[60] It is important to note these figures are absolute floors when it comes to comparing misidentification rates, as the studies included varied widely according to their practices.[61] Two other meta-analyses, including more similar studies, put the misidentification figures at 27% and 53% for simultaneous lineups, and 9% and 16 % for sequentials.[62]

Critics of the sequential procedure point out that in simultaneous lineups witnesses make more correct identifications and fewer false rejections, or a failure to identify the culprit when present.[63] This is in fact true, as the main meta-analyses show correct identification rates as 54% and 50% for simultaneous procedures, and 43% and 35% for sequential lineups.[64] Some researchers claim the improved performance under simultaneous procedures could be due to an advantage in using relative judgment, as when the culprit is in the lineup he will look most like the witness' memory.[65] When the culprit is removed, there will be yet another photo most closely resembling the culprit, though it will be a misidentification. Other researchers have noted that since simultaneous procedures create more choices, some will be true and some will be false. What matters is the whether the additional choices skew in favor of correct identifications or degrade the total hit percentage by adding proportionately more misidentifications. When we examine the proportion of the numbers given in the meta-analyses above, we see that simultaneous procedures have significantly more false identifications. One study finds three times the number of false positives.[66] In comparison, simultaneous lineups only improved upon sequential procedures in correctly identifying suspects by a few percentage points, with the greatest outlier showing only an improvement by a third.[67]

Simultaneous procedures encourage and record a witness' "calculated guess."[68] These calculated guesses more often than not turn out to be wrong, but the court system has no way to filter out these incorrect choices, and juries rely heavily on them to pass judgment. Sequential procedures inhibit guessing, without diminishing correct choices to an appreciable degree.[69]

2. Lineup Instructions

A witness, often called in to a police station to make identification, could be excused for thinking the culprit is necessarily in a lineup.

Witnesses might rightly assume the police invested a great deal of preparation and work in constructing the lineups and presume the perpetrator is present.[70] This is why researchers label as biased any lineup viewing that is not preceded with a warning declaring that the culprit may not be present. Police must take some sort of action against this inherent bias.[71] Bias can also take the form of an investigator asserting that the police caught the culprit, or simply implying that a failure to identify someone is undesirable.[72]

In the first experiment testing the effects of lineup instructions, test subjects witnessed a staged crime.[73] The witnesses were later run through one of four lineups, in which the actual perpetrator was or was not present, and the instructions were or were not biased. The instructional bias included the "investigator's" stated belief that the culprit was present, and the absence of an option rejecting the lineup altogether.[74] The results were stark: When the perpetrator was absent, those with the biased instruction failed the test miserably, identifying an innocent person 78% of the time.[75] In contrast, those witnesses with the unbiased instruction only picked out the wrong person in 33% of the identifications. In the perpetrator-present, biased lineup, 100% of witnesses made identification, though only 75% were correct.[76] Of those in the perpetrator-present, *unbiased* lineup, 83% made an identification but all of them were correct.[77] What this test starkly demonstrates is that a biased instruction gets more identification, but those extra identifications are likely to be false.

A large number of experiments have followed similar procedures and tested the effects of biased lineups. A recent analysis of fourteen such studies confirms that instructions can greatly alter the outcome.[78] Biased instructions without any warnings lead to more correct identifications, in 55.9% of attempts, as compared to unbiased lineups with warnings, at 49.5%.[79] However, biased instructions also lead to more incorrect choices, 9.6% compared to 7.1%; in some experiments, witnesses without warnings made false accusations at twice the rate as those with notices.[80] The science supporting the negative effects of biased instructions has almost universal support among psychologists; 98% of scientists polled trust the evidence enough to testify in court.[81] The harm is clear, and there are few advantages to biased practices.

3. LINEUP COMPOSITION

A typical lineup procedure features the police showing the witness the suspect's photo with the photos of innocent individuals, known as foils or fillers. Scientists have identified two aspects of the procedure, size and content, as critical in influencing accuracy.[82] One can view lineup composition as the "how many" and "who" of eyewitness identification.

A. LINEUP SIZE

The number of individuals in the lineup may seem simple to understand, but is substantially more complex upon further review. The *nominal size* of the lineup refers to the raw number of individuals included.[83] Researchers grasped early on that this number says very little regarding the reliability of the identification, and instead refer to the functional size of the lineup when analyzing the procedure for suggestiveness. Functional size can best be understood as "the number of lineup members who provide a viable option for selection."[84] The distinction is critical because low functional size in lineups is known to substantially increase false identification rates.[85] The best way to understand the difference between nominal and functional size is to presuppose a white suspect in their mid-thirties, clean-shaven, and with red hair. Placed into a lineup with three African-Americans, a bearded white brunette, and one clean-shaven redhead, the "six-pack's" nominal size would be still be six. The functional size would be a very suggestive two, since four members of the lineup do not resemble the suspect or the description.

While identifying bias in such obviously deficient lineups is relatively easy, determining whether a procedure featuring greater resemblance among members is possible with a simple test accepted in many jurisdictions.[86] A lineup featuring a suspect is shown to non-witnesses, who are asked to pick out the subject.[87] The functional size is then determined by dividing the total number of non-witnesses exposed to the lineup by the number of correct suspect identifications. For instance, if a "six pack" were shown to ten uninvolved people, and two correctly identified the suspect, the functional size of the lineup would be a very good five.[88] This test operates under the belief that non-witnesses would identify at a random rate a suspect in an unbiased lineup, or one out of six times in the traditional "six pack."[89]

Having identified the proper method of gauging the functional size of a lineup, we now turn to the question of an ideal size lineup. What is clear is that increasing lineup size increases lineup accuracy, but at a diminishing rate.[90] Each additional member of the lineup decreases the chances of a misidentification at a lesser rate than the previous addition.[91] In other words, there is a ceiling on the effectiveness of adding lineup members.

Another aspect of lineup size is the number of suspects included in the lineup. Scientists have argued that single-suspect lineups are vastly superior to multiple-suspect lineups.[92] Fillers act as the control in the detective's experiment. A filler's value, innocence, is known to the police and the selection of a filler, known to the police to be innocent, immediately indicates that an identification is unreliable. Only one answer in a single-suspect lineup will result in prosecution. By contrast in a multiple-suspect lineup, there are fewer controls and the functional size, so important in preventing false identifications, drops dramatically. In addition to a greater risk of false identification, there are more witness' answers, potentially leading to more prosecutions.[93] Experiments show witnesses are willing to identify a known innocent in approximately 25% of multiple-suspect lineups.[94] Multiple-suspect lineups create an environment where identifications are more likely to lead to prosecutions, even as a quarter of identifications would be known to be wrong, and the detective's ability to discern the misidentification is restricted due to a smaller control group.

B. Lineup Content

There are two competing methods of selecting fillers for a lineup.[95] One common strategy is to select foils based on their resemblance to the suspect. It is easy to see the appeal of such a process, selecting photos based on their similarity to the suspect's photo. However, a suspect-similarity approach has a number of logical and practical problems. First, the detective's subjective assessment of the filler's similarity to the suspect will result in a considerable amount of variability in foil selection.[96] Each detective's lineup would be very different, with reliability suffering. Second, researchers have identified what they term "the back-fire effect" operating in the suspect-similarity approach.[97] The suspect, as the origin of the lineup, may objectively stand out in the procedure. In addition, the suspect-similarity approach's rational end would be a lineup of near-clones.[98] This would merely make it more difficult for the witness to make an accurate description, and arguably render her more likely to make a misidentification from among the very similar choices. Finally, and most damaging, are charges that in culprit-absent lineups the suspect-similarity approach renders the innocent suspect as the most similar to the culprit among lineup members and substantially contributes to the risk of misidentification.[99] Since the detective included the fillers based on their relationship to the suspect, logic dictates that the fillers will rarely, if ever, be more similar to the culprit than is the suspect. The fillers, after all, only look like the suspect and may bear no resemblance at all to the actual culprit.

Another method for selecting fillers is by similarity to the witness' description.[100] A lineup searching for a white culprit with a beard and long blonde hair would feature members sharing only these features. The fillers would all resemble the culprit in roughly the same degree, and there would be an objective standard to gauge similarity rather than reliance on the detective's subjective opinion. The description-similarity method faces a problem, however, when the witness description is not complete enough to form a strong lineup.[101] This problem suggests that the use of a hybrid, suspect/description-similarity approach may be necessary in some cases.

A recent meta-analysis comparing the results of experiments comparing the two approaches came just short of declaring the description-similarity method superior.[102] While the study noted a marked variability in the results, there was a noted tendency for description-similarity lineups to produce more correct identifications, 56% versus the suspect-similarity rate of 43%.[103] The study also noted that description-similarity lineups featured twice the rate of incorrect identifications, 15% versus 8% for suspect-similarity lineups.[104] In conclusion, the study argued there was "a compelling case" for basing filler inclusion on the description, but noted the experimental data was underdeveloped and inconclusive.[105]

4. Administrator Suggestiveness

Witnesses rarely pick a member of a lineup quickly, and the identification procedure often becomes a conversation about photographs between the investigator and the witness.[106] This conversation is problematic because the investigator knows the identity of the suspect and has an interest in the resolution of the case. The situation, unattended by defense council and rarely monitored, is ripe for an investigator's influence whether intentional or not.[107]

The potential for influence begins before the witness sees a photograph, with a call for the witness to come to the station to "identify the culprit" or "have a look at our suspect."[108]As discussed in the earlier section on procedure instructions, this influences the witness to be more likely to give an identification to a detective who seems to have the crime "all figured out." In addition, the officer conducting the investigation speaks from a position of power, as an expert in crime and an authority figure. It is not hard to imagine a certain level of intimidation, coupled with a real desire of the witness to assist police in solving the crime by picking the suspect out of a lineup.[109]

One of the central theories of eyewitness identification science is that the lineup is in fact an experiment testing a police hypothesis of guilt. It is well known in the scientific community that investigators will naturally test a hypothesis so as to prove the theory.[110]This is known as confirmation bias, as the investigator is looking to confirm the hypothesis, and is related to the more familiar self-fulfilling prophesy.[111] This sort of influence typically takes a benign form, often with a false identification being followed by an exhortation for the witness to "take another look".[112] Positive identifications can be accompanied by a smile or a run-down of the suspect's rap sheet.[113] Officers will sometimes innocently request the witness to examine the suspect's photo repeatedly, in what becomes a passive argument for a positive identification.[114] Finally, the administrator has the power to determine when the identification procedure comes to an end. The detective may continue with the lineup to see if the witness changes his mind, or "suddenly" recognizes the culprit as the suspect.[115] The ability to prolong the procedure is perhaps the clearest form of influence, as it is difficult to imagine an investigator continuing the lineup to see if the witness changes his mind *to pick a foil.*

In recent years there has been a great deal of scientific study examining the performance of lineups by knowing investigators.[116] These studies found higher rates of both correct and incorrect identification with the biased administrators.[117] As an interesting side note, there is science to suggest that the influencing behavior passes unnoticed by both the investigator and the witness, but is readily seen by an outside observer.[118] In addition, the administrators in these studies were undergraduates, who when compared to detectives had both less of an incentive to influence the witness and less skill or ability to do so.[119] Police officers experienced in administering lineups would likely be even more persuasive to a witness.

5. Witness Confidence

Witness confidence is perhaps the most studied aspect of eyewitness identification.[120] The Supreme Court included witness certainty as a factor indicating reliability, and a witness dead certain of the culprit's identity makes for compelling testimony.[121] What is also compelling is the level of unanimity in expert opinion on "certainty": confidence in general is a poor indicator of accuracy and is easily manipulated by investigators.[122] Virtually all experts polled agreed that the science "tends to prove" the above assertions, and a clear majority feel the science is "very reliable".[123] We shall consider each in turn.

Witness Confidence

- Poor indicator of identification accuracy
- Confident witnesses have a 30% error rate
- 20% of witnesses are overly confident
- Confirmatory feedback increases witness confidence

a. Confidence and Accuracy

Virtually all experiments regarding identification include a question about confidence in the witness' decision. This makes the data perfect for a meta-analysis, which shows an overall low rate in confidence as a predictor of accuracy; the rate is approximately 60% for a witness correctly identifying their accuracy, not much better than a 50-50 toss of a coin.[124] When the survey group is restricted to only those making an identification, the rate increases to approximately 70% of witnesses correctly estimating their accuracy.[125] Furthermore, studies indicate that highly confident and highly unconfident witnesses tend to be more accurate.[126] An archival analysis of real identifications also tends to support that "highly confident witnesses are much more prone to choose the suspect...than moderately confident ones."[127] These studies would seem to indicate ambivalence in the science of confidence and accuracy. But there are a number of factors that limit the utility of confidence.

First is the inherent inaccuracy of even the most confident witnesses, with approximately a 30% error rate.[128] Even the most confident witnesses are no guarantee of accuracy. [129] Second, the proportion of witnesses classified as "highly confident" is usually quite low, around 20% in studies.[130] In addition, there is the presence of pervasive over-confidence by all sectors of witnesses, running as high as 20%.[131] Furthermore, there is the problem of prosecutors taking only the most confident witnesses to trial.[132] While this would seem to eliminate the least accurate identifications, it in fact leads the jury to a false sense of security in the testimony. Studies of mock jurors conclude that jurors are extremely susceptible to highly confident, though inaccurate, eyewitness testimony.[133] One experiment tested highly confident witnesses in low-accuracy environments, featuring many estimator variables undermining the ability to make an identification and with an accurate identification rate of 33%.[134] These witnesses, totally confident and often totally wrong, were believed by the jury at twice their rate of accuracy, or 62% of the time.[135] The jurors were simply unable to assess the ability of the witness to observe, and instead looked only at the confidence of the identification. The jury, by hearing only these most confident of witnesses, misses out on the chance to critically analyze the witnessing environment. Finally, most studies indicate that witness confidence statements need to be obtained early, and are subject to influence by the justice system.[136]

B. Confidence Malleability

The concept that a witness' certainty can be altered shakes eyewitness testimony to its core. Upon making a selection, the typical eyewitness will seek out some feedback or confirmation that he's "got the right guy."[137] If the lineup administrator knows which lineup member is the suspect (as she often does), she can then provide feedback, tainting the most convincing aspect of the witness' testimony.

Experiments show a dramatic effect. In one such test, witnesses observed a crime in sub-prime conditions.[138] Those witnesses making a false identification (the majority) were then subject to either no response at all from the administrator, confirmatory feedback, or a truthful rejection of their identification. The witnesses were then asked about their confidence in the selection. The results were stark. The base confidence rate on a ten-point scale was 6.9 in those without feedback, compared with 8.8 in those told they had chosen the suspect.[139] The confidence dropped to 4.7 in those told they had the wrong guy. Three comments need be mentioned in light of these figures. First, these confidence rates reflect an already inflated confidence in accuracy. As mentioned above, witnesses tend to overestimate their ability to identify the culprit even without confirmatory feedback.[140] When coupled with the effects of feedback, confidence bears no relation to accuracy. Second, positive reinforcement brought the majority of observers into the "highly confident" category of witnesses, making it more likely they would be asked to testify. The witnesses would be a critical part of the prosecution's case, the jury would find them highly convincing, and under current practices there would be little ability to uncover the alteration of their confidence. Finally, witnesses still had a fairly strong degree of confidence even after learning they stood alone in their identification, further calling into question the value of confidence statements.

Confidence is highly malleable. Experiments show that the confidence effect is greater for those who have made a mistaken identification, and that an administrator's non-verbal cues can improve the witness' perception of the quality of their view.[141] Experts single out this "visual hindsight bias" as particularly damaging.[142] The witness' memory of the events, the actual evidence sought by the detective, is contaminated by this alteration.

The ease with which this influence occurs, and the special vulnerability of those incorrect witnesses the system must protect against, leads researchers to doubt the use of witness confidence in determining accuracy.[143] Despite widespread expert distrust, courts and jurors still place a great deal of trust in a highly confident witness. Because this trust shows no sign of weakening, the criminal justice system must seek reforms to improve the recordation of witness confidence statements. In a very real way, the witness' confidence itself becomes evidence.

III. Recommendations for Improving the Quality of Eyewitness Evidence

The problems listed above are serious and call eyewitness identification reliability into question. However, the vast majority of researchers do not seek to make the public and courts more skeptical, but the identifications more reliable instead. An unbiased lineup, free from unintentional contamination of the witness' memory, is the goal. As a result, experts have developed a number of alternative practices designed to curb or eliminate many of the problems inherent in current methods of identification collection. Many jurisdictions have adopted these measures. These six simple reforms would make eyewitness evidence more reliable and help to restore public confidence in the criminal justice system.

Six Recommended Reforms

- Cautionary Instructions
- Careful crafting of lineups
- Blind administration
- Sequential lineups
- Documenting witness confidence
- Exclusion of improper identification evidence

A. Cautionary Instructions

Perhaps the least expensive of all potential remedies, cautionary instructions would counter the natural expectation by many witnesses that the police have the culprit, and that an identification is a mere formality. Psychologists are in clear agreement that lineups are inherently biased towards witnesses making a choice, even an incorrect one.[144] Instructions simply warning witnesses that the culprit may or may not be present have the effect of reducing the rate of false identifications while having little effect on correct identifications.[145] Cautionary instructions have already been adopted in larger jurisdictions, but many smaller departments do not include them in lineups.[146] Cautionary instructions are easy to implement, virtually cost-free, and are effective. In light of these factors, smaller jurisdictions would have an easy time implementing the use of cautionary instructions in their lineup procedures, if such use were mandated.

B. Careful Crafting of Lineups

Choice of fillers and lineup size are important in the creation of an unbiased lineup. It should almost go without saying that all photographs should resemble each other in construction (all color or all monochrome, in front of the same background, all or none holding a mug shot card, etc.). Fillers should be chosen so as to resemble the description provided by witnesses, as opposed to the suspect.[147] This prevents the lineup itself from unnecessarily suggesting the suspect.[148] When the description of the culprit is incomplete or does not match the suspect, a combination of suspect- and description-fit techniques may be used.[149]

The size of the lineup is not as important as the composition, but experts seem to agree any fewer than six becomes problematic.[150] Since the use of six photos has become engrained in police practice, and any increase in nominal size would yield limited benefits, keeping the traditional "six pack" may be the best policy.

C. Blind Administrators

Blind administration of lineups would do much to eliminate bias.[151] The science is conclusive: when the administrator knows the identity of the suspect, there will be verbal and physical cues, whether intentional or not, and the parties will be unlikely to notice them.[152] Blind administrators would also help to prevent altering the witness' confidence, since there would be no chance for confirmatory feedback.

Putting blind administration into practice has been difficult, but there are a number of solutions. The simplest method is to utilize detectives or officers unassociated with the case. Police time is often at a premium, however, and extra officers are not always available. Some have suggested employing clerical personnel, since running a lineup requires little special training. A laptop would also be ideal.[153] Computer programs could automatically match photos to a description, laptops are portable and easy to use, and there would be no risk of confirmatory feedback or other bias. Finally, if none of these other methods are available the investigator could utilize the "folder system" to hide the photographs from her view. In this simple yet effective method, the investigator would gather the photos of the suspect and the filler, placing each in an individual folder. Pulling a filler folder out, the investigator would then shuffle the other folders, effectively disguising the location of the suspect. Placing the remaining filler folder on top, the lineup is ready for the witness.[154]

While a limited number of police departments have adopted blind administration, the experiences of other jurisdictions as laid out later in this section bode well for their use elsewhere.

D. Sequential Presentation of Lineups

Studies show a sequential procedure in a lineup greatly reduces the risk of a witness identifying an innocent suspect.[155] Sequential presentation eliminates guessing by the witness, which removes more misidentifications than correct selections from the system. Such procedures eliminate the use of relative judgment by witnesses, ensuring that identifications are more likely of the culprit and not merely someone resembling the criminal.

Implementing sequential lineups would need to be done in conjunction with the other rules, especially blind administration. In fact, sequential lineups without blind administration might feature more unintentional bias than the current system, since the investigator would know the witness was viewing the suspect.[156] The investigator may give cues, or urge the witness to study the photo more carefully. In contrast, the blind administration techniques mesh well with the sequential procedure, allowing the witness to independently view without bias the photos and compare them with her memory.

E. Witness Confidence Statements at Identification

Statements of witness confidence, so compelling to juries, are at their most pure and valuable immediately upon identification.[157] It is at this time, prior to any possibility of confirmatory feedback, that the memory should be recorded.[158] Using the witness's own words, as opposed to stock answers or even a numeric scale, would best preserve the evidence of the witness's confidence.[159]

F. Exclusion of Improper Eyewitness Evidence

Though exclusion may seem like an extreme solution, the problem of unnecessarily suggestive lineups is large, and the stakes are high. Many of the influences are so dangerous precisely because they are hidden and cannot be uncovered.[160] In addition, bright-line rules would prevent even unintentional influence. Adopting an exclusionary rule would cause police departments to immediately drop all suggestive procedures, leading to an immediate improvement in the quality of evidence.

Some exceptions could be carved out. For instance, police could use imperfect lineup results in investigations.[161] The real danger lies in the eyewitness testimony's effect on the jury. This type of exception would allow the police to conduct an imperfect lineup if the need arose, while protecting the jury from tainted evidence. An exception could also be made for culprits related to witnesses.[162] Studies show that misidentification of relatives is fairly rare.

G. Experience of Other Jurisdictions

Many jurisdictions have been open to reforming eyewitness identification methods. New procedures have been implemented in three ways. First, executive agencies have issued model policies presenting local law enforcement with best practices. In 2001 and 2005 respectively, the New Jersey and Wisconsin Attorneys General issued their model eyewitness procedures.[163] Both guides adopted measures similar to the ones outlined here, with the exception of the exclusionary rule. In addition, the guides explicitly state that they are advisory, leaving the matter open to local determination as to which practices to adopt. While these guides are less than fully satisfactory, they are a start and at least make law enforcement aware of the difficulties and the science in eyewitness identification.

Some law enforcement agencies have not waited for the courts or government to compel them to act and have adopted improved techniques on their own. Hennepin County, containing Minneapolis, is a notable example.[164] All five recommendations made in this article were adopted by the District Attorney's office as a pilot project. The Hennepin County D.A., now a U.S. Senator, wanted to prevent embarrassing wrongful convictions through more reliable eyewitness evidence. Despite some resistance to the new protocols from police, the new procedures were eventually accepted and used to great effect.[165] The agencies solved the greatest hurdle, finding genuinely blind administrators through the use of laptop computers to show the lineups. By the end of the pilot project, police chiefs were making plans to implement the procedures permanently.[166]

Legislatures have passed laws mandating improved techniques. In the most striking example, in 2009 the North Carolina Legislature adopted a host of reforms for eyewitness identification, including all the measures advocated in this paper.[167] What is notable about the new law is that it mandates all police agencies statewide to comply with the new procedures. It provides flexibility in blind administration, if none can be found, to preserve the ability of smaller jurisdictions to easily conduct lineups. It also strikes a reasonable balance in remedies for failure to follow the guidelines. The statute does not provide for exclusion of such identifications, but does render admissible such noncompliance as evidence of misidentification.

IV. Conclusion

DNA exonerations will continue for the foreseeable future. There is a backlog of innocence claims and of material to test. Innocent people are put in prison as a result of unreliable police procedures that manage to make them appear guilty. By far the leading contributor to wrongful conviction is eyewitness misidentification. Science now tells us that the way police have obtained identifications in the past is fatally flawed.

Many jurisdictions unfortunately continue to practice many of the worst identification procedures. In many areas across the country, the criminal justice system needs to regain the trust of the people. Law enforcement agencies need to adopt cautionary instructions, fairness in lineup composition, blind and sequential presentation, and appropriate recordation of witness confidence as their mandatory policy when obtaining eyewitness identifications. There is simply no excuse for further delay in making these critical improvements.

Endnotes

1. http://www.innocenceproject.org/.
2. The Justice Project, *Eyewitness Identification Procedures in Texas* (2008), http:// www.thejusticeproject.org/wp-content/uploads/texas-eyewitness-report-final2.pdf.
3. Gary L. Wells & Eric Seelau, *Eyewitness Identification: Psychological Research and Legal Policy on Lineups,* 1 Psych. Pub. Pol. and L. 765, 767-68 (1995) [hereinafter *Psychological Research*].
4. Gary L. Wells, Mark Small, Steven Penrod, Roy S. Malpass, Solomon M. Fulero, & C.A.E. Brimacombe, *Eyewitness Identification Procedures: Recommendations for Lineups and Photospreads.* 22 Law & Hum. Behav. 603, 617-19 (1998) [hereinafter *Recommendations*].

5. *Id.*
6. *See* Gary L. Wells, Amina Memon, & Steven Penrod, *Eyewitness Evidence: Improving Its Probative Value*, 7 PSYCHOL. SCIENCE IN THE PUB. INT. 45, 47 (2006) [hereinafter *Probative Value*] (explaining the century-long history of eyewitness science).
7. Steven E. Clark & Ryan D. Godfrey, *Eyewitness Identification Evidence and Innocence Risk*, 16 PSYCHONOMIC BULLETIN & REVIEW 22, 25 (2009).
8. *Probative Value, supra* note 7, at 48.
9. *Id.* at 51.
10. *Id.* at 53.
11. Mason v. Brathwaite, 432 U.S. 98 (1977).
12. BRIAN L. CUTLER & STEVEN D. PENROD, MISTAKEN IDENTIFICATION: THE EYEWITNESS, PSYCHOLOGY, AND THE LAW 87 (1995).
13. *Probative Value, supra* note 7, at 53; Clark & Godfrey, *supra* note 8, at 26.
14. CUTLER & PENROD, *supra* note 13, at 87.
15. Gary L. Wells & Deah S. Quinlivan, *Suggestive Eyewitness Identification and the Supreme Court's Reliability Test in Light of Eyewitness Science: 30 Years Later.* 33 LAW HUM. BEHAV. 1, 10 (2009) [hereinafter *Suggestive Identification*].
16. *Probative Value, supra* note 7, at 53.
17. CUTLER & PENROD, *supra* note 13, at 101.
18. Nancy Merkens Steblay, *A Meta-Analytic Review of the Weapon Focus Effect*, 16 LAW AND HUMAN BEHAVIOR 413 (1992).
19. *Id.* at 417.
20. *Id.*
21. Patricia Tollestrup, John Turtle, & John Yuille, *Actual Victims and Witnesses to Robbery and Fraud: An Archival Analysis*, *in* ADULT EYEWITNESS TESTIMONY: CURRENT TRENDS AND

DEVELOPMENTS 144-160 (David Ross, J. Don Read, & Michael Toglia eds., 1994).

22. *Id.* at 158.
23. *Id.* at 157.
24. *Id.*
25. Bruce W. Behrman & Sherrie L. Davey, *Eyewitness Identification in Actual Criminal Cases: An Archival Analysis*, 25 LAW HUM. BEHAV. 475, 485 (2001).
26. *Probative Value, supra* note 7, at 53.
27. Saul M. Kassin et al., *On the 'General Acceptance' of Eyewitness Testimony Research: A New Survey of the Experts,* AMERICAN PSYCHOLOGIST 56.5 (2001), at 405-416.
28. CUTLER & PENROD, *supra* note 13, at 104.
29. Christian A. Meissner & John C. Brigham, *Thirty Years of Investigating the Own-Race Bias in Memory for Faces: A Meta-Analytic Review.* 1 PSYCHOL. PUB. POL'Y & L. 3, 15 (2001).
30. Behrman & Davey, *supra* note 26, at 484.
31. *Id.* at 17.
32. CUTLER & PENROD, *supra* note 13, at 104.
33. Kassin et al., *supra* note 28, at 411.
34. *Suggestive Identification, supra* note 16, at 13.
35. *Probative Value, supra* note 7, at 54.
36. CUTLER & PENROD, *supra,* note 18, at 184.
37. Behrman & Davey, *supra* note 26, at 481.
38. Kassin et al., *supra* note 28, at 413.
39. *Suggestive Identification, supra* note 16, at 14.
40. *Id.*
41. Behrman & Davey, *supra* note 26, at 481; Kassin et al., *supra* note 28, at 413.
42. *Psychological Research, supra* note 4, at 765.
43. Clark & Godfrey, *supra* note 8, at 25.

44. *Eyewitness Identification Procedures in Texas, supra* note 2.
45. Clark & Godfrey, *supra* note 8, at 33.
46. *Probative Value, supra* note 7, at 63.
47. Neil Brewer & Matthew Palmer, *Eyewitness Identification Tests*, 15 LEGAL AND CRIMINOLOGICAL PSYCHOL. 77, 85 (2010).
48. *Psychological Research, supra* note 4, at 768.
49. *Id.*
50. *Recommendations*, supra note 5, at 614.
51. *Id.*
52. Dawn McQuiston-Surrett, Roy S. Malpass, & Colin G. Tredoux, *Sequential vs Simultaneous Lineups: A review of Methods, Data, and Theory*, 12 PSYCHOL. PUB. POL'Y & L. 137 (2006).
53. *Id.*
54. *Recommendations, supra* note 5, at 617.
55. *Id.*
56. *Id.* at 614; *Psychological Research, supra* note 4, at 770.
57. *Id.* at 614.
58. *Id.*
59. Clark & Godfrey, *supra* note 8, at 34; Nancy Steblay et al., *Eyewitness Accuracy in Sequential and Simultaneous Lineup Presentations: A Meta-Analytic Comparison*, 25 L. HUM. BEHAV. 459, 460 (2001).
60. Clark & Godfrey, *supra* note 8 at 34.
61. *Id.*
62. Steblay et al., *supra* note 60, at 463; CUTLER & PENROD, *supra* note 13, at 134.
63. McQuiston-Surrett et al., *supra* note 53, at 138-39.
64. Clark & Godfrey, *supra* note 8, at 34; Steblay et al, *supra* note 60, at 463.
65. *Id.* at 463.

66. Clark & Godfrey, *supra* note 8, at 34; Steblay et al, *supra* note 60, at 463; Cutler & Penrod, *supra* note 13, at 134.
67. *Id.*
68. Steblay et al, *supra* note 60, at 469.
69. *Probative Value, supra* note 7, at 63.
70. *Suggestive Identification, supra* note 16, at 6.
71. Cutler & Penrod, *supra,* note 13, at 115.
72. *Tests*, supra note 48, at 83.
73. Roy S. Malpass & Patricia G. Devine, *Eyewitness Identification: Lineup Instructions and the Absence of the Offender*, 66 Journal of Applied Psychol. 482 (1981).
74. *Id.* at 484.
75. *Id.* at 485.
76. *Id.*
77. *Id.*
78. Clark & Godfrey, *supra* note 8, at 32.
79. *Id.* at 33.
80. *Id.*
81. Kassin et al, *supra* note 28, at 413.
82. *Suggestive Identification, supra* note 16, at 7.
83. Brewer & Palmer, *supra* note 48, at 79.
84. *Id.*
85. *Id.*
86. Tollstrop, et al., *supra* note 22, at 151.
87. *Suggestive Identification, supra* note 16, at 7.
88. *Id.*
89. Cutler & Penrod *supra* note 13, at 124
90. *Probative Value, supra* note 7, at 62.
91. *Id.*

92. Brewer & Palmer, *supra* note 48, at 79.
93. *Id.*
94. Steblay et al., *supra* note 60, at 463
95. *Probative Value, supra* note 7, at 62.
96. Brewer & Palmer, *supra* note 48, at 80.
97. *Probative Value, supra* note 7, at 62.
98. *Id.*
99. Clark & Godfrey, *supra* note 8, at 30.
100. *Probative Value, supra* note 7, at 62.
101. Brewer & Palmer, *supra* note 48, at 80.
102. Clark & Godfrey, *supra* note 8, at 31.
103. *Id.*
104. *Id.*
105. *Id.*
106. *Psychological Research, supra* note 4, at 776.
107. *Suggestive Identification, supra* note 16, at 8.
108. *Recommendations, supra* note 5, at 627.
109. *Psychological Research, supra* note 4, at 776.
110. *Id*; Brewer & Palmer, *supra* note 48, at 82; *Suggestive Identification, supra* note 16, at 8.
111. *Recommendations, supra* note 5, at 627.
112. *Suggestive Identification, supra* note 16, at 8.
113. *Psychological Research, supra* note 4, at 778.
114. *Id.* at 777.
115. *Suggestive Identification, supra* note 16, at 8.
116. Brewer & Palmer, *supra* note 48, at 82-83.
117. *Id.*
118. *Id.*
119. *Id.*

120. Cutler & Penrod, *supra* note 13, at 95.
121. *Manson*, 432 U.S. at 114.
122. Kassin et al., *supra* note 28, at 411.
123. *Id.*
124. Cutler & Penrod, *supra* note 13, at 95.
125. Suggestive Identification, *supra* note 16, at 12.
126. Brewer & Palmer, *supra* note 48, at 87; *Probative Value, supra* note 7, at 66.
127. Berman & Davey, *supra* note 26, at 486.
128. *Suggestive Identification, supra* note 16, at 12.
129. Brewer & Palmer, *supra* note 48, at 87.
130. *Probative Value, supra* note 7, at 66.
131. *Id.*
132. *Recommendations, supra* note 5, at 14.
133. *Id.*
134. *Id.*
135. *Id.*
136. Brewer and Palmer, *supra* note 48, at 87.
137. *Id.* at 89.
138. *Psychological Research, supra* note 4, at 774-5.
139. *Id.*
140. *Probative Value, supra* note 7, at 66.
141. *Id.*; *Recommendations, supra* note 5, at 22; Brewer & Palmer, *supra* note 48, at 89.
142. *Probative Value, supra* note 7, at 67.
143. Cutler & Penrod, *supra* note 13, at 96.
144. Kassin et al., *supra* note 28, at 413.
145. *Recommendations, supra* note 5, at 629.
146. *Eyewitness Identification Procedures in Texas, supra* note 2.

147. Brewer and Palmer, *supra* note 48, at 90.
148. *Psychological Research, supra* note 4, at 776.
149. *Recommendations, supra* note 5, at 631.
150. *Id.*; Kassin et al., *supra* note 28, at 411.
151. Brewer & Palmer, *supra* note 48, at 82; *Suggestive Identification, supra* note 16, at 8.
152. *Id.*; *Recommendations, supra* note 5, at 627; *Psychological Research, supra* note 4, at 778.
153. *Probative Value, supra* note 7, at 63.
154. Bureau of Training and Standards for Crim. Justice, WI Off. Of Attorney Gen., Model Policy and Procedure for Eyewitness Identification (2005) *available at* http://www.doj.state.wi.us/dles/tns/eyewitnesspublic.pdf [hereinafter *WI Guide*].
155. Steblay et al., *supra* note 60, at 469; *Psychological Research, supra* note 4, at 770; Clark & Godfrey, *supra* note 8, at 34.
156. *Recommendations, supra* note 5, at 638.
157. Brewer & Palmer, *supra* note 48, at 87.
158. *Psychological Research, supra* note 4, at 780.
159. *WI Guide, supra* note 155, at 9.
160. *Psychological Research, supra* note 4, at 786.
161. Noah Clements, *Flipping a Coin: A Solution for the Inherent Unreliability of Eyewitness Identification Testimony.* 40 Ind. L. Rev. 271, 289-90 (2007).
162. *Id.*
163. Div. Crim. Just., N.J. Off. Of Attorney Gen., *Attorney General Guidelines for Preparing and Conducting Photo and Live Lineup Identification Procedures* (2001), *available at* http://www.nj.gov/oag/dcj/agguide/photoid.pdf; *WI Guide, supra* note 155.
164. Amy Klobuchar & Hilary Lindell Caligiuri, *Protecting the Innocent/Convicting the Guilty: Hennepin County's Pilot Project In Blind Sequential Eyewitness Identification,* 32 Wm. Mitchell L. Rev. 1 (2005).

165. *Id.* at 24.

166. *Id.*

167. N.C. Gen. Stat. § 15A-284.52 (2009).

Eyewitness Identification Reform: Is Texas Ready?

Christina M. Griffin*

I. Introduction

Recent advancements in DNA testing have precipitated a wave of exonerations in the United States.[1] The joy that the growing number of post-conviction DNA exonerations has brought to exonerees and their families has been accompanied by increased public scrutiny of our criminal justice system. These exonerations have called into question the effectiveness of current procedures intended to safeguard innocent individuals from wrongful convictions. Further justifying this scrutiny is the fact that the number of DNA exonerations likely represents only a minute fraction of all wrongful convictions, which some estimate to range anywhere from 5,000 to 100,000 each year.[2]

In response to these recent exonerations, numerous local and federal governments have commissioned investigations into the causes of wrongful convictions and have requested recommendations to prevent wrongful convictions in the future.[3] These investigations have

* Christina Griffin is a May 2010 graduate from the University of Houston Law Center. Following graduation, she interned at Dallas County Public Defender's Office, and currently works for the criminal defense firm Mark Morales & Associates, in the Austin area.

overwhelmingly concluded that mistaken eyewitness identification is the leading cause of wrongful convictions in the United States, accounting for more wrongful convictions than all other causes combined.[4] Recent reports indicate that eyewitness misidentification was involved in 77% of the over 250 wrongful convictions that have been overturned by post-conviction DNA testing in the US.[5]

In Texas, the nation's leader in post-conviction DNA exonerations, eyewitness misidentification accounted for as much as 85% of its 45 wrongful convictions.[6] Remarkably, these exonerations only represent the relatively small subset of cases where all three of the following statutory criteria for post-conviction relief based on DNA evidence were met: DNA evidence could be used as exculpatory evidence, DNA evidence was available for testing, and DNA evidence was in fact tested.[7] Therefore, the forty-five total exonerations presumably represent only a fraction of all wrongful convictions in Texas. If mistaken eyewitness identification accounted for 85% of these exonerations, then the total number of innocent individuals who have been wrongfully imprisoned or executed on the basis of mistaken identification must certainly be a staggering figure. Even more alarming is the fact that Texas also leads the nation in incarcerations and executions, thus amplifying the probability of incarcerating or executing an innocent individual.

Dallas County, Texas, has led the nation in exonerations since 2001, with a running total of nineteen overturned wrongful convictions.[8] A review of previously closed prosecution files by The Dallas News reportedly revealed a "law-and-order machine that focused on securing and bolstering eyewitness testimony, regardless of the victim's doubt or the lack of corroborating evidence."[9] The report asserted that eyewitness misidentification was the result of "ignored safeguards meant to protect the innocent."[10] Other counties in Texas have had more limited success with reexamining DNA evidence. The crime lab in Harris County, the state's largest county, is in the process of working "to achieve full legitimacy after being engulfed in scandal for years."[11] To date, all six of the wrongful convictions later overturned by DNA evidence in Harris County were predicated on mistaken eyewitness identifications.[12]

The effects of mistaken eyewitness identifications are significant. In its simplest form, each exoneration represents a mistake, a single instance in which an individual was wrongfully convicted. Stripping innocent persons of their individual liberty and incarcerating them for crimes they did not commit is a miscarriage of justice. Allowing the true perpetrator to evade prosecution and remain at large poses a security risk to the community. According to psychologist Rod Lindsay, "[t]he cost to society of inaccurate eyewitness identifications is twofold. . . .Not only are you convicting the innocent—or at least putting them through the process of having to get out of the situation—but the guilty are still out there doing the crimes."[13]

Furthermore, wrongful convictions are financially burdensome on the taxpayers. Experts calculate that over three million dollars have been spent incarcerating and later compensating the wrongfully convicted in Dallas County alone.[14] It is estimated that another $17 million have been spent at the state and local level in civil settlements and statutory compensations.[15]

In summary, recent DNA exonerations have sent shockwaves through the nation by exposing the weaknesses in our criminal justice system. Studies have revealed that the main cause of these wrongful convictions is mistaken eyewitness identification. Not only do mistaken eyewitness identifications undermine the goals of our criminal justice system, but they also greatly encumber state and local budgets. As the ranking state leader in exonerations, Texas certainly experiences the effects of mistaken eyewitness identifications and presumably stands to gain the most by improving the system. So what can Texas and other states do to reduce wrongful convictions caused by mistaken eyewitness identification?

This article addresses the issues surrounding mistaken eyewitness identifications, examining the causes of mistaken identifications and suggesting the adoption of more reliable eyewitness identification procedures based on decades of scientific research and the success of similar reform efforts in several states. This article is divided into three parts. Part II describes the inherent weaknesses of eyewitness identification by discussing two main sources of errors: "estimator variables," which cannot be controlled by the criminal justice system, and "system variables," which can be controlled by the criminal justice system. Both categories of variables are analyzed in the context of the eyewitness identification procedures administered by law enforcement personnel as well as the admissibility of eyewitness identification evidence in court. Part III focuses on the development of reforms aimed at improving the accuracy and reliability of eyewitness identification procedures and the subsequent emergence of recommendations endorsed by a number of criminal justice organizations. These recommendations, collectively referred to as "best practices," typically include the double blind administration and recording of lineup procedures, effective selection of "fillers" or "foils" in the lineup array, provision of cautionary instructions to the eyewitness prior to administering the lineup, and documentation of the eyewitness' confidence level if an identification is made. Finally, Part IV addresses the implementation of these changes at the state level by comparing the different legislative approaches and policy standards used by states. These options are then analyzed to determine what would work best in Texas, thus tailoring a path for reform in Texas, as well as other states considering reform measures.

II. The Causes of Eyewitness Misidentifications

Decades of research on eyewitness identification has revealed its unreliability and exposed certain variables that are prone to reduce an eyewitness's ability to make an accurate identification of a stranger.[16] These variables can be classified into two main categories: estimator variables and system variables. Each is discussed in the following sections.

A. Estimator Variables

Faulty eyewitness identifications are usually attributed to the frailties of memory and the influence of suggestive police procedures.[17] These factors, which are called "estimator variables,"[18] refer to the conditions surrounding a witness' observation of an event that may affect her memory of the incident. Factors that influence the accuracy of memory include lighting conditions, duration of the event, distance from the crime scene, age of the eyewitness, the presence of a weapon, stress, and cross-racial identification.[19] A more accurate understanding of the inherent deficiencies in human memory and perception can improve the way eyewitness identifications are used in court and the weight they are afforded by juries. For this reason, some reforms focus on the manner in which eyewitness identifications are presented to a jury. These reforms include instructing the jury about the shortcomings of eyewitness identification or videotaping the entire lineup procedure for use by the defense.[20]

Eyewitness identifications are "among the most commonly used and compelling evidence brought against criminal defendants" at trial.[21] The criminal justice system has historically relied on the judiciary to limit the danger of faulty eyewitness identification testimony in court.[22] Cross-examination has been the preferred method of shedding light on possible inaccuracies and scrutinizing the eyewitness testimony, while jury instructions have served to inform the jury of the burden of proof and to remind them of the inherent risk of eyewitness testimony.[23]

B. System Variables

The variables and procedures in the justice system that exacerbate the inherent weaknesses of eyewitness identifications and increase the risk of eyewitness error are known as "system variables."[24] Common system variables include suggestive lineup procedures, repetitive rehearsing, prosecution based on a single eyewitness and minimal corroboration, confirmative cues, and feedback before or after a lineup.[25] The remainder of this section will focus on two settings where system variables commonly affect witness identifications: during the administration of eyewitness identification procedure at the police station, and at trial.

The number of wrongful convictions exposed by DNA testing has sparked intense debate over the need to reform the design and execution of lineups and photographic arrays on which the police rely to identify suspects. These reform efforts focus on establishing additional procedural safeguards to limit the admissibility of tainted pretrial identifications, notwithstanding the level of certainty expressed by the eyewitness.

In a typical eyewitness identification, an eyewitness is asked to identify the suspect in either a live lineup or a photo array. Both live and photo lineups typically consist of the suspect and a given number of "fillers" or "foils," or individuals who are not suspects in the case. In live lineups, the eyewitness views the suspects and the "fillers" simultaneously in a row. In photo lineups, the eyewitness typically views six mug shot photographs (one of the suspect and five "fillers") displayed in two rows of three photographs each.[26]

Most eyewitness identification procedures used by law enforcement agencies today are non-blind simultaneous lineups or photo arrays.[27] A procedure is "blind" when the agent administering the lineup does not know who the suspect is.[28] "Simultaneous" refers to the method of presenting the suspect and fillers at the same time as a group, as compared to the sequential method, where witnesses view "fillers" and the suspect individually, one at a time, and are asked to make a decision about each before viewing the next.[29]

The United States Supreme Court has long recognized the "vagaries of eyewitness identification," admitting in a 1967 decision that "the annals of criminal law are rife with instances of mistaken identification."[30] Yet the ever-increasing number of exonerations has raised serious questions regarding the adequacy of the very procedural safeguards designed to prevent mistaken identifications. Today, studies reveal that of the 77% of wrongful convictions involving mistaken eyewitness identifications, 62% were based solely on one witness' misidentification.[31] The misidentification was the central cause of the conviction in 50% of the cases.[32] Reformers have long been cognizant of the evidentiary importance of eyewitness identification evidence in criminal trials and the weight it is typically afforded by juries. Today, the ever-increasing number of exonerations linked to eyewitness misidentifications has brought a more pronounced focus on the admissibility and treatment of eyewitness identification evidence in court.

Prior to 1972, there was a presumption that unnecessarily suggestive eyewitness identification procedures should be excluded as evidence at trial.[33] The Supreme Court later discarded this presumption and instead held that an eyewitness identification must be excluded only if the unnecessarily suggestive procedure created a substantial risk of mistaken identification.[34] In *Manson v. Brathwaite*, the Court established a two-prong test for the exclusion of eyewitness identification evidence, requiring the defense to show both that the procedure was suggestive and that it resulted in unreliable eyewitness evidence.[35] Thus, an eyewitness identification will be excluded if, based on the totality of the circumstances,[36] "the . . . identification procedure was so impermissibly suggestive as to give rise to a very substantial likelihood of irreparable misidentification."[37] The courts have placed particular importance on "reliability" as a critical factor in determining the admissibility of identification testimony.[38] This test remains the governing law on eyewitness identifications in most states today.[39]

In Texas, the courts have refused to deem eyewitness identifications "unreliable" where the totality of the circumstances revealed no substantial likelihood of misidentification despite "the corrupting effect" of a suggestive pretrial procedure."[40] Since 1975, Texas law has allowed for convictions based on the testimony of one eyewitness and for the elimination of prospective jurors on account of their unwillingness to convict based on such testimony.[41] For example, a criminal defendant can be convicted solely on basis of uncorroborated testimony of a sexual assault victim if the victim reports assault to anyone other than the defendant within a year.[42]

All of the recent DNA exonerees had the benefit of these protections against unreliable eyewitness identification evidence, yet these precautions were insufficient to prevent their wrongful convictions.[43] A lack of procedural safeguards specifically designed to protect against the use of eyewitness identifications gathered by impermissibly suggestive procedures that render them unreliable may be a contributing factor in many wrongful convictions. Some scholars allege that *Manson*'s "reliability" standard may in fact contribute to the number of wrongful convictions rather than reducing it.[44] In the words of one Houston defense attorney, "[m]eeting the 'impermissibly suggestive' burden is not easy."[45] Even cross examination "is largely useless for detecting witnesses who are trying to be truthful but are genuinely mistaken" because it serves to highlight the witness' sincerity.[46] Given that eyewitness identification is one of the most powerful types of evidence, it becomes very difficult for the defense to rebut once admitted. [47]

Such loose standards of admissibility have caused the jury to become the principle device for ascertaining the truth.[48] Thus, a second reason contributing to wrongful convictions is the juries' inability to accurately assess the credibility of the evidence.[49] Unfortunately, jurors tend to overvalue even highly unreliable identifications at the expense of undervaluing other, more accurate evidence.[50] Studies show that juries are prone to evaluate the identification evidence based on an assumption that the defendant must be guilty if the witness identified him, rather than considering why the witness might have erroneously identified an innocent defendant.[51] The latter takes into account certain conditions that have a clear causal connection to misidentification, like poor lineup composition and suggestive police procedures, but which have been largely absent in current courtroom discourse.

Since *Manson* was decided, hundreds of eyewitness identification studies have been conducted with a primary focus on the suggestiveness of identification procedures.[52] The studies have revealed inherent flaws in traditional eyewitness identification procedures, including the tendency of simultaneous procedures to cause eyewitnesses to make lineup selections based on "relative judgment" rather than on his/her own mental image of the perpetrator.[53] In other words, when eyewitnesses are faced with a typical lineup (whether a photo array or a live lineup), the available research strongly suggests that when the perpetrator is not included in the lineup, eyewitnesses tend to identify the individual who most closely resembles the suspect.[54] If the eyewitness is not informed that the perpetrator may not be included in the lineup and that the investigation will continue even if the eyewitness cannot make an identification at that time, the eyewitness may unintentionally identify an innocent individual who closely resembles the suspect.

Additionally, the unintentional suggestiveness of an eyewitness procedure increases when not administered by an investigator in a "blind" fashion.[55] Non-blind administrators often "provide unintentional, or at times deliberate, cues" and unnecessary "feedback" to the witness as to which individual to identify.[56] Witnesses, in turn, rely on such feedback to confirm their selections, even when they are mistaken.[57]

A third concern centers on the instructions provided to the eyewitnesses before the procedure is conducted. In the absence of instructions, "the eyewitness often assumes that the perpetrator of the crime is one of those presented in the lineup," which "often leads to the selection of a person despite doubts."[58] In blind procedures, the eyewitness would be told that the administrator does not know the identity of the suspect, thus eliminating the tendency of the eyewitness to infer clues from the administrator's demeanor.[59]

Scholars in the field generally agree that traditional eyewitness identification procedures administered by law enforcement personnel must be improved, if not revised entirely.[60] System variables, like estimator variables, play a significant role in the accuracy of eyewitness identifications. But unlike estimator variables, the criminal justice community and legislatures possess a greater ability to minimize suggestive influences.

Problematic Lineup Procedures
• Simultaneous presentation encourages mistaken identifications • Non-blind administrators may use suggestive practices • Lack of instructions may increase mistaken identification

III. Eyewitness Identification Reform: The Development of Guidelines and Best Practices

The social scientists who have helped shape reform policies based on decades of empirical research dedicated to improving the accuracy and reliability of eyewitness identifications are major players in the eyewitness identification reform movement.[61] Working in conjunction with law enforcement and legal practitioners, leading researchers began developing guidelines and best practices for law enforcement in the late 1990s.[62] Criminal justice organizations and scholars have also been major players in the reform movement; they have brought attention and legitimacy to these reform policies by acknowledging the flaws in eyewitness identification procedures in peer reviewed literature and by publically endorsing the changes in published reports.[63] These advocacy efforts are ultimately aimed at persuading state legislatures to adopt and implement these reform policies.

A. Best Practices

Acknowledging the research findings on memory and identification procedures, many criminal justice organizations have formally endorsed certain practices that tend to reduce the problems associated with suggestive identification procedures. Collectively, these reforms are referred to as "best practices." Although the specific reforms suggested vary somewhat depending upon the source, they generally involve some combination of the following:[64]

1. Effective selection of fillers that are based on the eyewitness' previous description of the suspect and designed to ensure that the suspect does not stand out in the lineup or photo array.
2. Cautionary instructions to the witnesses that:
    a. the perpetrator might not be in the lineup or photo array in order to reduce the risk of relative judgment
    b. the investigation will continue even if the witness does not make a positive identification; and
    c. where applicable, that the police official conducting the lineup does not know the identity of the suspect.
3. Double-blind administration, in which the person administering the lineup or photo array "should not be aware of which member is the suspect," in order to prevent feedback and any confirmation bias that may result. [65]
4. Documentation of the lineup procedure, including the photographs used and a photograph/videotape recording of the live lineup as well as all dialogue and witness statements made during the procedure.
5. A witness statement documenting the witness' level of confidence that the identified person is the actual suspect; the statement should be taken at the time of the identification and prior to any feedback.[66]
6. Sequential presentation.

Several of these best practice recommendations are not controversial.[67] In some cases, they are mere reiterations of several police departments' existing policies of informing witnesses that they should not feel obligated to make a positive identification or requiring that fillers be selected based on the description provided by the eyewitness.[68] However, there has been considerable debate regarding the use and effectiveness of sequential presentation over the traditional simultaneous method. Hence, the sequential presentation features in best practice recommendations are somewhat tentative.

Many psychological studies have overwhelmingly confirmed that presenting the individuals sequentially reduces the likelihood that a witness will exercise relative judgment, picking the person who most resembles the witness's memory of the perpetrator rather than making a selection based on actual recognition.[69] But some authorities argue that this method may decrease the likelihood of correct identifications as well.[70] According to one report, use of the sequential method accounted for a 15% loss of accuracy over that experienced with simultaneous lineup procedures.[71] In other words, eyewitness identifications were inaccurate 15% more often when administered in a sequential manner than in a simultaneous manner. Yet recent laboratory tests, like this one, have failed to deliver any comprehensive analysis regarding the effectiveness of the sequential method when accompanied with a blind administrator. Thus, many questions remain unaddressed.[72]

Two main efforts at field testing the "double-blind sequential" procedure have taken place recently. The first was a relatively uncontroversial 2003 study of a new photographic double-blind sequential lineup protocol used by several police departments in Hennepin County, Minnesota.[73] The results of this test were consistent with those predicted by the laboratory scientists, but made no explicit comparison to traditional practices.

The second field study took place in three Illinois jurisdictions in 2006. This report, known as "the Mecklenburg Report," became widely publicized and highly criticized for finding a higher rate of false identifications in sequential identification procedures.[74] The report appeared to contradict both the laboratory scientists' predictions and the minimal existing field data on eyewitness performance.[75] According to the Mecklenburg Report, the traditional method, consisting of a simultaneous lineup conducted by "not-blind" law enforcement personnel, produced a lower identification rate of innocent fillers and a higher identification rate of the correct suspect than the double-blind, sequential technique. Therefore, the recommendation was that the state not implement changes to the present lineup procedures until further research was undertaken to obtain a more comprehensive understanding of the results.[76]

The Mecklenburg Report was widely publicized and immediately drew both avid support and vigorous criticism.[77] Perhaps the greatest criticism regards the lack of a true control group; the Mecklenburg Report compared a non-blind simultaneous procedure with a blind sequential procedure.[78] By making this type of comparison, the Mecklenburg Report failed to clarify whether the favorable results from the non-blind, simultaneous procedure was attributable to the simultaneous nature of the procedure or the influence of the non-blind administrator.[79] This point is addressed in the Addendum to the Mecklenburg Report, which notes that the effect of blind administrators on simultaneous lineups is one of several questions to be addressed in future studies.[80] For this very reason, the Mecklenburg study is criticized as being inconsequential and therefore "not worth addressing."[81] Others criticize the Mecklenburg study for failing to comport with common sense and scientific research, as demonstrated by the conclusion that a witness's memory improves over time.[82]

B. Guidelines Endorsed by Criminal Justice Organizations

The American Psychology/Law Society (AP/LS) published a report in 1998, recommending four policies regarding eyewitness identifications that at the time represented "an emerging consensus among eyewitness scientists as to key elements that such a set of procedures must entail."[83] These recommendations included: cautionary instructions, effective selection of fillers, double blind administration, and recording statements of the witness' certainty.[84] The AP/LS recognized the superiority of sequential lineups, but refused to explicitly endorse it due to expense and implementation concerns.[85]

In 2002, the United States Department of Justice (DOJ) created a Technical Working Group for Eyewitness Evidence (TWGEYEE) and published a set of guidelines in collaboration with the National Institute of Justice entitled "Eyewitness Evidence: A Guide for Law Enforcement."[86] The DOJ Report recommended "non-suggestive" administration of identification procedures, but stopped short of explicitly endorsing the double-blind procedure.[87] The DOJ Report made several specific recommendations, including recommendations for instructions for sequential photo and live lineup procedures.[88] The DOJ report also recommended a host of detailed cautionary instructions, asking law enforcement personnel to advise eyewitnesses that the actual suspect may not be present in the lineup and that the investigation will continue even if the eyewitness is unable to identify the suspect.[89] It also emphasized the importance of effective foil selection, requiring law enforcement to ensure that the fillers match the eyewitness's previous description of the suspect to the extent possible.[90] Neither the DOJ Report nor the AP/LS Report recommended documentation of the identification procedure.

In 2006, the American Bar Association (ABA) Criminal Justice Section's Ad Hoc Innocence Committee to Ensure the Integrity of the Criminal Process released a report entitled *Achieving Justice: Freeing the Innocent, Convicting the Guilty.*[91] The recommendations of the ABA Report mirrored those of the AP/LS, except that it provided for double blind administration "whenever practicable" and supplied procedures for selection of foils.[92] In short, although there are some minor disparities between the various reports, overall there is much consensus.

IV. Eyewitness Identification Reform: The Implementation of Best Practices

A. The Current Status of Reform in Texas

There are no statewide standards for conducting eyewitness identifications today in Texas, and the majority of jurisdictions do not follow widely endorsed best practices.[93] The Justice Project published a public policy report in 2008 which evaluated existing policies in Texas police departments in four main areas: the quality of cautionary instructions provided to the eyewitness, the guidelines aimed at fairness in foil selection, the comprehensive documentation of the procedure and witness confidence, and the blind administration of the lineup.[94] Eighty-eight percent of law enforcement agencies in Texas had no written policies for conducting lineups, and of those that did, the policies were often vague, incomplete, and overwhelmingly failed to include best practices.[95] The director of state projects at The Justice Project, Edwin Colfax, stated that "[g]iven the fragile nature of eyewitness evidence and its documented role in wrongful convictions, it is essential that Texas require police to adopt written policies that include key reforms for ensuring the most reliable evidence possible."[96]

B. The Adoption of Best Practices in Other States

In response to recent DNA advancements, several states across the nation have successfully enacted eyewitness identification reform, and dozens more have considered such legislation.[97] The first to do so was New Jersey in 2001, followed by Illinois in 2003.[98] To date, nineteen states and the District of Columbia have adopted reform legislation.[99] However, the scale and scope of reform varies from state to state, sometimes even from jurisdiction to jurisdiction. There is little uniformity in the type of legislative model or the standards for identification procedures the states adopt.

1. Diverging Legislative Models

Some states choose to follow a prescriptive legislative model by establishing specific eyewitness identification procedures the police must follow. Between the years of 2005-2006, eleven states adopted prescriptive eyewitness identification legislation.[100] In 2002, Illinois established the Governor's Commission on Capital Punishment.[101] A year later, the Illinois legislature enacted the 2003 Death Penalty Reform Bill based on the Mecklenburg Study, which required two best practices: cautionary instructions and documentation of procedure & witness certainty.[102] The Illinois bill required law enforcement to issue all three suggested cautionary instructions to the witness and to record the lineup procedure by photograph or other means.[103] The legislature took a more cautionary approach with respect to sequential lineups, calling for a pilot study to investigate it further.[104]

Other states have relied upon their attorney general and other governmental bodies to implement statewide reform. The legislatures in Virginia and Maine, for example, established or considered task forces or commissions to study and make recommendations regarding eyewitness identification reform.[105] In addition to a task force, Pennsylvania also established a pilot project to study how effectively eyewitness identification procedures perform in the field.[106]

In some states, this approach has paved the way for the passage of reform bills, although such bills are frequently less expansive than the original recommendations. For example, the 2004 Virginia General Assembly directed the State Crime Commission to study mistaken eyewitness identifications, traditional lineup procedures, and sequential procedures.[107] The Commission returned less than a year later with six recommendations that embodied two general "best practices."[108] The first "best practice" was that written policies for conducting in-person and photograph lineups be developed, which coincided with the recommendation that a workgroup be established to develop model lineup policy.[109] With respect to a second "best practice," the Commission took a bold approach by recommending the exclusive use of the sequential method.[110] The Commission called for amendments to the training academy's lineup requirements to include only the use of the sequential method and for the inclusion of the sequential method as part of police training accreditation.[111] In addition, the Commission expended considerable effort to lobby for the designation of the state police as the repository for all lineup mug shots and queries.[112] These recommendations were largely incorporated into a 2005 bill, though it was silent with respect to the sequential method.[113]

On the other hand, the state legislatures in both Wisconsin and Maryland pursued the "Best Practices" Model for eyewitness identification reform.[114] The "Best Practices" Model requires police, the attorney general, or a training body to develop lineup procedures based on best practices or the Department of Justice Guidelines.[115] Some scholars champion this approach as "democratic experimentalism" whereby legislatures delegate rulemaking authority to local police agencies, which in turn gives them a stake in the problem-solving process and creates an institutional structure receptive to ongoing reform.[116]

As a response to the 2003 exoneration of Steven Avery, an innocent man who had served 18 years in prison after a jury had wrongfully convicted him on the basis of faulty eyewitness identification testimony, Wisconsin reformed its eyewitness identification procedures "from police agencies up, rather than the legislature down."[117] His case inspired Wisconsin Representative Mark Gundrum to create a task force to investigate "what went wrong" in Avery's case.[118] The task force's recommendations were then incorporated into a 2005 reform bill that focused on reducing wrongful convictions.[119] The bill required local law enforcement agencies to develop written lineup procedures in consideration of "model policies and policies adopted by other jurisdictions" that were "designed to reduce the potential for erroneous identifications" in light of the evolving best practices from social science.[120] Although the "content of police practice was neither legislatively nor judicially dictated to law enforcement agencies," the Wisconsin judiciary has enforced agency policies by excluding testimony relating to out-of-court identification procedures that failed to comply with proper policy and by leaving open the possibility that state courts could "hold a substandard policy to be itself unnecessarily suggestive."[121]

New Jersey essentially followed all three models. The Attorney General issued a set of guidelines in April 2001, which urged police departments to maintain written documentation of eyewitness identification procedures and implemented blind and sequential lineups.[122] That same year, New Jersey became the first state to officially adopt the recommendations issued by the Justice Department.[123] These reforms apply to all law enforcement, including sheriffs.[124] New Jersey is also an example of judicial reform. In July 2006, the New Jersey Supreme Court gave the guidelines teeth when it unanimously ruled that eyewitness identifications are inadmissible at trial unless a written record is kept of the procedure.[125]

2. Diverging Standards

While New Jersey was the first to implement blind and sequential lineups by order of the State Attorney General in 2001, followed by State Attorney General in Wisconsin in 2005, North Carolina became the first state to legislatively require statewide sequential double-blind lineups and photo array procedures without exception.[126] In 2010, Ohio adopted a "folder method" for blind and sequential photo lineups, among other identification procedures, as part of a comprehensive innocence investigation.[127] Ohio's "folder method" removes the inherent suggestiveness of the identification procedure by preventing the administrator from seeing which photo a witness is viewing. The Innocence and Justice Projects strongly recommend the use of the sequential double-blind method.[128] However, the Innocence Project has declined to include such recommendations in its reform package on the basis that it has "often prevented clear consideration of other important and accepted reforms."[129]

All four of these states (New Jersey, Wisconsin, North Carolina, and Ohio) have also adopted the other remaining best practices, including the provision of cautionary instructions, the use of effective foil or filler selection procedures, and the documentation of the identification procedures and witness certainty statements.[130] There also appears to be at least some consensus regarding the particular elements included in reform packages. Wisconsin, North Carolina, New Jersey, Maryland, and West Virginia all require written policies.[131]

Two states have enacted legislation which establishes both protocols for identification procedures and judicial remedies for non-compliance. Laws in North Carolina and Ohio now provide that trial courts shall consider evidence of a failure to comply with required identification procedures in adjudicating motions to suppress eyewitness identification.[132]

3. The Future of Reform in Texas

To date, Texas has seemingly embraced a "best practices" approach to eyewitness identification reform. Senator Rodney Ellis introduced legislation that sought to establish an innocence commission[133] and require police departments to create written policies for eyewitness identification practices (including the use of any best practices),[134] among other reform initiatives, in the Texas Legislature on November 10, 2008. Regarding eyewitness identification procedures, the reforms Senator Ellis proposed would have required each law enforcement agency to have a detailed written policy addressing:

1. the effective use of fillers,[135]
2. the issuance of cautionary instructions to eyewitnesses before beginning identification procedures,[136]

3. the use of double-blind administration procedures ("if practicable"),[137] and
4. the documentation of the identification procedure & witness certainty statements.[138]

With respect to the cautionary instructions, the bill would have required police administrators to tell the witness that the suspect might not be present, that the witness was not required to make an identification, and that the investigation would continue regardless of the result of the identification procedure.[139] With regard to documentation, the bill would have required identification procedures to be videotaped where practicable.[140] If videotaping was not possible, then the bill would have required that the person administering the identification procedure provide an explanation as to the absence of a recording.[141] If audiotaping equipment was available, then the bill would have required an audio recording of the identification procedure.[142] Also, if a blind administrator was not practicable, then the bill would have required law enforcement departments to find alternative methods to prevent administrators from "viewing the members of the [photo] array or lineup simultaneously with the witness or knowing the order of the presentation of the array or lineup to the witness."[143] The bill also would have required departments to develop a written policy addressing the manner in which identification procedures would be administered to illiterate persons or those of limited English language proficiency.[144]

This bill was substituted and passed in the Senate with few significant changes; even in its amended version, it required each agency to adopt, implement, or amend a detailed written policy based on scientific research on eyewitness memory and relevant policies and guidelines.[145] As amended, the bill still would have required written department identification policies addressing the four main issues mentioned above, which were central to the bill as originally drafted.[146] The revised bill would have allowed law enforcement departments to replace blind administration with an alternative procedure so long as it "prevents the opportunity to influence a witness."[147] The bill added a further measure, requiring "any other procedures or best practices."[148] This version was placed on the general calendar in the House but died at the end of the legislative session as a result of the end-of-session battle over voter identifications.[149] Thus, Texas' hopes of eyewitness identification reform have been delayed at least until the next session.

However, not all was lost this past legislative year in terms of eyewitness identification reform. The Texas Legislature created the Timothy Cole Advisory Panel on Wrongful Convictions.[150] The Panel was named after Tim Cole, who was posthumously pardoned by Gov. Rick Perry in March 2010 after DNA revealed he had been wrongfully convicted of a rape two decades ago.[151] This panel is currently working in conjunction with the Task Force on Indigent Defense to study a variety of issues relating to wrongful convictions, including the following: "the causes of wrongful conviction;" the "procedures and programs that may be implemented to prevent future wrongful convictions;" the "effects of state law on wrongful convictions;" and the desirability of a state "innocence commission to investigate wrongful convictions."[152]

Police departments should be permitted the flexibility to effectuate change in light of technological improvements, research developments, and the capabilities and financial restraints of each department. With that said, merely requiring local police agencies to adopt written policies is wholly insufficient. Ten years have passed since the DOJ Report was first issued and only a handful of states have adopted any reforms, whether as a matter of state constitutional law, evidence rules, or statute.[153] Additionally recalling The Justice Project's report which indicated that only 12% of police agencies in the entire state of Texas have written policies, it would be reasonable to assume that police departments will not make the recommended changes on their own, at least not anytime in the near future.[154] The Texas legislature should instruct local police agencies to adopt written policies consistent with best practices, but should allow for the implementation of divergent policies at the local level. Mandating particular procedures would likely risk the passage of any comprehensive reform package in Texas at this time.

V. Conclusion

Mistaken eyewitness identification is the leading cause of wrongful convictions in the United States and Texas. Because eyewitness identification testimony is one of the most widespread and compelling forms of evidence at trial, law enforcement personnel must take great care in collecting it and judges must later exercise equal care in admitting it at trial. Decades of research and empirical studies have identified certain aspects of traditional eyewitness identification procedures, called system variables, which increase the risk of misidentification. The criminal justice system has control over system variables, to some extent. Hence, any system variables contributing to misidentification can be minimized, if not completely eliminated. Even estimator variables, despite their inherent nature, can be remedied to some extent at the procedural level by treating the mind like a crime scene and acknowledging the existence of such variables before the jury.

In addition to identifying current deficiencies in the system, researchers, in collaboration with the criminal justice community, have also proposed a number of reforms to eyewitness identification procedures that can substantially cut the risk of misidentification and produce more reliable evidence. Several states have already embraced these reforms, each in their different way. Yet despite the divergent legislative approaches and particular standards employed, the motivation behind the change was the same: the preservation of justice.

The spark of reform has begun in Texas, but its full potential has yet to be realized. Texas must require law enforcement agencies to adopt written policies and procedures for eyewitness identifications in accordance with best practices. Our innocent citizens deserve that much.

Endnotes

1. *DNA Evidence*, N.Y. Times, June 18, 2009, *available at* http://topics.nytimes.com/topics/reference/timestopics/subjects/d/dna_evidence/index.html (last visited Aug. 25, 2010).
2. Richard A. Wise & Martin A. Safer, *A Survey of Judges' Knowledge and Beliefs About Eyewitness Testimony*, 40 Ct. Rev. 6, at 6 (2003).
3. Tanya Eiserer, *With Faulty Eyewitness Testimony Proving Problematic, Police Will Take Part In Federally Funded Study*, Dallas Morning News, Sept. 26, 2007, *available at* http://

www.dallasnews.com/sharedcontent/dws/news/localnews/stories/092607dnmetlineups.35fb3d4.html (last visited Aug. 23, 2010).

4. Samuel R. Gross et al., *Exonerations in the United States: 1989 through 2003*, 95 J. Crim. L. & Criminology 523, 523-560 (2005); *see also* Jim Dwyer, Peter Neufeld & Barry Scheck, Actual Innocence: Five Days to Execution and Other Dispatches from the Wrongly Convicted, NY: Penguin Books (2000); Ronald Huff, Arye Rattner, & Edward Sagarin, Convicted but Innocent, Thousand Oaks, Sage (1996); Gary L. Wells & Deah S. Quinlivan, *Suggestive Eyewitness Identification Procedures and the Supreme Court's Reliability Test in Light of Eyewitness Science: 30 Years Later*, 33 L. & Hum. Behav. 1, 2 (2008); Gary L. Wells et al., *Eyewitness Identification Procedures: Recommendations for Lineups and Photospreads*, 22 L. & Hum. Behav. 603, 604 (1998); Timothy P. O'Toole, *What's the Matter With Illinois? How an Opportunity Was Squandered to Conduct an Important Study on Eyewitness Identification Procedures*, Champion, Aug. 2006, at 18, *available at* http://www.nacdl.org/public.nsf/01c1e7698280d20385256d0b00789923/03c451bfa6487584852571e300634d51?OpenDocument (last visited Aug. 23, 2010).

5. Wells et al., *supra* note 4, at 605; Steve McGonigle & Jennifer Emily, *18 Dallas County Cases Overturned by DNA Relied Heavily on Eyewitness Testimony*, Dallas Morning News, Oct. 12, 2008, *available at* http://truthinjustice.org/dallas-eyewitness.htm (last visited Aug. 25, 2010); Innocence Project, *Facts on Post-Conviction DNA Exonerations*, *available at* http://www.innocenceproject.org/Content/351.php (last visited Aug. 25, 2010).

6. Brad Woodard, *Mistaken identifications under scrutiny as Texas leads nation in wrongful convictions*, KHOU-TV, Apr. 13, 2010, *available at* http://www.khou.com/news/local/Mistaken-identifications-under-scrutiny-as-Texas-leads-nation-in-wrongful-convictions-90772299.html (last visited Aug. 25, 2010); The Justice Project, Convicting The

INNOCENT: TEXAS JUSTICE DERAILED 6 (2009), *available at* http://www.thejusticeproject.org/wp-content/uploads/convicting-the-innocent.pdf (last visited Aug. 23, 2010).

7. Despite the staggering number of wrongful convictions, the remedies available to those seeking to prove their actual innocence are limited under the current system. Post-conviction DNA testing can only exculpate the select number of wrongful convictions in which DNA was a significant factor in the decision to convict in the first place, and where it is still available to be tested today. *See* Wells et al., *supra* note 4, at 649. According to one study, biologically-rich trace evidence is left behind in only a small fraction of murders, and almost no robberies or aggravated assaults. *See* Gary L. Wells et al., *From the Lab to the Police Station: A Successful Application of Eyewitness Research*, 55 AM. PSYCHOLOGIST 581, 589 (2000). Therefore, even if we could somehow identify those innocent individuals who are currently being incarcerated for crimes they did not commit, DNA testing would not be a viable option to prove actual innocence in the vast majority of those cases.

8. Steve McGonigle & Jennifer Emily, *18 Dallas County Cases Overturned by DNA Relied Heavily on Eyewitness Testimony*, DALLAS MORNING NEWS, Oct. 12, 2008, *available at* http://truthinjustice.org/dallas-eyewitness.htm (last visited Aug. 25, 2010).

9. *Id.*

10. *Id.*

11. Bradley Olson, *Backlog Woes Continue at HPD Lab*, HOUS. CHRON., Jan. 26, 2010, *available at* http://www.chron.com/disp/story.mpl/metropolitan/6836933.html (last visited Aug. 26, 2010).

12. Margery Malkin Koosed, *Reforming Eyewitness Identification Law and Practices to Protect the Innocent*, 42 CREIGHTON L. REV. 595, 599 (2009) (citing Roma Khanna, *Study: Witness Errors Lead Juries Astray*, HOUS. CHRON., Mar. 26,

2009, *available at* http://www.chron.com/disp/story.mpl/metropolitan/6342269.html (last visited Aug. 24, 2010)).

13. The Justice Project, Eyewitness Identification: A Policy Review 2, *available at* http://www.thejusticeproject.org/wp-content/uploads/polpack_eyewitnessid-fin21.pdf (last visited Aug. 23, 2010).

14. Jennifer Emily & Steve McGonigle, *Eyewitnesses still play key roles in cases where DNA, other evidence, is lacking*, Dallas Morning News, Oct. 4, 2008, *available at* http://www.dallasnews.com/sharedcontent/dws/dn/dnacases/stories/101308dnproDNArobbery.264af4b.html (last visited Aug. 23, 2010).

15. The Innocence Project, Sequential Lineups, *available at* http://www.innocenceproject.org/Content/151.php (last visited Aug. 23, 2010).

16. Sandra Guerra Thompson, *Judicial Blindness to Eyewitness Misidentification*, 93 Marq. L. Rev. 639, 643 (2009).

17. Daniel S. Medwed, *Anatomy of a Wrongful Conviction: Theoretical Implications and Practical Solutions*, 51 Vill. L. Rev. 337, 361–63 & n.179 (2006).

18. Thompson, *supra* note 16, at 643.

19. Elizabeth F. Loftus & James M. Doyle, Eyewitness Testimony: Civil and Criminal (2d ed. 1992).

20. Gary L. Wells, *Eyewitneess Identification Evidence: Science and Reform*, Champion, Apr. 2005, at 12, *available at* http://www.nacdl.org/public.nsf/698c98dd101a846085256eb400500c01/5c51d539cbda7fdc85256ff6005284fc?OpenDocument (last visited Aug. 26, 2010).

21. Barry C. Scheck & Peter J. Neufeld, Innocence Project, Eyewitness Identification Reform 1 (2006), *available at* http://www.nacdl.org/sl_docs.nsf/freeform/eyeID_attachments/$FILE/IP_Factsheet.pdf (last visited Aug. 25, 2010); *see also* Wells et al., *supra* note 4, at 604.

22. Jennifer L. Overbeck, *Beyond Admissibility: A Practical Look at the Use of Eyewitness Expert Testimony in the Federal Courts*, 80 N.Y.U. L. Rev. 1985, 194–205 (2005).
23. Britton Douglas, *"That's What She Said": Why Limiting the Use of Uncorroborated Eyewitness Identification Testimony Could Prevent Wrongful Convictions in Texas*, 41 Tex. Tech. L. Rev. 561, 576-579 (2009).
24. Thompson, *supra* note 16, at 644.
25. Wells et al., *supra* note 7, at 582.
26. This type of photo lineup is frequently called a "six pack."
27. National Institute of Justice, Eyewitness Identification: Simultaneous vs. Sequential Lineups (Mar. 2009), *available at* http://www.ojp.usdoj.gov/nij/topics/law-enforcement/eyewitness-identification/simultaneous-sequential.htm (last visited Aug. 23, 2010).
28. Daniel Schacter et al., *Policy Forum: Studying Eyewitness Investigations in the Field*, 32 L. & Hum. Behav. 3, 3 (2008) .
29. *Id.* at 3, *see also* National Institute of Justice, *supra* note 49.
30. United States v. Wade, 288 U.S. 218, 228 (1967); *see also* Mason v. Brathwaite, 432 U.S. 98, 107 (1977); Neil v. Biggers, 409 U.S. 188, 199–200 (1972); Stovall v. Denno, 288 U.S. 293, 301–02 (1967); Gilbert v. California, 288 U.S. 263, 264 (1967).
31. The Innocence Project, Understanding the Causes: Eyewitness Misidentification, *available at* http://www.innocenceproject.org/understand/eyewitness-misidentification.php (last visited Aug. 23, 2010).
32. *Id.*
33. Wells & Quinlivan, *supra* note 4, at 2 (citing to Stovall v. Denno, 288 U.S. 293 (1967)).
34. *Neil v. Biggers* , 409 U.S. 188, 199–200 (1972).

35. *Manson v. Brathwaite*, 432 U.S. 98, 113 (1977)(asserting that the five non-exclusive factors identified in *Neil* must be "weighed against the corrupting effect of any suggestive identification procedure" to determine the admissibility of eyewitness identification evidence).

36. The Court identified five non-exclusive factors, which include the following: the eyewitness' view of the perpetrator and degree of attention during the crime; the accuracy of the witness' prior description of the criminal; the length of time between the crime and identification; and the level of certainly demonstrated by the witnesses at the identification. *See Neil* , 409 U.S. at 199–200.

37. Simmons v. United States, 390 U.S. 377, 384 (1968); *see also* Madden v. State, 799 S.W.2d 683, 695 (Tex. Crim. App. 1990), *cert. denied*, 499 U.S. 954 (1991).

38. *Manson*, 432 U.S. at 113 (asserting that "reliability is the linchpin in determining the admissibility of identification testimony."); Loserth v. State, 963 S.W.2d 770, 772 (Tex. Crim. App. 1998); Sierra v. State, No. 01-07-00443-CR, 2008 Tex.App. LEXIS 6417, at *6 (Tex.App.—Houston [1st Dist.] Aug. 21, 2008).

39. Wells & Quinlivan, *supra* note 4, at 1.

40. *Id.; Sierra,* 2008 Tex.App. LEXIS 6417 at *9.

41. Sandra Guerra Thompson, *Beyond a Reasonable Doubt? Reconsidering Uncorroborated Eyewitness Identification Testimony*, 41 UC Davis L. Rev. 1526 n. 208 (2008) ("Unless a rule in effect requires additional investigation, there is no legal requirement that the police search for additional evidence once they obtain an eyewitness's statement identifying a suspect. Consequently, investigations often end with the eyewitness's identification of the suspect."). *See also*, John Council, *Witnesses to the Prosecution: Current and Former ADAs Who Helped Convict Exonerated Men Reflect*, Texas Lawyer (ALM Media, 2008), available at http://www.law.com/jsp/tx/PubArticleTX.jsp?id=1202421991854&slreturn=1&hbxlogin=1#.

42. Tex. Code Crim. Proc. Ann. art. 38.07 (Vernon Pamph. Supp. 2004); *see also* Smith v. State, No. 12-02-00240-CR, 2004 Tex.App. LEXIS 4487, at *5 (Tex.App.—Tyler May 12, 2004).

43. *See generally* Edward Connors et al., *Convicted by Juries, Exonerated by Science: Case Studies in the Use of DNA Evidence to Establish Innocence After Trial*, United States Dep't of Justice (1996), *available at* http://www.ncjrs.gov/pdffiles/dnaevid.pdf (last visited Aug. 23, 2010).

44. Richard A. Wise et al., *A Tripartite Solution to Eyewitness Error*, 97 J. Crim. L. & Criminology 807, 819 (2007); *see also* Manson v. Brathwaite, 432 U.S. 98, 113 (1977) (setting forth the reliability standard for admission of eyewitness identification evidence).

45. John T. Floyd, *DNA Exonerations Question Eyewitness Testimony: Flawed, Suggestive Photo Lineups Resulting in Eyewitness Misidentification and Wrongly Convicted*, Oct. 29, 2008, *available at* http://www.johntfloyd.com/comments/october08/29a.htm (last visited Aug. 23, 2010).

46. Wells et al., *supra* note 4, at 609.

47. *Id.*

48. William David Gross, *The Unfortunate Faith: A Solution to the Unwarranted Reliance Upon Eyewitness Testimony*, 5 Tex. Wesleyan L. Rev. 307, 310 (1999).

49. Richard S. Schmechel et al., *Beyond the Ken? Testing Jurors' Understanding of Eyewitness Reliability Evidence,* 46 Jurimetrics J. 177, 178 (2006).

50. Loftus & Doyle, *supra* note 19, at 1-8.

51. Steven E. Clark & Ryan D. Godfrey, *Eyewitness Identification Evidence and Innocence Risk*, 16 Psychonomic Soc'y Bull. & Rev. 22, 22-42 (2009).

52. Gary L. Wells, *Applied Eyewitness Testimony Research: System Variables and Estimator Variables*, 36 J. Personality & Soc. Psychol. 1546, 1546 (1978).

53. Schacter et al., *supra* note 50, at 3, *see also* SCHECK & NEUFELD, *supra* note 21, at 1.

54. *See id.*

55. Schacter et al., *supra* note 50, at 3.

56. SCHECK & NEUFELD, *supra* note 21, at 1.

57. Medwed, *supra* note 17, at 360; *see also* Amy Klobuchar, Nancy K. Mehrkens Steblay & Hilary Lindell Caligiuri, *Improving Eyewitness Identifications: Hennepin County's Blind Sequential Lineup Pilot Project*, 4 CARDOZO PUB. L. POL'Y & ETHICS J. 381, 390 (2006); SCHECK & NEUFELD, *supra* note 21, at 1.

58. SCHECK & NEUFELD, *supra* note 21, at 1.

59. *Id.* at 2.

60. *Id.* at 2.

61. Sandra Guerra Thompson, *What Price Justice? The Importance of Costs to Eyewitness Identification Reform*, 41 TEX. TECH. L. REV. 33, 36 (2008) (citing John T. Rago, *"Truth or Consequences" and Post-Conviction DNA Testing: Have You Reached Your Verdict?*, 107 DICK. L. REV. 845, 847 (2003)); THE JUSTICE PROJECT, EYEWITNESS IDENTIFICATION: A POLICY REVIEW 2, *available at* http://www.thejusticeproject.org/wp-content/uploads/polpack_eyewitnessid-fin21.pdf (last visited Aug. 23, 2010).

62. THE JUSTICE PROJECT, EYEWITNESS IDENTIFICATION, *supra* note 61, at 2.

63. *Id.*

64. SCHECK & NEUFELD, *supra* note 21, at 1–2.

65. Wells et al., *supra* note 4, at 604.

66. Scientific data indicates that witnesses most accurately gauge their true level of confidence at the time of the lineup (even though this confidence is not particularly accurate) and that over time, the trial preparation process tends to falsely inflate witness' confidence, thus leading to exaggerating statements

of confidence at trial. The Justice Project, Eyewitness Identification, *supra* note 61, at 3.

67. Brian Cutler et al., *Creating Blind Photoarrays Using Virtual Human Technology: A Feasibility Test,* 12 Police Q. 289, 290 (2009), *available at* http://pqx.sagepub.com/cgi/content/abstract/12/3/289 (last visited Aug. 23, 2010).

68. *Id.*

69. Curt A. Carlson, Scott D. Gronlund & Steven E. Clark, Lineup Composition, Suspect Position, and the Sequential Lineup Advantage, 14 J. Experimental Psychol: Applied 118, 118-128 (2008); *see also* Ryann M. Haw & Ronald P. Fisher, *Effects of Administrator-Witness Contact on Eyewitness Identification Accuracy,* 89 J. Applied Psychol. 1106, 1106-1112 (2004); Scheck & Neufeld, *supra* note 21, at 1–2.

70. American Bar Association Criminal Justice Section, Achieving Justice: Freeing the Innocent, Convicting the Guilty 34 (Paul Giannelli & Myrna Raeder eds., 2006); *see also* Gary Wells, *Does the Sequential Lineup Reduce Accurate Identifications in Addition to Reducing Mistaken Identifications?... Yes, but...* (2005), *available at* http://www.psychology.iastate.edu/faculty/gwells/SequentialNotesonlossofhits.htm (last visited Aug. 23, 2010).

71. Steven Penrod, *Identification Evidence: How Well are Witnesses and Police Performing?* 18 Crim. Just. 36, 37–45 (2003).

72. *See* Scheck & Neufeld, *supra* note 21, at 2.

73. Klobuchar, Steblay & Caligiuri, *supra* note 57, at 390

74. *See generally* Schacter et al., *supra* note 50; Klobuchar, Steblay & Caliguri, *supra* note 57; Medwed, *supra* note 17; O'Toole, *supra* note 4.

75. *See* Sheri H. Mecklenburg et al., *Report to the Legislature of the State of Illinois: The Illinois Pilot Program on Double-Blind, Sequential Lineup Procedures* 42–47 (2006), *available at* http://www.chicagopolice.org/IL%20Pilot%20on%20Eyewitness%20ID.pdf (last visited Aug. 23, 2010).

76. *Id.* at 64–65.

77. Shacter et al, *supra* note 50, at 4.

78. *Id.*

79. O'Toole, *supra* note 4, at 19.

80. Sheri Mecklenburg, *Addendum to the Report to the Legislature of the State of Illinois: The Illinois Pilot Program on Sequential Double-Blind Identification Procedures* 2–6 (2006), *available at* http://eyewitness.utep.edu/Documents/IllinoisPilotStudyOnEyewitnessIDAddendum.pdf (last visited Aug. 23, 2010).

81. Klobuchar, Steblay & Caligiuri, *supra* note 57, at 361-63.

82. O'Toole, *supra* note 4, at 19.

83. Wells et al., *supra* note 4, at 7.

84. *Id.*

85. Wells et al., *supra* note 4, at 639-41.

86. *See generally* United States Dep't of Justice, Eyewitness Evidence: A Guide for Law Enforcement (1999), *available at* http://www.ncjrs.gov/pdffiles1/nij/178240.pdf (last visited Aug. 23, 2010).

87. *See id.* at 17–20.

88. *Id.* at 34–36.

89. *Id.* at 31–32.

90. *Id.* at 29–31.

91. *See generally* American Bar Association Criminal Justice Section , *supra* note 70.

92. *Id.* at 25.

93. The Justice Project, Convicting The Innocent, *supra* note 6, at 6–7; *see also* The Justice Project, *New Study Documents Lack of Lineup Policies in Texas Law Enforcement Agencies*, Nov. 18, 2008, *available at* http://www.thejusticeproject.org/press/new-study-documents-lack-of-lineup-polices-in-texas-law-enforcement-agencies/ (last visited Aug. 23, 2010).

94. The Justice Project, Convicting The Innocent, *supra* note 6, at 7–8.

95. *Id.* at 6–7; *see also* Jennifer Emily & Steve McGonigle, *Eyewitnesses still play key roles in cases where DNA, other evidence, is lacking*, Dallas Morning News, Oct. 4, 2008, *available at* http://www.dallasnews.com/sharedcontent/dws/dn/dnacases/stories/101308dnproDNArobbery.264af4b.html (last visited Aug. 23, 2010).

96. The Justice Project, *New Study Documents Lack of Lineup Policies in Texas Law Enforcement Agencies*, Nov. 18, 2008, *available at* http://www.thejusticeproject.org/press/new-study-documents-lack-of-lineup-polices-in-texas-law-enforcement-agencies/ (last visited Aug. 23, 2010).

97. The Justice Project, *New Study Documents Lack of Lineup Policies in Texas Law Enforcement Agencies*, Nov. 18, 2008, *available at* http://www.thejusticeproject.org/press/new-study-documents-lack-of-lineup-polices-in-texas-law-enforcement-agencies/ (last visited Aug. 23, 2010). *See also*, National Association of Criminal Defense Lawyers (NACDL), *State Legislation: Eyewitness Identification Reform available at* http://www.nacdl.org/sl_docs.nsf/freeform/EyeID_legislation(last visited Aug. 23, 2010).

98. The Justice Project, *New Study Documents Lack of Lineup Policies in Texas Law Enforcement Agencies*, Nov. 18, 2008, *available at* http://www.thejusticeproject.org/press/new-study-documents-lack-of-lineup-polices-in-texas-law-enforcement-agencies/ (last visited Aug. 23, 2010). *See* also, National Association of Criminal Defense Lawyers (NACDL), *State Legislation: Eyewitness Identification Reform available at* http://www.nacdl.org/sl_docs.nsf/freeform/EyeID_legislation(last visited Aug. 23, 2010).

99. These states include: California, Connecticut, Georgia, Hawaii, Illinois, Maine, Maryland, Massachusetts, Michigan, Missouri, New Hampshire, New York, Oregon, Pennsylvania, Rhode Island, Vermont, Virginia, West Virginia, and Wisconsin. *See* National Association of Criminal Defense

Lawyers (NACDL), *State Legislation: Eyewitness Identification Reform available at* http://www.nacdl.org/sl_docs.nsf/freeform/EyeID_legislation(last visited Aug. 23, 2010).

100. These states include: Illinois; Connecticut; Georgia; Hawaii; Massachusetts; Michigan; New Hampshire; New York; Pennsylvania; Rhode Island; Vermont; and West Virginia. *See* Scott Ehlers, Nat'l Ass'n of Criminal Def. Lawyers Legislative Affairs Dir., *Eyewitness ID Reform Legislation: Past, Present and Future* 12–13, *available at* http://www.nacdl.org/sl_docs.nsf/freeform/eyeID_attachments/$FILE/Ehlers-July06.ppt (last visited Aug. 23, 2010).

101. *Id.* at 3.

102. S.B. 472, 93rd Gen. Assemb., Reg. Sess. (Ill. 2003).

103. *Id.*

104. *Id.*

105. H. 906, 122nd Leg., First Reg. Sess. (Me. 2005); S.B. 946, 2005 Leg., Reg. Sess. (Pa. 2005); H.B. 2632, 2005 Leg., Reg. Sess. (Va. 2005).

106. S.B. 947, 2005 Leg., Reg. Sess. (Pa. 2005).

107. H.R.J. Res. 79, 2004 Leg., Reg. Sess. (Va. 2004).

108. Virginia State Crime Comm'n, Mistaken Eyewitness Identification, H.D. 40, Reg. Sess., at 18-19 (2005).

109. *Id.* at 19.

110. *Id.*

111. *Id.* at 19.

112. *Id.* at 19.

113. *See generally* H.B. 2632, 2005 Leg., Reg. Sess. (Va. 2005).

114. S.B. 863, 2006 Leg., Reg. Sess. (Md. 2006); A.B. 648, 2005-2006 Leg., Reg. Sess. (Wis. 2005). The Maryland legislation died in the House. *See* Ehlers, *supra* note 100, at 14.

115. Ehlers, supra note 100, at 14.

116. Koosed, *supra* note 12, at 612 (citing Katherine Kruse, *Instituting Innocence Reform: Wisconsin's New Governance Experiment*, 2006 Wis. L. Rev. 645, 687–689 (2006)).

117. *Id.* at 612.

118. Wisconsin Rep. Mark Gundrum created the Avery Task Force in 2004. *See* Keith A. Findley, *Re-Imagining Justice*, 12 Wis. Defender 11, 12–13 (2004), *available at* http://www.wisspd.org/html/publications/docs/wdefwinter04.pdf. (last visited Aug. 24, 2010).

119. *Id.* at 13–16; *see also* A.B. 648, 2005-2006 Leg., Reg. Sess. (Wis. 2005).

120. A.B. 648, 2005-2006 Leg., Reg. Sess. (Wis. 2005).

121. Koosed, *supra* note 12, at 613 (citing Katherine Kruse, *Instituting Innocence Reform: Wisconsin's New Governance Experiment*" 2006 Wis. L. Rev. 645, 687–689 (2006)).

122. Memorandum from John J. Farmer, Jr., New Jersey Attorney General 4, 10 (Apr. 18, 2001), *available at* http://www.state.nj.us/lps/dcj/agguide/photoid.pdf (last visited Aug. 24, 2010).

123. *Id.* at 1.

124. *Id.*

125. State v. Cook, 847 A.2d 530, 592 (N.J. 2004).

126. Thompson, *supra* note 61, at 36 (citing N.C. Gen. Stat. § 15A-284.52(b)(2) (2007)).

127. S.B. 77, 128th Gen. Assemb., Reg. Sess. (Ohio 2010).

128. *See, e.g.,* Innocence Project, *Eyewitness Identification Reform*, *available at* http://www.innocenceproject.org/Content/Eyewitness_Identification_Reform.php (last visited Aug. 25, 2010); The Justice Project, *Eyewitness Identification*, *available at* http://www.thejusticeproject.org/convicting-the-innocent/tx-eyewitness-id/ (last visited Aug. 25, 2010).

129. Koosed, *supra* note 12 citing The Innocence Project, Sequential Lineups, *available at* http://www.

innocenceproject.org/Content/151.php (last visited Aug. 23, 2010)).

130. Sandra Guerra Thompson, Law Found. Professor of Law and Criminal Justice Inst. Dir., Univ. of Hous. Law Ctr., Remarks on Eyewitness Identification Before the Timothy Cole Advisory Panel on Wrongful Convictions (Apr. 22, 2010).

131. *See, e.g.,* Innocence Project, *Maryland: State Eyewitness Identification Reform Policies, available at* http://www.innocenceproject.org/news/LawViewstate5.php?state=md (last visited Aug. 25, 2010); Innocence Project, *New Jersey: State Eyewitness Identification Reform Policies, available at* http://www.innocenceproject.org/news/LawViewstate5.php?state=nj (last visited Aug. 25, 2010); Innocence Project, *North Carolina: State Eyewitness Identification Reform Policies, available at* http://www.innocenceproject.org/news/LawViewstate5.php?state=nc (last visited Aug. 25, 2010); Innocence Project, *West Virginia: State Eyewitness Identification Reform Policies, available at* http://www.innocenceproject.org/news/LawViewstate5.php?state=wv (last visited Aug. 25, 2010); Innocence Project, *Wisconsin: State Eyewitness Identification Reform Policies, available at* http://www.innocenceproject.org/news/LawViewstate5.php?state=wi (last visited Aug. 25, 2010).

132. H.B. 1625, 2007 Legislature, Reg. Sess. (N.C. 2007); S.B. 77, 128th Gen. Assemb., Reg. Sess. (Ohio 2010).

133. S.B. 115, 81st Gen. Assemb., Reg. Sess. (Tex. 2008).

134. S.B. 117, 81st Gen. Assemb., Reg. Sess. (Tex. 2008).

135. *Id.*

136. *Id.*

137. *Id.*

138. *Id.*

139. *Id.*

140. *Id.*

141. *Id.*

142. *Id.*

143. *Id.*

144. *Id.*

145. *See* S.B. 117, 81st Gen. Assemb., Reg. Sess. (Tex. 2009); *see also* Texas Legislature Online, *Bill History: SB 117, available at* http://www.capitol.state.tx.us/BillLookup/History.aspx?LegSess=81R&Bill=SB117 (last visited Aug. 25, 2010).

146. *See* S.B. 117, 81st Gen. Assemb., Reg. Sess. (Tex. 2009); *see also* Texas Legislature Online, *Bill History: SB 117, available at* http://www.capitol.state.tx.us/BillLookup/History.aspx?LegSess=81R&Bill=SB117 (last visited Aug. 25, 2010).

147. S.B. 117, 81st Gen. Assemb., Reg. Sess. (Tex. 2009).

148. *Id.*

149. *See generally* Texas Legislature Online, *Bill History: SB 117, available at* http://www.capitol.state.tx.us/BillLookup/History.aspx?LegSess=81R&Bill=SB117 (last visited Aug. 25, 2010).

150. H.B. 498, 81st Gen. Assemb., Reg. Sess. (Tex. 2009).

151. *See generally* S.R. 124, 81st Gen. Assemb., Reg. Sess. (Tex. 2009).

152. H.B. 498, 81st Gen. Assemb., Reg. Sess. (Tex. 2009).

153. Thompson, *supra* note 16, at 667.

154. *Accord* The Justice Project, Convicting The Innocent, *supra* note 6; *see also* Thompson, *supra* note 61, at 36.

B. Custodial Interrogation and Confessions

Reducing False Confessions Through Video Recording

Tanya M. Broholm*

I. Introduction

> The "bad" cop slams his hand on the wooden table in front of me and then grabs my shaking arm. He points his massive finger at the lonely blue vein poking through my tan skin. "That's where they're going to stick that needle you wetback. You know you're getting the death penalty for this. I know you did it and I'm sick of your bull shit," the officer yells as he stands up. He grabs the oversized black swivel chair that seemed to go unnoticed as it forgetfully spun in counter clock wise circles in the right corner of the small interrogation room.

* Tanya Broholm (University of Houston Law Center J.D. 2010) was a fifth grade math and science teacher before law school. It was here that she became dedicated to working to protect the rights of every human being, including every child and every person accused of a crime. Currently she is working as a business immigration attorney in Houston.

> After 3 days of a seemingly never-ending nightmare, I am tired, scared, hungry and confused. I feel like a starved dog being beaten in the alleyway. I just can't fight this anymore. I don't know what's going on. I don't know why I'm here. I just want to go home. As my confusing thoughts seem to swim chaotically like a little goldfish in the Atlantic Ocean, I am brought back into my harsh reality by that chair. The bad cop picks up the swivel chair with his right arm, and like a quarterback trying to make a touchdown from the 45 yard line, throws it with all his might at my head. Luckily, I duck in time to miss the metal backing of the chair, but I am unable to escape the fury of the spinning wheels as they slam into my head and I am knocked out of my chair.[1]

Christopher Ochoa recounts with disgust the interrogation in an Austin, Texas, police station that began his twelve-year prison nightmare. After being convicted of rape and murder based on his false confession during this brutal interrogation, Ochoa realized that he had been a victim of the very system he had trusted his entire life. The physical and psychological interrogation techniques used against Ochoa persuaded him that at that moment anything would be better than allowing this torture to continue, so he began repeating the story that the interrogators had developed about the crime, agreeing with their conclusions, and making the confession they wanted him to make. There was one problem: his confession was false.[2] Ochoa falsely confessed under pressure by the interrogators' use of coercive tactics.[324] It would take twelve years and one DNA test to conclusively prove that Mr. Ochoa had been innocent the entire time.[4] Those are years that he can never get back. Ochoa was a victim of improper interrogation techniques.[5] This injustice could have been avoided. After first making the false confession, Ochoa quickly realized that the police interrogation tactics had made him say something that he knew he needed to retract.[6] But, he could not take back the statements because he was so scared, and he thought no one would listen to his account of the coercive interrogation.[7] Ochoa needed a way to prove that the techniques used in the interrogation room actually pressured him to such a point that he gave a false confession.[8] He did not get his proof until many years later. Had a video recording been made of the entire interrogation, there would have been a clear record of the interrogator's behavior which would have allowed the fact-finder to assess the reliability of his confession and which, ultimately, could have prevented this tragedy.

Surely, no one would confess to a crime they never committed, would they? Surprisingly, the statistics tell us otherwise. Although it is difficult, if not impossible, to estimate the number of false confessions, police-induced false confessions "are of sufficient magnitude to demand attention."[9] More than 250 cases of interrogation-induced false confessions within the last twenty years have been documented.[10] Looking at these cases helps "provide abundant evidence that police-induced false confessions continue to occur regularly."[11] A confession by a suspect, whether accurate or not, provable or entirely improbable, increases the chances of conviction.[12] The danger is that false confessions beget wrongful convictions.

As the Ochoa case teaches us, false confessions can be induced by psychologically manipulative and threatening conduct during police interrogations. While some safeguards are in place to protect suspects and make them aware of their constitutional rights, the stories of the brutality and intimidation of some police practices during interrogations are "scary, threatening and inhumane."[13] Although not the norm, improper practices represent a demonstrated problem that can be prevented. Thus, additional safeguards should be considered to help reduce the risk of false confessions and consequential miscarriages of justice.

Part II of this article explores the current constitutional safeguards deriving from due process rights and the right against self-incrimination. This details the various statutes and Supreme Court decisions that have defined the scope of this privilege against self-incrimination and the protection of individual liberty, as well as the effects that these current safeguards have had on current police interrogation practices.

Next, Part III explores what happens when constitutional safeguards are ignored, and, instead, unconstitutionally coercive police interrogations occur, sometimes involving the use or threat of physical violence. While most police interrogations follow the constitutionally mandated procedures, some do not. When police interrogations employ psychologically coercive tactics to extract confessions from the accused, whether those tactics are legal or not, they increase the likelihood that an innocent person will be wrongly convicted while the true culprit escapes justice.

Finally, Part IV proposes an important additional safeguard to reduce the number of false confessions extracted based on coercive police interrogation techniques: videotaping interrogations in their entirety. One of the best ways to ensure that police interrogations follow constitutionally mandated procedures is to require that all police interrogations be videotaped in their entirety, beginning when the suspect arrives. Videotaping will ensure that the police adhere to the due process requirement that confessions be voluntarily given and ensure that innocent people do not confess falsely. The traditional secrecy surrounding interrogations allows police officers to stray from constitutionally mandated procedures, occasionally utilizing unconstitutional manipulation and even torture. If videotaped, however, these unconstitutional actions will be exposed, allowing for a more accurate due process assessment of the interrogation.

This section discusses some of the practical considerations of implementing this practice as well as some of the benefits that video-recorded police interrogations can offer. Video-recorded interrogations aid the police by protecting them against false claims by suspects of manipulation, coercion, and torture. It also considers the how recording will assist jurors in the fact finding process. Additionally, this section explores how recording police interrogations can help reduce the number of manipulated confessions that are false and have a significant likelihood of leading to wrongful convictions.

II. Current Safeguards Against Self-Incrimination During Police Interrogations

A. *Brown v. Mississippi:* Confessions Obtained by Means of Police Violence Violate the Due Process Clause

The Fifth Amendment privilege against self-incrimination defines the way in which confessions can be obtained during custodial police interrogation as well as determines when received confessions can be utilized against defendants. [14]

During the last century, the Supreme Court has crafted various tests that have helped to clarify the boundaries of this privilege. In 1936, the Court announced that a confession extracted by means of police brutality cannot be used against the defendant because it violates the due process clause.[15] The *Brown v. Mississippi* case involved three African Americans who were arrested in connection with the murder of a white farmer in Mississippi.[16] After the body was discovered, police officers believed they "knew" who did it and arrested an African-American man named Mr. Ellington.[17] The officers also arrested Ed Brown and Henry Shields, two other African American men.[18] Officers took Mr. Ellington to the scene of the murder and asked him to confess to the crime, but he insisted that he was innocent.[19] After adamantly denying having anything to do with the murder, a group of white men joined the officers and "encouraged" Mr. Ellington to confess by tying a rope around a tree, hanging him from his neck.[20] They then let him down and asked him to confess again.[21] He still proclaimed his innocence.[22] He was again grabbed and hung from the tree.[23] After being let down a second time, he continued to maintain his innocence.[24] The Deputy then savagely whipped him.[25] When he still refused to confessed he was allowed to go home, only to be arrested the following morning and beaten with leather straps and metal buckles until he finally confessed.[26] The other two suspects were arrested received similar torture but were told that if they confessed to their involvement in the murder, the torture would stop.[27] Eventually all three men provided the police officers with false, coerced confessions.[28]

During the police interrogation, the suspects were tortured, beaten, strung from trees and whipped.[29] Even though extracted through such an inhumane process, the defendants' confessions were used against them at trial, which resulted in their convictions.[30] The Supreme Court, however, saw the physical torture used to extract the defendant's confession as inconsistent with the constitutional right to liberty.[31] In reversing the lower court's convictions of the three men, the Court noted that the constitution's Due Process Clause protects the liberty of all suspects and requires that before a person's liberty is curtailed the accused must be provided with a fair trial.[32] A significant goal of the Due Process clause is to protect suspects from being coerced into making self-incriminating confessions that are extracted by torture and thus not comporting with this constitutional protection.[33] After Brown, confessions obtained by means of physical violence and torture cannot be used against suspects accused of a crime.

B. *MIRANDA V. ARIZONA:* VOLUNTARINESS STANDARD

In 1966, the Court defined the scope of the Fifth Amendment's privilege against self- incrimination and required that before custodial police interrogations can begin, suspects must be made aware of their rights to remain silent and be provided counsel.[34] The Court in *Miranda* held that "the prosecution may not use statements, . . . stemming from custodial interrogation of the defendant unless it demonstrates the use of procedural safeguards effective to secure the privilege against self-incrimination."[35] In *Miranda*, officers came to Ernesto Miranda's home and arrested him on suspicions of kidnapping and sexual assault.[36] At the police station, the victim identified Miranda as the perpetrator, and he was thereafter taken into an interrogation room.[37] Questioning immediately began, and Miranda was not made aware of his rights to remain silent or his right to counsel prior to questioning.[38] After two hours of questioning, investigators had managed to extract a written confession from Miranda. The bottom of the confession included a statement saying that this confession was made by Miranda with "full knowledge of my legal rights, understanding any statement I make may be used against me," and that he had knowingly waived those rights.[39] The problem with this confession was that actually the suspect had not been made aware of his rights during the interrogation process.[40]

The Court was concerned that the defendant was coerced into incriminating himself, and that constitutional safeguards afforded him by the Fifth Amendment were not observed. Therefore, in addition to prohibiting physical torture during custodial police interrogations as announced in *Brown v. Mississippi*, the Court in *Miranda*, further announced that the Fifth Amendment includes protections against psychological torture. The Court, relying on the Due Process Clause, based its decision on "the roots of our concept of American criminal jurisprudence [and] the restraints society must observe consistent with the Federal Constitution in prosecuting individuals for crime."[41] The Court wanted to employ "adequate protective devices [...] to dispel the compulsion inherent in custodial surroundings."[42] Police interrogations that employ manipulative, psychologically threatening, and coercive tactics go against the underlying protections afforded by the Fifth Amendment's privilege against self-incrimination.[43]

Thus, *Miranda v. Arizona* stands for the proposition that during custodial police interrogations, the suspect has, among other rights, the right to remain silent and the right to counsel during interrogation in order to prevent coerced self-incrimination. Furthermore, suspects must be made aware of these constitutional rights, and knowingly and voluntarily waive these rights, before any confession can be used against the suspect later. The Court noted that the goal of the *Miranda* warnings, as they are often referred to, is to eliminate the psychological pressures that often accompany custodial police interrogations.[44] Since *Miranda*, police officers typically read Miranda warnings to suspects upon detainment. The fundamental goal of these warnings, as expressed by the Supreme Court, is to reduce the instances of manipulated confessions that are false and to safeguard the privilege against self-incrimination.[45] The warning requires that prior to any questioning, the defendant must be "warned that he has a right to remain silent, that any statement he does make may be used as evidence against him, and that he has a right to the presence of an attorney, either retained or appointed."[46] A suspect "may waive effectuation of these rights, provided the waiver is made voluntarily, knowingly and intelligently."[47]

C. Problems with *Miranda*

The Court assumed that that a system of standardized warnings would empower suspects to assert their rights. The Court considered some of the realities of the interrogation process and how these warnings would fit into this process. Standardized warnings often have a counterproductive effect and can be perceived as largely ineffective.[48] Every American has heard the *Miranda* warnings as they are nonchalantly issued by police officers over and over again on their favorite shows, and even most children can even recite them by heart. But few know how these warnings are actually meant to change the interrogation process. Few understand the warnings' importance. And because of this lack of understanding of the true meaning of *Miranda*'s warning, few suspects know to insist on a strict adherence to the rules. Instead, they assume that the phrase is something the officers simply mumble as the handcuffs are put on, not knowing that these warnings, if seriously taken, are quite effective and can change the underlying nature of the interrogation process. The Court considered the reality of the interrogation process and how these warnings would fit into this process. The Court in *Miranda* even noted that interrogators "induce a confession out of trickery."[49] Interrogators are instructed to use psychological tactics on suspects who are knowledgeable of their constitutional rights in order to eliminate the effectiveness of the accused's understanding of their rights.[50] Often the suspect is given the warning, but then interrogators "point out the incriminating significance of the suspect's refusal to talk."[51] The implication is that the only reason that the suspect does not want to talk to the interrogators is that he or she has something to hide. The Court in *Miranda* noted that interrogation training manuals, applaud this technique noting that "few will persist in their initial refusal to talk . . . [if this technique] is employed correctly."[52] This tacit "usually has a very undermining effect."[53]

Skirting around the safeguards our justice system has in place limits the effectiveness of the protections. In order to comport with the spirit of *Miranda*, suspects must have a real choice about whether or not they are going to make a statement or whether or not the interview continues. The problem is that the major safeguard we have in place, the *Miranda* warnings, allows for significant deviations from the anticipated protections of the Constitution. This can cause the interrogation process to become a twisted game, whose goal is not to seek the truth, but instead to seek a confession, even if this confession is false.

The current safeguards may be somewhat effective but not as effective as they need to be. The danger with false confessions is that they threaten the very "quality of criminal justice in America by inflicting significant and unnecessary harms on the innocent."[54]

III. Current Police Interrogation Practices that Contribute to Obtaining False Confessions

Police compliance with the law is one of the most important aspects of a democratic society.[55] While most police interrogations follow constitutionally mandated procedures, some do not. Even if most interrogation practices across the United States adhere to *Miranda* requirements that suspects be made aware of their rights in order that confessions be voluntarily given, [56] when interrogators disregard the safeguards our justice system has in place, the goals of the interrogation process become significantly compromised.

A. Physical Torture: Third Degree Methods Have Become the Exception to the Rule

The use of physical torture during an interrogation can force suspects to talk. However, because the interrogation process is a search for the truth, the goal should not be simply to force the suspect to say what the interrogator wants. The goal of the interrogation process is to find out what happened and what this person knows. The statements provided during the interrogation process should be fact-based and accurate. This goal is undoubtedly compromised when physical torture is used. By condemning the use of physical coercion, the Supreme Court brought about a shift in the types interrogation tactics utilized by interrogators to extract confessions from suspects. Physical torture, often referred to as a third degree method, had declined as a tool of interrogation, even by the time *Miranda* was decided. The Court in *Miranda* noted that while physical torture as an interrogation strategy has "undoubtedly [become] the exception now, . . . [it is still] sufficiently widespread to be the object of concern."[57]

The Court in *Miranda* cites three cases that describe some of the physical nightmares that suspects were subjected to during police interrogations and how these coercive techniques influenced the suspect's willingness to confess and undermined the reliability of the statements they made.[58] Physical torture can be clearly seen in cases like *Brown v. Mississippi* in which the accused was whipped and beaten.[59] However, the Court notes that physical torture can also be accomplished by depriving suspects of food,[60] forcing a suspect to submit to lie detector tests after begging to go to the restroom,[61] forcing a suspect to continue answering questions while sleep deprived,[62] forcing a suspect to lie on cold boards,[63] forcing a suspect to continue questioning under such rough man-handling from interrogators that the suspect sustained multiple broken bones, bruises and injuries requiring over eight months of medical care to remedy, [64] and simply persisting to interrogate for too long of a period of time.[65]

The *Miranda* Court noted that "some policemen still resort to physical force to obtain confessions."[66] The court noted that "[t]he use of physical brutality and violence is not, unfortunately, relegated to the past or to any part of the country."[67] The Court even recounts an interrogation where "the police brutally beat, kicked and placed lighted cigarette butts on the back of a potential witness under interrogation for the purpose of securing a statement incriminating a third party."[68]

As late as the 1980s, Texas officers use a process known as water boarding to physically coerce suspects into providing a confession during interrogations.[69] Water boarding is a "term is used to describe several interrogation techniques."[70] The suspect "may be immersed in water, have water forced into the nose and mouth, or have water poured onto material placed over the face so that the liquid is inhaled or swallowed."[71] Water boarding is "real drowning that simulates death."[72] The "victim experiences the sensations of drowning: struggle, panic, breath-holding, swallowing, vomiting, taking water into the lungs and, eventually, the same feeling of not being able to breathe that one experiences after being punched in the gut."[73] In the early 1980s, "U.S. military tribunals and U.S. judges . . . examined certain types of water-based interrogation [techniques] and found that they constituted torture."[74] Officers were employing these tactics during interrogations "in order to coerce confessions."[75] The "prosecutors charged a Texas sheriff and three of his deputies with violating prisoners' civil rights by forcing confessions."[76] "The sheriff was sentenced to 10 years in prison" for his use of physical torture during an interrogation.[77]

Physical torture can coerce suspects into doing whatever it takes to get the pain to stop, even if it means giving a confession that they know is false. Physical torture breaks the suspect's spirit. Confessions extracted under these conditions cannot be seen as voluntary and are often viewed by courts as coerced and unreliable.[78] The Texas Penal Code recognizes the defense of duress and will not admit statements made through the use of torture.[79] Although physical coercion during interrogation is classified as duress and is impermissible, in order to make themselves available to this defense and get any confession made under such circumstances to not be used against them, suspects must be able to prove that torture actually occurred.[80] This is a very difficult hurdle to jump: if the interrogation was not recorded, the suspect does not have proof of what actually occurred.

The purpose of the interrogation process is to discover the truth. If the suspect during the interrogation voluntarily wishes to offer additional information to investigators to help solve the case, then that information should be accepted. In order for the purpose of the interrogation process to be effectuated, any statements made, should accurately direct the interrogation process through the true facts of the case so that the investigation yields accurate results.

When physical torture is used to pressure suspects during the interrogation process, not only is this a "flagrant violation of [the] law by the officers of the law, but it involves . . . the dangers of false confessions, and it tends to make police and prosecutors less zealous in the search for objective evidence."[81] The Court in *Miranda* quoted a statement by the National Commission on Law Observance and Enforcement, which expressed that, "if you use your fists, you are not so likely to use your wits."[82] The Court in *Miranda* reinforced the clear concept that physical torture, regardless of whether it results in a true or false confession, is not a tactic that can be legally employed during police interrogations, citing Lord Sankey's thought that "it is not sufficient to do justice by obtaining a proper result by irregular or improper means."[83] The *Miranda* Court notes that "physical coercion is not, however, [t]he only hallmark of an unconstitutional inquisition."[84] No longer do we see as many cases like *Brown v. Mississippi* in which the suspects were physically tortured.[85] Instead police techniques and the interrogation process has become a game of conning suspects into confessing to crimes.[86]

B. Psychological Abuse: A Current Police Practice that Contributes to False Confessions

Police interrogations are often strategically designed to induce stress. The goal is to overcome the resistance of a suspect, a goal that is reinforced through tactics often found in police training manuals.[87] The problem lies in the fact that the various deceptive techniques used during the interrogation process often create confusion in the minds of the suspect and lead to a confession that is unreliable and false. This danger is magnified in suspects whose background makes them particularly vulnerable to psychologically manipulative and high-pressure interrogation techniques. The threat of torture can be as effective as actual pain in destroying a suspect's resistance. Some concerned activists assert that "[t]actics that [can] cause . . . false confession[s] are common as dirt and used in police departments everywhere in the United States."[88] The prevalence of wrongful convictions based on false confessions confirms this assertion.[89]

The interrogation practice that has most often led to false confessions is psychological manipulation.[90] The Court in *Miranda* stressed that "the modern practice of in-custody interrogation is psychologically rather than physically oriented."[91] The psychological techniques that often define custodial police interrogations are not considered by courts to be inherently unconstitutional.[92] The *Miranda* Court, however, on the other hand, was mindful that "illegitimate and unconstitutional practices get their first footing . . . by silent approaches and slight deviations from legal modes of procedure."[93]

The goal of a police interrogation is to discern the truth.[94] All of the safeguards that our justice system currently have in place should further this goal. And all of these policies point to one overriding thought: the constitutional foundation underlying the privilege against self-incrimination is the idea that a government must at all times maintain a certain level of respect to protect "the dignity and integrity of its citizens."[95] When interrogations rely on psychological ploys, the reliability associated with free choice often fades and the potential for compulsion becomes great.[96] The following sections address the variety of psychologically coercive techniques often used during custodial interrogations.

1. Teaching the Tricks: How Interrogators Are Instructed to Employ Psychologically Manipulative Tactics to Extract Confessions

As the *Miranda* Court recognized, "[i]nterrogators are sometimes instructed to induce a confession out of trickery."[97] When this occurs, the interrogation process shifts from truth-finding to case-closing. The goal becomes extracting a confession from the suspect so that the case can be closed quickly.[98] Once interrogators come to believe a suspect is guilty, a psychological phenomenon called tunnel vision begins to define the remainder of the interrogation process.[99] It generally "originates during the initial police investigation of a crime."[100] The investigation "may become distorted by the desire to alleviate the pressure that comes from not being able to assure the public that the offender has been caught and the community is safe."[101] Guided by a desire "to solve cases quickly, the stress [that results] may contribute to investigative tunnel vision."[102] Investigators can "find it difficult to live up to their nearly mythical image as highly competent crime solvers."[103] Tunnel vision is a process by which, either intentionally or more commonly, unintentionally, once a suspect has been arrested in connection with a crime, investigators begin to focus their investigation and interrogation solely on the suspect often ignoring or discounting other relevant, exculpatory information. [104]

Interrogators presume detained suspects are guilty and then focus their interrogation process on extracting a confession. Interrogators use various methods in order to "persuade" the suspect to give a confession. But, police interrogations that rely too heavily on psychological games and tricks can lead to confessions that are unreliable and false.[105] After reviewing leading police training manuals, the Court in *Miranda* argued that even the most "enlightened and effective" interrogation techniques relied on psychological manipulation, intimidation, and trickery thus threatening to overbear a suspect's free will and violate his or her privilege against self-incrimination.[106] Interrogators "use of deception has become the functional alternative to the use of [physical] coercion."[107] The manipulation surrounding modern interrogations has become "more subtle, more invasive, and more total."[108]

In *Bram v. United States*, the Supreme Court announced a firm prohibition against the use of confessions obtained though any sort of threats or promises.[109] However, as the Court in *Miranda* notes, "interrogation[s] . . . take place in privacy."[110] This level of "privacy results in secrecy and this in turn results in a gap in our knowledge of what in fact goes on in the interrogation rooms."[111] Without additional safeguards, such as recording, in place, once an interrogation has been conducted, it can become difficult to review the conditions under which a confession was made in order to determine if the given confession was obtained through the use of suggestive or prohibited tactics.

The "Reid Technique" is a popular and controversial method of questioning used during police interrogation.[112] In his article, Criminal Interrogation and Confessions, Inbau describes how officers are often trained under this technique to use the interrogation process to wear down the resistance of the suspect.[113] Some would argue the technique is used to override the suspect's free will.[114] If the initial investigation conducted by the officers indicates that the suspect committed the crime, the Reid Nine Step approach to interrogation is used to elicit confessions from unwilling suspects.[115] To use the Reid Technique, the interrogator begins by isolating the suspect in order to increase his or her anxiety.[116] Behavior symptoms, which are to be used to gauge the guilt or innocence of suspects, "become more revealing as anxiety in the suspect increases."[117] The Reid Technique's analysis of verbal and non-verbal cues is inherently flawed.[118] When they find cues that they perceive as deception, investigators correlate this with admissions of guilt.[119] However, the cues that the Reid Techniques considers when assessing deception can actually be caused by "nervousness, fear, confusion, [and] hostility" which are responses that many people experience when faced with stress.[120] When investigators base their interrogation on these overly simplified assumptions, they begin to assume that the suspect is being deceitful and then begin to employ psychologically manipulative pressure to extract a confession.[121] Interrogators often "misattribute the cause of the confession as being an internal response to the person's actual guilt while discounting situational factors such as stress or coercion which may not be readily apparent to an observer."[122]

When using the Reid Technique, an interrogator first attempts to get suspects to confess by increasing their anxiety and then using the physical reactions to this anxiety as admissions of guilt. This circular process tricks suspects into confessing by increasing the anxiety whenever the suspect continues to proclaim their innocence. By raising the anxiety to a high level, suspects are "persuaded" into confessing to what they did.[123]

As the interrogation continues, the suspect is confronted by officers who exaggerate the negative consequences of and positive incentives to confessing. Ofshe and Leo describe how "interrogators manipulate the individual's analysis of his immediate situation and his perceptions of both the choices available to him, and of the consequences of each possible course of action."[124] The interrogator is instructed to lead the suspect into believing that confessing is the rational and appropriate choice.[125] While these techniques can sometimes be useful to elicit a confession from a truly guilty suspect who continues to profess his innocence, they can also have the effect of manipulating a suspect into manufacturing a false confession.

In this phase of the interrogation process, the interrogator often also suggests scenarios that might have influenced suspect's bad behavior and then offers justifications that help minimize the moral guilt associated with that crime.[126] Ofshe, in criticizing the use of the Reid Technique during interrogations, describes how interrogators format "a less heinous, less morally unacceptable version of the crime."[127] Interrogators express a willingness to compromise and accept a less serious version of the crime.[128] The central problem with this offer of leniency is that "what makes it effective is that it offers harsh punishment for silence and a benefit for confessing."[129] With the crime minimized in the suspect's mind, interrogators persuade suspects that confessing now is the best solution, and the reward is that the interrogation will end. Punishment is portrayed as minimal. So the accused believe that while they might receive a mild punishment of some sort, after they confess they can go home and return to their lives. This leads "suspects to see confession as an expedient means of escape."[130] Ofshe warns that the Reid Technique is fundamentally flawed because it "motivate[s] the initial decision to make the admission through threat and promise."[131]

In addition to minimizing the consequences and maximizing the rewards of confessing, the interrogators have another powerful weapon in their arsenal of tricks: evidence, whether real or simply manufactured. The use of false evidence during interrogations is a psychological trick that courts have not found to be illegal.[132] Bolstering evidence with false assertions are psychological tricks that are legal. Interrogators start by assessing the knowledge that the suspect has about the crime. Thereafter, they have the creative freedom to make up physical or testimonial evidence that implicates the suspect. Innocent suspects "can be convinced by interrogators' false assertions that there is strong evidence against them."[133] The "folder method" is one of the most commonly used methods to begin the false accusations stage of the interrogation process.[134] The "interrogator walks in and plops a thick file on the desk (which is likely from another case) suggesting the investigation is nearly complete, so this will be the last opportunity" for the suspect to confess if he wants any sort of leniency.[135] The folder method is then followed with detailed evidence "known" to the interrogator that implicates the accused. Ofshe testifying as an expert witness in *Oregon v. Pickens*, warned that people "criticize [the folder method] because it is deceptive, [because] it rel[ies] on deception."[136]

2. The Danger of Deception Defining the Interrogation Process

During the interrogation process, the use of false evidence purportedly implicating a suspect and other forms of deception can be an extremely powerful force that often causes suspects to confess to crimes they never committed. Not only might suspects confess due to intimidation, they may also be persuaded to believe they are in fact guilty. Research confirms the frailty and malleability of the human memory.[137] A person's memory is very susceptible to suggestion. In the context of criminal investigations this reality should remain in the forefront of the minds of investigators during the interrogation process.

In 1996, a study was conducted to see if people who were falsely accused based on false evidence would confess to a mistake they never made.[138] Seventy-nine people participated in a typing study.[139] The goal, as they were told, was for the participants to test out a computer program, but under no circumstances were they to press the ALT key, because that would crash the computer program.[140] The testers called out letters and the participants typed the corresponding letter on the key pad.[141] After typing a few letters, the screen went blank.[142] The tester would then return to the room and ask the participant if they had pressed the ALT key.[143] The participants adamantly denied it.[144] But then to measure the effect of confronting suspects with false evidence during the interrogation process, participants were told that an onlooker, an undercover tester posing as a fellow participant, had seen the participant press the ALT key.[145] After hearing the false evidence implicating them, 94% of the innocent participants signed what was in fact a false confession, admitting to pressing the ALT key, even offering explanations for why they accidently hit the wrong button, such as "I hit it with the side of my hand right after you called out the 'A'."[146] The false evidence implicating the participants led some to create an entire story describing the how the mistake had been made. Some actually became convinced that they had pressed the wrong button.[147] Similarly, when presented with false evidence suspects can often begin to believe that they actual committed the crime of which they have been accused. [148]

It has "been shown repeatedly that memory is quite malleable and unreliable."[149] In an experiment conducted by psychologist Elizabeth Loftus, participants were given four stories from their childhood allegedly provided by a family member.[150] One of the stories is about the participant being lost in the mall for hours as a child only to be reunited with their parents by an elderly woman, but the story is in fact entirely false.[151] Even though not initially remembering the story, the more the experiment went on, and with just a little prompting, participants began "remembering" details about the stories and began truly believing that the incident had taken place.[152] Surprisingly, the study "repeatedly revealed that the human brain can create memories out of thin air with some prompting."[153]

3. Vulnerable Groups Are Particularly Susceptible to Psychologically Manipulative Interrogation Techniques

Both of the studies mentioned in the previous section were conducted on adult participants of average intelligence, socio-economic status, and full understanding of the English language.[154] But not every suspect that comes into the interrogation room is well equipped. Clearly, aggressive and psychologically coercive techniques can negatively affect all types of suspects.[155] However, there are some categories of suspects who are even more vulnerable to psychologically manipulative and high-pressure interrogation techniques. Suspects with mental deficiencies, cultural or language barriers, and those who are intoxicated or are juveniles have a greater tendency to give false statements during interrogations that involve fear, intimidation, manipulation and undue pressure.[156]

A suspect is particularly vulnerable because his or her "memory is malleable by virtue of his/her youth, naiveté . . . [and possibly unusual cultural background,] lack of intelligence, stress, fatigue, alcohol, or drug use."[157] These vulnerable groups of people as a whole seem to be more trusting of the interrogation process and the authorities who are conducting it.[158] These groups of suspects are "particularly susceptible to producing unreliable statements in response to the isolation, fear, and intimidation of police interrogation settings, particularly if prompted by explicit or implied promises or threats such as being freed to go home or getting a better or worse result at trial, or false evidence implicating them."[159]

A sad example of a vulnerable suspect being psychologically manipulated during the interrogation process is in the case of "Delbert Ward, an introverted, easygoing but frail 59-year-old farmer with an IQ of 69."[160] Ward's story is chronicled in the movie Brother's Keeper.[161] In Ward's case,"[f]ollowing long hours of intense questioning and surrounded by five or six 250-pound state troopers, Ward signed a false confession of murdering his own brother."[162] Through the examination of some other evidence it was discovered that Mr. Ward was in fact innocent.[163] The clinical psychologist who interviewed Ward later warned that "Delbert would likely have been so nervous and confused at the time of his interrogation that he would have agreed with anything."[164] His ability to reason had been worn down, and his major focus was not "on the questions he was being asked, but on getting out of that unfamiliar, threatening environment."[165]

False evidence implicating suspects can be very persuasive in convincing innocent and vulnerable suspects to confess to a crime they never committed. Because memory is malleable and subject to manipulation, it should be treated like physical evidence from a crime scene in order to avoid contamination. Unfortunately, psychological manipulation and trickery is not ordinarily unconstitutional and happens quite frequently during interrogations.[166] These techniques often heavily influence the validity and reliability to the information extracted from the suspect.[167] "The longer police interrogate a suspect, emphatic about his guilt and peppering their interrogation with details of the crime, the more likely a suspect is to become convinced himself,"[168] leading to suspects providing a confession that is false. The American Judicature Society's Conference on Wrongful Convictions of the Innocent concluded that "interrogation misconduct, including suggestive, coercive, or misleading theories as well as subconscious biases, is a primary systemic cause of wrongful convictions."[169]

The basic problem with false confessions is that a jury cannot tell that the confession they are relying on to convict a suspect is false. A jury often does not know how the confession was extracted or what interrogation techniques were used in the hours before the suspect actually produced the confession upon which the jury is basing their decision. Sadly, "jurors often place almost blind faith in the evidentiary value of confession evidence."[170] This fact often remains true even when, the "confession [i]s not accompanied by any credible corroboration [. . .or even when] and there [i]s compelling evidence of the Defendant's factual innocence."[171] Jurors simply hear a confession and typically consider that confession as conclusive evidence of guilt.

IV. Recording Interrogations Help Reduce False Confessions

A. How Electronically Recording the Entire Interrogation Furthers the Goal of Ensuring a Non-Coerced Interrogation

The purpose of the interrogation process is to determine the truth, to determine what the suspect knows without forcing them to accept the interrogators assessment of the situation.[172] It should not be just about eliciting incriminating statements and admissions from those already presumed guilty. Nor should an investigator's aim be "to elicit a confession from an unwilling suspect."[173] Instead, the interrogation process should aim to produce voluntary statements. The *Miranda* warnings further the underlying goals of the interrogation process by guaranteeing the 1) reliability of the confession, and 2) protecting the right of the suspect to reach an autonomous decision.[174]

Benefits of Video Recording Interrogations

- Discourages disreputable practices
- Creates a reviewable record
- Costs are minimal
- Discourages false claims of coercion

A report of the New Jersey Supreme Court has recently found that "[a] contemporaneous electronic record of suspect interviews has proven to be an efficient and powerful law enforcement tool" when used in police stations across the United States.[175] By creating a permanent record of exactly what occurred, disputes about how suspects were treated by officers can be eliminated.[176] An Oregon police department which began video recording the interrogation process positively reports that "if a picture is worth a thousand words, it's been [our] experience that a video is worth ten thousand."[177] Although Texas does require that the actual statement be audio recorded,[178] without being able to see what lead up to this confession, oftentimes, the entire story is not being told. "Electronic recording should begin when [the] custodial interrogation,"[179] and any discussion of the incident, begins.

By having an electronic video version of the entire interrogation process, the fact-finders will have more information upon which to base their assessment of the suspect's guilt or innocence. The jury can see and hear "precisely what was said and done, including whether suspects were forthcoming or evasive, changed their versions of events, and appeared sincere and innocent or deceitful and guilty."[180] Although many states and individual police stations have implemented their own recording mandate for police interrogation,[181] because coercive tactics undermine constitutional rights, a statewide policy is appropriate.

B. The Costs and Benefits of Video Recording the Entire Interrogation Process

Although sometimes officers were initially hesitant to record the interrogation process, in jurisdictions where electronic recording of the entire interrogation process has already been implemented, once they started this practice, they nearly "uniformly agree that recording [is] invaluable."[182] Currently, electronically recording interrogations is done, in some form, across hundreds of departments encompassing twenty-six states.[183] Recording "has been done for years by many police agencies large and small throughout the United States . . . [and] their experiences have been uniformly positive."[184]

The concerns in the minds of officers who have not had the experience of recording custodial interrogations in their entirety are generally: (1) they are concerned about the costs associated with purchasing the electronic equipment; (2) they are concerned that recording will hinder the interrogation if the equipment fails; and (3) they are concerned that recording will limit the interrogation and litigation process.

1. Concerns with Costs Associated with Purchasing the Electronic Equipment

The initial "costs associated with electronic recordation [. . .] is minimal."[185] Money spent on the electronic equipment necessary to video record, is a cost that "comes [largely] on the front end, and they diminish once the equipment and facilities are in place equipment, [and] training has been given to" the officers.[186] Of the "police officers throughout the country, [discussing the idea of requiring electronic recording], very few mentioned cost as a burden, and none suggested that cost warranted abandoning recordings."[187] Installation of "cameras and microphones, wired to a control room where the interrogation can be monitored and recorded onto a DVD is approximately $5,000."[188] The up-front costs are not prohibitively expensive and the "savings continue so long as electronic recording continues."[189] The savings include reducing the costs of litigation associated with determining the various interrogation tactics used during the process and arguments about whether the confessions made should be excluded. Thus, video recording the interrogation process saves money in the long run.[190]

2. Concerns that Recording Will Hinder the Interrogation If the Equipment Fails

Another concern of officers resisting the electronic recordation of interrogations is the potential consequences or remedies of a failure to record based on the recording device malfunctioning. In the Truro Police Department manual on electronic recording of interrogation and interviews, there are interesting procedures in place for when the recording device malfunctions.[191] If the recording machine is not working, officers should consider either "defer[ring] the interrogation until an operable recording device can be obtained . . . or if is impractical to defer the interrogation continue the interrogation without a recording device," continuing the interview but employing even stricter procedures such as having two or more officers present in the room and having the suspect consent to an interrogation without recordation.[192] If recording is impossible and it is impractical to defer the interrogation, interrogators should first ask the suspect to consent to an interrogation without a recording device, and document that consent "in some manner, such as in a signed statement by the suspect or in the officer's interview or case report."[193] The interrogation should continue, but any confession made would be presumptively inadmissible, but that presumption could "be overcome by a preponderance* of the evidence that the statement was made voluntarily."[194] Any unrecorded statement should be "view[ed] with caution."[195] The benefit to officers is that recorded statements, however, would be presumed voluntary. The burden of proof would then shift to the suspect's counsel to put forth clear and convincing evidence to overcome the presumption that the recorded statement be admissible. Thus, if the suspect's statements are recorded, the shifting of the burden of proof would further aid officers and prosecutors in the investigation process.

3. Concerns that Recording Will Limit the Interrogation and Litigation Process

Documentation of the conditions under which the confession was produced can be an invaluable tool when the case goes to trial. Police officers often wonder if they can adequately develop their case if the interrogation is video recorded. Officers have been concerned that suspects would shut down at the idea of a camera recording the interrogation,[196] thus leaving interrogators unable to do their job. But jurisdictions that have the requirement in place have found that videotaping the interrogation process is beneficial because it serves to "document how . . . confessions were arrived at."[197] Officers "don't [even] have to tell the suspect that the interrogation is being recorded."[198] But if there is a camera video "recording every minute of an interrogation, . . . if there's [ever] a dispute about what happened, both the police and the suspect are protected."[199] Video recording the interrogation process further benefits officers in that it protects police officers' ability to do their jobs."[200] Video recording nearly eliminates the need to take

* The burden of proof normally required in a civil (non-criminal) action. It is generally understood to require proof that the plaintiff's case is "more likely than not" true, or that over 50% of the believable evidence is in the plaintiff's favor. In criminal cases, a party may be required to carry this burden of proof to raise or refute the admissibility of an item of evidence or a defense. The burden to prove a defendant's guilt of a crime, however, always rests with the prosecution and requires proof beyond a reasonable doubt.

officers off the street so as to testify in court to prove the confession was voluntarily given, thus saving valuable police and court resources. Instead, jurors are allowed to see exactly what conditions led to the suspect's confession.

Video recording interrogations would "certainly make it more difficult to claim confessions were coerced."[201] When suspects present themselves in court, they are often cleaned up and on their best behavior. It is easy to present this cleaned up front to the court, however, if video recording the entire interrogation was required; the fact-finder can see exactly how the suspect looked and acted before being cleaned up for court.[202] Fact-finding should not just be about telling the jury what they should or should not believe. Let them see and experience the suspect's actions during the interrogation and draw their own conclusions. The Montana Police Department recounts how "one video showed a suspect giggling when he described beating children."[203] The videotape helped the jury see more than just a confession or a cleaned up defendant. The jury saw the background, who the suspect was, and how the investigation progressed. This information is critical in guiding a jury to truth and justice. The department described the experience of video recording the entire interrogation process as "100 percent positive."[204]

Video recording the entire interrogation process also "would discourage disreputable interrogation tactics, protect real confessions from challenge in court, and help identify false ones after the fact – there's really very little downside."[205] With a video record of exactly what transpired during the interrogation, the public can be assured that officers are treating people who are in police custody with the constitutionally mandated level of respect.[206] Knowing that the interrogation process was being recorded would reinforce in the officer's mind that torture, whether physical or psychological, should not be used, and it would serve to prove that, in fact, it had not been used. If the interrogation is recorded and a jury is able to see that an interrogation was conducted using psychologically manipulative tactics, studies show that the jury is not able to "appropriately discount confession evidence–even when they judge the confession to be coerced and involuntary."[207] The commonly "held but false belief of most jurors is that a person would not confess to a crime she did not commit short of physical abuse or torture." [208] The major benefit of video recordation, therefore, is that it reduces the risk that impermissible interrogation practices were used to coerce a suspect into providing a statement in the first instance.[209] This helps to ensure that any confessions made during any interrogation were in fact made voluntarily. Video "recordation [serves to] protect and enhance the police officers' credibility, and protect against complaints of police misconduct."[210]

Video recordation can also provide a more accurate and complete evidentiary record of "what transpired during the interview if the police record from the very beginning of the interview."[211] By video recording the entire interrogation process, it can "result in a reduction in Miranda admissibility motions and hearings[, because] the voluntariness of the defendant's confession is typically apparent from viewing, or listening to, the recording."[212] Recordings "allow the judge and jury to better understand the demeanor of the defendant outside the courtroom."[213] The Colorado Police Department enthusiastically praised recording as being "invaluable to us [in] resolving disputes regarding [the voluntariness of] confessions."[214] Video recording the entire interrogation is beneficial in that it furthers the truth-searching goal of the investigation process by enhancing the integrity of the system and the accuracy of its results.[215] Video recording can help preserve evidence in such a way that the accuracy of the interrogation process can be readily judged. Another benefit that recording can provide is that it allows the officers to focus on what the suspect is saying rather than be distracted by note-taking. Not only can note-taking be a distraction to the officers conducting the interview, but it can also make suspects feel extremely anxious, and uncomfortable when every answer they provide is being scribbled down on a pad.[216] Attempting to write down everything the suspect says can lead to large chunks of information being missed and can often become time consuming and tedious.[217] Recording allows officers to ask questions at a more a natural pace, rather than being overwhelmed with having to try write down every answer.[218] A more conversational pace that is not interrupted by the delays of note-taking reduces some of the anxiety associated with the interrogation process and allows for a more natural discovery of the truth.

V. Conclusion

"Texas District Judge Bob Perkins [who] ordered Christopher Ochoa's release from a life sentence after DNA tests proved his innocence. . . stated that Ochoa suffered a fundamental miscarriage of justice."[219] The saddest reality of this situation is that it did not have to happen. The confession Ochoa made after a weekend-long interrogation was both physically and psychologically coerced. The interrogation process was not conducted in accordance with the safeguards our system has in place. However, because of a lack of clear evidence establishing the coercive nature of his interrogation process, the false confession was admitted during his trial, and Christopher Ochoa was wrongly convicted. He should not have lost twelve years of his life. Today, as a forty-three year old attorney, he describes the longing in his heart as he thinks about the lives of his friends and family and imagines what could have been. The relationships he could have formed. The children he could have had. The memories he could have made.[220] And he is not alone in having suffered this tragic fate at the hands of the government that was supposed to protect him.

Without some sort of accountability or review mechanism, it is difficult, if not impossible, to stop the dangerous interrogation tactics—some legal and some not—that are often currently employed during the interrogation process. Video recording the entire interrogation process, beginning when any discussion of the crime begins, will go a long way to prevent false confessions from being made based on unconstitutional or psychologically manipulative police interrogation tactics. Because it is very difficult, if not impossible, for a juror to distinguish between compelled and voluntary statements, video recording will help eliminate compelled statements, show the fact finder the exact interrogation process under which a confession was made, and ultimately help to end the injustices associated with wrongful convictions.

Endnotes

1. Telephone Interview with Christopher Ochoa, in Madison, Wis. (Jan. 28, 2010) [hereinafter Ochoa Interview] (notes on file with author).

2. *Id.*
3. *Id.*
4. *Id.*
5. *Id.*
6. *Id.*
7. *Id.*
8. *Id.*
9. Richard A. Leo, *The Problem of False Confessions in America*, CHAMPION, Dec. 2007, at 30 (describing false confessions as the leading cause of wrongful convictions). The article examines and describes numerous cases where suspects were convicted based on false confessions without any physical proof to confirm the suspect's confession. *Id.* "These studies reveal that false confessions are therefore not an anomaly but a systemic feature of American criminal justice, despite procedural safeguards such as *Miranda* rights and a constitutional prohibition against legally coercive interrogation techniques." *Id.*
10. *Id.*
11. *Id.*; *see infra* at notes 125-128 and accompanying text.
12. Ian Herbert, *The Psychology and Power of False Confessions*, 22 THE OBSERVER 10, 12 (2008) (discussing a confession corrupts any other evidence that the jury is presented with to the point to the point that there can never be such a thing as harmless error in association with false confessions).
13. *See* Ochoa Interview, *supra* note 1.
14. U.S. CONST. AMEND. V ("No person shall . . . be compelled in any criminal case to be a witness against himself.")
15. Brown v. Mississippi, 297 U.S. 278, 281-82 (1936).
16. *Id.*
17. *Id.*
18. *Id.*

19. *Id.*
20. *Id.*
21. *Id.*
22. *Id.*
23. *Id.*
24. *Id.*
25. *Id.*
26. *Id.* at 282.
27. *Id.*
28. *Id.*
29. *Id.* at 281.
30. *Id.*
31. *Id.* at 285.
32. *Id*
33. *Id*
34. *Miranda v. Arizona*, 384 U.S. 436 (1966).
35. *Id.* at 444
36. *Id.* at 491-92.
37. *Id.*
38. *Id.*
39. *Id.*
40. *Id.*
41. *Miranda*, 384 U.S. at 439.
42. *Id.* at 458.
43. *Id.* at 482.
44. *Id.* at 467.
45. *Id.*
46. *Id.* at 444-45.
47. *Id.*

48. Marvin Zalman, *Welsh S. White's Miranda's Waning Protections: Police Interrogation Practices After Dickerson* (2002), *available at* http://www.allbusiness.com/legal/3502341-1.html (analyzing White's article which discusses the effects that the *Miranda* opinion has had on modern interrogations and how interrogators have learned to adapt to Miranda thus reducing its effectiveness).

49. *Miranda*, 384 U.S. at 453.

50. *Id.*

51. *Id.* at 454.

52. *Id.*

53. *Id.* at 453.

54. Leo, *supra* note 9, at 30.

55. *See generally* National Research Council, *A Fairness and Effectiveness in Policing: The Evidence, available at* http://www.nap.edu/openbook.php?record_id=10419&page=47 (last visited Mar. 6, 2010) (describing current police practices and operations that contribute to public safety and crime prevention).

56. *Id.*

57. *Miranda*, 384 U.S. at 447.

58. *Id.* at 446.

59. *Brown*, 297 U.S. at 278.

60. *Miranda*, 384 U.S. at 447.

61. *Id.*

62. *Id.*

63. *Id.*

64. *Id.* at 446.

65. *Id.* at 447. The Court in *Miranda* reviewed Fred Inbau's training manuals, which explained that officers encourage and actively promote lengthy interrogations: "Criminal offenders... ordinarily will not admit their guilt unless

questions under conditions of privacy, and for a period of perhaps several hours." *Id.* Length of interrogation is one of the strongest determinants of its success. *Id.*

66. *Miranda*, 384 U.S. at 446.

67. *Id.*

68. *Id.*

69. Evan Wallach, *Waterboarding Used to Be a Crime*, WASH. POST, Nov. 4, 2007, *available at* http://www.washingtonpost.com/wp-dyn/content/article/2007/11/02/AR2007110201170.html (condemning the dangerous effects, both to the physical body and to the truth telling process, when interrogators use using waterboarding as an interrogation technique).

70. *Id.*

71. *Id.*

72. *Id.*

73. *Id.*

74. *Id.*

75. *Id.*

76. *Id.*

77. *Id.*

78. *Miranda*, 384 U.S. at 468.

79. TEX. PENAL CODE ANN. § 8.05 (Vernon 2003).

80. *Id.*

81. *Miranda*, 384 U.S. at 447.

82. *Id.* at 447-48.

83. *Id.* at 447.

84. *Id.* at 448.

85. *Id.*

86. *Margaret L. Paris,* Forum: Faults, Fallacies, and the Future of our Criminal Justice System: Trust, Lies and Interrogation, 3 VA. J. SOC. POL'Y & L. 3, 11 (1995) (arguing that modern

interrogation techniques now focus on psychological tricks and lies that force suspects to confess to interrogator's version of the story).

87. *Id.* at 12; *Miranda*, 348 U.S at 447.

88. *Recording Police Interrogations Make Loads of Sense*, Grits for Breakfast, (2008) http://gritsforbreakfast.blogspot.com/2008/07/recording-police-interrogations-makes.html (last visited Mar. 3, 2010) (arguing that interrogators use psychological tactics "that convince the suspect they have no other choice but to confess, even if in order to do so police must lie, threaten or bully the suspect when they try to exercise other options like refusing to answer questions. Recording interrogations would discourage disreputable interrogation tactics, protect real confessions from challenge in court, and help identify false ones after the fact - there's really very little downside").

89. Leo, *supra* note 9, at 30.

90. Richard A. Leo, *From Coercion to Deception: The Changing Nature of Police Interrogation in America*, CRIME, L. AND SOC. CHANGE, 35, 37 (2009) ("Not only do police now openly and strongly condemn the use of physical force during interrogation, they also believe that psychological tactics are far more effective at eliciting confessions. The use of deception has, in effect, become a functional alternative to the use of coercion. With this change, police power in the context of interrogation has acquired new meaning: it has become more subtle, more invasive, and more total, effectuated through psychological manipulation rather than physical violence"); Saul M. Kassin et al., *Police-Induced Confessions: Risk Factors and Recommendations,* 34 LAW. OF HUM. BEHAV. 3, 12 (2010) (discussing the dangerous effects of current police interrogation practices).

91. *Miranda*, 384 U.S. at 448.

92. *Id.*

93. *Id.*at 459 (citing Boyd v. United States, 116 U.S. 616 (1886)).

94. *Id.* at 447.

95. *Id.* at 460.

96. *Id.* at 453.

97. *Id.*

98. Kassin et al., *supra* note 90, at 12.

99. Keith A. Findley & Michael Scott, *The Multiple Dimensions of Tunnel Vision in Criminal Cases*, 2 WIS. L. REV. 323 (2006) (discussing the human tendency of interrogators to be unable to remain open-minded during the investigation process leading to dangerous injustice in the criminal justice system).

100. *Id.*

101. *Id.*

102. *Id.*

103. *Id.* at 324.

104. Kassin et al., *supra* note 90, at 12.

105. *Miranda*, 384 U.S. at 468.

106. *Id.*

107. Leo, *supra* note 90, at 37.

108. *Id.*

109. 168 U.S. 532 (1897).

110. *Miranda*, 384 U.S.at 448.

111. *Id.*

112. *See* John Reid, Investigator Tips, http://www.reid.com/educational_info/r_tips.html [hereinafter Investigator Tips] (last visited Mar. 3, 2010) (discussing the details of the Reid Interrogation Technique).

113. *See generally* Fred E. Inbau et al., CRIMINAL INTERROGATIONS AND CONFESSIONS (2004) (discussing the goals, benefits, and process guiding the Reid Interrogation Technique).

114. *Id.*

115. The nine steps of the Reid technique include: 1.The Positive Confrontation 2. Theme Development 3. Handling Denials 4. Overcoming Objections 5. Procuring and Retaining the Suspect's Attention 6. Handling the Suspect's Passive Mood 7. Presenting an Alternative Question 8. Detailing the Offense 9. Elements of Oral and Written Statements. *See* John Reid, The Reid Nine Steps of Interrogations, http://www.reid.com/training_programs/r_interview.html. (last visited Mar. 4, 2010).

116. Investigator Tips, *supra* note 112.

117. John Reid, Behavior Analysis Interview, http://www.reid.com/services/r_behavior.html [hereinafter Behavior Analysis Interview] (last visited Mar. 4, 2010) (describing what behavior interrogators should look for when attempting to determine the guilt or innocence of a suspect).

118. Saul Kassin, *A Critical Appraisal of Modern Police Interrogations, in* INVESTIGATIVE INTERVIEWING: RIGHTS, RESEARCH, REGULATION 207, 213 (Tom Williamson ed., 2006) (discussing the flaws inherent in the Reid Technique's behavior analysis assessment of guilt).

119. Investigator Tips, *supra* note 112.

120. Kassin, *supra* note 118.

121. *Id.*

122. Daniel T. Gilbert & Patrick S. Malone, *The Correspondence Bias,* 117 PSYCHOL. BULL. 21, 21-38 (1995) (describing interrogators tendency to overvalue dispositional reasons for observed behavior while undervaluing the effect that the present interrogation situation could be having on the suspect).

123. Kassin, *supra* note 118, at 213 (describing how interrogators correspondingly increase the anxiety and pressure associated with the interrogation as the length of the interrogation increases). This practice often has the psychological effect of convincing suspects to do whatever it takes to get pressure of the interrogation to subside. *Id.*
124. Richard J. Ofshe & Richard A. Leo, *The Decision to Confess Falsely: Rational Choice & Irrational Action*, 74 Denv. U. L. Rev. 979, 985 (1997) (discussing how innocent suspects are manipulated into confessing by well-trained detectives). "False confessions are not caused by what the courts allow police to do, but rather, by what some detectives do despite court prohibition." *Id.* Ofshe is a psychologist. *Id.* at 979.
125. *Id.*
126. *Id* at 986.
127. John Reid, Critics Corner (1997), http://www.reid.com/educational_info/critictestimony [hereinafter Critics Corner]. Richard Ofshe was the psychologist called to provide his expert opinion on the Reid Technique in *Oregon v. Pickens. Id.* He argued that the Reid Technique was flawed in that it is entirely based on deception. *Id.*
128. *Id.*
129. *Id.*
130. Saul M. Kassin, *The Psychology of Confessions,* 4 Ann. Rev. of L. and Soc. Sci. Behav.193, 198 (2008) (arguing that the "modern police interrogation, a guilt-presumptive process of social influence during which trained police use strong, psychologically oriented techniques involving isolation, confrontation, and minimization of blame to elicit confessions).
131. Critics Corner, *supra* note 128.
132. *See* Ofshe & Leo, *supra* note 124.
133. *Id.* at 985.

134. Robert Owens, Coerced (False) Confessions, http://www.fd.org/pdf_lib/Coerced%20False%20Confessions.pdf (last visited Mar. 3, 2010).

135. *Id.*

136. Critics Corner *supra* note 128.

137. Elizabeth Loftus, *Creating False Memories*, 277 Sci. Am. 70, 70-75 (1997) (discussing her experiment on people regarding childhood memories which furthers her proposition that the human memory is quite malleable).

138. Saul M. Kassin & Katherine L. Kiechel, *The Social Psychology of False Confessions: Compliance, Internalization, and Confabulation*, 7 Psychol. Sci. 125, 126-128 (1996) (describing a study conducted at Williams College to examine the reaction that false, incriminating evidence can have on the willingness of individuals to confession to crimes they never committed and internalize guilt associated with have actually committed the crime).

139. *Id.*

140. *Id.*

141. *Id.*

142. *Id.*

143. *Id.*

144. *Id.*

145. *Id.*

146. *Id.*

147. *Id.*

148. *Id.*

149. *See* Loftus, *supra* note138, at 72.

150. *Id.*

151. *Id.*

152. *Id.*

153. *Id.*
154. Kassin & Kiechel, *supra* note 139, at 125; Loftus, *supra* note138, at 72.
155. Richard P. Conti, *The Psychology of False Confessions*, 2 J. of Credibility Assessment and Witness Psychol. 14, 23 (1999) (discussing the psychological and social factors that influence innocent suspects to give self-incriminating false statements during police interrogation).
156. *Id.*
157. *Id.*
158. *Id.*
159. *Id.*
160. *Id.*
161. Joseph Berlinger & Bruce Sinofsy, Brother's Keeper (1992), http://www.docurama.com/productdetail.html?productid=NV-NVG-5605-NVG-9542.
162. Conti, *supra* note 156, at 24.
163. *Id.* at 23.
164. *Id.*
165. *Id.*
166. *Id.*
167. *Id.*
168. Herbert, *supra* note 12, at 12.
169. *Id.*
170. Robert Owens, Coerced (False) Confessions, http://www.fd.org/pdf_lib/Coerced%20False%20Confessions.pdf (last visited Mar. 3, 2010) (collecting the observations of a federal public defender).
171. *Id.*
172. Kassin et al., *supra* note 90, at 12.
173. Behavior Analysis Interview, *supra* note 117.

174. *See Miranda*, 384 U.S. at 436.

175. Report of the Supreme Court Special Committee on Recordation of Custodial Interrogations 33-34 (2005), *available at* http://www.judiciary.state.nj.us/notices/reports/cookreport.pdf [hereinafter N.J. Supreme Court Report].

176. *Id.*

177. Thomas P. Sullivan, *Police Experience with Recording Custodial Interrogations* (2004), *available at* http://www.innocenceproject.org/docs/Police_Experiences_Recording_Interrogations.pdf..

178. Tex. Code Crim. Proc. Ann. § 38.22(3) (Vernon 2005). Texas requires recordation of statements of an accused made as a result of custodial interrogation. *Id.* In order for a confession to be admissible, oral statements must be recorded. *Id.* Texas law enforcement officers are not required to record the entire custodial interrogation as a precondition to admissibility. *Id.*. *See* N.J. Supreme Court Report, *supra* note 176, at 11-12.

179. Sullivan, *supra* note 178, at 7.

180. N.J. Supreme Court Report, *supra* note 176,.at 33-34.

181. *See* Sullivan, *supra* note 178.

182. *Id.* at 7.

183. *Id.* at A1-A10.

184. *Id.* at Introduction.

185. National Association of Criminal Defense Lawyers, http://www.nacdl.org/sl_docs.nsf/freeform/MERI_attachments/$FILE/NACDL_Factsheet MERI_Support_Quotes.pdf (last visited Mar. 24, 2010).

186. Sullivan, *supra* note 178, at 24.

187. N.J. Supreme Court Report, *supra* note 176.

188. *Id.*

189. Sullivan, *supra* note 178, at 7.

190. *Id.* at 23-4.

191. Electronic Recording of Interrogations (2004), www.municipalpoliceinstitute.org/.../2.17%20Electronic%20Recording%20of%20Interrogations.doc.

192. *Id.*

193. *Id.*

194. *Id.*

195. *Id.*

196. N.J. Supreme Court Report, *supra* note 176,.at 29.

197. *Id.*

198. *Recording Police Interrogations Make Loads of Sense*, *supra* note 88.

199. *Id.*

200. *Id.*

201. N.J. Supreme Court Report, *supra* note 176,.at 33-34.

202. *Id.*

203. Sullivan, *supra* note 178, at 7.

204. *Id.*

205. *Id.*

206. *Id.*

207. Richard A. Leo & Brittany Lui, *What Do Potential Jurors Know About Police Interrogation Techniques and False Confessions?*, at 6 (2009) http://papers.ssrn.com/sol3/papers.cfm?abstract_id=1404078.

208. *Id.*

209. Sullivan, *supra* note 178, at 7.

210. N.J. Supreme Court Report, *supra* note 176,.at 33-34.

211. *Id.* at 33.

212. *Id.*

213. *Id.* at 34.

214. Sullivan, *supra* note 178, at 7.
215. *See* Thomas P. Sullivan, Police Experience with Recording Custodial Interrogations (2004), http://www.innocenceproject.org/docs/Police_Experiences_Recording_Interrogations.pdf.
216. *Id.*
217. *Id.*
218. *Id.*
219. Owens, *supra* note 135, at 2.
220. *See* Ochoa Interview, *supra* note 1.

Of Crimes, Confessions, and Convictions: Reducing Wrongful Convictions Attributable to False Confessions

Hillary K. Valderrama*

> "To ignore the possibilities of fixing the causes of unjust convictions is to render invisible the living witnesses, the fugitives from the unreal dream of wrongful incarceration."[1]

I. Introduction

Robert Miller first became a suspect in a series of brutal rapes and murders when his blood type matched evidence left at the scenes of the crimes.[2] Miller "was a regular user of drugs, and he believed that someone had slipped PCP into something he had ingested" when police first interrogated him.[3] During the ensuing interrogation, he

---

* Hillary Valderrama is an attorney licensed in Texas. She graduated summa cum laude from the University of Houston Law Center in May 2010.

made several incriminating statements.[4] Miller was tried for capital murder,[5] and the jury watched the interrogation (complete with his confession) during the trial.[6] The prosecuting attorney had a litany of damning evidence straight from Miller's own mouth to use in his closing argument:

> [Miller] knew what rooms [the victims] were in. He knew how the rooms were decorated. He knew precisely how the killer got into the houses. He knew how the killer and why the killer disconnected the telephone lines so [the victims] wouldn't, couldn't call out. And he told you exactly what the killer was thinking. And there's only one person on the face of this earth that knew that, and that's him right there.[7]

Not surprisingly, Miller was convicted of capital murder and given two death sentences.[8] On its face, the Miller prosecution seemed straightforward: a tragic crime and a fitting punishment. There was just one problem: Robert Miller was innocent.[9]

Despite the wealth of procedural protections observed in his case,[10] Robert Miller had been convicted of a crime he did not commit and sentenced to die.[11] This unsettling result raises serious questions about the integrity of the criminal justice system, perhaps especially in capital cases. In particular, how does the system fail innocent suspects like Robert Miller and the victims of the crimes for which they are convicted?

The Miller investigation and prosecution suffered from a myriad of shortcomings.[12] First, detectives considered another individual a "strong suspect" and continued to investigate the crimes for up to six months after the prosecutor charged Miller with capital murder.[13] But it is far from clear that the prosecution ever made Miller's defense attorney aware of the existence of another suspect.[14] Next, the confession itself was suspect. The twelve-hour interrogation was "a numbing drone of hallucination, interrogation, exorcism, revival, and nonsense."[15] Miller "cut[] off the conversation and denie[d] that he was present" at the scenes of the crimes over 130 times during the course of the interrogation.[16] Miller only suggested that the killer left his underwear at the scene after he had "suggested virtually every stitch or tool[] that a rapist might have carried," including gloves, pants, slacks, coats, and shirts.[17] As one observer noted, "[f]or every flimsy statement that could be tied to the crime, there [were] dozens of details that Miller was just wrong about."[18] Even the judge who presided over Miller's retrial declined to allow the videotaped confession into evidence, holding that the interrogation did not even meet the standard of admissibility for an admission.[19]

Perhaps most troubling was the system's reaction to Miller's protestations of innocence. Miller's "new public defenders encouraged [him] to accept a deal with prosecutors that offered him life without parole" rather than pursue a new trial.[20] The prosecuting authority "at first disputed the[] validity" of DNA evidence suggesting Miller was innocent.[21] Later, prosecutors observed that the DNA tests proved only that Miller did not sexually assault the victims but left open the possibility that he murdered them.[22] When a suspect whose DNA matched the crime scene evidence was found, prosecutors offered him a "'straight life sentence'" if he would "implicate Robert Miller in the crimes."[23] One high-ranking official allegedly told Miller's attorney that the state was "going to needle [his] client."[24] In the end, DNA tests proved that Miller was not the rapist and still it took another six long years before he was released from prison.[25]

As Robert Miller's case illustrates, confessions are among the most powerful evidence a prosecutor can present to a judge or jury. The Supreme Court has recognized the uniquely persuasive nature of confessions.[26] Studies illustrate that that seventy-three "percent of juries will vote to convict even when admissions have been repudiated by the defendant and contradicted by physical evidence."[27] As a result, false confessions are a source of major concern in the criminal justice system.

According to one commentator, "[f]alse confessions have long been one of the leading causes of miscarriages of justice in the United States."[28] For many people, it may be difficult if not impossible to believe that an innocent individual would confess to a crime she did not commit.[29] This is particularly true given that the use of physical brutality to obtain confessions has become increasingly uncommon in the United States.[30] However, though obtaining reliable estimates of the occurrences of false confessions is difficult, it is increasingly clear that false confessions do result in wrongful convictions in a significant number of cases. One source notes that "about [twenty-five percent] of those exonerated by DNA made incriminating statements, gave false confessions, or took guilty pleas."[31] Another expert suggests that due to the difficulty of proving that a confession is in fact false, "the cases that are discovered most surely represent the tip of an iceberg."[32] In any event, the incidence of wrongful convictions stemming from false confessions can properly be described as "high and unsettling."[33]

Wrongful convictions carry extremely high social costs[34] above and beyond the imposition of potentially harsh criminal sanctions upon innocent individuals. First, wrongful convictions are a serious threat to public safety given that the actual perpetrators frequently go on to commit additional crimes when an innocent person is convicted in their stead.[35] In addition, one jurisdiction has concluded that "even where charges do not result in conviction, the pendency of charges based upon false confessions can impose tremendous burdens upon the accused and their families, as well as the victims and their families."[36] Next, given that "false confessions are obtained more frequently in high-profile or capital cases,"[37] wrongful convictions predicated on such evidence threaten to undermine public confidence in capital punishment. Shockingly, over the course of one 14-year study, "[w]ith a handful of exceptions, everyone on [the] list of exonerees was sentenced to death or to a long term of imprisonment."[38] All but 7% "were sentenced to ten years in prison or more," while more than three quarters "were sentenced to at least twenty-five years."[39] Perhaps most appalling was the fact that "more than half were sentenced to life imprisonment or to death."[40] As one commentator noted, as long as "the American criminal justice system is prepared to accept the imposition of such . . . life-ending punishments, we cannot be complacent about any possibility that they might be unjustly enforced."[41] Finally, wrongful convictions also run counter to the spirit of the American criminal justice system[42] and offend traditional notions of justice.[43] They undermine public confidence in the criminal justice system[44] and dilute the message of moral condemnation that accompanies criminal convictions.[45]

Preventing injustices resulting from false confessions is a topic ripe for legislative attention for a variety of reasons. As an initial matter, the activities of groups like The Innocence Project and the exoneration of several hundred falsely convicted individuals[46] has drawn public attention to the issue. Stories of false confessions have even cropped up in mainstream movies and television series.[47] According to several scholars, "[f]alse confessions are the primary cause of wrongful convictions in many cases – especially those involving high-profile murders and sexual offenses."[48] Wrongful convictions involving such serious offenses can have serious repercussions, up to and including the execution of innocent individuals.[49] Moreover, literature documenting the occurrences of wrongful convictions related to false confessions has advanced enough to offer policymakers reasoned suggestions for dealing with the issue.[50]

This article argues that reforms are needed to avoid wrongful convictions based on false confessions and to maintain the integrity of the criminal justice system. Part II defines false confessions and the various types of false confessions identified by researchers. Part III describes existing procedural safeguards available to defendants and explores why such safeguards are largely ineffectual in eliminating the danger of wrongful convictions based on false confessions. These protections include *Miranda* warnings prior to interrogation, the due process voluntariness requirement, and the provision of jury instructions and the admission of expert testimony regarding false confessions. Part IV explores measures that jurisdictions can adopt to more effectively guard against wrongful convictions due to false confessions, including reforms to interrogation and police practices, recording requirements, expanded availability of jury instructions and expert testimony in order to alert juries to the hazards of confession evidence, and enhanced requirements for the admissibility of confessions. Part V concludes by suggesting that the most feasible and effective measures jurisdictions can adopt are recording interrogations and requiring the exclusion of confessions that are not supported by substantial corroborating evidence.

II. Definitions and Types of False Confessions

As the name implies, a false confession is "an admission of guilt followed by a narrative statement of what, how, and why the confessor committed the crime."[51] In general, false confessions are discovered in one of four ways. Officials may become aware that no crime was committed,[52] as in fact tended to happen in the eighteenth and nineteenth centuries.[53] New evidence may sometimes show that "it was physically impossible for the confessor to have committed the crime."[54] In other situations, "the real perpetrator, having no connection to the defendant, [may be] captured and implicated."[55] Finally, "DNA and other scientific evidence [may] affirmatively establish the confessor's innocence."[56] It is notoriously difficult to estimate the incidence of false confessions,[57] but they are likely to occur more often than commonly believed. Saul Kassin, the leading researcher on the psychology of false confessions, observes that "contrary to the widespread belief that people do not confess to crimes they did not commit, the pages of American history betray large numbers of men and women who were wrongfully prosecuted, convicted, imprisoned, and sometimes sentenced to death on the basis of false confessions."[58]

There are three widely accepted types of false confessions.[59] Perhaps the most widely known type is the compliant false confession, where the suspected "[is] induced to confess through the processes of police interrogation."[60] Suspects may confess "in order to escape a stressful custodial situation, avoid physical or legal punishment, or gain a promised or implied reward."[61] A compliant false confession is an "act of public capitulation by a suspect who knows that he or she is innocent but perceives that the short-term benefits of confession . . . outweigh the long-term costs."[62] However, there are two other types of false confessions: voluntary false confessions and internalized false confessions. In voluntary false confessions, "people claim responsibility for crimes they did not commit without prompting or pressure from police."[63] Internalized false confessions involve situations "in which innocent but vulnerable suspects confess and come to believe they committed the crime in question."[64] This belief may be "accompanied by false memories" indicating the suspect's guilt.[65] Experts theorize that in certain situations, "people develop a profound distrust of their own memory that renders them vulnerable to manipulation from external cues."[66] Cues from authority figures may be key in creating such distrust and planting the seeds of belief in guilt.[67] Understanding the differences between these types of false confessions is important in understanding the intricate interplay between psychology and law enforcement that can ultimately lead to false confessions.[68]

Three Types of False Confessions

- Induced by police pressure or promises
- Voluntary false confessions
- Internalized false confessions by vulnerable suspects

III. Existing Procedural Safeguards Are Insufficient to Adequately Guard Against Wrongful Convictions Predicated on False Confessions

A. Why *Miranda* Is Inadequate to Prevent Wrongful Convictions Based On False Confessions

There is some debate as to whether any of a defendant's constitutional rights provide useful protection against false confessions.[69] As a leading scholar observes, "[n]one of [the constitutional provisions commonly used to challenge the admissibility of evidence in criminal trials] currently provides much protection against the admission of unreliable or false confessions into evidence at trial."[70] Moreover, "[s]uspects who falsely confess to crimes that they did not commit tend to be particularly vulnerable."[71] This category includes suspects who have mental deficiencies and those who hail from "unusual cultural backgrounds," as well as juveniles, intoxicated suspects, and those who are simply anxious "to *appear* cooperative."[72] These issues may be difficult if not impossible for police officers to adequately address in all instances. This tends to support the argument that procedural remedies that focus on the defendant's constitutional rights (like *Miranda*) do little, if anything, to ensure the substantive truth of the defendant's confession.

Though *Miranda v. Arizona*[73] provided important safeguards for the rights of suspects as well as the integrity of criminal trials generally, the procedural safeguards it set forth have been unsuccessful in ensuring that confessions are freely given, as Justice Warren perhaps envisioned.[74] An early study including a nearly twenty-year period following *Miranda* found that false confessions contributed to one-tenth of the wrongful convictions in study.[75] A subsequent study concluded that "the interrogation techniques employed by the police in serious high-profile cases are at least as likely to produce false confessions today as they were" at the end of the previous study.[76] Commentators have attributed *Miranda*'s ineffectiveness in this area to a number of factors.[77]

1. *MIRANDA*'S PROTECTIONS HAVE BEEN WEAKENED BY A NUMBER OF EXCEPTIONS

In addition, the Supreme Court has moved away from *Miranda*'s sweeping pronouncement that "[e]ven without employing brutality, . . . the very fact of custodial interrogation exacts a heavy toll on individual liberty and trades on the weakness of individuals."[78] While the Court has declined to overrule *Miranda*,[79] its support has been almost grudging.[80] Even the iconic right to silence is riddled with exceptions.[81] For example, a suspect's unwarned statement may be used in the prosecution's case-in-chief if the statement is obtained due to public safety concerns.[82] If the police initially obtain a confession in violation of *Miranda*, in certain circumstances the prosecution can use a subsequent, identical confession obtained after *Miranda* warnings are administered.[83] Even if law enforcement officers neglect to give *Miranda* warnings, statements made by a suspect may nonetheless be used as impeachment* evidence.[84] Moreover, a suspect's custodial silence may be used against her if *Miranda* warnings have not been read to her,[85] which may give suspects incentives to speak with police. Finally, evidence the police obtain from unwarned statements may be admissible against the defendant even if the statements themselves are not.[86] These issues (among others) led one scholar to proclaim that "[n]ext to the warning label on cigarette packs, *Miranda* is the most widely ignored piece of official advice in our

---

* Discrediting a witness by showing that he/she is not telling the truth or does not have the knowledge to testify as he/she did.

society. Even when *Miranda* is violated, it is rare that a confession will be ruled inadmissible or that a suspect will go free."[87]

2. The Language and Substantive Content of *Miranda* Warnings May Be Difficult for Suspects to Understand

Though the Court's decision in *Miranda* required the states to make criminal suspects aware of certain procedural rights, it allowed the states considerable discretion in implementing these safeguards.[88] The Court's only criteria was that warnings must be "fully as effective [as those proposed by the Court] . . . in informing accused persons of their right of silence and in affording an opportunity to exercise it."[89] As a result, *Miranda* warnings are not uniform across the United States. In fact, one study found more than thirty different variations on *Miranda* warnings across the fifty states.[90] The grade level reading skills required to comprehend the warnings were similarly diverse, "ranging from the second grade to post-college."[91] More surprising was the fact that only 80% "of the warnings stated a suspect's continuing rights to silence and counsel," rights about which *Miranda* clearly requires law enforcement to inform suspects.[92]

These regional variations and deficiencies compound other systemic issues. For example, the substantive meaning of *Miranda* warnings is often unclear even to the public at large. In a study of college undergraduates, over a quarter of the participants believed that failure to cooperate with the police would be used against them in court even after receiving their *Miranda* warnings.[93] Over a third of the survey population believed that the police may continue to interrogate suspects after the invocation of the right to counsel, and nearly a quarter believed that waivers must be signed to be effective.[94] In addition, *Miranda* warnings issued in other languages (such as Spanish) may be incorrectly translated,[95] injecting additional confusion into the process.

3. It is Much Harder for Suspects to Invoke *Miranda* Rights Than to Waive Them

Practical aspects of *Miranda* warnings also make them inadequate to fully guard against false confessions. Invoking the various *Miranda* rights does not require any specific language, but the invocation must usually be clear and unambiguous to warrant the exclusion of subsequent statements.[96] This is problematic, given that "[s]uspects typically use language that leaves some doubt about their invocation or waiver of the right to counsel or silence."[97] Moreover, even if the suspect successfully invokes her right to remain silent, police may ordinarily reapproach the suspect after a reasonable amount of time has passed and begin interrogation anew.[98] Though law enforcement must cease *all* interrogation upon a suspect's invocation of the right to counsel, a suspect may initiate contact with law enforcement after doing so.[99] In addition, a new ruling by the Supreme Court allows police officers to reapproach even suspects who *have* successfully invoked their right to counsel after the suspect has been out of police custody for two weeks.[100]

In short, it is challenging for many suspects to invoke their rights with sufficient clarity to warrant suppression of any subsequent statements. Even if a suspect successfully navigates this challenge, law enforcement officers may have additional opportunities to interrogate suspects afterwards. These procedural issues may be particularly disadvantageous to vulnerable populations such as youthful or mentally disabled offenders, who may be less likely to clearly invoke *Miranda* rights in the first instance and more likely to reapproach law enforcement in the second. Even outright violations of *Miranda* can lead to admissible physical evidence, witnesses, and statements which can be used for impeachment purposes. Thus, *Miranda* fails to provide meaningful protection during custodial interrogations.

By contrast, waivers of *Miranda* rights are found rather frequently, with some studies suggesting that four out of every five suspects waives these important rights.[101] Suspects can make knowing and voluntary waivers of *Miranda* rights even when they are unaware of the nature of the specific criminal conduct the police are investigating.[102] Likewise, the Court has held that law enforcement officers' failure to inform a suspect that legal counsel has been retained for him does not invalidate the suspect's waiver of *Miranda* rights.[103] Given the comparative ease with which suspects may waive their *Miranda* rights, it is unsurprising that confessions are rarely ruled inadmissible.[104] One scholar notes that "it is not uncommon for suspects – especially highly suggestible ones such as the mentally handicapped, juveniles, and individuals unusually trusting of authority – to give false confessions (after waiving their *Miranda* rights) in response to police inducements that do not legally qualify as coercive or fundamentally unfair."[105]

4. Police Procedures in Issuing *Miranda* Warnings May Decrease Their Effectiveness, Especially with Vulnerable Suspects

Another practical concern is the manner in which law enforcement officers issue *Miranda* warnings. One scholar notes that police officers frequently engage in strategies designed to "maximize the likelihood of obtaining a waiver" of *Miranda* rights.[106] Police officers may "de-emphasize the potential importance of the *Miranda* rights" by reading them quickly or "deliver[ing them] in a perfunctory tone of voice and bureaucratic manner, implicitly suggesting that the warnings do not merit the suspect's concern."[107] Alternately, the officer may suggest that "the *Miranda* warnings are a mere formality."[108] Officers "may also attempt to persuade suspects to waive their *Miranda* rights" by "explicitly, if subtly, attempt[ing] to convince the suspect to waive his rights."[109] These tactics present ample reason for concern, given that "those suspects who are most likely to give a false confession . . . are least likely to invoke their *Miranda* rights to terminate police questioning."[110]

Additionally, law enforcement officers have developed extremely effective means of obtaining confessions despite *Miranda*'s requirements.[111] Indeed, *Miranda* itself did not "curb[] the use by police interrogators of such tactics as showing the suspect fake evidence, putting the suspect to a phony lie detector test that he is guaranteed to flunk, and making fraudulent offers of sympathy and help."[112] As a result, police "have developed and refined interrogation methods that are based on influence, manipulation, and deception."[113] Occasionally state courts have acted to limit the nature of deceptive tactics that police officers may use.[114] However, trickery is still generally permissible under the federal standard as long as the confession can be said to be voluntary under the "totality of the circumstances test."[115] This is particularly disturbing given that the Court's opinion in *Miranda v. Arizona* did not limit its disapproval of coercion to solely physical coercion.[116] In fact, *Brown v. Mississippi*[117] had firmly established that physical coercion and brutality were unconstitutional means of interrogation thirty years before *Miranda* was decided.[118] Instead, the Court specifically spoke to psychological pressure in *Miranda.*[119] As one commentator noted, "[i] n cases in which suspects do waive their rights, interrogations can be carried out much as they were before *Miranda*. In such instances *Miranda* is . . . virtually worthless as a safeguard against the specific interrogation practices that were characterized as abusive in the *Miranda* decision and cited as the empirical justification for *Miranda*'s reforms."[120] In short, though the type of physical coercion condemned by the Supreme Court in *Brown v. Mississippi*[121] has become relatively infrequent,[122] other types of coercion are still present in the interrogation rooms of America.

B. Why the Due Process Voluntariness Test Is Inadequate to Prevent Wrongful Convictions Based On False Confessions

Miranda is not the only protection afforded to criminal defendants. Critics of measures intended to reduce or eliminate false confessions might argue that the courts are in fact willing to consider the defendant's particular vulnerability in evaluating the voluntariness of the confession under the due process analysis. In fact, it was not long ago that the Supreme Court agreed that "as interrogators have turned to more subtle forms of psychological persuasion, courts have found the mental condition of the defendant a more significant factor in the 'voluntariness' calculus."[123] However, the due process requirement that any confession must be voluntarily made is far from a panacea for the problem of false confessions for several reasons.

First, though the courts consider the defendant's particular vulnerabilities, "coercive police activity is a necessary predicate to finding that a confession is not 'voluntary' within the meaning of the Due Process Clause of the Fourteenth Amendment."[124] While coercive police activities undoubtedly can contribute to the false confession dilemma,[125] such practices are not the exclusive means by which police obtain false confessions. Leading experts cite a number of different factors that can lead an innocent suspect to confess to a crime she did not commit. As an initial matter, "people have a naïve faith in the power of innocence to set them free."[126] Suspects may elect to speak with police officers initially out of a belief that they have nothing to hide. However, once an interrogation has begun, suspects may begin to feel "beleaguered and trapped."[127]

Moreover, police may still legally resort to a number of interrogation tactics that psychological studies have shown to result in false confessions. Two particular practices involving "trickery and deception" are of concern.[128] The first practice, known as "minimization," is defined as "the process by which a sympathetic investigator normalizes and minimizes the crime in question."[129] Minimalization "lead[s] people to infer that they will be treated with leniency if they confess, *even when no explicit promises are made.*"[130] Laboratory experiments strongly suggest that minimalization may persuade innocent suspects to confess to acts they did not commit.[131] The second tactic, called maximization, "involves a cluster of tactics designed to convey the interrogator's rock-solid belief that the suspect is guilty and that all denials will fail."[132]

The final tactic involves the use of false evidence.[133] Police interrogators often confront suspects with allegedly incontrovertible evidence of their guilt.[134] This evidence may take a number of forms, from fingerprints to blood types to failed polygraph results,[135] all of which are generally considered strong evidence. Such evidence "can alter people's perceptions, beliefs, memories, and behaviors."[136] In one study, the provision of false evidence "nearly doubled" the number of innocent subjects who signed a confession.[137] As one commentator noted, "[t]he power of false evidence to produce these effects is not surprising in light of the fact that people who know they are innocent may agree to confess as an act of compliance when they perceive that there is strong evidence against them, a belief that induces a state of despair and an urgent need of escape."[138] This observation seems to reinforce the Court's observation over forty years ago in *Miranda v. Arizona* that "the process of in-custody interrogation of persons suspected or accused of crime contains inherently compelling pressures which work to undermine the individual's will to resist and to compel him to speak where he would not otherwise do so freely."[139] Moreover, it highlights the fact that information so obtained is unreliable. However, under the Court's subsequent precedent, police may use deceit and trickery freely[140] and minimalization has yet to be addressed as a problem by the courts. Some states have held that the fabrication of evidence renders a confession involuntary, but even in such states false assertions do not render a confession involuntary.[141]

Though maximization, minimalization, and trickery may elicit false confessions from "average" suspects, such tactics may be unnecessary to elicit confessions from vulnerable groups of suspects. Certain groups have been found to be particularly susceptible to persuasion from authority figures like police officers. Psychological studies strongly suggest that juveniles are prone to offer false confessions and that this propensity is inversely related to the age of the suspect.[142] This is particularly problematic given that "[m]ore than [90%] of juveniles whom police seek to question waive their *Miranda* rights."[143] Individuals with mental disabilities are also more likely to offer false confessions for a number of reasons.[144] First, psychological studies link mental retardation to a host of personality traits that may predispose an individual to offer a false confession.[145] In addition, mentally retarded suspects have been found to be "more likely to yield to leading questions and change their answers in response to mild negative feedback."[146] The Supreme Court has even cited the elevated likelihood that mentally retarded suspects will confess to crimes they did not commit as a reason to prohibit the imposition of the death penalty for mentally retarded defendants.[147] Various mental illnesses (such as depression, antisocial disorder, attention deficit hyperactivity disorder (ADHD), and schizophrenia) also increase the likelihood that a suspect will offer a false confession.[148] Suspects hailing from "unusual cultural backgrounds" or who are under the influence of "alcohol or other drugs" may also be particularly likely to confess.[149] These risks are further compounded in the case of suspects who belong to multiple vulnerable groups.[150] These suspects are perhaps most at risk of internalized false confessions.[151]

In short, police utilize many interrogation tactics that may persuade even average suspects to confess to a crime they did not commit,[152] largely because the Court has held that the use of such tactics is generally insufficient to make a confession involuntary for due process purposes.[153] More susceptible suspects, including younger suspects and those suffering from mental retardation or mental illness, may be still more likely to confess under such circumstances.[154] Moreover, in some high-profile cases, individuals may offer voluntary false confessions with little or no provocation from the police at all.[155] In most jurisdictions judges must make a voluntariness determination without the benefit of a recording of the actual interrogation.[156] Due in part to these factors, "[t]he 'totality of the circumstances' test, while affording judges flexibility in practice, has offered little protection to suspects."[157]

C. Why the Admission of Expert Testimony Regarding False Confessions is Inadequate to Prevent Wrongful Convictions Based on False Confessions

The Supreme Court has held that defendants have the right to acquaint the jury with circumstances tending to affect the reliability of a confession, even when the trial court has found the confession to be voluntary for due process purposes.[158] Hence, at first glance, false confessions seem to be a problem uniquely suited to remediation by the admission of expert testimony. Though such testimony is always subject to the criticism that it may invade the province of the jury, [159] two larger questions loom in the background.

1. Expert Testimony Regarding False Confessions Is Insufficient to Mitigate the Impact a Confession Has on the Jury

The first and perhaps most important issue is that "[m]ock jury studies show that confessions have more impact than other potent forms of evidence and that people do not fully discount confessions even when they are judged to be coerced and even when it is logically and legally appropriate to do so."[160] There are several potential reasons for this. First, it seems illogical that a suspect would incriminate herself unless she was in fact guilty.[161] Next, "people are typically not adept" at detecting deception."[162] Research indicates that "neither lay people nor professionals accurately distinguish truths from lies."[163] Unfortunately, there is also research that indicates that while police officers are no better at detecting the truth than lay people, officers are in fact more likely to give credence to false confessions.[164] This creates a lamentable situation in which those who are entrusted with determining the course of an investigation may prematurely narrow their focus based on false information.[165] Finally, false confessions may be "persuasive and compelling" due to "content cues presumed to be associated with truthfulness."[166] Despite their best efforts, police interrogators may provide the suspect with details about the crime during the interrogation process.[167] When they do, it sets the stage for confessions that are "scripted in accordance with the police theory of the case . . . [and] directed by the questioner"[168] without regard for the truth of the confession.

2. Expert Testimony Regarding False Confessions May Be Inadmissible or Unduly Limited by Trial Courts

The second question is whether such testimony even meets the current standard of admissibility under current evidentiary standards. States vary in their evidentiary requirements, but the federal standard is often influential.[169] The federal standard for the admissibility of expert testimony is set forth in a series of well-known cases. Initially, expert testimony was subject to a rather rigorous evidentiary standard known as the *Frye* test: in order to be admissible in federal court, the data underlying the expert opinion had to be "sufficiently established to have gained general acceptance in the particular field in which it belong[ed]."[170] Later, the adoption of the Federal Rules of Evidence altered this standard to make admissible expert testimony which would "assist the trier of fact to understand the evidence or to determine a fact in issue."[171] Rather than requiring expert testimony to be based on generally accepted scientific tenets, the Federal Rules of Evidence only required that it meet three new criteria: it must be (1) "based on sufficient facts or data," (2) "the product of reliable principles and methods," and (3) demonstrable that "the witness has applied the principles and methods reliably to the facts of the case."[172] As the Supreme Court recognized, the adoption of the Federal Rules of Evidence broadened the scope of admissible expert testimony by eliminating *Frye*'s "general acceptance" requirement.[173] In its place, the Court held that expert testimony must be "scientifically valid" and relevant to the facts at issue.[174] The Court also set forth a number of criteria courts should consider in determining whether expert testimony is admissible under the new standard.[175] Chief among these factors was whether the science upon which the expert testimony was predicated could be or had been tested, as well as its rate of error, whether it had been subject to peer review and publication, and whether it was generally accepted.[176]

As the Court itself noted, the test for admissibility is flexible,[177] allowing trial courts great latitude in admitting expert testimony. In 2003, one commentator noted that "[a]bout half the states that ha[d] ruled on the issue [of the admissibility of expert testimony about false confessions] ha[d] excluded the expert testimony, some on the ground that it does not meet the *Frye* or *Daubert* standards relating to reliability of expert testimony."[178] There is some evidence suggesting that "courts appear to be receptive to expert testimony when the credibility of a confession is at issue."[179] However, even the most optimistic observers note the apparent reluctance of many courts to admit such evidence and observe that "[t]he key to admissibility of such expert testimony under *Daubert* . . . appears to be the particularity with which the research on false confessions is shown to have specific application to the defendant."[180] In cases where the expert has not sufficiently examined the particular defendant at issue, then, defendants may not be able to take full advantage of expert testimony.[181]

Moreover, it is still not clear that expert testimony regarding false confessions is regularly admitted.[182] As one commentator noted, there is little consensus as to whether or when expert testimony about false confessions should be admissible, even among jurisdictions adopting the same test for admissibility.[183] There are a number of reasons judges might reject such expert testimony: "not enough is understood yet about false confessions to satisfy *Daubert*, jurors know how to judge credibility and don't need expert testimony, and the admissibility of expert testimony lies within the discretion of the trial judge."[184] It is rare that trial court judges' evidentiary rulings are overturned on appeal, and ironically appellate courts may only be inclined to require the admission of expert testimony about false confessions in cases in which there is already evidence tending to suggest that the defendant is in fact innocent.[185] One scholar observes that rulings on the admissibility of expert testimony regarding false confessions "look more like ad hoc determinations in which the trial judge tries to assess whether the defendant was treated unjustly than reasoned explanations about expert testimony."[186]

Practically speaking, expert testimony about false confessions is unlikely to be sufficient standing alone to combat the impact of a defendant's confession.[187] As several researchers wrote, a confession "is inherently prejudicial and highly damaging to a defendant, even if it is the product of coercive interrogation, even if it is supported by no other evidence, and even if it is ultimately proven false beyond any reasonable doubt."[188] In light of the weight jurors give to confessions generally, expert testimony is unlikely to rehabilitate the defendant's case after confession evidence is introduced. While expert testimony could be useful to some defendants in conjunction with other legal strategies, the courts are frequently hesitant to admit such evidence under the current evidentiary standards.[189] This hesitance could be even greater in jurisdictions where judges must seek reelection and explain their rulings to a voting public that adheres to the "prevailing sentiment that no one would confess to something [s]he didn't do."[190] Also, in jurisdictions that have not adopted mandatory videotaping procedures, defendants are likely to need to testify about the alleged shortcomings of the interrogation itself.[191] This risks subjecting defendants to ordinarily inadmissible evidence for impeachment purposes and exposes them to cross-examination.[192] Though perhaps expert testimony regarding false confessions should be admissible,[193] it is unlikely to stem the growing tide of wrongful convictions without additional reforms.

D. Why the Provision of Jury Instructions about False Confessions Is Inadequate to Prevent Wrongful Convictions Based On False Confessions

Even critics of expert testimony support the use of jury instructions informing jurors about the risks of false confessions.[194] However, others "have doubts regarding the adequacy of jury instructions in dealing with concerns about . . . false confessions . . ."[195] Despite the limited evidence available on the effectiveness of jury instructions regarding false confessions, there are reasons to believe that jury instructions will be inadequate to mitigate such potent evidence. Broadly stated, concerns about jury instructions center on the likelihood that a trial judge will grant an instruction and on the effect such an instruction is likely to have on a jury.

First, defendants may not be able to persuade a trial judge to issue a jury instruction addressing false confessions. Jury instructions addressing special issues regarding the reliability of evidence first arose in the case *United States v. Telfaire*, where an appellate court upheld a trial judge's decision to instruct the jury about the risks inherent in eyewitness identifications.[196] Since then, defendants attempting to discredit eyewitness identifications have routinely requested jury instructions regarding factors that affect eyewitness identifications and indicia of unreliability. These requests have not been uniformly successful. Though the majority of the circuit courts do allow *Telfaire* instructions, most leave the decision to issue such instructions to the trial judge's discretion.[197] As a result, even jury instructions regarding the reliability of eyewitness identifications (a topic with a venerable body of scientific literature to support such instructions) are more a matter of judicial grace than of right.

While evidence regarding the prevalence of requests for jury instructions regarding false confessions is scarce and largely anecdotal, it supports the theory that defendants making such requests are largely unsuccessful. One court opined that jury instructions were unnecessary because "the truth or falsity of a confession is a factual determination, not a question of law, that hinges on credibility issues that are well within the abilities of jurors to sort out."[198] Another court "questioned the existence of authority for the proposition that oral admissions and confessions should be viewed with caution."[199] Even where jury instructions request jurors to independently consider the truth of a confession, specific warnings regarding the frequency and causes of false confessions are often lacking.[200]

Moreover, as discussed above, confessions are incredibly powerful and persuasive evidence to juries.[201] One commentator starkly summarized research on the impact of confessions in criminal trials as follows: "It has been shown that placing a confession before a jury is tantamount to an instruction to convict, even when the confession fails to accurately describe the crime, fails to produce corroboration, and is contradicted by considerable evidence pointing to a suspect's innocence. Even a demonstrably unreliable confession is likely to greatly confuse, mislead, and prejudice jurors against a defendant . . ."[202]

In short, judges are unlikely to issue cautionary jury instructions regarding false confessions. If such instructions are issued, it is unlikely that they will adequately convey the dangers and prevalence of false confessions. Finally, assuming that the instructions are given and are sufficiently detailed to fully inform jurors of the risks inherent in confessions, jury instructions are unlikely to significantly diminish the jury's reliance on the defendant's confession.

IV. Getting to the Truth: Preventing Wrongful Convictions Based on False Confessions

Because of the wide variety of factors that can contribute to false confessions,[203] it seems unlikely that a single reform measure could adequately address all or even most of these factors. However, there are a number of reforms available to policymakers that may significantly reduce the risk of wrongful convictions due to false confessions. The number of possibilities offers jurisdictions a great deal of flexibility in tailoring reform packages to local needs, including political feasibility and budget restraints.

A. Reforming Police and Interrogation Practices to Avoid False Confessions

Public safety is of paramount importance, and wrongful convictions predicated on false confessions detract from law enforcement's achievement of this goal.[204] Research strongly suggests that police practices can contribute to false confessions. Providing law enforcement officials with training describing the causes and characteristics of false confessions may help them more effectively identify false confessions and take remedial actions. Procedural safeguards restricting or eliminating the use of certain interrogation practices linked to false confessions can also reduce the number of false confessions. Requiring officers to diligently investigate evidence tending to contradict a suspect's confession will ensure that those that do occur are less likely to result in wrongful convictions. While these changes may seem cumbersome, preserving the integrity of the criminal justice system and ensuring that only those who actually committed a crime are convicted is well worth the investment. This is especially true when the death penalty is under attack, in part due to questions about the accuracy of the underlying convictions.[205]

As discussed in detail above, certain suspects may be more likely to offer false confessions regardless of the tactics police officers use during the interrogation.[206] Because the use of different interrogation tactics is less likely to prevent false confessions from these suspects, law enforcement officials should be trained to identify such suspects and take preventive measures.[207] Preventive measures could include the use of especially low-pressure interrogation techniques or the requirement that an attorney be present during all interrogations to assist the individual.[208] At a minimum, confessions from suspects in these groups should be viewed with caution and painstaking efforts should be made to corroborate such confessions due to their potential unreliability.[209]

Similarly, longer interrogation sessions are more likely to produce false confessions.[210] Though nine out of ten interrogations conducted by police in the United States lasts less than two hours, one study found that over 80% of the suspects who gave false confessions had been interrogated for over six hours.[211] 50% "were interrogated for more than twelve hours," with "[t]he average length of interrogation . . . 16.3 hours."[212] Though it is difficult if not impossible to isolate any ideal length of interrogation,[213] this evidence argues for limiting or eliminating lengthy interrogations in general. At a minimum, officers should be aware of the potential for false confessions after extended interrogations. Law enforcement agencies could adopt additional precautions, such as requiring an independent review of all the evidence in such cases to assess the reliability of the confession. Jurisdictions that are committed to preventing wrongful convictions may also consider prohibiting interrogations in excess of a given length (such as six hours), or imposing additional procedural requirements upon prosecutors attempting to admit evidence obtained during lengthy interrogation sessions.

The substantive content of an interrogation may also be problematic. A suspect's ability to provide details about a crime known only to the perpetrator is understandably powerful evidence of guilt. However, when police provide such evidence or lead suspects to such evidence during interrogations,[214] the results can be especially harsh. In Robert Miller's case, such a tactic led to a false confession that the prosecutor confidently told the jury reflected information only the true killer could have known.[215] Moreover, assuming that a suspect provides an accurate confession, such interrogation tactics can provide an able defense attorney with a tool to create reasonable doubt in the mind of a juror where none might otherwise exist. Police officers must be provided with training regarding the risk factors associated with false confessions and alerted to the need to keep such vital information from a suspect. In addition, the establishment of local review boards housed in police departments or prosecuting authorities could prove beneficial in a number of ways. Such boards could screen recorded confessions to alert prosecutors to instances where suspects were provided with information about the crime and where further investigation may be warranted. They could also assist local law enforcement departments to develop interrogation standards for future trainings.

Researchers have identified maximization, minimalization, and the use of false evidence as factors that also contribute to many false confessions.[216] Self-report data indicates that officers use both maximization and minimalization "with some degree of regularity," and all of these tactics are legally acceptable.[217] This problem is only exacerbated by the fact that "training and prior experience will bias investigators towards suspicions of untruth without any increase in the accuracy of their hunches."[218] Investigators are "more likely to assuredly pursue what is ultimately a false alarm,"[219] putting potentially innocent suspects at risk. The adoption of a more balanced interrogation protocol may address these issues. The United Kingdom's interrogation process, called PEACE, is just one example of such a protocol.[220] It was developed "in conjunction with police officers, psychologists and lawyers" in response to "a series of miscarriages of justice."[221] Fairness in the interrogation process is central to the PEACE system, and investigators are not allowed to use fabricated evidence or false statements during interrogations.[222] In addition to suggestions already discussed above,[223] the PEACE training package clearly states that "[t]he role of the police is to obtain accurate information from suspects."[224] Officers must "approach[interviews] with an open mind" and compare existing information with that provided by the suspect.[225] These procedures could help lessen the risk that investigators will focus on one suspect to the unfortunate exclusion of the true perpetrator by ensuring that officers properly account for contradictory evidence.[226] This system "has become respected in the international community," perhaps in part due to the fact that it makes the "interview and interrogation process . . . take[] a more conversational tone, rather than a confrontational one."[227] By avoiding tactics that have been shown to elicit false confessions and thoroughly and logically evaluating new evidence,[228] law enforcement authorities can substantially increase the accuracy of the criminal justice system.

Available evidence supports the proposition that "police officers do not want to obtain a false confession any more than a suspect wants to provide one."[229] Such confessions, "if exposed, can ruin hours of good police work and tarnish departmental reputation."[230] But there is ample evidence to conclude that despite the best efforts of police officers and prosecutors alike, innocent individuals are wrongfully convicted due to false confessions.[231] Widely utilized investigative tactics contribute to these convictions by elevating the likelihood of false confessions, which in turn raises the likelihood of convictions. Good intentions are not enough to prevent wrongful convictions predicated on false confessions. Training regarding the psychological forces and interrogation tactics that can lead to false confessions, coupled with changes in common interrogation and investigative practices, may not eliminate the problem entirely. Nevertheless, such reforms represent cautious advances that neither cripple law enforcement's efforts to secure justice nor abandon suspects' rights to the inexorable progress of the criminal justice system.

B. Recording Interrogations to Preserve a Complete Record of All Confessions

As another author addresses the mandatory recording of interrogations at length in this collection, its benefits are reiterated here only briefly. One commentator succinctly summarized the literature on mandatory recording this way: "Within the past decade, near-unanimity has emerged among policy groups and scholars to mandate recording of interrogations to reduce coercion, to minimize dangers of false confessions, and to increase the visibility and transparency of the process."[232] A California task force pragmatically observed that "[w]hile it is unlikely that all false confessions can ever be eliminated, the risk of harm caused by false confessions could be greatly reduced if police were required to electronically record the entirety of custodial interrogations of suspects in serious criminal cases."[233] In part, this may be due to the fact that recording reduces the likelihood that police officers will use the most aggressive interrogation tactics that are more likely to elicit false confessions.[234] And while recording interrogations protects defendants, the risk of lost confessions is relatively small.[235] Research indicates that "[i]n most instances, the ability to obtain confessions and admissions is not affected by recording."[236]

Moreover, it bears noting that defendants are not the only parties benefited by mandatory recording. First, though it may seem counterintuitive, mandatory recording of custodial interrogations provides tangible benefits to police departments. Recording interrogations can "protect police from false claims of abuse."[237] Because the ability to review electronic recordings of interrogations frees interrogators from the need to take notes, officers are able to focus on "suspects' demeanors and statements . . . [without having] to attempt to recall details about the interviews days and weeks later when recollections have faded."[238] Complete recordings can also serve as training tools and assist police departments to "improve interrogation techniques."[239] With these advantages, it is easy to see why "over 500 police departments throughout the country require the taping of interrogations."[240] In fact, as of 2008 one-fifth of the states had adopted some form of recording protocol,[241] and self-report data suggests that police generally favor electronic recording measures.[242]

Second, both the prosecuting authorities and the judiciary also benefit from mandatory recording rules. Prosecutors can more readily assess the accuracy of any claims of coercion based on the video evidence,[243] leading one prosecutor to exclaim that recording was "'the best thing [prosecutors] ever had rammed down [their] throats.'"[244] Evidence suggests that defense attorneys may be less likely to file motions to suppress "based on alleged coercion and abuse" when interrogations are recorded as well.[245] Recorded interrogations also provide judges with concrete, objective evidence to evaluate in determining whether *Miranda* warnings were properly issued and whether confessions were made voluntarily.[246] These recordings can be helpful in determining whether (as prosecutors often claim) the defendant has provided new information that was known only to the perpetrator of the crime or if the information was unintentionally supplied to the defendant during the course of the interrogation.[247] Finally, greater transparency in interrogation practices can increase public confidence in law enforcement officials.[248]

Though cost is frequently cited as a consideration urging caution or gradual adoption of this reform,[249] technological advances are likely to reduce costs in the future.[250] Even if such costs remain substantial, evidence suggests that often the "expenses . . . [associated with recording interrogations are] more than offset by saving officers' time in court, reducing motions to suppress, increasing the incidence of guilty pleas, saving defense costs in civil suits based on police coercion and perjury, and avoiding civil judgments based on wrongful convictions traced to false or coerced confessions."[251] When these costs are carefully weighed against the resulting benefits, it seems clear that mandatory recording is well worth the expense.[252]

In order to ensure that mandatory recording has the desired impact, legislatures should keep several factors in mind. First, it is important that the entire custodial interrogation be recorded.[253] Beginning the recording concurrent with the interrogation eliminates questions about compliance with *Miranda* by capturing the warnings.[254] Moreover, the Supreme Court has already noted the potential for abuse when only abridged versions of a defendant's original confession are obtained after *Miranda* warnings;[255] many of the same concerns would be present if the entire interrogation is not recorded.[256] In particular, partial recordings sacrifice many of the benefits of recording generally. Partial recordings leave judges, prosecutors, and defense attorneys with the same limited information regarding the interrogation practices that occurred prior to the start of the recording. Next, care should be taken to ensure that the camera focuses equally on the suspect and interrogator. Scientific evidence suggests that juries make more balanced determinations about whether a confession was coerced when the camera focuses equally on the suspect and on the interrogator.[257] In addition, legislatures should provide statutory remedies for failures to record. Possible remedies include lesser measures, such as the provision of jury instructions,[258] as well as exclusion. Because of the particularly strong nature of confession evidence, jury instructions alone are unlikely to adequately address failures to record. A properly limited exclusionary rule could encourage compliance with recording requirements[259] while protecting defendants. Exceptions for equipment malfunctions or showings of good cause would protect the state's interest in admitting confession evidence where recording was impossible.[260] The provision of a jury instruction regarding false confessions could provide additional protection for the defendant if the court finds the interrogation admissible. This compromise adequately balances the public's interest in the efficient administration of justice with the need to prevent wrongful convictions.

C. Predicating the Admissibility of Confessions on Clear and Convincing Evidence that the Confession is Accurate

Confession evidence can undoubtedly be both accurate and valuable evidence for law enforcement and prosecuting agencies.[261] Some commentators have proposed barring all use of custodial confession evidence,[262] but such proposals risk excluding even those confessions that are otherwise supported by strong evidence. Due to this cost, exclusionary measures should only be adopted cautiously when their benefits clearly outweigh the costs of exclusion.[263] However, the benefits of excluding only those confessions not supported by clear and convincing evidence outweigh the costs of exclusion.

Researchers have identified "tunnel vision" as a factor that contributes to wrongful convictions.[264] Tunnel vision is a term coined to describe the tendency for law enforcement and prosecution personnel to focus on one suspect to the exclusion of all others, even in the face of contradictory evidence.[265] This is a dangerous state of affairs for several reasons. First, when law enforcement officers obtain a confession from an individual suspected of wrongdoing, independent investigation into the facts of the crime frequently ceases.[266] This is problematic, as contradictory evidence may not even be discovered if law enforcement stops seeking such evidence.[267] In addition, if evidence pointing to the suspect's innocence is revealed, law enforcement and prosecutorial staff may continue to focus on the initial suspect even though an objective review of the evidence would not seem to support that focus.[268] This relentless focus on a single suspect simultaneously risks imprisoning an innocent person and allowing the true perpetrator to commit additional offenses.[269] Any requirement that obliges both law enforcement and prosecutorial staff to consider how a neutral third party, like a judge, would consider the evidence as a whole would encourage thorough investigations and meticulous consideration of all alternative suspects.

Admittedly, Supreme Court precedent provides defendants limited protection in this respect by requiring a minimal amount of evidence corroborating a confession in certain circumstances.[270] The Court reaffirmed this protection at least in part due to concerns centering on the reliability of confession evidence[271] and in doing so observed the importance of thorough, independent investigations of the crime notwithstanding the confession.[272] Even so, the protections afforded by this doctrine are so circumscribed as to be virtually worthless to most defendants. As an initial matter, corroboration is only required when there is doubt as to whether the offense itself was committed.[273] In many cases, there may be no doubt as to whether a crime has been committed. The rule is wholly inapplicable to these cases.[274] Even in the limited number of cases where confessions are subject to this rule, the corroboration requirement is exceedingly modest. According to the Court, "the corroborative evidence does not have to prove the offense beyond a reasonable doubt, or even by a preponderance, as long as there is substantial evidence that the *offense* has been committed . . ."[275] The prosecution need only offer substantial evidence to establish that the offense itself was committed; once the offense is established, the confession may be freely admitted and used to establish the defendant's guilt beyond a reasonable doubt.[276] While such a formulation ensures that a crime was in fact committed, it provides no protection against false confessions and in fact sanctions convictions resulting from such confessions as long as the crime itself is established by substantial evidence.

The gravity of the harm wrongful convictions cause, the systemic inclination to focus on a single suspect, and the inadequacy of existing safeguards to prevent false confessions from resulting in convictions all argue for a more rigorous standard for admitting confessions generally. A suspect providing an accurate confession should be able to provide law enforcement officers with sufficient detail that subsequent investigation could provide the corroborating evidence[277] that prosecutors could use to establish the admissibility of the confession. A suspect's refusal or inability to do so should indicate that further investigation is needed as the confession may not be reliable.[278] In fact, prosecutors already recognize the value of confessions that provide previously undisclosed or unknown information about crime and frequently direct jurors' attention to the suspect's uncanny familiarity with the crime during trials.[279] Requiring prosecutors to prove that confessions are accurate by clear and convincing evidence as a condition of admissibility merely ensures that the defendant in fact possessed such knowledge.[280] It also ensures that the jury is not presented with a confession whose evidentiary value is outweighed by its potential to confuse or mislead the jury,[281] a laudable goal in light of the particularly persuasive nature of confession evidence.[282]

It is undoubtedly true that "society's interest in apprehending, prosecuting and punishing criminals"[283] must be accorded the utmost respect. By the same token, at least in some circumstances, confessions can provide law enforcement and prosecutors alike with valuable information to protect the public.[284] However, conditioning the admissibility of confessions on the provision of clear and convincing evidence of factual accuracy does not preclude the use of confessions in all or even most cases. Such a condition merely requires that law enforcement and prosecutorial staff examine all available evidence, including that which tends to exculpate the defendant, in an objective light and amass sufficient evidence to convince a neutral arbiter that the confession is reliable. If the defendant committed the crime, she is likely to be able to provide investigators with leads to such evidence[285] and any burden is likely to be minimal. The defendant's inability or refusal to provide such leads should always alert law enforcement to the need to conduct additional investigation.[286]

D. Allowing Defendants to Obtain Jury Instructions and Expanding Defendants' Ability to Admit Expert Testimony Regarding False Confessions

As discussed above, neither providing jury instructions nor allowing expert testimony will completely remedy the problems posed by false confessions. Neither is adequate to guard against wrongful convictions in all cases. However, both jury instructions and expert testimony can make valuable contributions to efforts to address wrongful convictions predicated on false confessions. This is particularly true if defendants are allowed to utilize the combination of jury instructions and expert testimony.

If a confession is admissible, an instruction about false confessions alerts the jury to the possibility that the confession may be inaccurate. Jury instructions, which are inexpensive and relatively easy to issue,[287] may "counteract the possibility that jurors may not appreciate why someone would falsely confess to a crime."[288] However, courts may be reluctant to issue instructions on what may be perceived as a factual issue within the province of the jury.[289] Without legislative or judicial guidance encouraging the issuance of jury instructions regarding false confessions, many courts may refuse to do so. This refusal deprives defendants of an important protection against wrongful convictions predicated on false confessions. The addition of a pattern jury instruction regarding false confessions alerting jurors to the existence and causes of false confessions could hasten the trial courts' willingness to issue jury instructions in appropriate cases.

Similarly, expert testimony may at least acquaint the jury with the existence of false confessions and the factors that may elicit such a confession from an innocent suspect. Expert testimony regarding false confessions "falls well outside the common knowledge of prospective jurors and . . . would assist the jury in evaluating a defendant's alleged confession."[290] Opponents of admitting such testimony invariably cite the relative novelty of false confession research.[291] Like-minded courts argue that there is no reason to admit expert testimony on the subject because "there is no proof that 'the general public believes that a person who confesses must be guilty.'"[292] But commentators have cautioned against the relative novelty of false confession research for over ten years,[293] and whatever the state of literature was a decade ago, there seems to be a significant amount of consensus today that certain practices are more likely to produce false confessions. As early as 1999, while false confession research was still in its formative stages, one commentator tentatively observed that "the admissibility of expert testimony based on the psychology of false confessions cannot be ruled out."[294] In fact, despite the fact that false confession research was a relative novelty, courts had found expert testimony on false confessions admissible under the *Daubert* standard as early as 1997.[295] Moreover, even if jurors are aware that suspects may confess to crimes they did not commit, "[s]uch a superficial inquiry [does] nothing to address the issue of what jurors know about why, how, and how often a particular event occurs."[296]

Understandably, in order to preserve the jury's fact-finding function, courts may wish to limit expert testimony to the interrogation practices and the psychological factors that may contribute to false confessions.[297] But such restrictions, while desirable, are not unique to expert testimony on false confessions. Expert testimony on battered woman's syndrome,[298] the symptoms and signs of child sexual abuse,[299] and the psychological state of the defendant[300] have all posed similar threats to the jury's function. In such cases, many courts concede the value of expert testimony in these areas and have successfully addressed these concerns by limiting (rather than eliminating) expert testimony.[301] Clear instructions to expert witnesses prohibiting any testimony about the expert's opinion on the accuracy of the confession at issue can preserve the jury's independence in criminal trials involving confessions as well.

Providing juries with cautionary instructions and allowing defendants to present reasonably limited expert testimony on false confessions are two imminently reasonable, cost-effective reforms that could pay large dividends. Judicial restraint in these areas, while understandable, deprives defendants of small but important protections against wrongful convictions. Cautionary instructions warn potentially unsuspecting jurors of the need to consider confessions objectively and completely evaluate all the evidence in the case. Expert testimony can inform jurors about the interrogation practices and psychological factors that may lead to false confessions, while leaving the ultimate determination as to the truthfulness of the particular defendant's confession in the jury's hands. Far from invading the jury's province, these measures merely ensure that the jury possesses the information it needs to arrive at a more accurate, reasoned verdict.

V. Conclusion

Though false confessions are not a recent development, advances in DNA testing have revealed that such confessions provide the foundation for wrongful convictions with alarming frequency. Wrongful convictions exact a heavy toll on both the innocent suspects and society as a whole. Public policy considerations (including the maintenance of public safety and the integrity of the criminal justice system) further compel the conclusion that wrongful convictions are a serious problem meriting widespread concern. Existing safeguards for defendants' rights have proved inadequate to protect defendants against the dangers of false confessions. Fortunately, an ever-growing body of research suggests that false confessions can often be prevented. Moreover, those which cannot be prevented can frequently be identified before they result in wrongful convictions.

While some courts and local law enforcement agencies have adopted measures to guard against wrongful convictions predicated on false confessions, legislative resolutions to this issue are far preferable. Legislators are uniquely positioned to determine which measures are likely to be most effective in their jurisdictions. In addition, legislative adoption of preventive measures ensures that these systemic problems in the criminal justice system are thoroughly addressed by popularly chosen representatives. Finally, legislation provides a consistency that is unlikely to be achieved through any other method.

In addressing the unique problem posed by wrongful convictions predicated on false confessions, a number of potentially effective preventive measures are available to legislators. First, law enforcement personnel are the first line of defense against false confessions. Law enforcement personnel may be unaware of the factors that can result in false confessions, including the particular factors that may predispose certain groups of suspects to confess to crimes they did not commit. Likewise, they may not know that certain commonly utilized police practices can elicit false confessions. Providing additional training for law enforcement personnel and restricting or eliminating the use of certain practices can reduce false confessions. Requiring supervisory review of interrogations leading to confessions can also provide several benefits. Such review adds another layer of protection for suspects who have confessed to crimes and allows law enforcement agencies to monitor the quality of their interrogation practices.

Second, mandatory recording of interrogations pays dividends far exceeding the relatively minimal costs involved. Recorded interrogations protect law enforcement officers from unwarranted civil suits claiming abuse by providing objective evidence to refute such claims. They also maximize scarce resources in the criminal justice system by providing judges with objective evidence for voluntariness determinations and discouraging defense attorneys from making unfounded exclusionary motions. In the event that the interrogation practices utilized were objectionable, recording ensures that the courts have the evidence needed to adequately protect defendants' rights. Given that technological advances have made recording much more cost-efficient in the last ten years, such requirements are imminently sensible.

Third, state legislatures should bar the use of confessions unless the prosecuting authority can prove by clear and convincing evidence that the confession is factually accurate. This is likely to be a controversial proposal, since exclusion is a harsh remedy and could potentially deprive the jury of important information. However, the uncommonly powerful nature of confession evidence coupled with the prevalence of false confessions merits such a measure for several reasons. Most importantly, a presumption of inadmissibility is not a per se rule excluding all confessions. To the contrary, it only restricts the use of confession evidence to those cases in which the prosecutor can provide clear and convincing evidence that the confession is factually accurate. Such a standard gives law enforcement and prosecutorial staff powerful incentives to carefully weigh evidence tending to contradict the confession and guards against the phenomena researchers have identified as "tunnel vision" by requiring thorough investigation to continue even after a confession is obtained. This standard also provides defense attorneys with the opportunity to alert the judge to any information the police may have provided to the suspect during the interrogation process, especially in jurisdictions that also choose to adopt recording requirements. A requirement that the judge make a preliminary finding on the admissibility of the confession would ensure that only confessions with some indicia of reliability reach the jury. This proposal does nothing more than ensure that the jury only hears reliable evidence whose probative value outweighs its potential to confuse or mislead jurors. This general premise has already been adopted in the Federal Rule of Evidence 403 and its state counterparts. There is no reason to believe that this important reform measure would unduly limit the use of confession evidence. Finally, legislators should encourage courts to issue jury instructions and permit expert testimony about false confessions. Currently, the provision of jury instructions about false confessions is more a matter of judicial grace than right. This is problematic because jurors may assume that a confession issued by the defendant and offered into evidence by the state must be accurate. As long as the criminal justice system leaves the determination of factual issues to the jury, care must be taken to ensure that the jury is alerted to unique or unusual issues requiring its particularly careful attention. Moreover, many courts are still reluctant to accept expert evidence regarding false confessions. Properly circumscribed expert testimony about false confessions can add to the jury's arsenal of fact-finding tools by acquainting jurors with a phenomenon outside of common knowledge without allowing an expert to pass on the ultimate question of a confession's accuracy. Like any type of science, research on false confessions is not infallible. Nevertheless, such research is dependable enough to meet the *Daubert* test and should be admitted in proper cases.

These preventive measures will undoubtedly require the investment of valuable resources which are likely to be scarce in the current economy. However, a failure to prevent wrongful convictions is itself costly, and false confessions frequently lead to wrongful convictions. Additionally, such measures are the only means that can adequately guard against wrongful convictions predicated on false confessions in cases where DNA evidence is unavailable. The stark reality is that the public attention garnered by the nearly three hundred exonerations has ensured that maintaining the status quo is no longer a viable option. Wrongful convictions undermine public confidence in the criminal justice system, the very confidence from which the system derives its legitimacy. Without that confidence, the public and the judiciary may refuse to support harsh criminal sanctions such as the death penalty. When innocent people are convicted for crimes they did not commit, criminals remain at large to prey upon the unsuspecting public. Police departments and prosecuting authorities alike may spend countless hours trying to address the harm these individuals cause, and all the while the state may continue to expend scarce tax dollars to imprison the innocent victims of the justice system. Legislators are uniquely positioned to translate these policy concerns into concrete measures to improve the accuracy of the criminal justice system, thus saving the state's precious resources and avoiding vast amounts of human suffering. The trust the public places in its elected representatives is nowhere more evident than when it implores them to see that justice is done. A failure to do so is no less than a betrayal of that trust and must be avoided at all costs.

Endnotes

1. Jim Dwyer, Peter Neufeld & Barry Scheck, Actual Innocence: Five Days to Execution and Other Dispatches from the Wrongly Convicted 250 (2000).
2. *Id.* at 79–80.
3. *Id.* at 80.
4. *See id.* at 93–101 (describing information Miller offered to investigators regarding the escape route, clothing items left at the scene, and the method of entry into the homes where the crimes occurred).
5. *Id.* at 81.
6. *Id.* at 84.
7. *Id.* at 83.
8. *Id.* at 84.
9. *See id.* at 87 (observing that DNA tests "clearly excluded Robert Miller . . . [as] the rapist of either dead woman.").

10. *See, e.g.*, Section III, *infra* (describing existing procedural protections and questioning their adequacy for preventing false confessions).

11. DWYER, NEUFELD & SCHECK, *supra* note 1, at 84, 87.

12. *See id.* at 80, 85–86, 94, 96–97, 101–02 (describing the shortcomings in the Miller investigation).

13. *Id.* at 85.

14. *Id.* at 86.

15. *Id.* at 80.

16. *Id.* at 94.

17. *Id.* at 96–97.

18. *Id.* at 101.

19. *Id.* at 102. The judge worded his decision rather strongly:

    There is nothing in these statements by defendant which would in any way be considered a confession. . . .In my view, . . . the statements made by the defendants in the taped interviews taken as a whole, or even divided into parts, do not constitute an 'admission' either. Mr. Miller's statements come to the detectives as visions and dreams–even images he receives from deceased grandparents and so forth.

    Virtually every item of information is hedged with 'maybe' this happened, 'probably' this occurred. Admittedly, after some prompting, he became more definite in certain answers. I get the impression, however, taking the statements as a whole, that Mr. Miller was attempting to tell the detectives what he believed they wanted to hear. And it is evident from the video that the detectives are directing many of his responses.

    To the extent defendant's statements are consistent with known facts, the consistencies are not such as to compel even probable cause to believe he committed these crimes.

    Id. at 102–03.

20. *Id.* at 101.

21. *Id.* at 92.

22. *Id.* at 93.

23. *Id.* at 95 (quoting a state official discussing the plea deal). Fortunately, the new suspect declined the offer. *Id.* at 95–96.

24. *Id.* at 79. The official, Ray Elliott, "headed all criminal prosecutions in the office of the Oklahoma City district attorney." *Id.* at 78. Elliott denies having made this comment and has since been elected a judge in Oklahoma County. *Id.* at 105–06.

25. *Id.* at 79, 96.

26. Atkins v. Virginia, 536 U.S. 304 (2002).

27. DWYER, NEUFELD & SCHECK, *supra* note 11, 92.

28. Richard A. Leo, Miranda *and the Problem of False Confessions, in* THE *MIRANDA* DEBATE: LAW, JUSTICE, AND POLICING 271, 272 (Richard A. Leo & George C. Thomas III eds., 1998).

29. DWYER, NEUFELD & SCHECK, *supra* note 12, at 92.

30. Leo, *supra* note 28, at 272.

31. North Carolina Center on Actual Innocence, *Causes and Remedies*, http://www.nccai.org/causes.html (last visited Jan. 25, 2010); *Regarding the Reauthorization and Improvement of the DNA Initiatives of the Justice For All Act of 2004: Before the Subcomm. on Crime, Terrorism & Homeland Security of the H. Comm. of the Judiciary*, XX Cong. 35 (2009) (statement of Barry C. Scheck, co-founder and co-director of the Innocence Project). Note that in some jurisdictions the percentage may be much higher. For example, in Illinois, "false confessions [were] a significant factor in eleven out of eighteen recent Illinois exonerations in capital cases." Marvin Zalman & Brad W. Smith, *The Attitudes of Police Executives Toward* Miranda *and Interrogation Policies*, 97 J. CRIM. L. & CRIMINOLOGY 873, 896 (2007) (footnote omitted).

32. Saul M. Kassin et al., *Police-Induced Confessions: Risk Factors and Recommendations*, 34 L. & HUM. BEH. XX, XX (forthcoming 2010).

33. Talia Fisher & Issachar Rosen-Zvi, *The Confessional Penalty*, 30 Cardozo L. Rev. 871, 877 (2008).

34. *See id.* at 879 (arguing that the police "externalize the enormous social costs of confessions, which include the pain and suffering of the wrongly convicted, the erosion of the criminal justice system's overall reliability, the stagnation of a law enforcement system that focuses almost exclusively on confessions, the moral costs to a society in which self-incrimination is the rule rather than the exception").

35. Cookie Ridolfi & Marjorie K. Allard, *Book Review: The Psychology of Interrogations and Confession: A Handbook*, 43 Santa Clara L. Rev. 1485, 1500 (2003) ("In addition to the unimaginable costs imposed on the person who has been wrongfully incarcerated, society also bears the public safety costs of the guilty perpetrator who has never been caught."); *see also* Anthony Head, *Guilty Until Proven Innocent*, Texas Super Lawyers, 2009, at 18 (noting that Dallas District Attorney Craig Watkins said that "in each of the convictions he'[d] worked to overturn, if a DNA match uncover[ed] the real criminal, it's been shown that the person had continued to commit crimes"); *see, e.g.*, Chris Smith, *Central Park Revisited*, New York Magazine, Oct. 21, 2002, *available at* http://nymag.com/nymetro/news/crimelaw/features/n_7836/ (last visited Mar. 23, 2010) (observing that while five innocent juveniles were convicted for the brutal attack of the Central Park jogger after they confessed, the real perpetrator went on to commit additional rapes and murder a pregnant woman while her children watched).

36. California Comm'n on the Fair Administration of Justice, Report and Recommendations Regarding False Confessions 2 & n.4 (2006), *available at* http://www.ccfaj.org/documents/reports/false/official/falconfrep.pdf [hereinafter CCFAJ Recommendations] (observing that one murder victim's family member "suffer[ed] nightmares for twelve years based upon an account of her daughter's rape and murder that was factually untrue").

37. Sharon Davies, *The Reality of False Confessions – Lessons of the Central Park Jogger Case*, 30 N.Y.U. Rev. L. & Soc. Change 209, 228 (2006) (footnote omitted).
38. Samuel R. Gross et al., *Exonerations in the United States: 1989 through 2003*, 95 J. Crim. L. & Criminology 523, 535 (2005).
39. *Id.*
40. *Id.* The authors noted that the group of exonerees was "a highly atypical group." *Id.*
41. Davies, *supra* note 37, at 228.
42. *See, e.g.*, Herring v. New York, 422 U.S. 853, 862 (1975) (describing the "ultimate objective" of the criminal justice system as ensuring that "the guilty [are] convicted and the innocent go free"); United States v. de Ortiz, 883 F.2d 515, 524 (7th Cir. 1989) (Easterbrook, J., concurring), *vacated on other grounds*, 897 F.2d 220 (7th Cir. 1990) ("Nothing we do as judges in criminal cases is more important than assuring that the innocent go free.").
43. *See, e.g.,* In re Winship, 397 U.S. 358, 372 (1970) (Harlan, J., concurring) (describing the reasonable doubt standard of proof as "bottomed on a fundamental value determination of our society that it is far worse to convict an innocent man than to let a guilty man go free").
44. *Cf.* Fisher & Rosen-Zvi, *supra* note 33, at 879 (observing that the social costs of confessions include "the erosion of the criminal justice system's overall reliability, the stagnation of a law enforcement system that focuses almost exclusively on confessions, the moral costs to a society in which self-incrimination is the rule rather than the exception.").
45. *Id.*
46. *See, e.g.,* The Innocence Project, *Know the Cases: Eddie Joe Lloyd*, http://www.innocenceproject.org/Content/201.php?phpMyAdmin=52c4ab7ea46t7da4197 (last visited Jan. 25, 2010) (describing the case of a mentally ill man who confessed to

a murder, spent nearly twenty years in jail, and was later exonerated based on DNA evidence).

47. *See, e.g., A&E Cold Case Files: The Interrogation / The Slide* (A&E television broadcast Jul. 1, 2006) (showing taped footage of the same false confession); THE INTERROGATION OF MICHAEL CROWE (Interrogation Film Productions 2002) (illustrating how a fourteen-year-old boy interrogated by the police regarding the murder of his younger sister confessed to a crime he did not commit).

48. Saul M. Kassin & Gisli H. Gudjonsson, *The Psychology of Confessions: A Review of the Literature and Issues*, 5 PSYCHOL. SCIENCE IN THE PUB. INT. 31, 49 (2004) (citations omitted).

49. *Cf.* Furman v. Georgia, 408 U.S. 238, 366–68 & n.156 (1972) (Marshall, J., concurring) (describing literature discussing wrongful convictions and concluding that "[w]e have no way of judging how many innocent persons have been executed but we can be certain that there were some.").

50. *See, e.g.,* TRUE STORIES OF FALSE CONFESSIONS 495–500 (Rob Warden & Steven A. Drizin eds., 2009) (offering policy recommendations after documenting over forty cases of false confessions).

51. Saul M. Kassin, *The Psychology of Confessions*, 4 ANNUAL REV. L. & SOC. SCI. 193, 194 (2008).

52. *Id.* at 194; *see also* Gross et al., *supra* note 38, at 538 (discussing the case of a mentally retarded woman who was imprisoned in Alabama after confessing to killing her newborn baby, despite the state's later discovery that she had "had a tubal ligation that was intact throughout the relevant period, making pregnancy impossible").

53. *See* DWYER, NEUFELD & SCHECK, *supra* note 1, at 88–89 (citing EDWIN M. BORCHARD, CONVICTING THE INNOCENT: ERRORS OF CRIMINAL JUSTICE (1932) (noting that "[t]he vanishing corpse is a recurring theme" in Professor Borchard's book on wrongful convictions).

54. Kassin, *supra* note 51, at 194.

55. *Id.*

56. *Id.*

57. *See* Kassin et al., *supra* note 32, at XX (observing that "the precise incidence rate [of false confessions] is not known").

58. Kassin, *supra* note 51, at 194.

59. Professors Leo and Ofshe developed a similar but slightly different typology of false confessions. *See* Richard A. Leo & Richard J. Ofshe, *The Social Psychology of Police Interrogation: The Theory and Classification of True and False Confessions*, 16 Studies in Law, Politics & Society 189 (1997) (describing false confessions in terms of stress compliant, coerced compliant, and persuaded false confessions). Professor Kassin's typology is utilized above for simplicity.

60. Kassin, *supra* note 51, at 195.

61. *Id.* Kassin identifies various examples of such incentives, including "being allowed to sleep, eat, make a phone call, go home, or, in the case of drug addicts, feed a drug habit." *Id.* (citation omitted).

62. *Id.*

63. *Id.* Kassin notes that this frequently occurs in high-profile cases, such as the kidnapping of the Lindbergh baby and the Black Dahlia murder. *Id.*

64. *Id.* (citation omitted).

65. *Id.*

66. *Id.* at 195–96 (citations omitted).

67. *See id.* at 196 (likening this phenomenon to "the creation of false memories . . . in psychotherapy patients" and noting that "[i]n both situations, an authority figure claims a privileged insight into the individual's past, the individual is isolated from others and in a heightened state of malleability, and the expert ultimately convinces the individual to accept a painful self-insight by invoking concepts like dissociation or repression").

68. *See infra* Sections III–IV.

69. *See generally* Leo, *supra* note 28, at 274–77 (discussing various constitutional safeguards and questioning their effectiveness in the context of confession evidence).

70. *Id.* at 275.

71. American Bar Association Criminal Justice Section, Achieving Justice: Freeing the Innocent, Convicting the Guilty 13–14 (Paul Giannelli & Myrna Raeder eds., 2006).

72. *Id.*

73. 384 U.S. 436 (1966).

74. *See Miranda*, 384 U.S. at 478 ("Any statement given freely and voluntarily without any compelling influences is, of course, admissible in evidence."); *supra* notes 31–33 and accompanying text (discussing prevalence of erroneous convictions due to false confessions in the United States).

75. Welsh S. White, Miranda's Waning Protections 144, 153 (2001) (citing Hugo Adams Bedau & Michael Radelet, *Miscarriages of Justice in Potentially Capital Cases*, 40 Stan. L. Rev. 21, 45, 173–79 (1987)).

76. *Id.* at 153 (citing Richard J. Ofshe & Richard A. Leo, *The Social Psychology of Police Interrogation: The Theory and Classification of True and False Confessions*, 16 Studies in Law, Politics, And Society 189, 194–207 (1997)).

77. *See, e.g.*, Leo, *supra* note 28, 275–77 (observing that *Miranda*'s limited protections are primarily concerned with procedural fairness rather than accuracy, and that even these protections "evaporates" after the suspect waives these rights).

78. *Miranda*, 384 U.S. at 455. It bears noting that in a footnote immediately following this quote, the Court observed that "[i]nterrogation procedures may even give rise to a false confession." *Id.* at 455 n.24. In the example the Court cited, the prosecutor vehemently denied that the suspect was beaten but conceded that "brain-washing, hypnosis, [and] fright"

could have been used to obtain the confession. *Id.* (citations omitted).

79. *See* Dickerson v. United States, 530 U.S. 428, 437–38 (2000) (holding that the Court's decision in *Miranda* was based in the Constitution and could not be legislatively altered).

80. *See id.* at 443–44 (observing that *Miranda* warnings "have become part of our national culture" and conceding that the Court's "subsequent cases have reduced the impact of the *Miranda* rule").

81. *See* Irene Merker Rosenberg & Yale L. Rosenberg, *A Modest Proposal for the Abolition of Custodial Confessions, in* THE *MIRANDA* DEBATE: LAW, JUSTICE, AND POLICING 142, 143–44 (Richard A. Leo & George C. Thomas III eds., 1998) (discussing a number of ways in which the Court has subsequently weakened central themes in the *Miranda* holding).

82. New York v. Quarles, 467 U.S. 649, 655–57 (1984). Notably, the officer need not in fact be motivated to protect public safety, as the test established by the Court is objective rather than subjective. *Id.* at 655–56.

83. *See* Oregon v. Elstad, 470 U.S. 298, 317–18 (1985) (holding that "a suspect who has once responded to unwarned yet uncoercive questioning is not thereby disabled from waiving his rights and confessing after he has been given the requisite *Miranda* warnings"). *But see* Missouri v. Seibert, 542 U.S. 600, 614–617 (2004) (holding that two confessions obtained in stationhouse interrogation were both inadmissible despite the fact that the defendant had been read *Miranda* warnings prior to the second confession).

84. Harris v. New York, 401 U.S. 222, 225–26 (1971).

85. *See* Fletcher v. Weir, 455 U.S. 603, 607 (1982) (in the absence of *Miranda* warnings, post-arrest silence may be used as impeachment evidence against defendants who testify in their own defense); Jenkins v. Anderson, 447 U.S. 231, 238 (1980) (same).

86. Michigan v. Tucker, 517 U.S. 433, 452 (1974) (holding that testimony of a third party whose identity defendant revealed to police officers during unwarned discussion was admissible despite the *Miranda* violation).

87. Patrick A. Malone, *"You Have the Right to Remain Silent":* Miranda *After Twenty Years, in* THE *MIRANDA* DEBATE: LAW, JUSTICE, AND POLICING 75, 76 (Richard A. Leo & George C. Thomas III eds., 1998).

88. *Miranda*, 384 U.S. at 490 ("[T]he Constitution does not require any specific code of procedures for protecting the privilege against self-incrimination during custodial interrogation. Congress and the States are free to develop their own safeguards for the privilege, so long as they are fully as effective as those described above in informing accused persons of their right of silence and in affording an opportunity to exercise it.").

89. *Id.*

90. Richard Rogers, Daniel W. Shuman & Eric Y. Drogin, Miranda *Rights . . . And Wrongs: Myths, Methods, and Model Solutions*, CRIM. JUSTICE, Summer 2008, at 4 (citing Jeffrey L. Helms, *Analysis of* Miranda *Reading Levels Across Jurisdictions: Implications for Evaluating Waiver Competency*, 3 J. FORENSIC PSYCHOL. & PRAC. 25 (2003)). In fact, one jurisdiction advises suspects that they have the right to remain silent "'until counsel is available,'" though *Miranda* itself seems to contemplate that the right to silence and counsel both continue throughout the interrogation process. *Id.* at 9 (citing Richard Rogers et al., *The Language of* Miranda *in American Jurisdictions: A Replication and Further Analysis*, 32 LAW & HUM. BEHAV. 124 (2008)); *Miranda*, 384 U.S. at 469–70.

91. Rogers, Shuman & Drogin, *supra* note 90, at 5.

92. *Id.*; *Miranda*, 384 U.S. at 469–70.

93. Rogers, Shuman & Drogin, *supra* note 90, at 4.

94. *Id.*

95. *Id.* at 8–9.

96. *See* Davis v. United States, 512 U.S. 452, 459–60 (1994) (requiring that defendant clearly and unambiguously request counsel in order to trigger the right to counsel). Some states have adopted standards which are more solicitous of suspects' rights. These states various either hold that "any statements that might be interpreted as an assertion of rights put[] an end to the interrogation" or impose a duty on law enforcement officers to ask additional questions to clarify the suspect's intent "when a suspect makes an ambiguous statement that could be an assertion of rights." Marc L. Miller & Ronald F. Wright, Criminal Procedures: The Police 589 (2007).
97. Miller & Wright, *supra* note 96, at 583.
98. Michigan v. Mosley, 423 U.S. 96, 105–06 (1975).
99. Edwards v. Arizona, 451 U.S. 477, 485–87 (1981); *see also* Minnick v. Mississippi, 498 U.S. 146, 150–56 (1990) (holding that police may not reinitiate questioning with suspects who have invoked the right to counsel even after counsel has been provided); Arizona v. Roberson, 486 U.S. 675, 686–88 (1988) (holding that police may not question suspects about any crime after she invokes her right to counsel).
100. Maryland v. Shatzer, 130 S.Ct. 1213 (2010).
101. Saul M. Kassin, *Confession Evidence: Commonsense Myths and Misconceptions*, 35 Crim. Justice & Beh. 1309, 1312 (2008) (citations omitted).
102. Colorado v. Spring, 479 U.S. 564, 572–75 (1987) (holding voluntary a confession made by a defendant who was questioned regarding a homicide following his arrest on an unrelated arms trafficking charge).
103. Moran v. Burbine, 475 U.S. 412, 421–22 (1986). Even so, the Court pointedly noted that it "share[d] respondent's distaste for the [police's] deliberate misleading of an officer of the court" and observed that "the 'deliberate or reckless' withholding of information [could be] objectionable as a matter of ethics." *Id.* at 423–24.
104. Malone, *supra* note 87, at 76.

105. Leo, *supra* note 28, at 277.
106. Richard Leo, *The Impact of* Miranda *Revisited*, *in* THE *MIRANDA* DEBATE: LAW, JUSTICE, AND POLICING 208, 216 (Richard A. Leo & George C. Thomas III eds., 1998).
107. *Id.*
108. *Id.*
109. *Id.*
110. Leo, *supra* note 28, at 276.
111. WHITE, *supra* note 75, at 99
112. Malone, *supra* note 87, at 76.
113. Leo, *supra* note 28, at 272.
114. *See* Miriam S. Gohara, *A Lie for a Lie: False Confessions and the Case for Reconsidering the Legality of Deceptive Interrogation Techniques*, 33 FORDHAM URB. L.J. 791, 803–08 (2006) (describing state court efforts to limit the use of deceptive tactics such as fabricated evidence or false information).
115. *Id.* at 798–99 (citing Frazier v. Cupp, 394 U.S. 731, 739 (1969)); *see, e.g.*, Illinois v. Perkins, 496 U.S. 292, 297–98 (1990) (citations omitted) (holding that *Miranda* warnings are not required when undercover officers question a prisoner in custody, noting that "*Miranda* forbids coercion, not mere strategic deception . . . Ploys to mislead a suspect or lull him into a false sense of security that do not rise to the level of compulsion to speak are not within *Miranda*'s concerns").
116. 384 U.S. 436, 448–56 (describing interrogation methods contained in popular interrogation manuals and noting that "the modern practice of in-custody interrogation is psychologically rather than physically oriented.").
117. 297 U.S. 278 (1936).
118. *Brown*, 297 U.S. at 282–86.
119. 384 U.S. at 448–49.
120. United States Department of Justice, Office of Legal Policy, *Report to the Attorney General on the Law of Pretrial*

Interrogation (February 12, 1986, with addendum of January 20, 1987), in THE *MIRANDA* DEBATE: LAW, JUSTICE, AND POLICING 95, 98 (Richard A. Leo & George C. Thomas III eds., 1998). Indeed, the same source observes that a subsequent edition of the very training manual cited with disapproval by the Court in *Miranda* contained the following statement in its subsequent edition: "'All but a few of the interrogation tactics and techniques presented in our earlier publication are still valid.'" *Id.* (citing FRED GRAHAM, THE SELF-INFLICTED WOUND 315–16 (1970)).

121. 297 U.S. at 282–86.

122. *See* DWYER, NEUFELD & SCHECK, *supra* note 1, at 92 ("Almost none of [the defendants who confess to crimes] come to modern courtrooms with physical scars from interrogation room beatings.").

123. Colorado v. Connelly, 479 U.S. 157, 164 (1986) (citing Spano v. New York, 360 U.S. 315 (1959)).

124. *Id.* at 167.

125. *See* Kassin, *supra* note 32, at 4 (internal citations omitted) (observing that in 15-20% of the exonerations since 1989 "police-induced false confessions were involved").

126. Kassin, *supra* note 101, at 1312.

127. *Id.* at 1313.

128. *Id.*

129. *Id.* The investigator may "suggest[] to the suspect that [the crime] was spontaneous, provoked, drug induced, peer pressured, an accident, or otherwise morally justified." *Id.*

130. *Id.* (citation omitted) (emphasis added). The lack of an explicit promise to infer such leniency is significant, as the Supreme Court has suggested that explicit promises of leniency might render a resulting confession involuntary. *See* Clanton v. Cooper, 129 F.3d 1147, 1159 (10th Cir. 1997) (citations omitted) (collecting cases holding that promises may render a confession coerced). *But see* United States v. Roman-Zarate, 115

F.3d 778, 783–84 (10th Cir. 1997) (holding that an officer's promise to advise the prosecuting authorities of defendant's cooperation did not constitute a promise of leniency and did not render defendant's confession involuntary).

131. *See* Kassin, *supra* note 101, at 1313 (describing an experiment in which 18% of the innocent sample group confessed to cheating on a problem after minimalization tactics were employed).

132. Kassin et al., *supra* note 32, at XX. Maximization "tactics include making an accusation, overriding objections, and citing evidence, real or manufactured, to shift the suspect's mental state from confident to hopeless." *Id.*

133. Kassin, *supra* note 101, at 1314.

134. *Id.*

135. *Id.*

136. Saul Kassin, *False Confessions: Causes, Consequences, and Implications for Reform*, 17 Current Directions in Psychological Science 249, 250 (2008).

137. Kassin, *supra* note 101, at 1314 (citations omitted).

138. *Id.*

139. Miranda v. Arizona, 384 U.S. 436, 467 (1966).

140. *See* Frazier v. Cupp, 394 U.S. 731, 739 (1969) (holding that the interrogating officer's false claim that defendant's co-conspirator had confessed to the crime was "relevant [but] insufficient . . . to make this otherwise voluntary confession inadmissible" under the totality of the circumstances test).

141. Kassin et al., *supra* note 32, at XX (describing cases from Florida and New Jersey).

142. *See id.* at XX (citations omitted) (observing that younger suspects are more likely to offer false confessions and invoke their *Miranda* rights less frequently); *see also* Christine S. Scott-Hayward, *Explaining Juvenile False Confessions: Adolescent Development and Police Interrogation*, 31 Law & Psychol. Rev. 53, 69 (2007) ("Tactics that, when used with

adults, might be seen as acceptable and useful tools to obtain reliable confessions only seem to increase the likelihood of false confession when used with juveniles.").

143. Kassin, *supra* note 136, at 251. The presence of a responsible guardian does not ameliorate the risk of false confessions from juveniles, "as adults often urge their youths to cooperate with police." *Id.* (citations omitted).

144. Kassin et al., *supra* note 32, at XX.

145. *Id.* The list of tendencies includes the following: "tendencies to rely on authority figures for solutions to everyday problems; please persons in authority; seek out friends; feign competence; exhibit a short attention span; exhibit memory gaps; lack impulse control; and accept blame for negative outcomes." *Id.*

146. *Id.* (citations omitted).

147. Atkins v. Virginia, 536 U.S. 304, 320–21 & n.25 (2002).

148. Kassin et al., *supra* note 32, at XX (citations omitted).

149. *See* American Bar Association Criminal Justice Section, *supra* note 71, at 13–14 ("Suspects who falsely confess to crimes that they did not commit tend to be particularly vulnerable, such as those intoxicated by alcohol or other drugs, or those overly eager to *appear* cooperative. The largest category of falsely confessing suspects consists of those with mental deficiencies or unusual cultural backgrounds.").

150. *See* Kassin, *supra* note 136, at 251 (citation omitted) ("To make matters worse, most justice-involved youth have diagnosable psychological disorders, putting them at 'double jeopardy' in the interrogation room.").

151. *See supra* notes 65–66 and accompanying text (describing internalized false confessions).

152. *See supra* notes 123–47 (describing police tactics and the effects they may have on suspects).

153. *See* Frazier v. Cupp, 394 U.S. 731, 739 (1969) (holding that the use of false evidence did not render an "otherwise

voluntary confession inadmissible" under the totality of the circumstances test).

154. *See supra* notes 139–47 and accompanying text (describing the heightened risk of false confessions due to police tactics in certain vulnerable groups).

155. *See* Kassin, *supra* note 51, at 195 (describing voluntary confessions); *see also* Kassin et al., *supra* note 32, at XX (describing several infamous instances of voluntary confessions, including the Black Dahlia murder, the kidnapping of the Lindbergh baby, and the murder of JonBenet Ramsey).

156. *See* Kassin et al., *supra* note 32, at XX (concluding that "[w]ithout bright lines for courts to follow, and without a complete and accurate record of what transpired during the interrogation process, the end result has been largely unfettered and unreviewable discretion by judges").

157. *Id.* at 32, at XX; *see also* Nadia Soree, Comment, *When the Innocent Speak: False Confessions, Constitutional Safeguards, and the Role of Expert Testimony*, 32 Am. J. Crim. L. 191, 206 (2005) ("[W]hile even the phrase used by every court in its review – 'totality of the circumstances' – would indicate a meaningful review, taking into account the entire environment of the interrogation and its effect on a given defendant, it seems these potential circumstances have become somewhat of a laundry list. Courts can use the totality test much like a checklist, maneuvering through and balancing the factors on one or the other side of the voluntariness scale, without careful review of any one factor to determine its actual coercive effect on the defendant, to arrive at the decision they wish to reach."). Kassin further opines that courts only exclude confessions in the most egregious of circumstances, and argues that this latitude encourages police officers to "push the envelope with respect to the use of arguably coercive psychological interrogation techniques." Kassin et al., *supra* note 32, at XX (citations omitted).

158. *See* Crane v. Kentucky, 476 U.S. 683, 690 (1986) (holding that the Constitution's guarantee of the opportunity to present a

complete defense "would be an empty one if the State were permitted to exclude competent, reliable evidence bearing on the credibility of a confession when such evidence is central to the defendant's claim of innocence.").

159. *See, e.g.*, Specht v. Johnson, 853 F.2d 805, 812 (10th Cir. 1988) (observing that in certain circumstances "testimony . . . by applying the law to the facts[] can be described as invading the province of the jury").

160. Kassin, *supra* note 101, at 7 (citations omitted). In one such study, mock jurors were presented with various versions of a "murder trial transcript." *Id.* (citing Saul M. Kassin & Holly Sukel, *Coerced Confessions and the Jury: An Experimental Test of the "Harmless Error" Rule*, 21 L. & Hum. Behav. 21, 27–46 (1997)). One of the transcripts informed participants that the defendant had confessed while "in pain and [being] interrogated aggressively by a detective who waved his gun in a menacing manner." *Id.* Though the participants "judged the statement to be involuntary and said it did not influence their decisions . . . , this confession significantly increased the conviction rate . . . even [when] subjects were specifically admonished to disregard confessions they found to be coerced." *Id.* Another analysis of actual cases reflected conviction rates ranging between 73% to 81% when defendants whose confessions were proven false pled not guilty and proceeded to trial. *Id.* (citations omitted).

161. *Id.* ("[G]eneralized common sense leads us to trust confessions the way we trust other behaviors that counter self-interest . . . while neglecting the role of situational factors. . . . [P]eople draw quick and relatively automatic dispositional inferences from behavior and then fail to adjust or correct for the presence of situational constraints.").

162. *Id.*

163. *Id.*

164. *Id.* (citations omitted).

165. *See* Scott-Hayward, *supra* note 142, at 53–54 (footnotes omitted) (describing the false confession of Allen Chesnet, who spent six months in jail following a false confession while "DNA tests showed that the blood at the crime scene was not Chesnet's [before] suspicion began to focus on a man about whom police had received a tip just hours after the murder"); Soree, *supra* note 157, at 202–05 (footnotes omitted) (detailing how teenager Stephanie Crowe's murder investigation focused almost exclusively on her brother Michael Crowe following his confession, despite the fact that police had also interviewed another individual with a criminal record and whose blood was later matched to DNA found on the victim's clothing).

166. Kassin, *supra* note 101, at 7. Kassin notes that "[o]ften [false confessions] contained not merely an admission of guilt but vivid details about the crime, the scene, and the victim that became known to the innocent suspect through leading questions, photographs, visits to the crime scene, and other secondhand sources invisible to the naïve observer." *Id.*

167. *See, e.g.*, Dwyer, Neufeld & Scheck, *supra* note 1, at 93–101 (describing the interrogation of Robert Miller and documenting several questions that provided Miller with information he later incorporated into his confession).

168. Kassin, *supra* note 101, at 8; Julie E. Bear & Scott A. Bresler, *Overshadowing Innocence,* Champion, Dec. 2007, at 16, 17–18 (explaining how one teenager who falsely confessed to a homicide had received details regarding the crime from the police officers and cautioning practitioners to "[k]eep in mind that the investigators and the media can contaminate a subject's knowledge about crime scene details").

169. *See* Margaret A. Berger, *False Confessions – Three Tales from New York*, 37 Sw. L. Rev. 1065, 1075 (2008) (footnotes omitted) ("To be admissible, expert testimony has to satisfy the *Daubert* test in federal court and in some state courts, and usually a 'general acceptance' *Frye* test in other states. The current law on allowing expert testimony on false confessions is far from settled or consistent in either type of jurisdiction.").

170. Frye v. United States, 293 F. 1013, 1014 (D.C. Cir. 1923).

171. Fed. R. Evid. 702.

172. *Id.*

173. *See* Daubert v. Merrell Dow Pharms., 509 U.S. 579, 588 (1993) (citing Beech Aircraft Corp. v. Rainey, 488 U.S. 153, 169 (1988)) ("Nothing in the text of this Rule establishes 'general acceptance' as an absolute prerequisite to admissibility. . . . [A] rigid 'general acceptance' requirement would be at odds with the 'liberal thrust' of the Federal Rules and their 'general approach of relaxing the traditional barriers to opinion testimony.'"). Although *Daubert* dealt with the admissibility of scientific testimony, the Court later clarified that the standard set forth in that case is applicable to all types of expert testimony. Kumho Tire Co. v. Carmichael, 526 U.S. 137, 147 (1999); *see Daubert*, 509 U.S. at 589 (discussing trial court judges' evidentiary obligations with regards to "all scientific testimony").

174. *See Daubert*, 509 U.S. at 592–93 ("Faced with a proffer of expert scientific testimony, then, the trial judge must determine at the outset, pursuant to [Federal] Rule [of Evidence] 104(a), whether the expert is proposing to testify to (1) scientific knowledge that (2) will assist the trier of fact to understand or determine a fact in issue. This entails a preliminary assessment of whether the reasoning or methodology underlying the testimony is scientifically valid and of whether that reasoning or methodology properly can be applied to the facts in issue."). It bears noting that though the Court cites Federal Rule of Evidence 104(a) for these requirements, the Court's analysis of Federal Rule of Evidence 702 led to much the same result. *See id.* at 591–92 (observing that certain text in Rule 702 went "primarily to relevance" or "fit" and noting that "Rule 702's 'helpfulness' standard requires a valid scientific connection to the pertinent inquiry as a precondition to admissibility").

175. *Id.* at 593–95.

176. *Id.*

177. *Id.* at 594 & n.12.

178. Welsh White, *False Confessions in Criminal Cases*, 17-WTR. Crim. Just. 5, 5 (2003) (citing Frye v. United States, 293 F. 1013 (D.C. Cir. 1923); Daubert v. Merrell Dow Pharms., Inc., 509 U.S. 579 (1993)).

179. Henry F. Fradella, Adam Fogarty, & Lauren O'Neill, *The Impact of* Daubert *on the Admissibility of Behavioral Science Testimony*, 30 Pepp. L. Rev. 403, 416 (2003).

180. *Id.* at 416; *see also* White, *supra* note 178, at 5 (discussing standards of admissibility of expert testimony regarding false confessions under both the *Frye* and *Daubert* standards).

181. *See* Fradella, Fogarty & O'Neill, *supra* note 179, at 416–17 ("When offering generalized data on false confessions from social psychological research, for example, the testimony of the expert may be properly limited to presenting data that false confessions do, in fact, exist, and the traits associated with those who give false confessions. Such an expert, however, may not extrapolate from such empirical research that a particular defendant's mental impairments led to a greater likelihood of confessing falsely.").

182. David A. Perez, Comment, *The (In)Admissibility of False Confession Expert* Testimony, 26 Touro L. Rev. 23, at 35–42 (observing that "[c]learly there is no consensus on either the federal or state level regarding the admissibility of false confession expert testimony" and arguing that such evidence fails the *Daubert* test); *see also* State v. Cobb, 43 P.3d 855, 867–69 (Kan. App. 2002) (holding inadmissible expert testimony proffered by Dr. Richard Leo, an expert in the field of false confessions, after concluding that such testimony "invades the province of the jury").

183. Berger, *supra* note 169, at 1075; *see also* Janet C. Hoeffel, *The Sixth Amendment's Lost Clause: Unearthing Compulsory Process*, 2002 Wis. L. Rev. 1275, 1339–40 (2002) (footnotes omitted) ("While federal courts have given expert testimony on false confessions a mixed reception, the majority of state courts have excluded the evidence. The usual panoply of reasons for the

exclusion follow: while a few courts have decided the evidence is unreliable, the vast majority exclude the evidence because it is not helpful to the finder of fact since it is within the common knowledge of the jurors, it invades the province of the jury to decide credibility or provides testimony on the ultimate issue, its probative value is outweighed by the possibility of juror confusion and waste of time, cross-examination and closing arguments are adequate safeguards against false confessions, or the testimony is not sufficiently linked to the facts of the case to be relevant.").

184. Berger, *supra* note 169, at 1075; *see also* White, *supra* note 178, at 5 (discussing arguments prosecutors make to exclude expert testimony about false confessions); Hoeffel, *supra* note 183, at 1339–40 (collecting reasons given by judges for exclusion of expert testimony about false confessions).

185. Janet C. Hoeffel, *The Gender Gap: Revealing Inequities in Admission of Social Science Evidence in Criminal Cases*, 24 U. Ark. Little Rock L. Rev. 41, 68–69 (2001) (citing United States v. Hall, 93 F.3d 1337 (7th Cir. 1996)).

186. Berger, *supra* note 169, at 1075 (footnote omitted).

187. *See supra* Section III.c.i (discussing the impacts of confessions and juries' susceptibility to confession evidence generally).

188. Steven A. Drizin & Richard A. Leo, *The Problem of False Confessions in the Post-DNA World*, 82 N.C. L. Rev. 891, 961 (2004). The same authors go on to note that "confessions (even if they are demonstrably false) almost always seal the defendant's fate – either by leading the innocent defendant to choose to accept a plea bargain, or, more commonly, by leading a judge or jury to wrongfully convict the factually innocent defendant." *Id.*

189. *See supra* Section III.c.ii (discussing the admissibility of expert testimony regarding false confessions under the *Frye* and *Daubert* tests).

190. Berger, *supra* note 169, at 1075–76.

191. *Id.* at 1076.

192. *Id.*

193. *See generally* Danielle E. Chojnacki, Michael D. Cicchini & Lawrence T. White, *An Empirical Basis for the Admission of Expert Testimony on False Confessions*, 40 Ariz. St. L.J. 1 (2008) (arguing that expert testimony regarding false confessions should be admissible under current evidentiary standards).

194. *See, e.g.*, Perez, *supra* note 182, at 74 (arguing that expert testimony regarding false confessions should be inadmissible because "[s]trategic opening statements, vigorous cross-examinations, and particularized jury instructions would help reinforce the jury's ability to detect an untrustworthy confession without unduly trampling upon the jury's role as the trier of fact"). One commentator noted that "various standard jury instructions on the voluntary nature of confessions have little value, or perhaps, are incapable, of providing any real value for detecting false confessions." John T. Rago, *A Fine Line between Chaos & Creation: Lessons on Innocence Reform From the Pennsylvania Eight*, 12 Widener L. Rev. 359, 436 (2006) (footnotes omitted). As a result, the jury instructions discussed in this paper refer not to general jury instructions regarding voluntariness but instructions targeted specifically to the issue of false confessions.

195. Edwin Colfax, *Fairness in the Application of the Death Penalty: Panel One—The Capital Crime*, 80 Ind. L.J. 35, 36 (2005).

196. 469 F.2d 552, 558–59 (D.C. Cir. 1972); *see also* Margery Malkin Koosed, *Reforming Eyewitness Identification Law and Practices to Protect the Innocent*, 42 Creighton L. Rev. 595, 620 (2009) (describing the origins of jury instructions about eyewitness identification and concluding that though such measures are imperfect, they may be a beneficial first step). Because of this, such jury instructions are frequently referred to by commentators and the courts as *Telfaire* instructions. *See, e.g.,* United States v. Tipton, 11 F.3d 602, 606 (6th Cir. 1993) (discussing the appropriateness of *Telfaire* instructions in the case at bar).

197. *See, e.g.*, United States v. Miranda, 986 F.2d 1283, 1285–86 (9th Cir. 1993) (citing United States v. Masterson, 529 F.3d 30, 32 (9th Cir. 1976)) (observing that the Ninth Circuit allows does not require trial court judges to issue special instructions regarding eyewitness evidence "[e]ven where the only evidence is identification evidence"); United States v. Brooks, 928 F.2d 1403, 1407–08 (4th Cir. 1991) (conceding that jury instructions might be proper but refusing to require them); United States v. Wilford, 493 F.2d 730, 735 (3d Cir. 1974) ("When convictions obviously turn on the testimony of eyewitnesses who are uncertain, unclear, or inconsistent, the difficulties raised by such evidence are manifest. In such circumstances, a cautionary instruction will help to obviate the danger of erroneous conviction."); United States v. Evans, 484 F.2d 1178, 1188 (2d Cir. 1973) (observing that an instruction may be appropriate but refusing to require the instruction in all cases).

198. Loomis v. Blades, No. CV-06-157-S-BLW, 2008 WL 50126, at *9 (D. Idaho Feb. 15, 2008).

199. Madrid v. State, 910 P.2d 1340, 1346 (Wyo. 1996).

200. *See, e.g.*, Tenn. Pattern Jury Instructions – Crim. §§ 42.11, 42.12 (2007) (instructing juries to independently assess the credibility of confessions and admissions against interest). In fact, one pattern jury instruction cautions jurors that they "must not disregard [any of the defendant's statements] without good reason." Tenn. Pattern Jury Instructions – Crim. § 42.12 (2007). This may enhance jurors' preexisting reluctance to disregard confessions, even when reason exists to do so. *See infra* note 202 and accompanying text (stating that a confession is "tantamount to an instruction to convict," even where contradictory evidence is introduced).

201. *See supra* notes 160–168 and accompanying text (describing studies indicating that juries were unlikely to discredit any confession, even given credible reasons to do so, and discussing the reasons and consequences of this effect in criminal trials).

202. Richard J. Ofshe & Richard A. Leo, *The Decision to Confess Falsely: Rational Choice & Irrational Action*, 74 Denv. U. L. Rev. 979, 1118 (1997).

203. *See supra* notes 69–78 (describing types of confessions and theories as to why innocent individuals confess to crimes they did not commit).

204. *See supra* note 35 and accompanying text (noting that wrongful convictions based on false confessions allow the actual perpetrators to commit additional crimes).

205. *See* Andrew Cohen, *Staying Executions After Expanding the Death Penalty, The Pendulum Swings Back*, 34-SPG. Hum. Rts. 21, 22 (2007) ("[A] newfound willingness by judges and prosecutors . . . to revisit old capital cases have led to many well-publicized exonerations of death row inmates, each one cutting into the core of confidence that people have about the reliability and accuracy of capital punishment. Since 1973, reports the Death Penalty Information Center, at least 120 people on death row have been exonerated for one reason or another. That list surely will grow in the months and years to come. Where is capital punishment likely to be at the end of this mini upheaval? I have no idea. But I am willing to offer an educated guess: the death penalty will exist in fewer states than it does now. And in those states where it still exists, capital procedures, from jury selection through lethal injection, will be subject to a much more rigorous judicial review. Politicians may be more willing to ensure that capital defendants get decent representation at trial, and when they do not, judges may be more willing to toss tainted convictions. And DNA, the latest 'great equalizer,' will loom in the background of every capital case that does not otherwise involve irrefutable evidence."); *see also Report of the Governor's Council on Capital Punishment*, 80 Ind. L.J. 1, 4 (2005) ("It is not possible to have a death penalty system that is both inexpensive, and at the same time capable of being relied upon to produce accurate and fair results. We are confident that the people of Massachusetts would insist on a death penalty system that

is extremely accurate and fair, despite the increased costs."); James S. Liebman, *Rates of Reversible Error and the Risk of Wrongful Execution*, 86 JUDICATURE 78, 82 (2002) (observing that Texas was one of five states in a nationwide study that "appear[ed] to have the highest overall risk of serious error" in capital cases).

206. *See supra* notes 142–151 and accompanying text. These groups include juveniles and individuals who are under the influence of drugs or alcohol or who have developmental disabilities, mental health issues, or unique cultural backgrounds. *Id.*

207. *See, e.g.*, General Order 01-33 from Broward County Sheriff Ken Jenne to All Personnel 5–6 (Nov. 17, 2001) (on file with author) [hereinafter "Broward County General Order"] (requiring annual training for detectives to identify developmentally disabled individuals and false confessions).

208. Especially in the area of juvenile interrogations, several jurisdictions provide that a juvenile has a right to have a parent or guardian present during an interrogation. *See, e.g.*, COLO. REV. STAT. § 19-2-511(1) (2009) (generally requiring the exclusion of statements made by juveniles during interrogations held without the presence of a parent or guardian). However, many studies suggest that this does not adequately safeguard juveniles' rights. *See* Larry Cunningham, *A Question of Capacity: Towards A Comprehensive and Consistent Vision of Children and Their Status Under Law*, 10 U.C. DAVIS J. JUV. L. & POL'Y 275, 342 (2006) (citing Thomas Grisso, *Juveniles' Consent in Delinquency Proceedings*, *in* CHILDREN'S COMPETENCE TO CONSENT 131, 137 (Gerald P. Koocher et al., eds., 1983) (observing that over 70% of parents present during their children's interrogations said nothing about whether the children should waive *Miranda* rights, while nearly a fifth "encouraged their children to speak to the police," and concluding that "the presence of a juvenile's parents during an interrogation actually adds very little to helping ensure that the child's rights are protected); *see also* Hillary B. Farber, *The Role of the Parent/Guardian in Juvenile Custodial Interrogations:*

Friend or Foe?, 41 AM. CRIM. L. REV. 1277, 1291–98 (2004) (discussing reasons why parental presence is not an adequate safeguard of juveniles' *Miranda* rights). Given that many of the concerns regarding suggestibility and a lack of understanding may also apply to other at-risk suspects, this article suggests the presence of an attorney during interrogations for all at-risk suspects to reduce the risk of false confessions.

209. *See, e.g.*, Broward County General Order, *supra* note 207, at 2–4 (outlining special interrogation procedures for use with developmentally disabled suspects and providing a two-level review process to identify false confessions prior to the filing of criminal charges).

210. *See* Dale E. Ives, *Preventing False Confessions: Is* Oickle *Up to the Task?*, 44 SAN DIEGO L. REV. 477, 491 (2007) (footnotes omitted) ("In particular, false confession researchers have assembled a considerable body of evidence that shows that the risk of a false confession increases with the length of the interrogation. Lengthy interrogations give rise to greater fatigue, uncertainty, confusion, fear, anxiety, stress, and despair on the part of the individual, all of which can increase the individual's desire to bring the interrogation process to a conclusion no matter the cost. In other words, the more prolonged the interrogation, the greater the likelihood that the individual will become fixated on the immediate benefit of confessing (removal from the interrogation process) to the neglect of the potential long-term consequences of falsely confessing (conviction and imprisonment.").

211. Drizin & Leo, *supra* note 188, at 948. It bears noting that the authors of the study were unable to determine the length of the interrogation in nearly two thirds of the sample; even so, this result illustrates a strong correlation between false confession and the length of interrogation. *See id.*

212. *Id.*

213. *See* Ives, *supra* note 210, at 492 ("[T]he research does not indicate the precise point at which one can say that the length of the interrogation has itself created a perceptively higher

risk of false confession. This is in part because it is not just the length of the interrogation that increases the potential for a false confession; it is also the individual's perception about how long the interrogation may last.").

214. *See, e.g.*, DWYER, NEUFELD & SCHECK, *supra* note 1, at 96–97 (recounting Robert Miller's confession that the killer had left his underwear at the scene of the crime, a detail he stumbled upon after suggesting "virtually every stitch or tools that a rapist might have carried," including gloves, pants, slacks, coats, and shirts). Interrogators may provide details of the crime to the suspect intentionally or unintentionally, but the end result is the same: such details enable innocent individuals to provide incredibly detailed confessions (including nonpublic information about the crimes) that may lead to their conviction. *See* Brandon L. Garrett, *Judging Innocence*, 108 COLUM. L. REV. 55, 89–90 (2008) (observing that several individuals who provided such confessions have been exonerated by DNA testing and noting that "[u]nless the person was an accomplice, if those details were truly nonpublic, they could have come only from law enforcement").

215. DWYER, NEUFELD & SCHECK, *supra* note 1, at 83.

216. *See supra* notes 129–132 and accompanying text (defining and describing these tactics in more detail).

217. Saul M. Kassin et al., *Police Interviewing and Interrogation: A Self-Report Survey of Police Practices and Beliefs*, 31 LAW & HUM. BEH. 381, 394 (2007).

218. Edward J. Sackman, *False Confessions: Rethinking a Contemporary Problem*, 16-WTR. KAN. J.L. & PUB. POL'Y 208, 227 (2007).

219. *Id.* at 228.

220. Steven M. Smith et al., *Using the 'Mr. Big' Technique to Elicit Confessions: Successful Innovation or Dangerous Development in the Canadian Legal System?*, 15 PSYCHOL. PUBL. POL'Y & L. 168, 184 (2009).

221. *Id.* at 183–84.

222. *Id.*

223. For example, the PEACE training package also requires officers to treat "vulnerable suspects" with "particular consideration." *Id.* at 184.

224. *Id.*

225. *Id.*

226. This phenomenon is frequently referred to as "tunnel vision." *See , e.g.*, Alafair Burke, *Neutralizing Cognitive Bias: An Invitation to Prosecutors,* 2 NYU J. L. & Liberty 512, 517 (2007) (footnote omitted) ("[A] leading cause of error is 'tunnel vision,' in which investigators and prosecutors hone their sights on one suspect, and then search for evidence inculpating him, to the neglect of exculpatory evidence or the consideration of alternative suspects."); Kent Roach & Gary Trotter, *Miscarriages of Justice in the War Against Terror*, 109 Penn. St. L. Rev. 967, 982–83 (2005) (footnotes omitted) (defining and discussing tunnel vision in the context of terrorism and noting that "[t]unnel vision is particularly likely to occur in cases where false confessions have been obtained from detainees"). Tunnel vision is another major contributor to erroneous convictions, and it can occur at both the investigative and prosecutorial levels. *See* Myrna Raeder, *What Does Innocence Have to Do With It?: A Commentary on Wrongful Convictions and Rationality*, 2003 Mich. St. L. Rev. 1315, 1327 (2003) (footnotes omitted) ("[T]he tunnel vision problem has been widely noted in wrongful conviction cases. Officers and prosecutors either don't realize the significance or accuracy of exculpatory evidence or on occasion affirmatively conceal it because they are convinced of the suspect's guilt."). At least one expert has suggested that additional training and a focus on "testing guilt by inquiring about the existence of evidence that contradicts" the defendant's guilt could be instrumental in combating wrongful convictions. *Id.* (footnotes omitted).

227. Smith et al., *supra* note 220, at 184.

228. *See also* Raeder, *supra* note 226, at 1327–28 ("A grounding in logic, as well as in avoiding practices that encourage false confessions, will lessen the possibilities of erroneous convictions.").

229. Sackman, *supra* note 218, at 227.

230. *Id.*

231. *See supra* notes 31–33 (describing estimates of convictions resulting from false confessions).

232. Barry Feld, *Police Interrogation of Juveniles: An Empirical Study of Policy and Practice*, 97 J. Crim. L. & Criminology 219, 304 (2006).

233. CCFAJ Recommendations, *supra* note 36, at 4.

234. *See id.* (noting that "taping leads to the improved quality of interrogation, with a higher level of scrutiny that will deter police misconduct and improve the quality of interrogation practices").

235. For a detailed discussion of the risks and costs of lost confessions in the context of *Miranda* warnings, *see* Paul Cassell, Miranda*'s Social Costs: An Empirical Reassessment (1996), in* The *Miranda* Debate: Law, Justice, and Policing 175, 175–90 (Richard A. Leo & George C. Thomas III eds., 1998).

236. Thomas P. Sullivan, *Electronic Recording of Custodial Investigations: Everybody Wins*, 95 J. Crim. L. & Criminology 1127, 1129 (2005).

237. *Id.* at 304–05; CCFAJ Recommendations, *supra* note 36, at 4 ("[T]aping provides the police protection against false claims of police misconduct.").

238. Sullivan, *supra* note 236, at 1129.

239. *See* Jeremy W. Newton, *False Confession: Considerations for Modern Interrogation Techniques at Home and War*, 9 J. L. & Soc. Challenges 63, 71 (2008) ("A complete recording could also allow police officers to improve interrogation techniques.").

240. CCFAJ Recommendations, *supra* note 36, at 4. Perhaps more surprising is that "[e]xperienced detectives from [departments that recorded a majority of custodial interrogations] report[ed] great satisfaction with the results of recorded interrogations, including but not limited to higher conviction rates, less time litigating unwarranted suppression motions, and fewer claims of police misconduct." *Id.*

241. Garrett, *supra* note 214, at 123 ("Six jurisdictions now require videotaping of at least some interrogations by statute, and in five more state supreme courts have either required or encouraged electronic recording of interrogations"); *see* Sullivan, *supra* note 236, at 1131–35; *see also* Sackman, *supra* note 218, at 230 ("Videotaped interrogations are either mandatory or commonplace in England, Australia, and Canada . . . all of which also use the adversarial system . . ."). Three states and the District of Columbia adopted legislation requiring recording, while five states have various types of recording requirements imposed by the court of last resort. *See* Sullivan, *supra* note 236, at 1131–35. There is a great deal of variety in recording requirements among the states. *See id.* (discussing various requirements and sanctions for failure to record interrogations). These requirements do not always require suppression of unrecorded confessions, though. *See* Lisa C. Oliver, Note, *Mandatory Recording of Custodial Interrogations Nationwide: Recommending A New Model Code*, 39 Suffolk U. L. Rev. 263, 268–75 (2005) (comparing recording requirements and sanctions for failure to comply).

242. Kassin et al., *supra* note 217, at 396 ("[A]lthough only 16% of the participants in our survey worked in jurisdictions where the electronic recording of interrogations was required (none were in states in which it was mandatory), 81% believed that interviews and interrogations should be fully recorded, from start to finish.").

243. *See* CCFAJ Recommendations, *supra* note 36, at 4.

244. Sullivan, *supra* note 236, at 1127 (quoting Alan K. Harris, Deputy Prosecutor, Hennepin County, Minnesota).

245. *Id.* at 1129 ("Defense motions to suppress based on alleged coercion and abuse drop off dramatically, and the few that are filed are easily resolved by the recording.").

246. *See* Feld, *supra* note 232, at 304–05 (noting that recording interrogations "provides an independent basis by which to resolve credibility disputes between police and defendants about Miranda warnings, waivers or statements"). Judges often lament the lack of such evidence where recordings are not available. *See* Sullivan, *supra* note 236, at 1130 (collecting cases where judges express frustration at the lack of objective evidence to resolve these disputes).

247. Feld, *supra* note 232, at 305.

248. Sullivan, *supra* note 236, at 1130.

249. *See, e.g.,* CCFAJ Recommendations, *supra* note 36, at 5 (observing that "[t]he only objection to mandating the recording of police interrogation heard by the Commission was to the potential cost of video recording, as compared to audio recording").

250. *See id.* ("We are optimistic that improved technology will reduce these costs in the future, and that positive experience with a requirement that all custodial interrogations in serious felony cases be audio recorded will convince all concerned that eventual conversion to video recording is well worth the cost.").

251. Sullivan, *supra* note 236, at 1130.

252. *See also* CCFAJ Recommendations, *supra* note 36, at 5 (footnote omitted) ("The cost of recording custodial interrogations must be measured against the cost of false confessions, which takes a devastating human toll upon those who are wrongfully charged, their families, the victims of crime, and their families. Closing a case with conviction of the wrong person based upon a false confession also leaves the real perpetrator at large, to victimize others. The costs of litigating claims of police misconduct that might have been deterred by taping, and the savings in avoiding false claims of police

misconduct should, in the long run, more than pay the costs of implementation of a mandate that all custodial interrogation in serious criminal cases be electronically recorded.").

253. Though it may be more challenging to record custodial interrogations that do not take place in police stations, portable recording devices make it technologically feasible. *See* Oliver, *supra* note 241, at 281–82 (discussing various methods of ensuring police can conduct recordings in the field). Recording custodial interrogations regardless of the setting seems to be the most prudent course of action, as the same benefits accompany recording generally.

254. Oliver, *supra* note 241, at 284. This tactic would also eliminate issues with what researchers have termed "recap bias," which indicates that "[a] viewer without the relevant background information will likely draw incomplete conclusions about why the suspect confessed, or the veracity of the confession itself," by providing the jury with context for the confession. Sackman, *supra* note 218, at 231.

255. *See* Missouri v. Seibert, 542 U.S. 600, 604–05 (2004) (discussing the practice of questioning suspects prior to administering *Miranda* warnings, obtaining a confession, and recording the post-warnings statement); *id.* at 609–13 & n.2, 613 (noting that "by any objective measure [the facts in *Seibert*] represent[ed] a police strategy adapted to undermine the *Miranda* warnings").

256. *See id.* at 609–13 & n.2 (concluding that the aims of the *Miranda* rule would be disserved by permitting the interrogation practices at issue).

257. *See* Newton, *supra* note 239, at 72–73 (footnotes omitted) (describing studies finding that "when the camera is focused on the suspect, the confession is judged as being the least coerced, more coerced when both the suspect and interrogator are recorded, and most coerced when the camera is focused on the interrogator").

258. *See, e.g.*, Commonwealth v. Giambattista, 813 N.E.2d 516, 533 (Mass. 2004) (holding that a defendant was entitled to

a jury instruction when the interrogating officer failed to maintain a recording of defendant's statements).

259. *See* Oliver, *supra* note 241, at 285 ("Without an exclusionary provision, police officers who use improper interrogation tactics might ignore the recording requirement to shield their coercive methods from public view. For recording requirements to be effective, there must be consequences for not following them.").

260. *Id.*; *see also Giambattista*, 813 N.E.2d at 531 n.19 (quoting State v. Cook, 847 A.2d 530, 547 (N.J. 2004)) ("In the exercise of its supervisory authority, the Supreme Court of New Jersey has recently established a committee to investigate whether to 'encourage' electronic recording of interrogations by imposing 'a presumption against admissibility of a non-recorded statement.'"); State v. Scales, 518 N.W.2d 587, 592 (Minn. 1994) (exercising the court's supervisory power to require recording of all custodial interrogations occurring at the police station, though providing for exclusion only in situations determined to be substantial violations); Stephan v. State, 711 P.2d 1156, 1162–63 (Ak. 1985) (holding that the unexcused failure to record the entire custodial interrogation would result in exclusion but listing circumstances that might constitute excused failures to record).

261. *Cf. Miranda*, 384 U.S. at 538 (White, J., dissenting) ("Particularly when corroborated, as where the police have confirmed the accused's disclosure of the hiding place of implements or fruits of the crime, such confessions have the highest reliability and significantly contribute to the certitude with which we may believe the accused is guilty.").

262. *See, e.g.*, Merker Rosenberg & Rosenberg, *supra* note 81, 142–52.

263. *Cf.* Jaffee v. Redmond, 518 U.S. 1, 9 (1996) (in the context of determining whether a communication should be privileged, observing that testimonial privileges are disfavored but may be justified by a public need sufficient to outweigh the loss of evidence).

264. *See supra* note 226 and accompanying text (discussing and defining tunnel vision).

265. *Id.*

266. *See* Boaz Sangero, Miranda *Is Not Enough: A New Justification for Demanding "Strong Corroboration" To A Confession*, 28 CARDOZO L. REV. 2791, at 2821 ("[T]he police investigation following the apprehension of a suspect is mostly focused on extracting a confession. Furthermore, once the confession is obtained, the investigation usually ceases.").

267. *See id.* ("Only a requirement for strong corroboration would effectively make it clear to investigators that their role is not limited to eliciting confessions.").

268. *See* Raeder, *supra* note 226, at 1327 ("Officers and prosecutors either don't realize the significance or accuracy of exculpatory evidence or on occasion affirmatively conceal it because they are convinced of the suspect's guilt.").

269. *See, e.g.,* Gary Craig, *Douglas Warney Denied Restitution for Wrong Murder Conviction, Decade In Prison*, ROCHESTER DEMOCRAT & CHRON., Feb. 11, 2010 (describing how an AIDS patient with psychiatric problems was convicted of a brutal murder and spent over ten years in prison due to a false confession); Head, *supra* note 35, at 18 (observing that a Texas prosecutor recounted that "in each of the convictions he'[d] worked to overturn, if a DNA match uncover[ed] the real criminal, it's been shown that the person had continued to commit crimes").

270. Smith v. United States, 348 U.S. 147, 152–53, 156 (1954) (citations omitted) ("The general rule that an accused may not be convicted on his own uncorroborated confession has previously been recognized by this Court, and has been consistently applied in the lower federal courts and in the overwhelming majority of state courts . . . All elements of the offense must be established by independent evidence or corroborated admissions, but one available mode of corroboration is for the independent evidence to bolster the

confession itself and thereby prove the offense 'through' the statements of the accused.").

271. *Id.* at 151–152 (citations omitted) ("[The rule's] purpose is to prevent 'errors in convictions based upon untrue confessions alone' . . . [T]he experience of the courts, the police and the medical profession recounts a number of false confessions voluntarily made. These are considerations which justify a restriction on the power of the jury to convict, for this experience with confessions is not shared by the average juror.").

272. *Id.* at 152 (emphasis added) (asserting that the "foundation [of the rule] lies in a long history of judicial experience with confessions and in the realization that *sound law enforcement requires police investigations which extend beyond the words of the accused*"). Notably, this was not the last time that the Court expressed a preference for independent corroborating evidence over confession evidence. *See, e.g.*, Miranda v. Illinois, 384 U.S. 436, 460 (1966) (citations omitted) ("To maintain a 'fair state-individual balance,' to require the government 'to shoulder the entire load,' to respect the inviolability of the human personality, our accusatory system of criminal justice demands that the government seeking to punish an individual produce the evidence against him by its own independent labors rather than by the cruel, simple expedient of compelling it from his own mouth."); Escobedo v. Illinois, 378 U.S. 478, 488–89 (1964) (footnotes omitted) ("We have learned the lesson of history, ancient and modern, that a system of criminal law enforcement which comes to depend on the 'confession' will, in the long run, be less reliable and more subject to abuses than a system which depends on extrinsic evidence independently secured through skillful investigation.").

273. *Smith*, 348 U.S. at 154. This rule is an incarnation of an earlier common law rule known as the corpus delicti rule. *See id.* at 153–54 ("The corroboration rule, at its inception, served an extremely limited function. In order to convict of serious crimes of violence, then capital offenses, independent proof

was required that someone had indeed inflicted the violence, the so-called corpus delicti rule.").

274. *See id.* at 154 (emphasis added) ("We choose to apply the rule, with its broader guarantee, to *crimes in which there is no tangible corpus delicti*, where the corroborative evidence must implicate the accused *in order to show that a crime has been committed.*").

275. *Id.* at 156 (emphasis added).

276. *See id.*

277. Sangero, *supra* note 266, at 2822.

278. *Id.* (arguing that such confessions are "very suspicious").

279. *See, e.g.*, *supra* note 7 and accompanying text (illustrating the use of this tactic in the prosecutor's closing argument in the Robert Miller case).

280. It should be noted that in jurisdictions adopting recording requirements, this requirement also provides defendants with the opportunity to draw the judge's attention to any information the police may have unintentionally provided to the defendant during the interrogation. *See supra* note 17 and accompanying text (describing how Robert Miller had gone through a multitude of clothing items at the interrogator's urging prior to indicating that the killer had left underwear at the scene of the crime).

281. *See* Fed. R. Evid. 403 ("Although relevant, evidence may be excluded if its probative value is substantially outweighed by the danger of unfair prejudice, confusion of the issues, or misleading the jury . . .").

282. *See supra* notes 160–168, 202 and accompanying text (describing the weight factfinders give to confessions).

283. Moran v. Burbine, 475 U.S. 412, 435 (1986).

284. *See* Fisher & Rosen-Zvi, *supra* note 33, at 874 (discussing the value of confessions generally); Jennifer J. Walters, Comment, *Illinois' Weakened Attempt to Prevent False Confessions by Juveniles: The Requirement of Counsel for the Interrogations*

of Some Juveniles, 33 LOY. U. CHI. L.J. 487, 521 (2002) (footnotes omitted) ("The public has an interest in solving crimes and a confession is a valuable way for police officers to determine what happened."); Lawrence Herman, *The Supreme Court, the Attorney General, and the Good Old Days of Police Interrogation*, 48 OHIO ST. L. J. 733, 735–36 (1987) (footnotes omitted) ("Although there is an ongoing debate about the percentage of cases that could not be solved without a confession, all concede that confessions are crucial in some cases."); Joseph P. Garin, Note, *Custodial Interrogation and the Right to Counsel:* People v. Houston, 1987 DET. C.L. REV. 547, 562 (1987) ("It is recognized by most that confessions are valuable law enforcement tools; but, how valuable confessions may be is a matter of controversy."). *But see* Michael Wald et al., *Interrogations in New Haven: The Impact of* Miranda, 76 YALE L.J. 1519, 1579 (1967) (footnotes and internal quotations omitted) ("In the year since the [*Miranda*] decision, however, a small but growing number of officials and commentators have come to the conclusion that the value of confessions in law enforcement has been grossly exaggerated. They argue that most cases can be solved by other investigative techniques.").

285. *See* Sangero, *supra* note 266, at 2821–2823.

286. *See id.*

287. *See* Steven B. Duke, *Does* Miranda *Protect the Innocent or the Guilty?*, 10 CHAP. L. REV. 551, 576 (2007) ("One remedy for unreliable confessions that neither takes up much time nor costs any money is cautionary jury instructions.").

288. Smith et al., *supra* note 220, at 174.

289. *See, e.g.*, Loomis v. Blades, No. CV-06-157-S-BLW, 2008 WL 501526, at *9 (D. Idaho Feb. 15, 2008) (stating that "[t]he lack of authority mandating [a jury instruction about false confessions made] sense, given that the truth or falsity of a confession is a factual determination, not a question of law, that hinges on credibility issues that are well within the abilities of jurors to sort out."). There are several problems

with this holding. First, as discussed at length above, false confessions are counterintuitive. Though determining the credibility of a confession is concededly the jury's responsibility, studies demonstrate that many individuals would be inclined to convict a defendant based on a confession even in light of contradictory evidence. Instructions do not invade the province of the jury; rather, they alert the jury to the need to exercise particular care in certain aspects of its duty. Moreover, false confession instructions need not direct the jury to discard a confession. On the contrary, depending on the way the instruction is drafted, it may do no more than to attempt to counteract the natural tendency to convict based on confession evidence.

290. Chojnacki, Cicchini & White, *supra* note 193, at 39.

291. *See, e.g.*, Perez, *supra* note 182, at 35 ("One reason the Court has explicitly avoided [addressing the admissibility of false confession testimony] might involve the relative infancy of false confession research.").

292. Chojnacki, Cicchini & White, *supra* note 193, at 39 (quoting State v. Free, 798 A.2d 83, 93 (N.J. Super. Ct. App. Div. 2002)).

293. *See, e.g.*, Paul G. Cassell, *The Guilty and the 'Innocent:' An Examination of Alleged Cases of Wrongful Conviction from False Confessions*, 22 Harvard J.L. & Pub. Pol'y 523, 589 (1999) ("It is not at all clear that acceptance of particular conclusions about false confessions yet exists given the preliminary nature of false confession research.").

294. Maj. James R. Agar, II, *The Admissibility of False Confession Expert Testimony*, 1999-Aug Army Law. 26, 43 (1999).

295. United States v. Hall, 974 F. Supp. 1198, 1204–05 (C.D. Ill. 1997) (finding that "the science of social psychology, and specifically the field involving the use of coercion in interrogations, is sufficiently developed in its methods to constitute a reliable body of specialized knowledge").

296. Chojnacki, Cicchini & White, *supra* note 193, at 39. The same commentator opined that "this reasoning badly misses the point . . . [and] would be akin to excluding expert testimony on battered women's syndrome because the general public already knows that people are capable of falsely testifying in court." *Id.* In both instances, environmental factors may predispose actors before the court to act in certain ways. *Id.*

297. *See id.* at 1205 (warning that expert testimony on the likelihood that the confession at issue in the case was in fact false would not be admitted and that such testimony would be limited solely to a general discussion of the "framework [of false confession research] which the jury can use to arrive at its own conclusions"). By contrast, psychologists who have examined a defendant may be allowed to testify to the likelihood that the defendant in the instant case falsely confessed. *See* Fradella, Fogarty & O'Neill, *supra* note 179, at 441 ("In contrast [to experts testifying about false confessions generally], though, psychologists and psychiatrists who have performed a clinical evaluation of the defendant are permitted to testify about the specific likelihood of a false confession from a defendant based upon their evaluation of the defendant, provided they have used generally accepted methods of clinical assessment.").

298. *See, e.g.*, Ibn-Tamas v. United States, 407 A.2d 626, 632–35 (D.C. Cir. 1979) (discussing the ways in which expert testimony about battered woman's syndrome could have invaded the province of the jury and concluding that when appropriately limited such testimony did not interfere with the jury's function); State v. Kelly, 478 A2d 364, 378 (N.J. 1984) ("The difficulty with the expert's testimony is that it *sounds* as if an expert is giving knowledge to a jury about something the jury knows as well as anyone else, namely, the reasonableness of a person's fear of imminent serious danger. That is not at all, however, what this testimony is *directly* aimed at. It is aimed at an area where the purported common knowledge of the jury may be very much mistaken, an area where jurors' logic, drawn from their own experience, may lead to a wholly incorrect conclusion, an area where expert knowledge would

enable the jurors to disregard their prior conclusions as being common myths rather than common knowledge.").

299. Yount v. State, 636 A.2d 50, 55–56 (Md. App. 1994) (noting and dismissing a "'last gasp' contention" that expert testimony on child sexual abuse impermissibly infringed upon the jury's credibility determination)

300. *See* United States v. Freeman, 357 F.2d 606, 619–20 (2d Cir. 1966) (discussing the relationship between psychological experts and the jury's role in the context of an insanity defense).

301. *See, e.g.,* State v. Kelly, 478 A.2d at 378 & n.13 (allowing limited expert testimony on battered woman's syndrome and describing cases in which other courts had done the same); People v. Cintron, 551 N.E.2d 561, 572 (N.Y. 1990) (finding that a trial court "acted within its discretion in permitting [] expert testimony" on "the reactions of a four-year old victim of sexual abuse"); *see also* State v. Ali, 660 A.2d 337, 351 (Conn. 1995) (citations and internal quotations omitted) (observing the critical difference between "testimony about the general behavior of victims and an opinion as to whether the instant victim is telling the truth is critical" and that the former is admissible while the latter is not).

C. Jailhouse Informants

Whispering Sweet Nothings: How Jailhouse Snitches[*] Subvert American Justice

Matthew W. Gilliam[†]

I. Introduction

Around 4:30 P.M., on December 8, 1981 in Canaveral Groves, Florida, "Trish," a seventeen-year-old woman, was brutally raped in her bedroom.[1] Threatening Trish with a box cutter, the man cut off her clothes and threw her onto her bed.[2] The rapist then proceeded to cut Trish 65 times with the box cutter and to rape her twice.[3] Trish originally described her assailant to the police as being 6 feet tall, around 180 pounds, with long blond hair and a mustache.[4]

* Most courts use the term "in-custody informant." Despite its negative connotation, however, this paper will use the term "jailhouse snitch." This is because our current American justice system has no effective way of separating truthful informants from lying informants. Because of that, as this paper will argue, courts and legislatures need to begin from the assumption that informant testimony is inherently unreliable. Using the term "snitch" instead of "informant" better expresses that notion.

† Matthew W. Gilliam is a J.D. Candidate (2011) at the University of Houston Law Center. He earned his B.A. in 2008 at the University of Texas at Austin.

Four days after the incident, Trish and her sister made the 46-mile trip to the nearby town of Port St. John.[5] Stopping at a Jiffy Mart to buy snacks, Trish thought she spotted the man who had raped her.[6] Trish's sister recognized the man as one of her old elementary schoolmates and thought his name was Walter.[7] A week later, Trish returned to the Jiffy Mart and saw the man again.[8] While the first time she saw him, the man looked shorter than the man who raped her, Trish thought this was because of the high heel shoes she wore.[9] Trish called the police, and Trish's sister identified the man as Walter Dedge.[10]

On January 8, 1982, police officers arrested Walter Dedge.[11] After seeing Walter's picture in a photo lineup, Trish's sister realized that it was not Walter who she saw in the Jiffy Mart, but his younger brother Wilton.[12] The Brevard County Sherriff's Office arrested Wilton Dedge the next day.[13] Trish positively identified Wilton Dedge as the man who had raped her.[14]

At trial, along with Trish's identification, the State relied on a positive identification from a scent dog, as well as the testimony of a hair analyst that Dedge could not be eliminated as the possible source of a pubic hair found in Trish's bed sheets.[15] Despite the fact that Dedge called five witnesses who testified that he had been in New Symra Beach at the time of the rape, the jury found Dedge guilty of burglary with assault, sexual battery with a weapon, and aggravated battery.[16] He was sentenced to 30 years in prison.[17]

On December 22, 1983, the Fifth District Court of Appeals of Florida reversed Dedge's conviction.[18] Finding that the trial judge improperly barred Dedge from putting on an expert witness to challenge the dog-scent evidence, the appeals court decided Dedge deserved a new trial.[19] In transport to Brevard County to request bail before his second trial, Dedge sat next to inmate Clarence Zacke.[20] Zacke had been found guilty in three different murder-for-hire plots and had been sentenced to 180 years in prison.[21] The next night, the prosecutor in Dedge's case got a phone call from Zacke's son who told him that Dedge had confessed to the crime to his father.[22]

At the bail hearing, Zacke testified that Dedge told him that he "raped and cut up some old hog."[23] Zacke also said that Dedge had told him that he drove his motorcycle more than 160 mph to make the 45-mile drive to Trish's home in 15 minutes and returned to his auto mechanic shop without anyone knowing.[24] Dedge's bail request was subsequently denied.[25] At the second trial, based on Trish's identification, the forensic hair analysis and Zacke's testimony, the jury again found Dedge guilty.[26] Instead of the original 30-year sentence, the judge sentenced Dedge to life in prison.[27]

Even though the prosecutors did not specifically promise Zacke anything for his testimony, he did receive a reduction in his sentence.[28] Moreover, this was not the first time Zacke had testified as a snitch.[29] In a previous murder trial, Zacke testified that the defendant had confessed to him.[30] Based in part on Zacke's testimony, this other defendant was sentenced to death.[31] From his original 180-year prison sentence, Zacke, by virtue of testifying twice, obtained a reduced sentence of sixty years or less with good behavior.[32]

While Zacke was busy reducing his sentence, Wilton Dedge sat in prison. In 2000, a judge granted Dedge's motion to conduct DNA analysis on both the semen sample and pubic hair from the rape.[33] Although the DNA test was inconclusive for the semen sample, the test on the pubic hair determined that it had not come from Dedge.[34] Based on this new DNA evidence, the appeals court granted Dedge a new trial.[35] Four years later, while awaiting trial, the court ordered a new advanced DNA test to be carried out on the semen sample.[36] This time the test confirmed that the DNA had not come from Dedge.[37] Based on a witness misidentification and the testimony of an unreliable jailhouse snitch, Wilton Dedge, an innocent man, had spent almost 22 years behind bars for a crime he did not commit.[38]

Unfortunately, Wilton Dedge has not been the only one to be convicted based in part on the false testimony of a jailhouse snitch.[39] Since the end of the moratorium on capital punishment in the 1970s, 111 death row inmates have been exonerated.[40] Accounting for 45.9 % of those cases, snitch cases are the leading cause of wrongful convictions in U.S. capital cases.[41] Wrongful convictions based on jailhouse snitch testimony occur for a number of reasons. First, because a jailhouse snitch can receive compensation in the form of a reduced sentence or a preferable prison transfer, he has a strong incentive to come forward to authorities.[42] This incentive is coupled with the small probability that the snitch will be prosecuted for perjury if he is later found to have fabricated the confession. These factors create an atmosphere of unreliability surrounding the testimony of a jailhouse snitch. Second, while cross-examination is thought to be fundamental to uncovering the truth in the American justice system, many times defense attorneys simply do not have the necessary pretrial information to conduct an effective cross-examination of a jailhouse snitch. These pretrial disclosures can include such things as a jailhouse snitches' criminal history, any prior inconsistent statements made to the authorities, any benefit the snitch is receiving for his testimony, and whether or not he has ever testified as a snitch in any other cases. Despite this, most states have failed to pass comprehensive legislation regarding the use of jailhouse snitches.[43] Third, sometimes law enforcement suffers from the syndrome of "falling in love with their snitch."[44] This may subconsciously cause tunnel vision in police and prosecutors, and make them focus only on the defendant as the true perpetrator.[45] Despite mitigating evidence or the obvious unreliability of a snitch, police officers and prosecutors still might construe this information in a way that confirms their original decisions.

This article will examine the unique difficulties posed by the use of jailhouse snitch testimony at trial. In addition to examining proposed solutions and the current state of the laws concerning snitch testimony, this article will argue that notwithstanding statutory protections, the Fourteenth and Fifth Amendments of the Constitution already require prosecutors to disclose pertinent information regarding the snitch's testimony.

Part II of this article investigates the problem in using jailhouse snitch testimony. Due to a combination of many different factors, jailhouse snitch testimony often tends to be unreliable. Part III of the article takes a look at various reforms targeting the problem of jailhouse snitch testimony. Reforms exist at both the investigative, pretrial, and trial level. While state legislators have passed some of these proposals into law in a few states, Texas, in particular, only recently began to regulate the use of jailhouse informants, and more comprehensive reform is necessary.

Part IV examines the United States Supreme Court case of *Brady v. Maryland* and its progeny. Because of problems with the *Brady* test, Part IV argues that prosecutors, when using a jailhouse snitch, have an independent constitutional due process requirement to share certain information with the defendant. This information should include such things as prior statements made by the snitch, the criminal history of the snitch, whether or not the snitch has testified in prior trials, and the outcome of those trials. Failing to disclose this information to the defendant should always constitute constitutional error and require reversal. Finally, Part V concludes that although requiring prosecutors to share this information would represent genuine progress, more reforms are necessary to ensure that defendants receive fair trials.

II. The Unreliability Dilemma

The use of jailhouse snitches poses a unique problem because of the strong incentive to lie that exists.[46] In return for his testimony, a jailhouse snitch can receive compensation in the form of a dismissal of charges, reduction of sentence, an increase in in-custody privileges, or the payment of cash upon his release. Often the agreement between the snitch and the prosecutor is understood and not formalized so the snitch can still testify that he has not been promised anything in return for his testimony.

In 1988, career jailhouse snitch Leslie Vernon demonstrated to the Los Angeles County Sheriff's Department how he was able to fabricate confessions of fellow inmates by using confidential information he obtained.[47] This demonstration prompted a Los Angeles County Grand Jury to investigate the use of jailhouse informants from 1989 to 1990.[48] The grand jury found that because jailhouse snitches often face long prison sentences, they are highly motivated to testify falsely.[49] In high profile cases, jailhouse snitches have even more incentive to provide false testimony.[50] One jailhouse snitch explained to the grand jury how snitches work together in cases:

> One informant acquires some information on the case. He may then relay that information to another informant who disseminates it to other informants. Each informant will then try the story out on police, changing a word here or there for slight variation. When an inmate previously unknown to other informants arrives in the informants' area in the jail,[51] the informants will discuss "booking"[52] him all day. [53]

Jailhouse snitches have developed ways to learn information regarding a case in order to fabricate false confessions.

The recent case of *U.S. v. Colomb*[54] perfectly demonstrates how the snitch system works in prison. On April 24, 2004, a federal grand jury indicted Mary Ann Colomb and her sons Edward Colomb, Sammy Davis, Jr., and Danny Davis with conspiracy to possess with intent to distribute cocaine and forfeiture.[55] In addition to those charges, Sammy Davis, Jr. was charged with distribution of cocaine base, possession of cocaine base with intent to distribute, and possession of a firearm in furtherance of a drug trafficking crime.[56] Mary Ann Colomb was also charged with possession of cocaine base with intent to distribute, possession of a firearm in furtherance of a drug trafficking crime and establishment of manufacturing operations.[57] Like Mary Ann, Edward Colomb was charged with possession of cocaine base with intent to distribute and possession of a firearm in furtherance of a drug trafficking crime.[58]

On three separate dates in September of 2004, less than two weeks before the scheduled trial date, the government disclosed to the Colombs their intention to use a total of sixteen new witnesses, all of whom where serving time primarily in a prison in Texas.[59] These witnesses had independently contacted the government offering to testify against the Colombs.[60] Ultimately, eleven of these witnesses testified against the Colombs.[61] Based in part on the testimony of these witnesses, all of the Colombs were found guilty.[62] Shortly after the trial, each defendant filed a motion for a new trial asserting that the testimony of the jailhouse snitches was unreliable and thus should have been excluded.[63]

During the trial, another U.S. Attorney[64] received a letter from Quinn Alex, an inmate housed at the Federal prison located in Three Rivers, Texas.[65] Alex claimed that one of the inmates who testified against the Colombs, Charles Anderson, offered to sell him some information about people going to trial.[66] Anderson made this offer while housed with Alex at the Three Rivers prison.[67] This information included pictures of one of the Colomb boys.[68] Anderson wanted $2,200 for the information.[69] Alex had his girlfriend transfer the money to Anderson's girlfriend.[70] Anderson, however, was transferred to another prison, and Alex never received the information.[71] Alex wrote the letter to the U.S. Attorney asking him to prosecute Anderson for stealing his money.[72] The government disclosed this letter to the Colombs while their trial was ongoing.[73] The Colombs made an oral motion for a mistrial. The trial court denied this motion, and the jury never learned of Alex's letter.[74]

Three days after the guilty verdict, Danny Davis' attorney interviewed and obtained an affidavit from an inmate imprisoned at a federal prison in Lafayette Parish.[75] This inmate, referred to as John Doe, had served time at Beaumont Low Federal Prison with many of the inmates who testified at the Colombs' trial.[76] Doe's statements described the information sharing that occurred between inmates in prison.[77] According to Doe, he saw some of the inmates who testified against the Colombs reviewing documents before they were scheduled to testify.[78] In addition to Doe's affidavit, the government also interviewed Quinn Alex.[79] Again, Alex told the same story and corroborated his statement with copies of wire transfers in the sum of $2,200.[80]

On August 31, 2006, the district court judge granted the Colombs' motions for a new trial.[81] The judge found that the Colombs' were deprived of the right to due process and the right to a fair trial when their motion for a mistrial was denied.[82] In addition to vacating the Colombs' guilty verdict, the court required the government to conduct an investigation into the jailhouse snitch problem before a new trial date could be set.[83] In December 2006, the government dropped the charges against the Colombs.[84]

Allegedly, this was not the first time these inmates had falsified their testimony. Many of the same inmates who testified against the Colombs also testified in the trial of Otis Jackson, Trina Jackson, and Timothy Cotton.[85] Cotton and the Jacksons were ultimately convicted of multiple drug conspiracy charges in a court presided over by the same judge as in the Colomb case.[86] In appealing the trial court's denial of a new trial based on newly discovered evidence, the defendants presented affidavits of eight inmates housed in the Beaumont federal prison.[87] These inmates claimed that a group of inmates, known as the "Hot Boyz," would receive materials, such as photographs and background information, on individuals who were being investigated or had been indicted.[88] An inmate in the "Hot Boyz" would then share this information with another "Hot Boyz" inmate allowing him to testify against an accused.[89]

Cotton and the Jacksons argued that the testimony of the "Hot Boyz" in their case required the court to grant them a new trial.[90]

In upholding the district court's refusal of a new trial, the Fifth Circuit found that the affidavits were merely impeachment evidence.[91] Because the affidavits contained no allegations that the "Hot Boyz" testified falsely in this specific trial, the new evidence could only be used to undermine the witnesses' testimony.[92] The court also found that the defendants had already cross-examined the witnesses about the information contained in the affidavits and that even without the testimony there was enough evidence to find Cotton and the Jacksons guilty.[93]

The story of the "Hot Boyz" is not unique to Texas or Louisiana. Jailhouse snitches in California have found numerous ways to discover information so they can snitch on defendants.[94] For example, some steal legal documents from other inmates' cells.[95] A snitch may even con other inmates into believing they are jailhouse lawyers.[96] The snitch can also twist a fellow inmate's statements about their innocence into a confession.[97] A snitch does not even have to be housed in the same facility to snitch on a defendant.[98] Veteran snitch Leslie Vernon White only needed a telephone and a last name to learn information about an inmate.[99] White would impersonate police officers and prosecutors to get information from law enforcement.[100] He would then fabricate records to show that he was in jail with the inmate.[101]

Courts have recognized these problems with jailhouse snitches. As the Fifth Circuit said, "it is difficult to imagine a greater motivation to lie then the inducement of a reduced sentence."[102] Allowing jailhouse snitches to testify falsely undermines the purpose of our justice system.[103] In order to combat this problem, some courts recognize the importance of broad disclosure when a jailhouse snitch testifies.[104] In cases with jailhouse snitch testimony, trial judges must play a more integral role in scrutinizing the testimony.[105] This is necessary because the jury does not possess the background knowledge to properly assess the testimony of a jailhouse snitch.[106]

The jailhouse snitch's motivation to falsify testimony is also coupled with the law enforcement and prosecutors' dependence on the testimony the snitch provides. In many instances, a prosecutor's case hinges on the testimony of a jailhouse snitch. Because of this reliance, police and prosecutors acquire a stake in the testimony of the informant. In some instances, a prosecutor may fall in love with her snitch and lose the ability to look at the evidence neutrally.[107] In her article, Professor Ellen Yaroshefsky interviewed former assistant United States Attorneys from the Southern District of New York about the use of cooperating witnesses.[108] Yaroshefky found a various numbers of factors led prosecutors to falsely believe that a cooperating witness was telling the truth. These factors included: (1) a lack of proper investigation, (2) insufficient evidence of guilt, (3) misplaced trust in cooperators, (4) rigid theory of the case, (5) cultural barriers, (6) attitudes of individual assistant prosecutors, (7) a lack of experience of the prosecutor, and (8) conduct of the proffer sessions.[109] Therefore, the police and prosecutors lack the necessary objectivity required to critically examine the snitch's story for accuracy.

Even when evidence exists that may exculpate the defendant, law enforcement and prosecutors still often believe the defendant is guilty.[110] Law enforcement, prosecutors, and even judges may develop tunnel vision and only take into account evidence that supports their original conclusions.[111] Law enforcement and prosecutors may encourage the testimony of jailhouse snitches to support the idea that they are convicting the correct individual.[112] This is especially true when law enforcement and prosecutors lack strong evidence and look to jailhouse inmates to bolster their case.[113] This tunnel vision is created by cognitive distortions, which can affect a prosecutor's ability to accurately interpret what she perceives.[114] These cognitive distortions include confirmation bias, hindsight bias, and outcome bias.[115] There can also be institutional pressures that cause police to focus on one individual.[116] Once police arrest an individual the focus of the investigation may shift towards proving that the police arrested the correct individual.[117] If that occurs, law enforcement may unwittingly encourage jailhouse snitches to create false confessions or may subconsciously fail critically to examine an accused's purported confession to a jailhouse snitch.[118]

Tunnel vision is especially troublesome in the context of *Brady* disclosures. Under *Brady*, prosecutors must only disclose information to the defendant that would cause the result of the trial to be different.[119] Cognitive biases and other pressures make it unlikely that prosecutors, and ultimately judges, will decide that certain information should be disclosed to a defendant.[120] Because a prosecutor must determine which evidence to share with the defendant prior to trial, and the *Brady* test is retrospective, it is difficult for a prosecutor to know before seeing the defense's theory what evidence needs to be disclosed.[121] Thus, the problem of law enforcement and prosecutors' dependence on jailhouse snitch testimony destroys an important safeguard against wrongful convictions.

In some instances, law enforcement officials and prosecutors actively seek out jailhouse snitches. For example, the Los Angeles County Grand Jury heard evidence that the Sheriff's Department intentionally placed new inmates with a group of known snitches in hopes of eliciting confessions.[122] In Pennsylvania, the district attorney's office had an implied agreement with a jailhouse snitch.[123] In return for not holding a sentencing hearing on the snitch's crimes, the snitch would inform the district attorney's office about any statements he heard from inmates awaiting trial.[124]

When a law enforcement agent or prosecutor entices a jailhouse snitch to secure a confession, she might be running afoul of constitutional principles. In *United States v. Massiah,*[125] the Supreme Court clearly established that a defendant's Sixth Amendment right to assistance of counsel attaches after indictment.[126] Therefore, law enforcement may not use a defendant's post-indictment, self-incriminating statement made to an agent of the government against him at trial.[127] The Supreme Court dealt specifically with self-incriminating statements made by a defendant to his cellmate in *United States v. Henry.*[128] In *Henry*, a Federal agent told a paid informant, in the same jail as Henry, the defendant, to "be alert to any statements made by the federal prisoners," but to not actively question the defendant regarding his charges.[129] Shortly after his release, the informant contacted the Federal agent and told him that Henry made self-incriminating statements to him.[130] The informant testified at trial about his conversations with Henry.[131] Based in part on his testimony, the jury found Henry guilty and he was sentenced to 25 years in prison.[132]

On appeal, Henry claimed the trial court violated his Sixth Amendment right to assistance by counsel by allowing the informant to testify.[133] In holding that Henry's Sixth Amendment right was violated; the Supreme Court found four factors determinative.[134] First, the informant had worked with the government for more than a year.[135] Second, the Federal agent knew the informant had access to Henry and would be able to converse with him.[136] Third, the government only paid the informant if he produced useful information.[137] Fourth, Henry made the statements during his imprisonment.[138] Even though the Federal agent told the informant not to actively question Henry, the Court thought the agent should have foreseen that such a result would occur.[139] Therefore, the government violated Henry's Sixth Amendment right to counsel by "intentionally creating a situation likely to induce Henry to make incriminating statements without the assistance of counsel."[140]

Proposed Solutions:

- Adopt law enforcement guidelines
- Require pretrial disclosure
- Conduct pretrial reliability hearings
- Require independent corroboration
- Provide jury instructions

An agreement between a jailhouse snitch and law enforcement does not in every circumstance violate a defendant's right to counsel. In a factual situation very similar to *Henry*, the Supreme Court found that a defendant's Sixth Amendment right to counsel was not violated. In *Kuhlman v. Wilson*,[141] police placed the defendant in the same cell as the snitch.[142] The snitch previously arranged with a police officer to listen to the defendant's conversations.[143] The police officer explicitly instructed to snitch not to ask the defendant questions, but to "keep his ears open."[144] The defendant confessed that he committed the crime to the snitch.[145] The snitch provided the defendant's statements to the police officer and later testified at trial.[146] The Supreme Court distinguished this case from *Henry* finding that in the present case, the snitch did not stimulate conversations with the defendant in order to elicit incriminating information.[147] The Court held that a violation of the Sixth Amendment's right to counsel only happens when a defendant demonstrates "that the police and their informant took some action, beyond merely listening, that was designed deliberately to elicit incrimination remarks."[148]

In interpreting *Massiah*, *Henry*, and *Wilson*, lower courts have created a two-prong test. To prove a Sixth Amendment right to counsel violation in the jailhouse snitch context, the defendant must show that (1) the snitch was a government agent; and (2) that the snitch deliberately elicited criminal statements from him.[149] The first prong of the test may be met when the government has an agreement with the snitch to target a specific defendant.[150] Under those circumstances, the government must also know that its actions will cause the snitch to ask the defendant questions regarding his incarceration.[151] The first prong might also be met when law enforcement or prosecutors create an "informant at large."[152] The second prong of the test requires action on part of the snitch in obtaining the information.[153] This action may take the form of the snitch questioning the defendant or the snitch deliberately using his position to learn incriminating information.[154]

III. Safeguards Against Unreliable Snitch Testimony

In order to combat the problem of wrongful convictions due to jailhouse informant testimony, a number of solutions have been proposed. Proposals have come from non-profits, professional organizations, and academia. Some of these proposals have been either codified or adopted as law enforcement guidelines. These safeguards apply at the investigative, pretrial, and trial levels.

A. Investigative Level Solutions

A large problem with the use jailhouse snitches, as well as snitches in general, is the lack of guidelines for law enforcement to follow. Currently the only the U.S. Attorney General and the California Department of Justice have law enforcement guidelines governing the use of snitches. While the Attorney General's guidelines specifically deal with the use of confidential informants, the guidelines also provide that certain requirements be met before federal law enforcement agents can use a prisoner as a confidential informant.[155] Thus the guidelines regulate both the decision to use an informant and the process for how federal law enforcement uses information from that informant.[156] The California

Department of Justice guidelines deal only with the use of jailhouse informants.[157] These guidelines demand prior approval by the senior assistant attorney general before the jailhouse snitch testimony is used. In making her decision, the senior assistant attorney general must consider: (1) whether or not the informant has passed a polygraph test, (2) whether or not there is a tape recording of the statements made by the defendant to the informant, (3) whether there is any corroborating evidence, (4) whether the informant has provided some inside information not attainable through public records, and (5) whether it is in the interest of justice for the jailhouse informant to testify. When the information provided by the jailhouse informant is only intended to be used for an investigative purpose, the California Department of Justice again requires prior approval by the Senior Assistant Attorney General based upon the reliability of the information to secure a warrant, the nature of the source of the information, the seriousness of the offense, and any corroborative evidence.

In addition to the federal and California guidelines, the American Bar Association ("ABA") has also made recommendations concerning the use of jailhouse informants.[158] In its recommendation, the ABA urges law enforcement not to convict an individual based solely upon the uncorroborated testimony of a jailhouse snitch.[159] The report urges that prosecutors follow a checklist when deciding whether or not to use a jailhouse snitch.[160]

In order to combat the problems associated with using jailhouse snitches, state law enforcement agencies should adopt guidelines and policies to aid in deciding when to use jailhouse snitch testimony.[161] In addition to adopting the above-mentioned guidelines, law enforcement agencies in other states should also consider increasing the recording requirements of the purported confession made to the snitch and all discussions between the jailhouse snitch and law enforcement.[162]

Another problem with jailhouse snitches, as well as snitches in general, is the lack of data regarding the number of snitches in the system.[163] Currently no law enforcement agency keeps track of how often snitches are used.[164] Law enforcement at both the state and federal level should begin to record when they use snitches.[165] This would provide transparency to the shadowy snitch system.

B. Pretrial Level

In order for defendants to be adequately prepared to cross-examine a jailhouse snitch, certain disclosures by the prosecution should first be made.[166] As Part IV of this paper argues, prosecutors must take the requirements of *Brady* more seriously in the context of snitch testimony. *Brady* material should include such factors as statements made by the snitch, incentives the informant has or will receive for his testimony, whether the snitch has testified against other defendants, and other inconsistent statements made by the jailhouse snitch.[167] Because the amount of information disclosed varies from prosecutor to prosecutor, detailed guidelines are necessary to ensure equal treatment. These guidelines could take the form of policies enforced by prosecutorial offices, statutes passed by state legislatures, or judicial decrees. For example, the Los Angeles County District Attorney's Office has extensive policies regarding the use of jailhouse snitches. Prior to using a jailhouse snitch as a witness, the prosecutor must receive approval from a Jailhouse Informant Committee.[168] All requests to this committee must be in writing.[169] The request must include the following: a brief description of the crime and the name and criminal history of the snitch; the evidence offered by the snitch; a description of the evidence corroborating the snitch's testimony; an analysis of the strengths and weaknesses of the case if the jailhouse snitch is not used; and any benefit promised to the snitch.[170] The guidelines also require the prosecutor to include in the written request whether the jailhouse snitch has offered to be a witness in the past or has testified before.[171] In addition to implementing an approval process, the guidelines also restrict the kind of information that can be shared over the telephone.[172] To fulfill their *Brady* obligations, the Los Angeles District Attorney's Office also preserves all records regarding jailhouse snitches.[173] While the Supreme Court has held that an open file policy is not necessary to comply with *Brady*, it certainly seems smart in the jailhouse snitch context.[174] Having such a policy would increase the likelihood of uncovering a dishonest jailhouse snitch.

The State of Illinois has already taken steps to require certain disclosure when prosecutors plan to use jailhouse snitch testimony in capital cases.[175] The Illinois statute requires that before the prosecution can use the testimony of a jailhouse informant in a capital case, they must first make a series of discovery disclosures to the defense.[176] These disclosures include: (1) the complete criminal history of the informant; (2) any "deal, promise, inducement, or benefit" the prosecutor has made or will make with the informant; (3) the statements made by the accused; (4) the time and place of the statements, the time and place of their disclosure to law enforcement, and the names of all individuals present when the statements were made; (5) whether the informant has ever recanted and if so, the time and place of the recantation, the nature of the recantation, and the names of all people present at the recantation; (6) other cases the informant has testified in and any promises, or inducements he received for that testimony; and (7) any other information relevant to the informant's credibility.[177] In addition to these pretrial disclosures, the prosecution must also disclose their intent to use the testimony of an informant.[178]

These types of disclosure requirements can also be put into effect by means of judicial decision. In 2000, Rocky Dodd appealed his capital murder sentence to the Supreme Court of Oklahoma.[179] Dodd claimed that the judge wrongfully excluded evidence that would impeach the testimony of a jailhouse snitch with prior inconsistent statements.[180] The Oklahoma Supreme Court agreed with Dodd reversing his conviction and ordering a new trial.[181] The court found that it is necessary to be exceedingly cautious when dealing with jailhouse snitch testimony, especially when the testimony is in return for some kind of benefit.[182] To ensure the defendant's attorney is prepared to cross-examine the snitch, the court expressly required that prosecutors disclose certain information at least ten days before trial.[183] The State must disclose the following information: (1) the complete criminal history of the informant; (2) any deal, promise, inducement, or benefit that the offering party has made or may make in the future to the informant; (3) the specific statements made by the defendant and the time, place, and manner of their disclosure; (4) all other cases in which the informant testified or offered statements against an individual but was not called, whether the statements were admitted in the case, and whether the informant received any deal, promise, inducement or benefit in exchange for or subsequent to that testimony or statement; (5) whether at any time the informant recanted that testimony or statement, and if so, a transcript or copy of such recantation; and (6) any other information relevant to the informant's credibility.[184]

To further improve the process, courts should conduct pretrial reliability hearings when jailhouse testimony is used.[185] At this hearing, the judge would hear the jailhouse snitch's testimony and be required to find that the testimony is sufficiently reliable before allowing the evidence to be presented to a jury. The judge would serve a gate-keeping function, increasing the chances that the jury would hear reliable snitch testimony. Again the Illinois statute requires these pretrial reliability hearings when a prosecutor plans to use jailhouse snitch testimony in a capital murder case. In those instances, the prosecution must prove that the snitch's testimony is reliable by a preponderance of the evidence. It is also possible that absent an express statute, courts already possess the power to conduct these reliability hearings under the applicable rules of evidence. For example, Federal Rule of Evidence 104 allows the court to determine preliminary questions concerning the qualification of a person to be a witness.[186] Many states have identical rules of evidence.[187] Some commentators have noted how these pretrial reliability hearings would parallel the hearing required for scientific or technical evidence under the Supreme Court's decision in *Daubert v. Merrell Dow*.[188] Just like expert witnesses, jailhouse snitches are "compensated" by one party, have inside knowledge, and present central evidence that is hard to corroborate or contradict.[189]

While, law enforcement and prosecutors possess the power to reward snitches, defendants are at a great disadvantage. They cannot provide the same incentives to an inmate in order to get him to testify on their behalf. Instead they must rely on goodwill and persuasion. To even the playing field the government could provide a defendant a means to reward a snitch who testifies on his behalf.[190] This might consist of an independent authority that determines when to award benefits to defense snitches.[191]

C. Trial Level

Similar to the use of accomplice testimony, states should enact statutes refusing to allow convictions solely based upon uncorroborated jailhouse testimony.[192] In Texas, the first law concerning the use of in-custody informants was passed during the 81st Legislative Session in 2009.[193] Senate Bill 1681 bill, authored by Senator Juan Hinojosa, amended Chapter 38 of the Code of Criminal Procedure by adding article 38.075.[194] The bill required independent corroboration of any testimony offered by a jailhouse informant.[195] Thus, an individual can no longer be convicted based solely on the testimony of a jailhouse informant.[196] This bill was filed without the Governor's signature and became effective September 1, 2009.[197]

This new law is a step in the right direction; it places the same corroboration burden on the government as applicable to the use of accomplice testimony.[198] Accomplice testimony and jailhouse informant testimony, however, are vastly different. When accomplices testify, they usually make self-incriminating statements placing themselves in risk of criminal prosecution. This creates an internal safeguard in assuring that the accomplice's testimony is reliable. When a jailhouse informant testifies, that safeguard no longer exists. Because the informant's testimony is independent from the underlying crime, he or she does not face the same self-incrimination risk as an accomplice. The importance of ensuring the reliability of a jailhouse informant's testimony is therefore greater.

In addition to corroboration requirements, juries should be instructed as to the unique problems of coming to a verdict when faced with jailhouse snitch testimony.[199] This instruction might tell the jury to consider certain factors such as the snitch's incentive to lie, whether the snitch has testified at other trials, and any inconsistent statements the snitch has provided. Currently California, Connecticut, Montana, and Oklahoma require jury instructions when a jailhouse snitch testifies.[200]

IV. Brady v. Maryland:[201] An Independent Legal Basis for Requiring the Disclosure of Jailhouse Snitch Information

Although it would be wise for states to pass legislation controlling the use of jailhouse snitches, prosecutors already have a constitutional duty under the Fifth and Fourteenth Amendments to disclose certain information before allowing a snitch to testify.[202] This duty stems from two discordant concepts in the criminal justice system: the adversary model and the state's interest in seeing that justice is done.[203] Because of these competing concepts, in some instances the prosecutor must abandon his role of advocate and share information with the defendant.[204]

While the Supreme Court decision of *Brady v. Maryland*[205] is the most important case requiring disclosure of certain evidence, the Court has long recognized some duty to share evidence with a defendant. Since 1935, violations of the Fourteenth Amendment's Due Process Clause have been found when a prosecutor deliberately presents perjured testimony.[206] Furthermore, a Due Process Clause violation occurs when a prosecutor fails to correct the testimony of a witness that he knows to be false.[207] Such subtle factors as the motivation behind a witnesses' testimony might be determinative of guilt or innocence.[208] The prosecutor has an affirmative obligation to ensure the truthfulness of witness testimony so that the defendant's life or liberty is not infringed in violation of the Fourteenth Amendment.[209]

In *Brady*, the Court explicitly required a prosecutor to share certain information with the defendant.[210] *Brady* involved the failure of the prosecution to share statements of an accomplice indicating that he had actually committed the killing, not the defendant.[211] Brady, however, did not discover his accomplice's confession to the actual homicide until after he was found guilty, sentenced to death, and his conviction was affirmed.[212]

The Supreme Court found that the prosecution's failure to divulge the statement in *Brady* violated the Due Process Clause of the Fourteenth Amendment.[213] The Due Process violation occurs when the prosecution fails to disclose evidence that is "material either to guilt or to punishment irrespective of the good faith or bad faith of the prosecution."[214] This duty stems from the importance to society in a defendant receiving a fair trial.[215]

Since the *Brady* decision, the Court has had difficulty determining the circumstances in which a prosecutor must disclose evidence and what standard to apply when this failure occurs. In *U.S. v. Giglio*,[216] its first decision applying the *Brady* requirement, the Court was faced with a situation in which the prosecution failed to disclose a promise made to a key government witness that he would not be charged for his role in the crime if he testified.[217] Because the Government's case depended almost entirely on the testimony of that witness, the Court found that the prosecution was required to share any information that might undermine the witness' credibility.[218] The Court interpreted *Brady* to require a new trial "if the false testimony could . . . in any reasonable likelihood have affected the judgment of the jury."[219]

In *U.S. v. Agurs,*[220] the Supreme Court muddied *Brady*'s requirement of materiality* by creating different standards for different requests made by the defendant.[221] The Court distinguished three different situations in which *Brady* applies and the varying applicable standards.[222] The first situation is one in which a prosecutor presents testimony that she knows or should have known is false.[223] In those cases, the Court applies a strict standard of materiality.[224] The second situation occurs when there is a pretrial request for specific evidence by the defendant.[225] In those cases a reversal is necessary when the suppressed evidence might have affected the outcome of the trial.[226] The third and final situation arises when there is no request for evidence or only a general request for *Brady* evidence.[227] A failure to disclose in that situation causes a constitutional error only if the omitted evidence creates a reasonable doubt that did not otherwise exist.[228]

The materiality standard of *Brady* was cleaned up only nine years later in *U.S. v. Bagley*.[229] The Court disavowed *Agurs*' distinction between the different standards of materiality.[230] The Court collapsed the category requiring a specific request into the category not requiring a request, holding that evidence is material "only if there is a reasonable probability that, had the evidence been disclosed to the defense, the result of the proceeding would have been different."[231] A "reasonable probability" was defined by the Court as a "probably sufficient to undermine the confidence in the outcome."[232]

In a vigorous dissenting opinion, Justice Marshall argued that withheld evidence which might impeach the prosecution's only witness could not be harmless error.[233] Justice Marshall found it necessary to return to the underlying interest that *Brady* sought to protect.[234]

* In the context of motions for a new trial based on the prosecution's failure to disclose exculpatory evidence pursuant to Brady v. Maryland, "material" refers to whether the omission is sufficiently serious to warrant a new trial.

By making the requirements of *Brady* so unclear, Justice Marshall thought prosecutors would have a hard time knowing when certain evidence needed to be disclosed to the defendant.[235] In order to take the burden off prosecutors, Justice Marshall interpreted *Brady* to place an affirmative duty on the prosecutor to disclose all information that might be reasonably favorable to a defendant's case.[236] This requirement of disclosure would be compatible with the underlying goal of a trial, which is to ensure the defendant receives a fair trial.[237] In balancing the dual roles of a prosecutor – one of zealous advocacy and the interest in determining the truth – Justice Marshall found that for the purposes of *Brady* "the prosecutor must abandon his role as an advocate and pore through his files, as objectively as possible, to identify the material that could undermine his case."[238] The standard articulated by the majority allows prosecutors to withhold large amounts of evidence favorable to the defendant.[239] Unlike the majority, Justice Marshall would subject a *Brady* violation to a harmless-error review and reverse unless it is clear beyond a reasonable doubt that the withheld evidence would not have affected the outcome of the trial.[240]

The Supreme Court's interpretation of *Brady* was liberalized in 1995.[241] In determining whether a *Brady* violation has occurred the cumulative effect of the withheld evidence must be examined.[242] If the cumulative effect of the withheld evidence raises a reasonable probability that the outcome of the trial would have been different if disclosed, reversible error occurs.[243] The Court expanded on the definition of materiality espoused by the *Bagley* and reiterated that a defendant does not need to show that he would have been acquitted had the suppressed evidence been disclosed.[244] Evidence is material not if it would cause a different outcome in the trial, but whether without the disclosure the defendant received a trial "resulting in a verdict worthy of confidence."[245]

Despite the disclosures required by *Brady*, juries may still not find out about the motivations behind a jailhouse snitch's testimony. Now, instead of making concrete promises, prosecutors have an incentive to make open-ended promises so as not to trigger mandatory disclosure.[246] Furthermore, the *Brady* test is backwards-looking. Because a police officer may not include necessary information in her written reports or may not share this information with prosecutors, *Brady* material might only be discovered after an individual is convicted.[247] For example, police officers in Chicago and New York City kept two sets of files.[248] The police officers kept the investigative report, but only gave the public version of that report to prosecutors.[249] The *Brady* test also assumes that the prosecution actually has information to disclose. In the recent decision of *Van de Kamp v. Goldstein*,[250] the Supreme Court held that prosecutorial immunity shields prosecutors from liability for failing to properly maintain *Brady* and *Giglio* material.[251] Because of this, prosecutors are not incentivized to maintain comprehensive records concerning jailhouse snitches. Failing to document possible jailhouse snitch impeachment evidence leaves the defendant with no effective way to cross-examine the snitch. Therefore, the defendant cannot undermine the jailhouse snitch's testimony in front of the jury.[252] Even when a defendant discovers exculpatory material, it is unlikely he will be successful in his *Brady* claim. A study of 210 *Brady* claims brought in cases in 2004 found that 83% of those claims were unsuccessful.[253]

A prosecutor also may determine that evidence need only be disclosed when it changes *her* mind about the guilt/innocence of a defendant.[254] Under this test it is extremely unlikely that a prosecutor will disclose jailhouse snitch information, because such testimony merely confirms in the minds of law enforcement and prosecutors that the defendant actually committed the crime. As discussed previously, a prosecutor sees exculpatory evidence through a prism. Due to confirmation hindsight and outcome biases, she may only interpret evidence as supporting her original determination that the defendant is in fact guilty.[255] That being the case, the prosecutor may conclude that a snitch's criminal history, previous statements, and previous experiences providing snitch testimony will not affect the outcome of the trial and need not be disclosed.

While the Due Process Clause requires prosecutors to share certain information prior to going to trial, that same information does not need to be shared prior to the defendant entering into a binding plea agreement.[256] About 90% of those charged with felonies plead guilty.[257] However, this 90% includes innocent individuals.[258] When faced with a jailhouse snitch's concocted confession, an otherwise innocent defendant might feel pressured into pleading guilty. In those instances, not sharing exculpatory evidence and allowing innocent people to plead guilty is incongruous with the fundamental notions of the American justice system.

Three different solutions can help fix disclosure problems in the jailhouse snitch arena. First, District Attorney Offices need to implement guidelines to document their encounters with jailhouse snitches. These guidelines should mirror those of the Los Angeles County District Attorney's Office.[259] Prosecutors ought to establish an information system that includes such things as any promises made to the snitch, any prior statements made by the snitch, and any other times the snitch has or has offered to testify against another inmate. Failing to properly memorialize this information takes the teeth away from the *Brady* doctrine. The effectiveness of *Brady* entirely depends on prosecutors preserving possible exculpatory evidence.

Second, prosecutors can have an open-file discovery policy in cases where they plan to use snitch evidence.[260] This can be mandated in the form of state statutes or prosecutorial office policies. While the Supreme Court has held that *Brady* does not require prosecutors to have a *general* open-file discovery policy, in the *specific* context of jailhouse snitch testimony, such a policy would aid in the search for justice.[261] An open-file discovery policy would lighten the already heavy burden on prosecutors. They would no longer be required to decide whether certain evidence required disclosure, but instead would allow the defendant access to all jailhouse snitch material. This would ensure that the defendant's attorney could adequately cross-examine the jailhouse snitch.

Third, courts should find reversible error every time a prosecutor fails to disclose evidence concerning a jailhouse snitch. Justice Marshall was correct in saying withheld impeachment evidence cannot be harmless error.[262] This is especially true when this withheld evidence would uncover the false testimony of a snitch. Under the current standard articulated by the courts, a defendant's *Brady* claim is rarely successful.[263] Hindsight bias and the backward looking nature of the *Brady* test create high barriers to any defendant who challenges jailhouse snitch testimony. Courts, however, have stressed the importance of impeachment evidence.[264] When a prosecutor offers the testimony of a jailhouse snitch, she essentially asks the jury to believe the snitch's story. Not disclosing evidence that shows the motivations behind the snitch's testimony distorts the jury's deliberation process. To fix this dilemma, courts should lower the bar and find reversible error when the government does not reveal jailhouse snitch evidence to the defendant.

V. Conclusion

There is a common street saying that "snitches get stitches."[265] While this statement may hold true on the streets, inmates know the value of fabricating confessions. If they make up a story about your fellow prisoner confessing, they can receive a reduced sentence, an increase in privileges and a host of other benefits. Often times, because of implicit deals or incomplete discovery, the jury never learns about the snitches' motivation to testify. Permitting unreliable jailhouse snitch testimony not only adversely affects individual defendants, but undermines the fundamental notions of our criminal justice system.

The current criminal justice system does not possess the means to ferret out the truthful snitches from the untruthful snitches. Only a handful of states have legislation concerning the use of jailhouse snitch testimony.[266] Even in those states, the laws do not comprehensively deal with the jailhouse snitch problem. When a jailhouse snitch testifies, states should require pretrial reliability hearings, disclosure of relevant snitch material, independent corroboration, and jury instructions.

Under *Brady*, prosecutors must share certain evidence with the defendant.[267] The current requirements under *Brady* and its progeny, however, still allow prosecutors to convict individuals with unquestioned jailhouse snitch testimony.[268] Prosecutors and courts need to do a better job of exposing the motivations behind a snitch's testimony to the jury.

How many more stories like those of Wilton Dedge or the "Hot Boyz" must come to light before legislatures and the courts adequately address the jailhouse snitch dilemma? Now is the time to tackle these difficult questions before another innocent person is placed behind bars due to untrustworthy jailhouse snitch testimony.

Endnotes

1. Leonard LaPeter, *21 Years, 10 months, 23 days, for a Crime He did not Commit: Guilty Until Proven Innocent*, St. Petersburg Times, Nov. 14, 2004 at 1A.
2. *Id.*
3. *Id.*
4. *Id.*
5. *Id.*
6. *Id.*
7. *Id.*
8. *Id.*
9. *Id.*
10. *Id.*
11. *Id.*
12. *Id.*
13. *Id.*
14. *Id.*
15. The Justice Project, In-custody Informant Testimony: A Policy Review 11 (2007).
16. LaPeter, *supra* note 1.
17. *Id.*
18. The Justice Project, *supra* note 15, at 11.
19. *Id.*
20. *Id.*
21. LaPeter, *supra* note 1. Specifically, Zacke had tried to hire two different hit men to kill a witness in a drug smuggling case against him. He then tried to hire another hit men to murder one of the original hit men. In jail, he then attempted to hire a fellow inmate to kill the state attorney who originally prosecuted him. *Id.*

22. *Id.*
23. *Id.*
24. *Id.*
25. *Id.*
26. *Id.*
27. *Id.*
28. The Justice Project, *supra* note 15, at 12.
29. *Id.*
30. *Id.*
31. *Id.* Zacke later recanted his testimony in an interview with a freelance writer. *Id.*
32. *Id.* While Zacke successfully reduced his original sentence, in 2005 a jury convicted him of raping his adopted daughter and he was sentenced to five consecutive life sentences. The Justice Project, In-custody Informant Testimony: A Policy Review 12 (2007).
33. LaPeter, *supra* note 1. DNA testing was not originally available in 1981. *Id.*
34. *Id.*
35. *Id.*
36. *Id.*
37. *Id.*
38. *See* The Justice Project, *supra* note 15, at 13.
39. This paper addresses the problems of jailhouse snitches and does not specifically deal with the problems of using snitches who are not in custody. Many of the solutions proposed in this paper, however, also apply to snitches in general. An individual may also start out as a jailhouse snitch and then turn into a street snitch when released. *See 48 Hours Mystery: Hannibal Unmasked* (CBS television broadcast Apr. 24, 2010) *available at* http://www.cbsnews.com/video/watch/?id=6428964n (Scott Kimball made up a story while in federal prison about a

murder-for-hire plot involving his cellmate's girlfriend. Based on his story, Kimball was released from prison and worked as a paid FBI informant. While working as an informant, Kimball murdered four people.).

40. Northwestern University School of Law Center on Wrongful Convictions, The Snitch System: How Snitch Testimony Sent Randy Steidl and Other Innocent Americans to Death Row 3 (2004); *see also* David R. Dow, Executed on a Technicality: Lethal Injustice on America's Death Row 120 (2005) (noting that in more than two dozen capital cases, Texas prosecutors have relied heavily on jailhouse snitches).

41. *Id*; *see also* Samuel R. Gross et al., *Exonerations in the United States 1989 Through 2003*, 95 J. Crim. L. & Criminology 523, 543-44 (2005) (explaining that roughly 50% of wrongful murder convictions involved perjurious testimony, usually by jailhouse snitch or other witnesses who received benefits for their testimony).

42. Because men make up approximately 93% of the prison population, I will use the male pronoun when referring to jailhouse snitches. Bureau of Justice Statistics, Prisoners in 2008 2 (2009). That is not to say that every jailhouse snitch is a man. *See* John Grisham, The Innocent Man (2006) (in John Grisham's nonfiction book regarding a wrongful conviction in Oklahoma, the jailhouse snitch was a woman).

43. *See* Cal. Penal Code § 1127a (2009); 725 Ill. Comp. Stat. 5/115-21 (Supp. 2009); Tex. Code Crim. Proc. Ann. art. 38.075 (Vernon 2009).

44. *See* Alexandra Natapoff, *Beyond Unreliable: How Snitching Contribute to Wrongful Convictions*, 37 Golden Gate U. L. Rev. 107, 111-12 (2006).

45. *See generally* Keith A. Findley & Michael S. Scott, *The Multiple Dimensions of Tunnel Vision in Criminal Cases*, 2006 Wis. L. Rev. 291 (2006).

46. *See* ROBERT M. BLOOM, RATTING: THE USE AND ABUSE OF INFORMANTS IN THE AMERICAN JUSTICE SYSTEM 63 (2002).
47. COUNTY OF LOS ANGELES, CALIFORNIA, 1989-90 LOS ANGELES COUNTY GRAND JURY: INVESTIGATION OF THE INVOLVEMENT OF JAIL HOUSE INFORMANTS IN THE CRIMINAL JUSTICE SYSTEM IN LOS ANGELES COUNTY 1 (1990), *available at* http://www.ccfaj.org/documents/reports/jailhouse/expert/1989-1990%20LA%20County%20Grand%20Jury%20Report.pdf.
48. *Id.*
49. *Id.* at 10.
50. *Id.* at 18.
51. The grand jury found that the Los Angeles Sheriff Department houses all the snitches together in the same area that is known as the "snitch tank" within the jail. *Id.* at 9.
52. "Book" means to provide information to law enforcement. *Id.* at 16.
53. COUNTY OF LOS ANGELES, CALIFORNIA, *supra* note 47, at 18.
54. 448 F. Supp. 2d 750 (W.D. La. 2006).
55. *Id.* at 751.
56. *Id.*
57. *Id.*
58. *Id.*
59. *Id.* at 751-52. The government already had 16 jailhouse snitches lined up to testify against the Colombs. Radley Balko, *Guilty Before Proven Innocent: How Police Harassment, Jailhouse Snitches, and a Runaway War on Drugs Imprisoned an Innocent Family*, REASON, May 2008, *available at* http://reason.com/archives/2008/04/14/guilty-before-proven-innocent.
60. *Colomb*, 448 F.Supp.2d at 752.
61. *Id.* Although there are no transcripts from the trial, the jailhouse snitches claimed they had sold narcotics to the

Colombs. The government offered no evidence to corroborate the snitches' testimonies. *See* Balko, *supra* note 59.

62. *See Colomb*, 448 F. Supp. 2d at 752-53.
63. *Id.* at 753.
64. This U.S. Attorney, Joseph T. Mickel, was not involved in the Colombs' trial, but worked in the same office. *See* Balko, *supra* note 59.
65. *See Colomb*, 448 F. Supp. 2d at 753.
66. *Id.*
67. *Id.*
68. *Id.* at 757.
69. *Id.* at 753.
70. Balko, *supra* note 59.
71. *Id.*
72. *Id.*
73. *Colomb*, 448 F. Supp. 2d at 753-54.
74. *Id.*
75. *Id.* at 756.
76. Balko, *supra* note 59.
77. *Colomb*, 448 F. Supp. 2d at 756.
78. *Id.*
79. *Id.* at 756-57.
80. *Id.* at 757.
81. *Id.* at 750, 758.
82. *Id.* at 755.
83. *Id.* at 758.
84. Balko, *supra* note 59.
85. *See Colomb*, 448 F. Supp. 2d at 753 n.6; United States v. Jackson, 254 Fed. Appx. 434, 442-44 (5th Cir. 2007).

86. *Jackson*, 254 Fed. Appx at 441-42; *See Colomb*, 448 F. Supp. 2d at 753 n.6.
87. *Jackson*, 254 Fed. Appx at 442-43.
88. *Id.* at 443
89. *Id.*
90. *Id.* at 442.
91. *Id.* at 444-45.
92. *Id.*
93. *Jackson*, 254 Fed. Appx. at 445-48.
94. *See* Ted Rohrlich & Robert W. Stewart, *Jailhouse Snitches; Trading Lies for Freedom*, L.A. TIMES, Apr. 16, 1989, *available at* http://www.snitching.org/docs/Trading_Lies_for_Freedom.pdf. Access to the internet might also increase the jailhouse snitches' ability to fabricate confessions. *See* Valerie Alter, *Jailhouse Informants: A Lesson in E-Snitching*, 10 J. TECH. L. & POL'Y 223 (2005).
95. *Id.*
96. *Id.*
97. *Id.*
98. *Id.*
99. *Id.*
100. *Id.*
101. *Id.*
102. U.S. v. Cervantes-Pacheco, 826 F.2d 310, 315 (5th Cir. 1987).
103. *See* Northern Mariana Islands v. Bowie, 243 F.3d 1109, 115 (9th Cir. 2001). The mission of the justice system is "utterly derailed by unchecked lying witnesses, and by any law enforcement officer who finds it tactically advantageous to turn a blind eye to the manifest potential for malevolent disinformation." *Id.*

104. *See* Carriger v. Stewart, 132 F.3d 463, 479 (9th Cir. 1997) ("Criminals who are rewarded by the government for their testimony are inherently untrustworthy, and their use triggers an obligation to disclose material information to protect the defendant from being the victim of a perfidious bargain between the state and its witness."); *see also* Lee v. U.S., 343 U.S. 747, 757 (1952) ("The use of informers, accessories, accomplices, false friends, or any of the other betrayals which are 'dirty business' may raise serious questions of credibility. To the extent that they do, a defendant is entitled to broad latitude to probe credibility by cross-examination and to have the issues submitted to the jury with careful instructions.").
105. *See* United States v. Swiderski, 539 F.2d 854, 860 (2nd Cir. 1976); D'Agostino v. State, 823 P.2d 283, 284 (Nev. 1991).
106. *See D'Agostino*, 823 P.2d at 284 ("A legally unsophisticated jury has little knowledge as to the types of pressures and inducements that jail inmates are under to 'cooperate' with the state and to say anything that is 'helpful' to the state's case.").
107. Natapoff, *supra* note 44, at 111-12.
108. Ellen Yaroshefsky, *Cooperation with Federal Prosecutors: Experiences of Truth Telling and Embellishment*, 68 FORDHAM L. REV. 917, 921 (1999).
109. *Id.* at 932-33.
110. *See* Keith A. Findley & Michael S. Scott, *The Multiple Dimensions of Tunnel Vision in Criminal Cases*, 2006 WIS. L. REV. 291, 299-304 (2006) (describing how Steven Avery was prosecuted and convicted of rape based on a victim's eyewitness testimony despite strong alibi evidence, and another likely suspect who was well known to law enforcement).
111. Findley, *supra* note 110, at 292.
112. *Id.* at 293.
113. *Id.* at 358-59.
114. *Id.* at 307.

115. Individuals with confirmation bias only look for information that supports their conclusions and try to avoid conflicting information. Hindsight and outcome bias makes law enforcement and prosecutors more likely to view their original decision as correct after they attain a conviction. *Id.* at 309-22.
116. *Id.* at 323-27.
117. *Id.* at 326.
118. *See* Findley & Scott, *supra* note 110, at 327-28.
119. *See* United States v. Bagley, 473 U.S. 667 (1985).
120. *Id.* at 351.
121. *Id.* at 352.
122. County of Los Angeles, California, *supra* note 47, at 57-68; *see also* Ted Rohrlich, *Authorities Go Fishing for Jailhouse Confessions*, L.A. Times, Mar. 4, 1990, at A1.
123. Commonwealth v. Moose, 602 A.2d 1265, 1267 (Pa. 1992).
124. *Id.* at 1266-68. The snitch sat in county jail for three years waiting to be sentenced. *Id.* at 1270.
125. 377 U.S. 201 (1964).
126. *Id.* at 206.
127. *Id.* at 207.
128. 447 U.S. 264, 265 (1980).
129. *Id.* at 266.
130. *Id.*
131. *Id.* at 267.
132. *Id.*
133. *Id.* at 268.
134. *Id.* at 270-71.
135. *Id.*
136. *Id.*
137. *Id.*

138. *Id.* at 273-74. The Court found that an incarcerated individual might be "particularly susceptible to the ploys of undercover government agents." *Id.* at 274.

139. *Id.* at 271.

140. *Id.* at 274.

141. 477 U.S. 436 (1986).

142. *Id.* at 439.

143. *Id.*

144. *Id.*

145. *Id.* at 440.

146. *Id.*

147. *Id.* at 459-61.

148. *Id.* at 459.

149. *See* Depree v. Thomas, 946 F.2d 784, 793 (11th Cir. 1991); Lightbourne v. Dugger, 829 F.2d 1012, 1019 (11th Cir. 1987); United States v. Johnson, 4 F.3d 904, 910 (10th Cir. 1993); State v. Hernandez, 842 S.W.2d 306, 313 (Tex. App.—San Antonio 1992, pet. ref'd).

150. *See* United States v. LaBare, 191 F.3d 60, 65-66 (1st Cir. 1999); United States v. Birball, 113 F.3d 342, 346 (2nd Cir. 1997); United States v. Panza, 750 F.2d 1141, 1152 (2nd Cir. 1984).

151. *See Henry*, 447 U.S. at 271.

152. *See* United States v. Sampol, 636 F.2d 621, 638 (D.C. Cir. 1980); Maia Goodell, Note, *Government Responsibility for the Acts of Jailhouse Informants Under the Sixth Amendment*, 101 Mich. L. Rev. 2525, 2532-38 (2003). The government creates an "Informant at large" when it implicitly or explicitly tasks an inmate to snitch on fellow prisoners. *Id.*at 2532. For example, the snitch in *Commonwealth v. Moose* was a "snitch at large." *See Moose*, 602 A.2d at 1266-68.

153. *See Wilson*, 447 U.S. at 459; Westbrook v. State, 29 S.W.3d 103, 118 (Tex. Crim. App. 2000).

154. *See Westbrook*, 29 S.W.3d at 118.

155. *See Attorney General's Guidelines Regarding the Use of FBI Confidential Sources, available at* http://www.fas.org/irp/agency/doj/fbi/chs-guidelines.pdf.

156. *Id.*

157. California Department of Justice – Division of Criminal Law, *Jailhouse Informant Policy, available at* http://www.aclu.org/files/pdfs/drugpolicy/cadojinformantpolicy.pdf.

158. American Bar Association Section of Criminal Justice, *Report to the House of Delegates, available at* http://meetings.abanet.org/webupload/commupload/CR209700/relatedresources/ABAInformant%27sRecommendations.pdf.

159. *Id.*

160. Specifically, the prosecutor should review the following factors: (1) the extent to which the statement is confirmed, (2) the specificity of the alleged statement, (3) how detailed the statement is and whether it contains information only known to the perpetrator, (4) whether or not the statement contains information that the snitch could have learned independently and not through the perpetrator, (5) the general character of the snitch, (6) in request or agreement for benefits because the snitch agreed to testify, (7) whether the snitch has given reliable information to law enforcement in the past, (8) whether the snitch has ever previously claimed to receive statement while in custody, (9) whether the snitch has every testified in a previous trial, (10) whether the snitch any record of the statement made by the accused, (11) the circumstances under which that record was taken, (12) how the report of the statement was taken by the police, (13) any other evidence that may increase or decrease the credibility of the snitch, and (14) any relevant information contained in available registry of informers. *Id.*

161. Alexandra Natapoff, Snitching: Criminal Informants and the Erosion of American Justice 187-88 (2009).

162. *See* Northwestern University School of Law Center on Wrongful Convictions, *supra*, note 40, at 15.

163. *Id.* at 103-04. The U.S. Department of Justice, however, reports that in 2007, 14% of all federal defendants received a sentencing departure for cooperation. *Id.* at 104.

164. *Id.*

165. *Id.* at 179-80.

166. Natapoff, *supra*, note 160, at 192-94; Northwestern University School of Law Center on Wrongful Convictions, *supra*, note 40 at 15; *See* The Justice Project, *supra* note 16, at 3.

167. *See* Natapoff, *supra*, note 160, at 192-94.

168. Los Angeles County District Attorney's Office, Legal Policies Manual 187 (2005), *available at* http://www.aclu.org/files/pdfs/drugpolicy/ladapolicyoninformants.pdf.

169. *Id.*

170. *Id.* at 187-88.

171. *Id.* at 188.

172. *Id.* at 189. Under the guidelines, the District Attorney's Office can only disclose confidential information with unknown prosecutors or law enforcement members after receiving verification and then only if there is a need to know basis for the information. *Id.*

173. *Id.* at 190. These records include all notes, memoranda, computer printouts, or any records of promises made, payments made, or rewards given to jailhouse snitches, the last known location of the snitch, records relating to the cell assignments of the snitch and all memoranda concerning the snitch. *Id.*

174. Kyles v. Whitley, 514 U.S. 419, 437 (1995).

175. *See* 725 ILCS 5/115-21 (Supp. 2009).

176. *Id.*

177. *Id.*

178. *Id.*

179. Dodd v. State, 993 P.2d 778, 780 (2000).

180. *Id.* at 782. The snitch had recanted after a preliminary hearing only to later assert the truthfulness of his testimony. *Id.* Dodd's appeal specifically dealt with the trial court's refusal to let him admit two letters written by the snitch regarding his recantation. In the first letter, written to an investigator involved in another murder case, the snitch stated that despite his recantation he still believed the District Attorney's Office would offer him leniency. *Id.* On the same day, the snitch wrote another letter to an assistant in the District Attorney's Office about a different murder case. *Id.* The snitch told the assistant that he was no longer "afraid … and no longer [has] to lie … for anyone in this world-especially the OK County D.A.'s Office." *Id.* The snitch also said that, "the testimony from me in this case about a confession that you both asked & wanted from me-you'll not get-because as you very well know-there wasn't one." *Id.*

181. *Id.* at 785.

182. *Id.* at 783.

183. *Id.* at 784.

184. *Id.*

185. *See* Natapoff, *supra,* note 160, at 194-95; The Justice Project, *supra* note 16, at 3.

186. *See* Fed. R. Evid. 104(a).

187. *See* Tex. R. Evid. 104(a); N.J. R. Evid. 104(a); Ohio R. Evid. 104(a).

188. *See* Natapoff, *supra* note 44 at 112-29 (offering sample motions and memorandums in support of pre-trial snitch reliability hearings and citing *Daubert v. Merrell Dow Pharmaceuticals,* 509 U.S. 579 (1993)).

189. *See* George C. Harris, *Testimony for Sale: The Law and Ethics of Snitches and Experts,* 28 Pepp. L. Rev. 1, 3-4, 31, 49-58, 71 (2000).

190. *See* NATAPOFF, *supra*, note 160, at 186-87.

191. *Id.*

192. *See* THE JUSTICE PROJECT, *supra* note 15, at 4.

193. *See* Act of May 20, 2009, 81st Leg., R.S., ch. 1422, § 1, art. 38.075, 2009 Tex. Gen. Laws 4480.

194. *Id.*

195. *Id.*

196. *See* art. 38.075.

197. *Program Updates & Final Legislative Wrap-Up*, (Tex. Criminal Justice Coal., Austin, Tex.) 2009, at 4.

198. Article 38.14 of the Texas Criminal Code of Procedure requires the testimony of an accomplice to be corroborated by other independent evidence connecting the defendant to the crime. TEX. CODE CRIM. PROC. ANN. art. 38.14 (Vernon 2009).

199. *See* NATAPOFF, *supra*, note 160, at 197-99; THE JUSTICE PROJECT, *supra* note 16, at 5.

200. *See* State v. Patterson, 886 A.2 777, 790 (Conn. 2005); State v. Grimes, 982 P.2d 1037, 1042 (Mont. 1999); Dodd v. State, 993 P.2d 778, 784 (Okla. Crim. App. 2000); CAL. PENAL CODE § 1127a (2009). It should be noted, however, that some of these states differ as to when the jury instruction is necessary. For example, Connecticut requires a jury instruction whenever a jailhouse snitch testifies, while in Montana a jury instruction is only required when the informant testifies for personal gain rather than an "an independent law enforcement purpose." *Compare Patterson*, 886 A.2d at 790 (requiring a jury instruction when a jailhouse informant testifies), *with Grimes*, 982 P.2d at 1042 (holding "that when a government informant motivated by personal gain rather than some independent law enforcement purpose provides testimony, a cautionary instruction is the more prudent course of action").

201. 373 U.S. 83 (1963).

202. *See generally* Brady v. Maryland, 373 U.S. 83 (1963); Giglio v. United States, 405 U.S. 150 (1972); United States v. Agurs, 427 U.S. 97 (1976); *Bagley*, 473 U.S. 667; Kyles v. Whitley, 514 U.S. 419 (1985); Strickler v. Greene, 527 U.S. 263 (1999).
203. *See Bagley*, 473 U.S. at 696 (Marshall, J., dissenting); *see also* Standards for Criminal Justice: Prosecution Function and Defense Function Standard 3-1.2(c) (3d ed. 1993).
204. *Bagley*, 473 U.S. at 696-97.
205. 373 U.S. 83 (1963).
206. Mooney v. Holohan, 294 U.S. 103 (1935).
207. Napue v. Illinois, 360 U.S. 264 (1959).
208. *Id.* at 269.
209. *See id.*
210. *Brady*, 373 U.S. at 86.
211. *Id.* at 84.
212. *Id.*
213. *Id.* at 88.
214. *Id.*
215. *Id.* at 87 ("Society wins not only when the guilty are convicted but when criminal trials are fair; our system of the administration of justice suffers when any accused is treated unfairly.").
216. 405 U.S. 150 (1972).
217. *Giglio*, 405 U.S. at 151.
218. *Id.* at 154.
219. *Id.*
220. 472 U.S. 97 (1976).
221. *See Agurs*, 427 U.S. 97.
222. *Id.* at 103-12.
223. *Id.* at 103-04.
224. *Id.*

225. *Id.* at 104.
226. *Id.* at 106.
227. *Id.* at 107.
228. *Id.* at 114.
229. *See Bagley*, 473 U.S. 667.
230. *Id.* at 682.
231. *Id.*
232. *Id.*
233. *Id.* at 685.
234. *Id.* at 696-704 (Marshall, J., dissenting).
235. *Id.*
236. *Bagley*, 473 U.S. at 695-96.
237. *Id.*
238. *Id.* at 696-97.
239. *Id.* at 701-02.
240. *Id.* at 696.
241. *See Kyles*, 514 U.S. 419.
242. For example, in the *Kyles* case the prosecution withheld six eyewitness statements, records of an informant's initial call to the police, the tape recording between the informant and officers, one of the statements given by the informant, evidence which indicated Kyles was not at the scene of the crime, an internal police memorandum calling for the seizure of Kyles' trash after the informant suggested evidence might be found there, and evidence indicating the informant had committed other crimes at the crime scene. *Id.* at 428-29.
243. *Id.* at 422.
244. *Id.* at 434.
245. *Id.*

246. *See* R. Michael Cassidy, *"Soft Words of Hope:" Giglio, Accomplice Witnesses, and the Problem of Implied Inducements*, 8 Nw. U. L. Rev. 1129, 1131-32 (2004).

247. *See* Natapoff, *supra* note 160, at 93-94; *see also* Randall Coyne, *Dead Wrong in Oklahoma*, 42 Tulsa L. Rev. 209, 215 n.76 (2006) ("Police investigators have no legal duty to put all information they gather into written reports. Consequently, once the police have decided that a particular suspect is guilty, evidence inconsistent with this theory--and potentially exculpatory--is likely to be disregarded and not written down.").

248. *See* Natapoff, *supra*, note 160, at 23.

249. *Id.*

250. 129 S.Ct. 855 (2009).

251. *Id.* at 858-59.

252. *See* Hoffa v. United States, 383 U.S. 293, 311 (1966) ("The established safeguards of the Anglo-American legal system leave the veracity of a witness to be tested by cross-examination.").

253. *See* Stephanos Bibas, *The Story of Brady v. Maryland: From Adversarial Gamesmanship Toward the Search for Innocence?*, *in* Criminal Procedure Stories (Carol Steiker ed., 2005).

254. *See id.*

255. *See supra* text accompanying note 115.

256. U.S. v. Ruiz, 536 U.S. 626 (2002).

257. Scott W. Howe, *The Value of Plea Bargaining*, 58 Oka. L. Rev. 599, 600 2005).

258. Rodney Uphoff, *Convicting the Innocent: Aberration or Systemic Problem?*, 2006 Wis. L. Rev. 739, 796-802 (2006).

259. *See supra* p. 21 and note 169.

260. *See* Peter A. Joy, *Brady and Jailhouse Informants: Responding to Injustice*, 57 Case W. Res. L. Rev. 619, 640-42 (2007)

(advocating that head prosecutors adopt an open file discovery policy).

261. *See Kyles*, 514 U.S. at 437 ("We have never held that the Constitution demands an open file policy (however such a policy might work out in practice)."); *see also Strickler*, 527 U.S. at 283 n.23.

262. *See Bagley*, 473 U.S. at 695 (Marshall, J., dissenting).

263. *See supra* p. 32 (in 210 *Brady* claims brought in 2004, 83% of the claims failed).

264. *See Napue*, 30 U.S. at 269; *Giglio*, 405 U.S. at 154; *Bagley*, 473 U.S. at 695.

265. *See* Urban Dictionary, http://www.urbandictionary.com/define.php?term=snitches+get+stitches (last visited May 1, 2010); *see also Jim Rome is Burning: Delonte West Correspondence Piece* (ESPN television broadcast Apr. 24, 2009), *available at* http://www.twitvid.com/D3D97.

266. *See supra* note 43.

267. *See supra* Part IV.

268. *See* Frazier v. United States, 419 F.2d 1161, 1176 (D.C. Cir. 1969) (Burger, C.J., dissenting) ("Guilt or innocence becomes irrelevant in the criminal trial as we flounder in a morass of artificial rules poorly conceived and often impossible of application.").

IV. Improving the Adversary System through Discovery

Reciprocal Discovery: Eliminating "Trial by Surprise" for Both Sides

Ryan King*

I. Introduction

When it comes to criminal pre-trial discovery in Texas, the district attorney's offices in some of Texas' biggest counties have voluntarily enacted what is known as an "open file" policy.[1] Under this system, they provide the contents of their prosecution files to the defense counsel, although Texas law does not require them to do so.[2] Recently, there has been a growing movement to statutorily require such "open file" policies. Focusing on prosecutorial disclosure,[3] however, less attention has been paid to defense disclosure and under what circumstances defense attorneys should be required to open their files to the prosecution.

In 2005, the Texas Senate attempted to pass Senate Bill 560, which would have created disclosure obligations for both the prosecution and defense attorneys that far surpass current requirements.[4] It would have

* Ryan King, University of Houston Law Center, J.D., 2010; Yale University, B.A. Political Science, 2005. I would like to thank Professor Thompson for her help and guidance on this project, as well as the Tarrant County District Attorney's Office for demonstrating and explaining their discovery procedures and sparking the idea for this paper.

statutorily mandated discovery equivalent to an "open file" policy for the prosecution, including disclosure of witness statements and police reports.[5] But it would also have required defense counsel to turn over any witness statements they collected in their investigation, as well as alert the prosecution to any affirmative defenses they planned to introduce at trial (i.e., alibi, self-defense, mistake, etc).[6]

But the bill failed to pass.[7] This proposed law deserves further consideration, especially as it pertains to the disclosure of witness statements for parties, police reports, and affirmative defenses. Requiring disclosure of these types of information for both the defense and prosecution will better enable courts to fulfill their role in seeking the truth and discourage trial by surprise.

Part II begins with a discussion of the classic debate of the 1950s and 1960s over the proper scope of criminal discovery laws, the prosecutor's constitutional discovery requirements, and the prosecutor's role in criminal discovery. Part III examines the rise and constitutionality of alibi notice statutes, as well as the defense attorney's role in discovery. Part IV examines the evolution of Texas discovery law, its current law, and the proposed changes in the failed Senate Bill 560 of 2005, concluding that the bill's purposes should be reconsidered, especially as they relate to disclosure of witness statements for both defense and prosecution, disclosure of police reports, and defense notification to the prosecution of its intended defenses at trial.

II. The Classic Discovery Debate of the 1950s and 1960s

The original common law rule of pretrial discovery in American criminal courts held that, unless legislation provided otherwise, the judiciary lacked any inherent authority to order pretrial discovery in criminal cases.[8] In nearly all states during the early 1900s, criminal discovery operated only through the informal mutual exchange of information between the defense attorney and prosecutor or through pre-trial hearings.[9] But by the late 1930s, formal pretrial discovery rules were beginning to be adopted by many jurisdictions. By the 1940s, a majority of the states had adopted their own criminal pretrial discovery rules by recognizing a discretionary authority of the trial court to control the trial process.[10] Most of the statutes focused on the court's discretion to require the prosecutor to reveal what evidence the state had in its possession; however, some states required defense counsel to provide the prosecutor with advance notice if they intended to present an alibi defense.[11]

During the same time frame, many more jurisdictions were adopting full and open pretrial discovery statutes in the civil arena.[12] With the liberalization of civil discovery that allowed for the disclosure of depositions, interrogatories, production of documents and the like, observers around the country began discuss whether the same type of expansion should be adopted in the criminal courts.[13] Throughout the 1950s and 1960s, one of the "classic debates in the field of criminal procedure" revolved around how expansive defense discovery could and should be, with suggestions ranging from making it wide open to maintaining the status quo.[14]

As a long-time champion of broad criminal defense discovery, Supreme Court Justice Brennan argued that the criminal trial should seek to underscore a "quest for the truth," which was best achieved through expansive discovery similar to civil trials.[15] But unlike the civil arena, there are additional concerns in criminal trials: the presumption of innocence and the privilege against self-incrimination.[16] Proponents of broader discovery rules seized on these limitations, arguing that the defense could not be required to disclose anything without violating these rights, but that the truth seeking function would still be served if the prosecution had broader disclosure obligations.[17]

Opponents of broad discovery rules argued that the adversary system relied on equal discovery for both sides.[18] If both sides could not benefit, then neither side should benefit.[19] They also pointed to other constitutional safeguards provided for the defendant that put the government at a disadvantage.[20] For example, the defendant has a right to remain silent and therefore is "immune from question or comment on his silence."[21] The prosecution's burden of proof is "beyond a reasonable doubt," of which all twelve jurors must be convinced.[22] Also, the rules of evidence and the exclusionary rule can prevent improper evidence from being presented to a jury in determining guilt.[23] In the end, they argued that these safeguards were offset by any informational imbalances and available resources in favor of the government.[24] They wanted to maintain the status quo.

Furthermore, opponents of broad discovery argued that if prosecutors were required to disclose more information to defendants, it would increase the chance of perjury by the defendant on the witness stand and precipitate an increase in witness intimidation out of court. If a defendant has all the prosecution's information, then he may craft his story with false testimony to make his defense more believable and take advantage of false weaknesses in the case.[25] Also, if he knows the identities of the witnesses against him (as in civil cases), then he may bribe or intimidate them so they will not testify against him.[26] Since the government may not try a person twice for the same crime,[27] defendants would have an incentive to commit perjury themselves and harass witnesses to thwart the prosecution. This is especially true for the most violent criminals, who will likely be facing long prison terms anyway. Critics of these arguments viewed the perjury argument as an "old hobgoblin," arguing that the civil discovery regime did not increase odds of successful perjury or witness intimidation and that it would be no different in the criminal system.[28] Furthermore, they argued that the truth seeking function of the court still outweighed these concerns.

This debate, which took place concurrently with the expansion of civil discovery, shifted the balance in favor of those who wanted more pretrial discovery for the defense. In 1966, the Supreme Court commented on the matter, emphasizing "the growing realization that disclosure, rather than suppression, of relevant materials ordinarily promotes the proper administration of criminal justice" and noting "the expanding body of materials . . . favoring disclosure in criminal cases."[29] Modern discovery statutes all provide for some form of disclosure by the defense, and the trend throughout the years has been to broaden the prosecution's disclosure obligations.[30]

While this debate during the 1950s and 1960s convinced jurisdictions that the defense needed to be provided with some prosecutorial disclosure mechanisms, the practices across jurisdictions varied widely. While many saw reducing "trial by surprise" as a good thing, there is nothing in the Constitution that speaks to reducing "trial by surprise." In fact, the Supreme Court and the federal courts have continued to hold that in most instances "discovery which is unavailable pursuant to statute may not be ordered based on principles of due process because 'there is no general constitutional right to discovery in criminal cases.'"[31] Texas courts have reiterated this same position.[32] However, there is one major exception: When the prosecutor has evidence that tends to show the innocence of the defendant, they must turn that evidence over to the defense prior to trial.[33] As this paper demonstrates, this rule gives little guidance to a prosecutor.

A. Constitutional Discovery Requirements

In 1963, the United States Supreme Court issued its landmark holding in the case of *Brady v. Maryland*,[34] permanently shaping the prosecution's required disclosures of evidence to defense counsel. The facts of the case are as follows: Low on money, Brady and Boblit hatched a scheme to rob a bank; however, they needed a fast getaway car, so they conspired to steal the new Ford Fairlane that one of Brady's friends, William Brooks, had recently bought.[35] One night, Brady and Boblit placed a log in the road, and waited for Brooks to drive by.[36] When William drove up, Brady and Boblit knocked him unconscious as he got out of his car to remove the log.[37] They took his car, drove him to a secluded field ten miles away, where either Brady or Boblit strangled Brooks to death with a shirt.[38]

Both men gave a series of statements prior to trial: Brady claimed that both he and Boblit agreed to kill William, but that Boblit actually committed the murder without Brady's help.[39] In a series of four out of five statements, Boblit claimed that Brady had committed the murder. However, in a crucial fifth statement, Boblit admitted to knocking the victim, William, unconscious and strangling William himself.[40] Prior to trial, Brady's defense counsel requested to examine Boblit's extrajudicial statements but only examined the first four; the prosecution withheld the fifth statement incriminating Boblit.[41]

Both men were tried separately for murder in the perpetration of robbery and the juries found them both guilty.[42] Under Maryland law, the jury decides whether the punishment will be life imprisonment or death.[43] Despite the fact that at trial each blamed the other for actually killing William, both juries sentenced the men to death.[44]

Later, Brady's appellate counsel uncovered the previously undisclosed fifth statement and moved for a new trial based on this newly discovered evidence which had been suppressed by the prosecution.[45] The Supreme Court reviewed the appeal and held that "the suppression by the prosecution of evidence favorable to an accused upon request violates due process where the evidence is material either to guilt or to punishment, irrespective of the good faith or bad faith of the prosecution."[46] The majority opinion by Justice Douglas reasoned that "a prosecution that withholds evidence on demand of an accused which, if made available, would tend to exculpate him or reduce the penalty helps shape a trial that bears heavily on the defendant."[47] Conceding that the prosecution in this case did not withhold the evidence as a "result of guile," the Court nonetheless expressed the opinion that "[s]ociety wins not only when the guilty are convicted but when criminal trials are fair; our system of the administration of justice suffers when any accused is treated unfairly."[48]

The basic premise of *Brady* still holds true: Due process requires access to evidence that casts doubt on the prosecution's case or proves the innocence of the accused. In the cases that followed *Brady*, however, the Supreme Court severely limited the ability of a defendant to benefit in any practical way from the rule in *Brady*. Instead of providing prosecutors with any practical rules for determining what evidence must be disclosed before trial, *Brady* and its progeny merely established an appellate review process by which courts can monitor whether the *failure* to disclose exculpatory evidence rose to the level of reversible error.

Nearly 20 years later, the Court severely limited the reach of *Brady* in the 1985 case of *United States v. Bagley*.[49] Bagley was indicted for violation of federal narcotics and firearms statutes, and prior to trial his counsel filed a discovery motion requesting "any deals, promises or inducements made to [government] witnesses in exchange for their testimony."[50] In response, the government produced two signed affidavits by their principal witnesses recounting their undercover dealings with Bagley, which also contained statements that the affidavits were made without any "threats, rewards or promises of reward."[51] The two witnesses testified and Bagley was convicted of the narcotics charges (but not the firearms charges).[52]

After Bagley's conviction, his counsel received copies of contracts made between the Bureau of Alcohol, Tobacco and Firearms (ATF) and the two adverse witnesses that contradicted the affidavits statement that no rewards were given for their testimony.[53] In fact, the later-discovered contracts revealed that the ATF agreed to pay the witnesses based on the information they furnished.[54] Defense counsel filed a *Brady* motion based on the non-disclosure of the contracts, arguing that the defense could have used this information for impeachment.[55] The district court disagreed, finding that "beyond a reasonable doubt" the disclosure of the contracts would not have affected the outcome of the case.[56] The appellate court agreed with Bagley and reversed his conviction, stating that automatic reversal was required when the government failed to disclose requested impeachment evidence that respondent could have used to conduct an effective cross-examination.[57]

In the end, the Supreme Court reversed the appellate court.[58] The majority disagreed with the proposition that non-disclosure of impeachment evidence requires automatic reversal;[59] rather, constitutional error requiring reversal only occurs when the non-disclosed evidence is "material" to the outcome of the trial.[60] The court defined "materiality" under the *Brady* standard as "a reasonable probability that, had the evidence been disclosed to the defense, the result of the proceeding would have been different" and defined a "reasonable probability" as a probability that is sufficient to undermine confidence in the outcome.[61] According to the Court, this standard applies to prosecutorial failure to disclose favorable evidence to the defense, whether or not the defense makes a request for that evidence.[62] Therefore, if a reviewing court's confidence in the case is undermined to the extent it feels that the evidence would have changed the outcome of the case, it can reverse the conviction even if the defense never requested the evidence.[63] The decision demonstrates much confidence in the ability of reviewing courts to determine whether a judge or jury would have decided the case differently. Thus, while not directly narrowing the reach of *Brady*, the Court effectively narrowed a defendant's right to a new trial in the face of clear *Brady* violations.

In 1995, the Supreme Court decided *Kyles v. Whitley*,[64] a case which underscores the potential for judicial arbitrariness in deciding how much evidence will be considered legally "material." Kyles was convicted of first-degree murder and sentenced to death by a Louisiana jury.[65] After his appeal, it was discovered that the State did not disclose the following evidence: (1) six contemporaneous eyewitness statements taken by the police that had varied descriptions of the killer; (2) statements made by "Beanie," a police informant who did not testify at trial; and (3) a computer printout of the license plates of the cars present at the scene of the crime that did not include Kyles' license plate.[66] Kyles was denied relief by all state level courts and subsequently filed a federal habeas petition.[67] He argued that withholding the evidence favorable to his defense violated his due process rights under *Brady*.[68] Both the federal district court and the Fifth Circuit Court of Appeals denied him relief.[69] However, the Supreme Court disagreed with all four reviewing courts and remanded the case to the trial court for a new trial.[70] In the Court's view, the "disclosure of the suppressed evidence to competent counsel would have made a different result reasonably probable."[71]

The Court found that pretrial disclosure of the statements of the eyewitnesses who identified Kyles as the killer would have "markedly" weakened the prosecution's case and strengthened the defense's case due to their dissimilar descriptions of the killer at the scene of the crime.[72] The Court also found that, had "Beanie's" statements been disclosed, the defense could have attacked the thoroughness or good faith of the police investigation and questioned the probative value of certain physical evidence.[73] The statements were inconsistent and the police showed a "remarkably uncritical attitude" toward Beanie despite the fact that "Beanie" seemed anxious to see Kyles arrested for the murder.[74] Finally, while the list of crime-scene license plates was less exculpatory, it could have further called into question "Beanie's" statements and refuted a prosecution argument that Kyles' car was at the scene.[75]

While all other reviewing courts disagreed as to the materiality of this evidence, one court—the Supreme Court—found in its discretion that the evidence was sufficient to meet the *Brady* standard. The number of reviewing courts can be seen as favorable, since Kyle's claim was finally validated by the Supreme Court. On the other hand, one can also view it as troubling that Kyles was forced to remain in jail when he was not given a fair trial.

Perhaps most importantly, the Court further explained that the prosecutor alone is assigned the responsibility to gauge the likely net effect of all non-disclosed evidence, because only she will know what evidence remains undisclosed.[76] Thus, the Supreme Court left the initial disclosure decision entirely up to the prosecutor, leaving any review of this decision to post-conviction appellate review.[77] The Supreme Court demonstrated faith in all prosecutors when it wrote that, "this mean[t], naturally, that a prosecutor anxious about tacking too close to the wind will disclose a favorable piece of evidence [to the defense]."[78]

While an overwhelming majority of prosecutors will deserve the respect that the Court placed on them, the question still remains: What if Bagley or Kyles had never come across the evidence that the prosecutors decided they did not want to turn over? Would they have ever received the fair trial that our legal system says they deserve? In both cases, the prosecutors were never questioned as to any impropriety behind the lack of disclosures. If the prosecutors were not acting in bad faith, how could a court disagree with their decision? A better approach would give prosecutors practical guidance as to what they should disclose. If the Court had listed specific items that needed to be disclosed before trial, including such things as police reports and written statements, then we might avoid these troubling decisions not to disclose evidence. In addition, defense counsel would have the ability to detect and address weaknesses in the government's case before an unfair trial took place and the accused spent years in jail awaiting a fair trial.

B. Special Role of the Prosecutor to Seek Justice and "Truth"

Prosecutors have a different role than most attorneys in that they are expected to "seek justice" as opposed to merely seeking convictions.[79] In other words, they are not expected to win at all costs. In an essay dating back to 1854, George Sharswood recognized that while the defense attorney should "exert all his ability, learning and ingenuity in such a defense, even if he should be perfectly assured in his own mind of the actual guilt of the prisoner," a lawyer should never prosecute "a man whom he knows or believes to be innocent."[80] The American Bar Association, influenced by the essay in drafting its first "Canons of Ethics" in 1908,[81] still maintains this position today. The ABA's ethical standards for prosecutors state that "the duty of the prosecutor is to seek justice, not merely to convict."[82] Similarly, the Model Rules of Professional Conduct point out that prosecutors are "ministers of justice."[83] Perhaps most famously, the Supreme Court in *Berger v. United States* stated that a prosecutor's interest "is not that it shall win the case, but that justice shall be done."[84]

This "seeking justice" standard is not without critique, however. Fred Zacharias argues that the "do justice" standard's "vagueness leaves prosecutors with only their individual sense of morality to determine just conduct" as opposed to an objective standard that would truly advance the public interest.[85] A report by the special committee of the District of Columbia Bar Association, appointed to study the application of the Model Rules of Professional Conduct to government lawyers, stated that "the public interest is too amorphous a standard to have practical utility in regulating lawyer conduct."[86] It has also been argued that assistant prosecutors' decisions may be subconsciously influenced to maximize convictions in order to seek professional advancement, which can influence their ability to "do justice."[87]

However, while the "do justice" standard is broad, Bruce Green argues that it encompasses more specific objectives that flow from our constitutional and statutory scheme and that represent "what it means for the sovereign to govern fairly."[88] In Texas, these objectives are specifically enumerated in Rule 3.09 of the Texas Rules of Disciplinary Conduct regarding "Special Responsibilities of a Prosecutor."[89] Most importantly, the Texas rules require the prosecutor to "refrain from prosecuting or threatening to prosecute a charge that the prosecutor already knows is not supported by probable cause,"[90] to "make timely disclosure to the defense of all evidence or information known to the prosecutor that tends to negate guilt or mitigates the offense," and to disclose all known unprivileged mitigating information in connection with sentencing.[91] Essentially, as it relates to discovery, the law requires the prosecutor to seek justice by disclosing information that bears on the truth of the charges against the defendant.

While most prosecutors can be trusted to fulfill their role to do justice, the statutory scheme for pretrial discovery should serve to better guide them and reduce the amount of discretion as it applies to discoverable evidence and information. This will reduce the amount of information that, as we have seen, can so easily fall through the cracks without any prosecutorial misconduct whatsoever. The following section addresses the Texas discovery statute,[92] and argues that it currently provides insufficient guidance for the prosecutor.

III. The "Two Way" Street Movement and Reciprocal Discovery

As discussed above, the classic debate of the 1950s and 1960s ultimately focused on whether discovery should be more open for the defense.[93] The discussion assumed that the privilege against self-incrimination, due process and the right to silence would bar the defense from having equal disclosure requirements. However, prosecutors began to question this assumption, arguing that they deserved all the benefits of the adversarial system as much as the defense. They argued that the avoidance of trial by surprise required both sides to have equal access. [94]

One of the rare forms of discovery available for prosecutors in a few states derived from alibi notice statutes.[95] Typical alibi notice provisions require the defense to give pretrial notice of the intention to present an alibi defense.[96] In 1964, thirteen states had such provisions on their books, although many defense attorneys questioned the constitutionality of these laws.[97] However, it was not until after the open discovery debate receded that the Supreme Court would rule that alibi notice statutes are constitutional.[98]

In 1970, the Supreme Court took up the issue in *Williams v. Florida*[99] and provided a rationale that opened the door to broader provisions for prosecutorial pre-trial discovery than merely alibi notice. The *Williams* case involved a 1968 Florida alibi notice rule[100] modeled after statutes in Ohio, New York, and New Jersey.[101] The statute required a defendant, on written demand from the prosecuting attorney, to give notice in advance of trial if the defendant intended to claim an alibi and to furnish the prosecuting attorney with information as to the place where he claimed to have been and the names and addresses of the alibi witnesses he intended to use.[102] After Williams was arrested for robbery, and prior to his trial, his counsel challenged the statute's requirements on the grounds that it violated the Due Process Clause and the Fifth Amendment privilege against self-incrimination.[103] The district court denied the motion, and the appellate court affirmed.[104]

Despite its objection, the defense complied with the court order and gave the prosecution the name and address of its alibi witness, Mary Scotty.[105] Scotty claimed that Williams was with her at her apartment during the time of the robbery.[106] Supplied with her contact information, the prosecution was able to summon Scotty to the State Attorney's Office for an interview on the morning of the trial prior to her taking the stand.[107] At trial, Scotty gave dates and times that did not match up with her morning interview.[108] The prosecuting attorney was then able to use her prior testimony to impeach her accuracy and truthfulness during trial.[109] Furthermore, the prosecutor was able to anticipate her testimony and offered rebuttal testimony of an officer who claimed that Scotty had asked him for directions at the time when she claimed to be inside the apartment.[110]

The Supreme Court upheld the alibi notice statute, rejecting constitutional challenges under the Fifth and Fourteenth Amendments.[111] The Court rejected the Fourteenth Amendment claim, stating that the adversary system was not a "poker game in which players enjoy an absolute right always to conceal their cards until played."[112] Because alibis are easy to concoct, "[t]he State's interest in protecting itself against an eleventh-hour defense is both obvious and legitimate."[113] The Court found "ample room" in the adversary system for notice requirements like Florida's that are "designed to enhance the search for truth" by "insuring both the defendant and the State ample opportunity to investigate certain facts crucial to the determination of guilt or innocence."[114] Since the prosecution was also under a duty to disclose its rebuttal witnesses to the defense, the rule did not deprive Williams of due process or a fair trial.[115]

As to the Fifth Amendment argument, the Court asserted that criminal defendants are "frequently forced" to testify themselves or call other witnesses in order to "reduce the risk of conviction."[116] When the State presents a compelling case against the accused, it can work against the defense to offer the testimony of the defendant or of other witnesses by inadvertently providing the State with further ammunition.[117] Nonetheless, this dilemma between choosing silence and presenting a defense does not violate the privilege against compelled self-incrimination because "the pressures generated by the State's evidence may be severe but they do not vitiate the defendant's choice to present an alibi defense and witnesses to prove it."[118] Though it may be a tough choice, the defendant still has a choice. The Court concluded that "the pressures that bear on his pre-trial decision are of the same nature as those that would induce him to call alibi witnesses at trial."[119] Since the defendant was only "compelled . . . to accelerate the timing of his disclosure," the Fifth Amendment was not violated.[120]

The Supreme Court did put some restrictions on alibi notice statutes three years later in *Wardius v. Oregon*.[121] At the time, Oregon had an alibi notice statute in place that was similar to Florida's but differed in one major respect.[122] Like Florida's, Oregon's statute required the defense to declare its intention to present an alibi defense, along with the date, time and location of the defendant's claimed alibi and the names and addresses of supporting witnesses, five days before trial.[123] Unlike Florida, the state was under no reciprocal obligation to disclose its rebuttal information.[124] The penalty for failure to give notice of an alibi defense was exclusion of any alibi evidence at trial.[125]

In this case, Wardius had been charged with the unlawful sale of narcotics, which, according to the indictment, occurred earlier in the day before the arrest.[126] At trial, the State put on its case against him and rested.[127] To rebut the state's case, the defense called Colleen McFadden, who testified that she and Wardius were at a drive-in movie during the night in question.[128] After the jury heard the testimony, the prosecutor objected because the defense had failed to give proper notice of the alibi defense.[129] The judge sustained the objection and struck McFadden's testimony.[130] Then Wardius himself took the stand to tell the jury he was at the drive-in.[131] Once again, the defense was not allowed to put on the evidence due to the violation of the alibi notice rule.[132] Wardius was convicted and sentenced to eighteen months in prison.[133]

On appeal, the defense conceded that the required alibi notice had not been filed, but argued that the law should be struck down because it did not require the prosecution to notify the defense of its rebuttal information.[134] The Supreme Court agreed, holding that the Due Process Clause of the Fourteenth Amendment required that an alibi notice requirement must impose a reciprocal rebuttal evidence requirement on the prosecution.[135] Notwithstanding the defendant's failure to inform the prosecution of his intent to present an alibi defense, any alibi notice statute that does not require identical disclosure from the prosecution cannot be enforced against a defendant.[136]

In reaching its conclusion, the Court reiterated its position that "the Due Process Clause has little to say regarding the amount of discovery which the parties [in a criminal case] must be afforded . . . it does speak to the balance of forces between the accused and his accuser."[137] It is "fundamentally unfair" for a state to require alibi notice of defendants in the "search for truth" so as to reduce "trial by surprise" while failing to require the same of the prosecution.[138] To do so would be to subject the defendant "to the hazard of surprise concerning refutation of the very pieces of evidence which he disclose to the state."[139]

Williams opened the door to prosecutorial discovery of information from the defense, but *Wardius* limited this discovery in that the state may not require the defense to disclose information unless the prosecution must do the same.

A. The Role of Defense Counsel and Its Relation to the Search for Truth

The Sixth Amendment to the United States Constitution provides that "[i]n all criminal prosecutions, the accused shall enjoy the right . . . to have the Assistance of Counsel for his defense."[140] In interpreting this right, the Supreme Court has stated that "zealous and loyal representation" is required[141] and that counsel has an "overarching duty to advocate the defendant's cause."[142] Of course, zealous advocacy has its limits. A defense attorney may not, for example, present perjured testimony if the defendant insists on taking the stand and testifying falsely. As the Supreme Court stated in *Nix v. Whiteside*,

> that duty [of loyalty] is limited to legitimate, lawful conduct with the very nature of a trial as a search for truth. Although counsel must take all reasonable lawful means to attain the objectives of the client, counsel is precluded from taking steps or in any way assisting the client in presenting false evidence or otherwise violating the law.[143]

Texas has also adopted this premise in the Texas Disciplinary Rules of Professional Conduct: "A lawyer shall not knowingly offer or use evidence that the lawyer knows to be false."[144]

However, while the defense attorney may not provide false evidence to the court, this does not mean that he or she is under the same obligation as prosecutors in the "search for the truth." In fact, "'some defense lawyers report that they have avoided the ethical dilemma . . . because they follow a practice of not questioning the client about the facts in the case and, therefore, never 'know' that a client has given false testimony.'"[145] In *United States v. Wade*,[146] the Supreme Court stated that "defense counsel has no comparable obligation to ascertain or present the truth."[147] It explained that defense counsel must defend their clients whether they are guilty or not.[148] Even if the defense counsel knows that the prosecution is presenting truthful evidence, he or she is permitted to "put the State to its proof" and "put the State's case in the worst possible light."[149] So while defense attorneys may not suborn perjury, the role they play is not to ascertain the truth but rather to prevent the conviction of their clients.

With this in mind, the discovery laws should be constructed so as to allow defense attorneys to fully test the state's case. However, under certain circumstances, prosecutors should be aided in ascertaining the truth by providing them with the tools to test the case that the defense puts forward. These tools include alibi notice, as well as notice of other defenses. By imposing certain disclosure requirements on the defense, prosecutors would have a better opportunity to aid the court and jury in their roles as truth finder.

IV. Reforming Texas Discovery Law to Improve the Search for Truth

A. The Development of the Current Texas Law

In 1965, Texas adopted its most recent version of the Texas Code of Criminal Procedure.[150] In this version, Texas enacted the statutory baseline language for the discovery statute that remains to this day.[151]

Although there have been some significant additions over time, discussed below, it is clear that Texas law envisions limited discovery in criminal cases, focusing primarily on prosecutorial disclosure. With the exception of expert witnesses who will testify at trial,[152] disclosure of evidence is expected only of the prosecution. Thus, discovery is not a "two way street" in Texas, as there is no reciprocal discovery requirement. However, it is important to note that this original 1965 language was adopted hot on the heels of the classic debate of the 1950's and 1960's. Before the 1970 *Williams* holding that opened the door to allowing prosecutorial discovery through alibi notice statutes, many assumed that prosecutorial discovery was constitutionally unavailable.

According to the original 1965 statute, the State could not request any defense discovery; however, the defense could seek discovery of the State's case if it met a series of hurdles.[153] If a defendant could show "good cause," "materiality," and "possession by the state," the court in its discretion could require the state to produce evidence and to "permit inspection, copying and photographing of any designated documents, papers, written statement of the defendant, books, accounts, letters, photographs, [or] objects or tangible things not privileged."[154] The statute did not allow for a court to order production of the written statements of witnesses or work product of the state or its investigators, including their notes and reports.[155]

The current version of the law, while virtually the same, has incorporated two slight changes that are relevant to this discussion.[156] The first is that if expert testimony is being offered at trial (by either the prosecution or the defense) the court has the discretion to order the parties to disclose the name and address of the expert that the party intends to offer at trial.[157] This only refers to expert, not lay, witnesses.[158] Significantly, this is the closest that the Texas discovery rules come to allowing the prosecutor to get any discovery from the defense in the typical case. Second, if the defense seeks a discovery order and shows "good cause" for needing the information, the court no longer has discretion to deny the order.[159] Rather, the court must require the State to disclose the evidence or information.[160]

As to the defense's burden of "good cause, materiality, and possession by the state," there is little guidance as to what "good cause" means apart from the "materiality" standard.[161] Courts have construed "good cause" to be shown by proving the evidence is "material" to the case.[162] The "materiality" standard adopted by Texas essentially follows the Supreme Court's *Brady* line of cases. To be "material" means "that the evidence would create a reasonable doubt that did not otherwise exist."[163] Therefore, "the mere possibility that an item of undisclosed information might have helped the defense" does not establish materiality.[164]

What is important to note about current discovery law in Texas is that it assigns a great deal of discretion to the trial court. Essentially, the prosecutor is only required to turn over what the trial court requires. Beyond evidence that is exculpatory, the prosecutor will only be required to turn over what the defense convinces a court it should be allowed to see. Without any practical guidance on what a defense attorney can expect from a prosecutor, the rulings from jurisdiction to jurisdiction may be unpredictable and vary according to the disposition of the court. Furthermore, the state may not be required to disclose the two items that may prove to be the most helpful in allowing a defense attorney to discover if exculpatory material exists: police reports and witness statements. Lastly, the statute does not have any alibi notice provision in order to keep the prosecutor from being surprised at trial.

B. Failed Attempt at Real Reform and Guidance

During the 79th Regular Session of the Texas Legislature in 2005, both chambers of the Texas Congress attempted to pass legislation aimed at changing the existing discovery statute. The first piece of legislation, House Bill 969, became law on September 1, 2005.[165] This modest bill merely removed the court's discretion to deny defense discovery when "good cause" is shown.[166] The Senate, on the other hand, proposed Senate Bill 560, a more comprehensive statute that would have provided far more guidance and clarity to both parties as to what information and evidence must be provided prior to trial and would have done so without requiring court involvement. In doing so, it would have allowed for far more automatic discovery for both the defense and the prosecution.[167] Although the legislation was thought to have support from both prosecutors and criminal defense attorneys, it did not make it out of the reconciliation process of the conference committee in the

House.[168] Although it did not pass, this bill should be reconsidered for passage, especially certain aspects of the bill that would aid the courts in their search for the truth.

The bill's most salient attempt at change, and likely what caused its downfall, was to create broader obligations for the defense as well as the prosecution that surpassed the current requirements.[169] It was a trade-off. Prosecutors would have been required to turn over more discoverable material to defense attorneys, but defense attorneys would also have been required to do the same, though to a slightly lesser degree. Senate Bill 560 was ambitious in the scope of the proposed changes, and many of its provisions should be re-considered in the future.

C. Features of Senate Bill 560

If Senate Bill 560 had passed, no longer would defense attorneys be required to show "good cause" or "materiality" for discoverable information. As long as the information was listed in the statute, the prosecution would have had to turn it over as long as it was in the "possession, custody or control of the state or any of its agencies."[170] By the same token, the defense would have had to do the same.[171] The defense would have been able to get much more information than it could have previously, but at the cost of providing information to the prosecution.[172] Following the Supreme Court's rationale in *Williams* and *Wardius*, nothing inherent in the Constitution forbids a reciprocal discovery regime.

By eliminating the "good cause" discretion of the court, both defense attorneys and prosecutors would know what information they can expect from each other. Throughout Texas, uniformity would have been achieved by giving equal treatment of discovery to both attorneys, regardless of their jurisdiction. This would be especially helpful to defense attorneys who practice in multiple counties. It would also relieve the criminal courts of preliminary involvement in discovery.

Under Senate Bill 560, the list of items automatically discoverable by the defense would have substantially increased. Although this list is not exhaustive, the relevant additions are presented here.[173] The proposed statute would not only have required the prosecution to turn over the written and recorded statements of the defendant[174] (which a court can currently order)[175], but would have expanded the requirement to include "any written record containing the substance of any oral statement ... made before or after arrest, in response to interrogation by any person whom the defendant believed to be a peace officer."[176] The state would also have been required to turn over the names and addresses of all witnesses it intended to call at trial, including any experts (which a court can currently order) as well as any reports produced by those experts.[177] Furthermore, a prosecutor would have been required to turn over all written or recorded statements of any witness it intended to call at trial, which specifically included both the offense report created by law enforcement personnel (more commonly known as the "police report") and any written expert reports.[178]

But while the prosecution's discovery obligations would have increased under Senate Bill 560, so would the defense's obligations.[179] A defense attorney would have had to disclose its full list of intended witnesses (not including the defendant), along with their names and addresses and any written or recorded statements made by them.[180] This would include any expert testimony and reports made by those experts.[181]

Under the current Texas rules, no party to a criminal case is required to turn over the statements of its witnesses prior to trial, including statements in police reports.[182] However, under Texas Rule of Evidence 615, after a witness (other than the defendant) has testified on direct examination, the court, on motion of a party who did not call the witness, shall order opposing counsel to produce any statement of the witness that is in their possession and that relates to the subject matter concerning which the witness has testified for the examination and use of the moving party.[183] Does this make practical sense? A strong contradiction underlies our law that recognizes the importance of written witness statements made prior to trial by requiring their disclosure but no sooner than immediately after they testify. How can opposing counsel have any chance of a meaningful review if given the statement at the last possible moment before cross-examination? If one purpose of our criminal justice system is to seek the truth, requiring disclosure of written witness statements in advance would better serve this purpose.

Features of Senate Bill 560:

- Automatic defense discovery of prosecution evidence.
- Prosecution *and defense* disclosure of witness list including experts, as well as biographical information and prior statements.

By requiring advance disclosure of witness statements, both parties would be able to properly to investigate the importance of such statements, which would reduce trial by surprise for both parties. Defense counsel and prosecutors view evidence very differently. A prosecution team will naturally be led towards evidence that favors conviction, and a defense team will naturally be led towards evidence that casts doubt on the defendant's guilt. With more disclosure, the underlying rationale of *Brady* will be better served by increasing the likelihood that all exculpatory evidence is exposed prior to trial. This gives the defense a chance to pursue further evidence that may be exculpatory and that the prosecution failed to investigate. Conversely, the prosecution would be able to anticipate rebuttal evidence and to avoid being ambushed by unexpected defense evidence. With more information, prosecutors would also be better equipped to seek justice by dropping charges when appropriate.

Prior disclosure of statements may also lead to quicker resolutions of cases. The more information a defense attorney knows prior to trial, the better the advice she can give to her client on whether or not to plead guilty. This would reduce the expense of going to trial and would administer justice more expeditiously. Conversely, the prosecution may also discover exculpatory information that leads to the dropping of charges.

Roughly half of the states have discovery provisions that provide for disclosure of the written or recorded statements of prospective prosecution witnesses,[184] with slightly less than half of these states providing for disclosure of the substance of oral statements made by these witnesses.[185] Approximately seventeen states provide for the disclosure of the recorded statements of the defense witnesses included in its witness list.[186]

The rationale for requiring disclosure of witness statements applies equally to advance disclosure of both expert and police reports. Like witness statements, they may lead the investigation for both parties in different directions, providing for a fuller discovery of the evidence. Currently, several states require automatic discovery of police reports, viewing them as a critical source for defense preparation.[187] Likewise, expert reports may lead to differing conclusions but are also often filled with highly technical language that requires substantial research to understand. Requiring disclosure in advance would foster in-depth understanding and questioning of expert and police witnesses.

A majority of states, including Texas, require the defense to give notice of certain defenses. Currently, the federal system and more than forty states also require the defendant to give advance notice of the intent to raise an alibi defense.[188] The federal system and nearly all states, including Texas, require notice of the insanity defense.[189] Approximately a dozen states require the defendant to give notice in advance of trial of various defenses beyond alibi and insanity.[190]

Senate Bill 560 also attempted to create an alibi notice requirement for the defense similar to those discussed previously in the *Williams* line of cases, but the bill went much further.[191] In addition to requiring notice of intent to raise an alibi defense, the defense would also have been required to disclose its plans to offer evidence as to any defense listed in Chapter 8 or 9 of the Texas Penal Code, which includes insanity, mistake of fact or law, duress, entrapment, and defense of self or of third persons, among others.[192] In accordance with the due process requirements of the *Wardius* holding,[193] the prosecution also would have had to disclose the names and addresses of its rebuttal witnesses to any defense it plans to rebut.[194]

Using the same rationale underscoring the *Williams* decision and the initial enactment of the alibi statutes across other states, Texas should adopt these defense notice provisions. Alibis are a "hip pocket" defense that can be easily prepared and fabricated even during trial, and can catch a prosecutor off guard.[195] If false defenses are based on false testimony, giving a prosecutor time to investigate and prepare for them will deflate their effectiveness and discourage their use at trial by the defense.[196]

Investigating an affirmative defense may require a different mode of investigation as well. With affirmative defenses, there may be an independent investigation required of other witness stories, which can cause needless delay if discovered during trial.[197] By requiring pretrial disclosure, the time and costs associated with delay will be lessened.[198] Additionally, if a prosecutor discovers that the evidence in favor of the affirmative defense is likely true, he may drop the charges. By requiring prior disclosure of affirmative defenses, false defenses will have less impact at trial, defendants maybe deterred from putting forth false defenses in the first instance, and truthful defenses may end the case before prosecution even occurs.

V. Conclusion

Although "open file" discovery of prosecution files should be permanently implemented in Texas, more consideration should be given to defense discovery obligations as well. Allowing both sides more opportunity to "seek the truth" and properly investigate their cases is best achieved through reciprocal discovery. While our criminal justice system cannot tolerate unfairness to accused and should demand that trials be fair, fairness to society also demands that prosecutors have the opportunity to investigate defense evidence before trial so as promote the search for truth. A broader discovery rule that includes reciprocal discovery would ensure truly fair trials, and Texans could be confident that the final outcomes of criminal trials are just.

Endnotes

1. *See* Alex Branch, *Tarrant County's Electronic Open-File System Seen as Gold Standard for Reducing Wrongful Convictions*, Star Telegram, Mar. 18, 2010; John Council, *New Open File Policy Includes Appellate Info*, Tex. Law., Oct. 6, 2008, http://www.law.com/jsp/tx/PubArticleTX.jsp?id=1202425008168 (last visited Sep. 17, 2010) (discussing Dallas County and Denton County open-file systems); Press Release, Harris County District Attorney's Office, Houston, Tex., DA Begins New Discovery Agreement (Mar. 2, 2009) (on file with author) (detailing discovery of police reports and witness statements).

2. Tex. Code Crim. Proc. Ann. art. 39.14 (West 2009)

3. The Justice Project, http://www.thejusticeproject.org/state/texas/ (last visited Mar. 14, 2010).

4. S.B. 560, 79th Leg., Reg. Sess. (Tex. 2005).

5. *Id.*

6. *Id.*

7. House Committee on Criminal Jurisprudence, Texas House of Representatives, A Report to the House of Representatives 80th Texas Legislature 24 (Interim Report 2006), *available at* http://www.house.state.tx.us/committees/reports/79interim/criminalJurisprudence.pdf (last visited Aug. 27, 2010).

8. *See* Wayne R. LaFave et al., Criminal Procedure § 20.1(a) (5th ed. 2009); Lemon v. Supreme Court, 156 N.E. 84, 84-5 (N.Y. 1927) (Cardozo, J.)

9. *See* Robert L. Fletcher, *Pretrial Discovery in State Criminal Cases*, 12 Stan. L. Rev. 293, 295-97 (1960); LaFave et. al, *supra* note 8, at § 20.1(a).

10. *See* Lafave et al., *supra* note 8, at § 20.1(a).

11. *Id.*

12. *Id.*; *see also* F. James, G. Hazard & J. Leubsdorf, Civil Procedure § 5.2 (4th ed. 1992).

13. *See* LaFave et al, *supra* note 8, at § 20.1(a)(citing Wiliam J. Brennan, *The Criminal Prosecution: Sporting Event or Quest for the Truth*, 1963 Wash. U. L. Q. 279 (1963)).

14. See LaFave et al., *supra* note 8, at § 20.1(a).

15. *See* Brennan, *supra* note 13, at 291.

16. *Id.*

17. *See* Michael Moore, *Criminal Discovery*, 19 Hastings L.J. 865, 916 (1968); LaFave et al., *supra* note 8, at § 20.1(a); *see also* Kenneth Pye, *The Defendant's Case for More Liberal Discovery*, 33 F.R.D. 47, 82 (1963).

18. Kenneth Pye, *The Defendant's Case for More Liberal Discovery*, 33 F.R.D. 47, 82 (1963).
19. *See* Thomas A. Flannery, *The Prosecutor's Case against Liberal Discovery*, 33 F.R.D. 47, 74 (1963).
20. *See* LaFave et. al, *supra* note 8, at § 20.1(a).
21. *See* United States v. Garsson, 291 F. 646, 649 (S.D.N.Y. 1923) (Hand, J.); Flannery, *supra* note 19, at 74.
22. Flannery, *supra* note 19, at 74.
23. *Id.*
24. *Id.* at 79.
25. *Id.* at 80.
26. *Id.* at 74.
27. U.S. Const. amend. V; Green v. United States, 355 U.S. 184, 187–88 (1957).
28. State v. Tune, 98 A.2d 881, 894 (N.J. 1953) (J. Brennan dissenting).
29. Dennis v. United States, 384 U.S. 855, 879 (1966).
30. *See* LaFave et. al, *supra* note 8, at § 20.1(c).
31. City of New York v. Gentile, 248 A.D.2d 382, 669 N.Y.S.2d 854 (2nd Dept. March 2, 1998) (citing Weatherford v. Bursey, 429 U.S. 545, 559 (1977)).
32. Page v. State, 7 S.W.3d 202, 206 (Tex. App.—Fort Worth Oct. 7, 1999, rehearing overruled Dec. 13, 1999, pet. for discretionary rev. refused Sept. 13, 2000, rehearing on pet. for discretionary rev. denied Nov. 22, 2000); *see* Barcroft v. State, 881 S.W.2d 838, 840 (Tex. App.—Tyler 1994).
33. Brady v. Maryland, 373 U.S. 83, 87 (1963).
34. *Id.*
35. *See* Stephanos Bibas, *The Story of* Brady v. Maryland*: From Adversarial Gamesmanship Toward the Search for Innocence?* in CRIMINAL PROCEDURE STORIES 1, 4 (Carol Steiker ed., 2005).

36. *Id.*
37. *Id.*
38. *Id.*
39. *Id.*
40. *Id.*
41. *Id.*
42. Brady v. Maryland, 373 U.S. 83, 84 (1963).
43. *Id.*
44. *Id.*
45. *Id.*
46. *Id.* at 87.
47. *Id.* at 87–88,
48. *Id.* at 87.
49. United States v. Bagley, 473 U.S. 667 (1985).
50. *Id.* at 669–70.
51. *Id.* at 670.
52. *Id.*
53. *Id.*
54. *Id.* at 671.
55. *Id.* at 672.
56. *Id.* at 673.
57. *Id.* at 674.
58. *Id.* at 668.
59. *Id.* at 677.
60. *Id.* at 678.
61. *Id.* at 682.
62. *Id.*
63. *See id.*
64. Kyles v. Whitley, 514 U.S. 419 (1995).

65. *Id.* at 421.
66. *Id.* at 429.
67. *Id.* at 422
68. *Id.*
69. *Id.*
70. *Id.* at 454.
71. *Id.* at 441.
72. *Id.* at 441 (the state's principal witness described the assailant as "5'4" to 5'5", 140 pounds and medium build," a description closer to "Beanie's" size than Kyles', who was six feet tall and thin).
73. *Id.* at 445–46.
74. *Id.*
75. *Id.* at 450.
76. *Id.* at 437–38.
77. *Id.*
78. *Id.* at 439.
79. Berger v. United States, 295 U.S. 78, 88 (1935).
80. *See* Bruce Green, *Why Should Prosecutors Seek Justice?*, 26 Fordham Urb. L.J. 607, 612–613 (1999) (citing George Sharswood, An Essay in Professional Ethics (F.B. Rothman 5th ed. 1993)).
81. *See* Green, *supra* note 80, at 613 (citing *Canons of Ethics*, 33 ABA Rep. 575 (1908)); *see also* Russell G. Pearce, *Rediscovering the Republican Origins of the Legal Ethics Code*, 6 Geo. J. Legal Ethics 241, 243 (1992).
82. American Bar Association, Standards for Criminal Justice: The Prosecution Function 3-1.2(c) (1992).
83. Model Rules of Prof'l Conduct R. 3.8 cmt. 1 (2004).
84. *Berger*, 295 U.S. at 88.

85. *See* Fred Zacharias, *Structuring the Ethics of Prosecutorial Trial Practice: Can Prosecutors do Justice?*, 44 Vand. L. Rev. 45, 48 (1991).

86. See Roger C. Cramton, *The Lawyer as Whistleblower: Confidentiality and Government Lawyer*, 5 Geo. J. L. Ethics 291, 299 (1991) (citing Report By The District of Columbia Bar Special Committee of Government Lawyers And the Model Rules Of Professional Conduct, *reprinted in* The Wash. Law., Sept.-Oct. 1998, at 53 (Sep.-Oct. 1988)).

87. *See* Albert Alschuler, *The Prosecutor's Role in Plea Bargaining*, 36 U. Chi. L. Rev. 50, 106 (1968).

88. *See* Green, *supra* note 80, at 634.

89. Tex. Disciplinary R. Prof. Conduct § 3.09(a) (2005).

90. *Id.*

91. *See id.* at § 3.09(d).

92. Tex. Code Crim. Proc. Ann. art. 39.14 (West 2009)

93. *See supra* notes 8–30 and accompanying text.

94. *See* LaFave et al., *supra* note 8, at § 20.1(d).

95. *See* David M. Epstein, *Advance Notice of Alibi*, 55 J. Crim. L,, Criminology, & Pol. Sci. 29, 30 (1964).

96. *Id.*

97. *Id.*

98. *Id.*

99. Williams v. Florida, 399 U.S. 78 (1970).

100. Fla. R. Crim. P. R. 1.200 (1968) (currently Fla. R. Crim. P. Rule 3.200 (2010))

101. Fla. R. Crim. P. R. 3.200 Committee Notes – 1968 Adoption (referencing N.Y. Code of Crim. Proc. 295-L (1935); Ohio Rev. Code Ann. 2945.58 (1953) (enacted in 1929); N.J. Super. & Cnty. Ct. Crim. Prac. R. 3:5–9 (1948) (enacted in 1934)).

102. *Williams*, 399 U.S. at 79.

103. *Id.*
104. *Id.* at 80.
105. *Id.* at 80–81.
106. *Id.* at 81.
107. *Id.*
108. *Id.*
109. *Id.*
110. *Id.*
111. *Id.* at 86.
112. *Id.* at 82.
113. *Id.*
114. *Id.*
115. *Id.* at 81.
116. *Id.* at 83.
117. *Id.*
118. *Id.* at 84.
119. *Id.* at 85.
120. *Id.*
121. Wardius v. Oregon, 412 U.S. 470 (1973).
122. *Id.* at 472 n. 2; *Id*, at 472 n. 3.
123. *Id.* at 472 n. 2; *Id*, at 472 n. 3..
124. *Id.* at 472 n.3.
125. *Id.* at 473.
126. *Id.* at 472.
127. *Id.*
128. *Id.* at 473.
129. *Id.*
130. *Id.*
131. *Id.*

132. *Id.*
133. *Id.*
134. *Id.*
135. *Id.* at 472.
136. *Id.*
137. *Id.* at 474.
138. *Id.* at 475–6.
139. *Id.* at 476.
140. U.S. Const. amend. VI.
141. Nix v. Whiteside, 475 U.S. 157, 188 (1986).
142. Strickland v. Washington, 466 U.S. 668, 688 (1984).
143. *Nix*, 475 U.S. at 990.
144. Tex. Disciplinary R. Prof. Conduct § 3.03 (2005).
145. Geoffrey C. Hazard et al., The Law and Ethics of Lawyering 648 n.4 (4th ed. 2005) (quoting ABA Comm. on Ethics & Prof'l Responsibility, Formal Op. 353 n.9 (1988)).
146. United States v. Wade, 388 U.S. 218 (1967).
147. *Id.* at 256.
148. *Id.* at 257.
149. *Id.*
150. S.B. 107, 59th Leg. (Tex. 1965).
151. Tex. Code Crim. Proc. Ann. art. 39.14 (West 2009).
152. *Id.*
153. Tex. Code Crim. Proc. Ann. art. 39.14 (1966) (principle language is identical to the latest 2009 version).
154. *Id.*
155. *Id.*
156. Tex. Code Crim. Proc. Ann. art. 39.14 (West 2009).
157. Tex. Code Crim. Proc. Ann. art. 39.14 (West 2009). This change occurred in 1999.

158. Badillo v. State, 255 S.W.3d 125 (Tex. App. - San Antonio 2008); Osbourn v. State, 92 S.W.3d 531, 535-36, n. 2 (Tex. Crim. App. 2002).
159. Tex. Code Crim. Proc. Ann. art. 39.14 (West 2009). This change occurred in 2005. H.B. 969, 79th Leg., Reg. Sess. (Tex. 2005).
160. *Id.*
161. Rodriguez v. State, 513 S.W.2d 22 (Tex. Crim.App. 1974).
162. *Id.*
163. Jimenez v. State, 838 S.W.2d 661, 666 (Tex.App.—Houston [1st Dist.] 1992); Quinones v. State, 592 S.W.2d. 933 (Tex. Crim. App. 1980).
164. *Jimenez*, 838 S.W.2d at 666.
165. H.B. 107, 79th Leg., Reg. Sess. (Tex. 2005).
166. *Id.*
167. S.B. 560, 79th Leg., Reg. Sess. (Tex. 2005).
168. House Committee on Criminal Jurisprudence, *supra* note 7, at 24.
169. S.B. 560, 79th Leg., Reg. Sess. (Tex. 2005)
170. S.B. 560, 79th Leg., Reg. Sess. (Tex. 2005) (Proposed Art. 39.1 §1(a)).
171. S.B. 560, 79th Leg., Reg. Sess. (Tex. 2005) (Proposed Art. 39.1 §2(a)).
172. *Id.*
173. S.B. 560, 79th Leg., Reg. Sess. (Tex. 2005) (Proposed Art. 39.14 would also have required the prosecution to turn over the prior criminal record of the defendant and any witness it intended to call under § 1(a)(4),(5), as well as all documents in connection to any searches or seizures under §1(a)(6), any real evidence obtained from or belonging to the defendant under §1(a)(7) and any plea agreement, grant of immunity, or other agreement for testimony issued by the state's attorney under §1(a)(10)).

174. S.B. 560, 79th Leg., Reg. Sess. (Tex. 2005) (Proposed Art. 39.1 §1(a)(2)).
175. Tex. Code Crim. Proc. Ann. art. 39.14 (West 2009)
176. S.B. 560, 79th Leg., Reg. Sess. (Tex. 2005) (Proposed Art. 39.1 §1(a)(3)).
177. *Id.* (Proposed Art. 39.1 §1(a)(9)).
178. *Id.* (Proposed Art. 39.1 §1(a)(2)).
179. *Id.* (Proposed Art. 39.14 would also require the defense to disclose any known criminal convictions of a witness it intends to call at trial, not including the defendant under § 2(a)(2), and any real evidence under § 2(a)(3)).
180. *Id.* (Proposed Art. 39.1 §2(a)(4)).
181. *Id.* (Proposed Art. 39.1 §1(a)(5)).
182. Tex. Code Crim. Proc. Ann. art. 39.14 (West 2009).
183. Tex. R. Evid. 615(a).
184. *See* LaFave et al., *supra* note 8, at § 20.3(i); *see e.g.,* N.C. Gen. Stat. § 15A-903(a)(1) (2010); Colo. R. Crim. P. 16(a); Ill. Sup. Ct. R. 412(a); Minn. R. Crim. P. 9.01; Miss. U.R.C.C.C. 9.04(A); Mo. R. Crim. P. 25.03(A); N.M. Dist. Ct. R. Crim. P. 501(A); Wash. Super. Ct. Crim. R. 4.7(a); *see also* Cal. Penal Code. § 1054.1 (West 2009) (encompassing reports of statements).
185. *See* LaFave et al., *supra* note 8, at § 20.3(i).
186. *See* LaFave et al., *supra* note 8, at §20.5(f); *see, e.g.,* Cal. Penal Code § 1054.3 (West 2009); Fla. R. Crim. P. 3.220(d)(1)(B)(i); Minn. R. Crim. P. 9.02(Subd.1)(4)(a); *see generally* Vitauts M. Gulbis, *Annotation, Right of Prosecution to Discovery of Case-Related Notes, Statements, and Reports-State Cases*, 23 A.L.R. 4th 799, 803 (1983).
187. *See* LaFave et al., *supra* note 8, at § 20.3(k); *see, e.g.,* Ariz. R. Crim. P. 15.1(b)(3); Fla. R. Crim. P. 3.220(b); Idaho Crim. R. 16(b); Mich. Ct. R. 6.201(B)(2); N.H. R. Super. Ct. 98(A)(2)(i); N.J. Crim. R. 3:13-3(c)(8).

188. *See* LaFave et al., *supra* note 8, at §20.5(b); Fed. R. Crim. P. 12.1(a); *see e.g.,* Neb. Rev. St. § 29-1927 (2010); Mich. Comp. Laws Ann. § 768.20(1) (West 2010); Alaska R. Crim. P. 16(c)(5); Ariz. R. Crim. P. 15.2(b); Colo. R. Crim. P. 16(II)(d); Fla. R. Crim. P. R. 3.200; Haw. R. Penal P. 12.1(a); Ill. Sup. Ct. R. 413(d); Me. R. Crim. P. 16A(b)(3). .

189. *See* LaFave et al., *supra* note 8, at §20.5(c); Fed. R. Crim. Proc. 12.2(a); Tex. Code Crim. Proc. Ann. art. 46C.051 (West 2009); *see e.g.,* Okla. Stat. Ann. tit. 22, § 1176(A) (West 2003); La. Code Crim. P. Ann. art. 726 (2010); N.Y. Crim. Proc. Law § 250.10(3) (McKinney 1994).

190. *See* LaFave et al., *supra* note 8, at §20.5(d); *see e.g.,* N.C. Gen. Stat. § 15A-905(c)(1) (2010); Alaska R. Crim. P. 16(c)(5); Ariz. R. Crim. P. 15.2(b); Ark. R. Crim. P. 18.3; Ill. Sup. Ct. R. 413(d); N.J. Ct. R. 3:12-1.

191. S.B. 560, 79th Leg., Reg. Sess. (Tex. 2005) (Proposed Art. 39.1 §2(b)).

192. *Id.*; *see also* Tex. Penal Code Ann. § 8–9 (West 2009).

193. Wardius v. Oregon, 412 U.S. 470 (1973); *see also supra* notes 121–139 and accompanying text (discussing the Court's reasoning and holding in *Wardius*).

194. S.B. 560, 79th Leg., Reg. Sess. (Tex. 2005).

195. *See* Epstein, *supra* note 95, at 32.

196. *Id.*

197. *Id.* at 33.

198. *Id.* at 33.

VI. Creating Avenues to Uncover Actual Innocence

A. Access to DNA Testing: A Texas Case Study

Justice Denied: How Texas Courts Are Misinterpreting Chapter 64 and Improperly Denying Post-Conviction DNA Testing

Jennifer L. Hopgood*

DNA testing has an unparalleled ability both to exonerate the wrongly convicted and to identify the guilty. It has the potential to significantly improve both the criminal justice system and police investigative practices.

--Chief Justice John Roberts[1]

I. Introduction

As of August 4, 2010, forty-two men have been exonerated in Texas by DNA testing, after serving a collective 548 years in prison for crimes they did not commit.[2]

On February 4, 2009, the Texas Senate closed the day's legislative session with a somber remembrance for one of the forty-two Texans

* Jennifer Hopgood graduated from University of California, Berkeley and hopes to work as a prosecutor in her hometown of Austin, Texas after graduating from the University of Houston Law Center in May 2011.

who have been exonerated by DNA testing. Timothy Brian Cole died in prison after having spent thirteen years incarcerated for a crime he did not commit.[3] Cole was freed by death; his innocence posthumously proven when DNA evidence was finally tested and inculpated another man of the crime.[4] With Cole's family gathered in the Senate Chamber, Senate Resolution 124 was read aloud before the gathered Texas Senators, guests, and public:

> WHEREAS, Timothy Brian Cole always maintained his innocence, and in 2008 DNA evidence finally proved he had been wrongly incarcerated for the crime of another; . . . Although his life ended in prison, Tim Cole conducted himself with great courage, placing truth and integrity above even his freedom; he is deeply missed by those he cherished, but they may now take some solace in the knowledge that he has been vindicated before the world and is mourned by all who learn his tragic story; now, therefore, be it RESOLVED, That the Senate of the State of Texas, 81st Legislature, hereby pay special tribute to the life of Timothy Brian Cole and that profound sympathy be extended to the members of his family; and . . . when the Senate adjourns this day, it do so in memory of Timothy Brian Cole.[5]

While Timothy Cole, Army veteran, Texas Tech student, and beloved family member is now dead, Cole's death may not be in vain. Galvanized by the tragedy of Cole's wrongful conviction and his posthumous exoneration, the Texas Legislature passed HB 498 in 2009, establishing the Timothy Cole Advisory Panel on Wrongful Convictions ("TCAP").[6] The task force is just one result of the efforts of Texas legislators and others involved in the Texas criminal justice system to ensure that only the guilty are convicted. For example, during the 2009 Texas Legislative session, Senator Rodney Ellis introduced several bills that sought to implement best practices in several different areas, including eye-witness identification, writs based on scientific evidence, procedures during confessions, and improving the post-conviction DNA statute.[7] Although those bills were not passed because of an unrelated dispute that stopped passage of almost all bills during the 2009 session,

Texans, such as those on the Timothy Cole Advisory Panel, are working tirelessly both to improve the integrity of the criminal justice system and to ensure that innocent people are not convicted of crimes they did not commit.

This paper focuses on one component of the criminal justice process: post-conviction DNA testing. Part II focuses on both the history of Chapter 64, Texas's post-conviction DNA testing statute, and the manner in which Texas courts have interpreted this statute in ruling on whether to allow or deny incarcerated people access to DNA testing. Unfortunately, weaknesses in the statute have caused appellants who seem to have compelling cases to be denied testing. Specifically, courts have erroneously denied testing in three particular areas: (1) where the defendant is unable to prove before testing that biological material exists; (2) where courts have placed on the defendant the burden to prove both that evidence exists in a testable condition and that the evidence has been maintained in a proper chain of custody; and (3) where a defendant has failed to adequately explain why DNA testing was not previously conducted.

Part III analyzes the 2009 proposed amendment, which would remedy the third weakness of the statute. The 2009 bill, which was not enacted for reasons unrelated to the bill, attempted to increase access to DNA testing by deleting the requirement that a convicted person must sufficiently explain why DNA testing was not done previously. This bill should be resubmitted and passed during the 2011 legislative session.

Finally, Part IV makes recommendations for additional statutory reform to correct the remaining two weaknesses in the statute: the Legislature must clarify both the procedure by which to determine that biological material exists and the burden of proof the State has in establishing the existence of testable evidence and proper chain of custody.

Texas' post-conviction DNA statute is a crucial component in the attempt to strengthen our criminal justice system: to ensure that the actually innocent are not wrongfully convicted. However, we need a stronger post-conviction DNA testing statute so that justice is not denied to those attempting to prove their actual innocence.

II. THE HISTORY AND JUDICIAL INTERPRETATION OF CHAPTER 64

In 2001, the Texas Legislature enacted Chapter 64 of the Texas Code of Criminal Procedure.[8] Provided certain requirements are met, Chapter 64 requires post-conviction DNA testing of evidence containing biological material.[9]

As of February 10, 2010, Texas state and federal courts had issued 467 opinions that mentioned the statute. [10] Analyzing Texas appellate courts' interpretations of the statue provides greater insight into the weaknesses of the post-conviction DNA testing statute. Three sections of the statute seem to have weaknesses; in other words, courts are using these sections to deny testing in cases that seem to have compelling reasons to allow testing. First, courts are placing the burden on the defendant to prove that biological material exists before the evidence is tested. Second, contrary to statutory intent, the courts have placed on the defendant the burden of proof in establishing whether testable evidence exists and whether this evidence has been in a proper chain of custody. And third, a defendant can be denied testing if he fails to adequately explain why testing has not previously been conducted.

A. THE HISTORY OF CHAPTER 64

The Texas Legislature enacted the post-conviction DNA testing statute to "increase the ability to prevent wrongful convictions . . . [and] to establish procedures for the preservation of evidence containing DNA and postconviction DNA testing."[11] With the advances in DNA testing, the Legislature recognized the need to reform "obsolete" statutes that "unnecessarily inhibit[ed] the use of [biological evidence]."[12] As part of the statutory reform in the area of DNA testing, the Legislature also passed a companion statute that requires the preservation of evidence containing biological material.[13]

The Legislature subsequently amended Chapter 64 in 2003 and 2007.[14] In 2003 the Legislature made five changes to the statute, including important revisions to two sections that will be analyzed in this paper.[15] First, an attorney will now be appointed only upon showing of "reasonable grounds" rather than automatically upon the filing of a Chapter 64 motion.[16]

Second, the statute was amended to clarify the burden of proof required by the movant*: a preponderance of the evidence is required to establish that the defendant would not have been convicted if the DNA results were exculpatory.[17] The change was made to "undo the [CCA's] imposition of a higher burden in the *Kutzner* case" and clarify that "the standard of proof for DNA testing is a preponderance of the evidence."[18] The Legislature did not intend for a defendant to prove "'actual innocence,'" as under a habeas claim—only that "there is a 51% chance that the defendant would not have been convicted."[19] Furthermore, the 2003 amendment "clarifies that the defendant does not have to meet a two-prong test of not having been prosecuted or convicted . . . ."; "prosecuted" was deleted from the statute, requiring a convicted person to only have to prove that he would not have been convicted if exculpatory DNA evidence had been presented at trial.[20]

B. Statute-Based Reasons for Denial, January 1, 2008 to March 16, 2010

In order to assess the efficacy of Chapter 64, to determine whether courts are actually granting testing, and identify any weaknesses that might exist in the statute, an analysis was conducted of all appellate opinions that related to Chapter 64 during a twenty-six month period.[21] Between January 1, 2008 and March 16, 2010, Texas state and federal courts issued 104 opinions regarding Chapter 64.[22]

The reasons courts have denied, or in the rare instance allowed, testing were categorized based on the specific section of the statute relied upon by the court for the denial or granting of testing. There are nine reasons why testing is being denied. Three of these reasons reveal weaknesses in the statute and a need for legislative correction: (1) an ambiguity in the method to establish that biological material exists; (2) confusion as to who bears the burden of proof in establishing that evidence in a testable condition exists and has been maintained in a proper chain of custody; and (3) an almost impossible burden for a

* A person who applies to or petitions a court or judge for a ruling in his or her favor.

convicted person to provide an adequate explanation of why evidence was not previously subjected to DNA testing.[23] The other six reasons for denial appear to be consistent with the dictates of the statute: (1) there is a lack of proof that newer testing techniques ought to be used; (2) identity was not or is not an issue; (3) the movant cannot establish that he would not have been convicted if exculpatory results had been obtained; (4) the movant was not convicted and therefore cannot file a motion; (5) the movant did not submit properly formatted, sworn affidavits; or (6) no reason is given. The last category exists because there is no requirement for courts to provide a reason for denying testing.[24]

Twenty-nine cases were excluded from this section because the courts did not rely on Chapter 64 in their decisions: Chapter 11 motions were filed instead of appeals based on Chapter 64 (two cases)[25]; lack of jurisdiction (three cases)[26]; appeals were time-barred and the courts did not rule on the merits of the motions (four cases)[27]; a motion should have been filed under a different chapter instead of a Chapter 64 motion (one case)[28]; denial was based on procedural requirements unrelated to Chapter 64 (six cases)[29]; constitutional challenges (two cases)[30]; an abatement to the trial court after the defendant dismissed his attorney (one case)[31]; a petition for writ of mandamus[*] was denied because the trial court had ruled on the petitioner's motion for DNA testing and appointment of counsel after he had filed the motion with the appellate court (one case)[32]; dismissals of federal civil rights claims (two cases)[33]; dismissals from federal court because the petitioners failed to show a "denial of a federal constitutional right" (three cases);[34] and ruling that movants are not required to attend the hearing on the motion (two cases).[35] Additionally, two other cases were excluded because the appellate courts remanded the cases: one for procedural reasons[36] and one for addition briefing.[37]

* A legal action seeking an order issued by a superior court to compel a lower court or a government officer to perform mandatory or purely ministerial duties correctly.

1. The *Catch-22* of Proving Evidence Contains Biological Material: How the Court of Criminal Appeals Has Created an Untenable Burden on the Movant (Three Motions Denied)

As mandated by section 64.01(a), "[a] convicted person may submit to the convicting court a motion for forensic DNA testing of evidence containing biological material."[38] A defendant must establish "that there is biological evidence"* in order "to meet her threshold burden of showing that there is even any 'evidence containing biological material' to be tested."[39] This requirement makes sense in cases where the evidence that the defendant is requesting to be tested has been destroyed or was never collected: the State cannot test evidence that either no longer exists or never existed.[40] However, in *Swearingen v. State*, the Court of Criminal Appeals ("CCA") interpreted the statute in a way that leads to absurd results that the Texas Constitution disallows; moreover, the CCA's reasoning in *Swearingen* contradicts its own explanation of acceptable judicial interpretation of statutes.[41]

In 2000, Larry Ray Swearingen was found guilty of capital murder and sentenced to death for the 1998 murder of Melissa Trotter.[42] Swearingen requested testing of ligature (specifically, pantyhose that were used to strangle the victim) and articles of the victim's clothing for the presence of touch DNA, asserting that STR DNA† testing has yielded results in extracting touch DNA.[43] The CCA denied testing of the victim's clothing and the ligature because Swearingen failed to prove that "biological material existed" on either the clothing or ligature.[44]

In explaining the reason for its denial, the CCA noted that the statute "does not describe a method for determining the existence of biological material."[45] The CCA then notes that, in the absence of legislative clarification regarding a method for determining the existence

* Biological evidence is defined as evidence that is commonly recovered from crime scenes in the form of hair, tissue, bones, teeth, blood, or other bodily fluids.

† A chromosome contains sequences of repeating nucleotides known as short tandem repeats (STRs). An individual inherits one copy of an STR from each parent, which may or may not have similar repeat sizes. The number of repeats in STR markers can be highly variable among individuals, which make these STRs effective for human identification purposes.

of biological material, the CCA has previously held that "a mere assertion or a general claim that existence of biological material is probable will fail to satisfy the appellant's burden."[46] Swearingen argued that a plain reading of the statute could lead to "the deprivation of DNA testing simply because of the inability to ascertain whether or not biological material exists."[47] This quote, taken from *Routier*, referred to a rape kit that was never conclusively established to ever have existed.[48] In *Routier*, the CCA correctly interpreted the statute: Routier never established that a rape kit ever existed.[49] Conversely, in *Swearingen*, the ligature and the clothing the victim wore at the time of her death do still exist.[50]

When a statute is ambiguous, a court is permitted to consider "*extra*textual factors" in "seek[ing] to effectuate the 'collective' intent or purpose of the legislators who enacted the legislation."[51] However, the Texas Legislature is "*constitutionally entitled* to expect that the Judiciary will faithfully follow the specific text that was adopted."[52] The purpose of Chapter 64 is to "increase the ability to prevent wrongful convictions."[53] Even assuming for the sake of argument the statute is vague, the CCA is not effectuating the intent of our Legislature; rather, the CCA is ignoring the intent of the Texas Legislature and creating an almost impossible burden for defendants. The CCA circumvented statutory intent by holding that Swearingen had failed to meet his "threshold burden" to have testing done of the very clothes worn by the victim when she was murdered and of the ligature used to strangle her. Given this impossible holding and the absence of any indication that the CCA is going to overturn its decision in *Swearingen*, the Legislature must follow the CCA's suggestion and clarify the method for determining the existence of biological material so that the CCA will allow testing of evidence. Surely the Legislature did not intend to create a *Catch-22* situation in which a petitioner has to test the evidence to prove that biological evidence exists before the tests can be ordered.

As the CCA noted in *Swearingen*,[54] the Legislature needs to clarify the method for determining the existence of biological material. Only this correction will establish a burden that a defendant can satisfy and, thus, be able to prove the existence of biological material on evidence. Otherwise, a court can, or will feel compelled to, as the CCA did in *Swearingen*, deny testing of all evidence absent only the most obvious presence of biological materials as the CCA did in *Swearingen*, creating an almost impossible burden that a defendant will rarely satisfy. Part IV.A discusses remedies for this apparent statutory *Catch-22*.

2. Who Must Prove That Evidence Is Testable and Has Remained in a Proper Chain of Custody?

Article 64.01(b) requires that a movant may request testing only of evidence that was both "secured in relation to the offense that is the basis of the challenged conviction" and "was in the possession of the state during the trial of the offense. . . ."[55] Upon receiving a motion for post-conviction DNA testing, section 64.02(a)(2) mandates that the convicting court shall "require the attorney representing the state to take one of the following actions . . .": (1) deliver the evidence to the court or (2) explain why the state is unable to deliver the evidence.[56] The state has sixty days after receipt of the motion to comply with this requirement for production or provide an explanation why the evidence cannot be produced.[57]

a. A Movant Must Plead with Strict Particularity Regarding the Evidence He Seeks to Have Tested (Five Motions Denied)

A movant must identify the items that he wishes to have tested and establish that they were in possession of the state at the time of the trial.[58] In addition, the appellant must "allege . . . that DNA was taken and exists . . . or might have existed in the past."[59] Some appellate courts have held that, in order to meet the statutory requirements, the appellant must specify with great particularity which evidence he is seeking to have tested.[60] Therefore, in order to strictly comply with the courts' interpretation of the statute, a movant must list with great detail and specificity the evidence he wishes to have tested and establish that this evidence was secured in relation to the offense and was in possession of the state during the trial.

b. The Unfortunate Cases of Missing or Destroyed Evidence (Ten Motions Denied)

In the twenty-six month analysis period, there are ten cases that illustrate the unfortunate scenario where evidence has been lost or destroyed, a result, in part, of the fact that prior to 2001 the State was not required to keep evidence.[61] Fortunately, the opinions indicate a good faith effort by the State to locate evidence.[62] *Hurley v. State* is an excellent example of the court and state following the requirements of article 64.02(a)(2) and making a concerted effort to locate missing evidence.[63] As the court noted, "[t]he trial court ordered the district attorney to turn over the DNA evidence from appellant's case, or to explain in writing to the court why the evidence could not be delivered."[64] The State, in response to the trial court's order, submitted affidavits from the Addison Police Department, the Dallas County District Clerk's Office, and a forensics lab.[65] Each entity stated that no evidence could be found.[66] The district clerk surmised that, because no evidence had ever been in its custody, the court reporter probably disposed of any trial evidence.[67] Because the state ascertained the existence, or lack thereof, of evidence, the appellant was able to learn for certain if evidence still existed to be tested.

In re Bowman is another example of the court and state following the statutory requirements of article 64.02(a)(2): the court ordered the State to locate evidence or explain why no evidence could be delivered to the court.[68] The district court in Tom Green County "ordered the district attorney's office to investigate and report whether any biological evidence had remained from the criminal investigation two decades earlier."[69] In its response to the court, the district attorney stated that "neither its office nor the police department had possession of any evidence collected during the criminal investigation."[70] Though semen evidence had been introduced at the trial, it no longer existed, and, therefore, the court denied appointment of counsel because no testing could be done.[71]

In these ten cases, we see examples of the State searching for evidence and, if the evidence could not be located, presenting witness testimony and affidavits attesting to searches done to locate evidence. Unfortunately, as the next section will show, some courts do not require the State to follow the statute.

c. How Courts Have Misinterpreted the Requirements of 64.03(a)(1)(A)and Created an Erroneous Burden of Proof on the Movant (Two Motions Denied)

Section 64.03(a)(1)(A) states that a convicting court may order DNA testing only if the *court* finds that the evidence:

1. still exists;

2. is in a condition making DNA testing possible; *and*
3. has been subjected to a chain of custody sufficient to establish that it has not been substituted, tampered with, replaced, or altered in any material respect . . .[72]

There is debate regarding who has the burden to establish that evidence still exists in a testable condition and has been in a proper chain of custody. In fact, the CCA accepted *Garcia v. State* on review to "address whether the statute places a burden upon the appellant to make these showings as a predicate to obtaining post-conviction DNA testing."[73] However, the CCA did not rule on the burden issue because it denied the motion on other grounds.[74] The CCA has yet to rule on who has the burden to prove that evidence exists in a condition that allows for DNA testing and has been kept in a proper chain of custody.

From January 2008 to March 2010, the Fourteenth District Court of Appeals ruled twice that the appellant has the burden of satisfying the requirements of article 64.03(a)(1)(A) and has failed to meet that burden. In *Durden v. State*, the appellant submitted an affidavit from the Harris County Medical Examiner's Office ("MEO") dated December 2004, stating that the office was in possession of the two hairs found on the victim. [75] The court denied the motion for two reasons. First, despite the fact that the trial court had previously approved the movant's request for DNA testing of the hairs, the court held that the affidavit failed to establish that the MEO "was in possession of the hairs *when the trial court denied appellant's motion for post-conviction DNA testing* or that the hairs still exist[ed]" or that the hairs [we]re in a condition that ma[de] testing possible.[76] So, the Fourteenth Court of Appeals requires a movant to prove anew that both requirements have been met each time he submits a motion for DNA testing and even when compliance with the statutory requirements has already been proven in earlier proceedings. This holding is contrary to the plain meaning of the statute and, thus, is not a permissible statutory interpretation.[77] Now, every time a motion is denied, the court requires that the defendant obtain a new affidavit stating that the evidence was in compliance with the statute contemporaneously with the trial court's denial the defendant's motion. To require a movant to obtain affidavits each time a motion is submitted places an undue burden on the petitioner, particularly indigent defendants and also burdens the state agents who are required to complete these redundant affidavits.

Moreover, the court denied testing because the appellant "ma[de] no assertions in his motion or affidavit regarding whether the hairs ha[d] been subjected to a sufficient chain of custody and offer[ed] no evidence regarding this issue. Thus, appellant ha[d] failed to satisfy his burden of proving that the hairs ha[d] been subjected to a sufficient chain of custody."[78] In order to avoid this second reason for denial, a movant could include a section in the affidavit in which the state agency could attest to the evidence having been in a proper chain of custody. However, the court fails to indicate what amount of proof it considers sufficient in order for the movant to satisfy the court-imposed burden of proving a proper chain of custody.[79]

In *Delacruz v. State*, the Fourteenth Court of Appeals once again denied a motion for testing because the "[t]rial court found that appellant had failed to demonstrate that any biological evidence exists and is in a condition making DNA testing possible."[80] Again, the trial and appellate courts failed to require the State to comply with section 64.02(a)(2) and explain why the State was unable to deliver the evidence.[81]

While the opinion in *Lara v. State* concerned constitutional rights, the opinion reveals that at least one trial court in Harris County is also placing an impermissible burden on the convicted person to prove the evidence still exists and is in a testable condition.[82] The court denied the motion because "[t]he defendant was unable to show that the evidence still existed or that, if it did exist, that it could be tested."[83] The State submitted affidavits stating that the appellant "failed to establish that (1) evidence still exists; and (2) this evidence is in a condition making DNA testing possible."[84] If the trial court were enforcing the requirements of the statute, the State's affidavits would not be focused on the appellant's failure to establish information that the state is legally required to furnish. Rather, the State is required by article 64.02(a)(2) to explain "why the state cannot deliver the evidence."[85]

In contrast to the holdings of the Fourteenth Court of Appeals and at least one Harris County criminal court, some courts are following the statutory mandate and requiring the State either to deliver the evidence to the court or to explain why the State cannot comply with the request to deliver the evidence. For example, the El Paso appellate court noted that the trial court, in following the dictates of the statute, "made findings that the DNA evidence still existed, was in a condition that would make DNA testing possible, and had been subjected to a chain of custody sufficient to establish that it had not been substituted, tampered with, replaced, or altered in any material respect."[86] Likewise, in *Robinson v. State* the trial court ordered the state to deliver the physical evidence or explain in writing why the evidence could not be delivered.[87] These trials courts are correctly placing the burden of proof on the state, just as the statute mandates.

3. If Testing Not Previously Conducted, Movant Must Prove Lack of Fault or Prove Either DNA Testing Was Not Available or Could Not Provide Probative Results

a. A Movant Faces an Almost Impossible Task of Making a "Particularized Showing" of Lack of Fault (Six Motions Denied)

The movant must show that evidence was not previously tested "through no fault of the convicted person, for reasons that are of a nature such that the interests of justice require DNA testing."[88] In order to meet this burden of persuasion, a movant must make a "particularized showing of the absence of fault whenever she invokes article 64.01(b)(1)(B)."[89] Courts use the lack of a particularized showing to deny motions for DNA testing; in this particular twenty-six-month analysis period, testing was denied six times for this reason.[90] Otherwise, courts have reasoned, a defendant could purposely choose to not test evidence during trial in order to preserve the issue on appeal.[91] To quote one court: "To hold otherwise would allow defendants to 'lie behind the log' by failing to seek testing because of a reasonable fear that the results would be incriminating at trial but then seeking testing after conviction when there is no longer anything to lose."[92]

The purpose of the statute makes sense from both a public policy and jurisprudential perspective; defendants cannot be allowed to block DNA testing as a dishonest strategy to stave off the finality of their sentence. Additionally, an appellant can, under this provision, meet the burden of persuasion if "he can demonstrate that the incremental probative value of testing a discrete item of biological material was not reasonably apparent at the time of trial."[93] However, problems can arise with this requirement if a defense attorney chooses to not have DNA tested that might prove exculpatory.

The CCA in *Skinner* held that a movant is barred from testing evidence even if his trial attorney's miscalculation and misjudgment is proved post-conviction.[94] Henry Watkins Skinner was convicted of capital murder and sentenced to death for the 1993 murders of Twila Busby, his live-in girlfriend, and her two adult sons.[95] Among the items that have not been tested are knives, Busby's rape kit, a bloody dishtowel, and a windbreaker that is likely to have belonged to Busby's uncle, who is widely believed to be the murderer.[96]

The CCA denied Skinner's motion for DNA testing because his "defense counsel's decision to forgo testing was a reasonable trial strategy."[97] Skinner's trial attorney employed the defense strategy of claiming that the State "conducted a shoddy investigation" because, as this attorney opined later, he feared that some of the evidence had Skinner's DNA on it.[98] The CCA concluded that even if it were to consider post-trial evidence, such as the recanting of incriminating testimony of a neighbor, that evidence did not require the CCA to "retrospectively second-guess a trial strategy that seemed reasonable at the time . . ."[99]

In crafting its opinion, the CCA failed to consider two significant facts. First, Skinner's trial attorney, Harold Comer, had previously prosecuted Skinner twice when Comer was the Gray County District Attorney.[100] Second, after resigning as the District Attorney in 1992, the Texas State Bar "suspended Comer for mishandling money from a seized drug fund.[101] While mishandling of money does not implicate a lawyer's ability to defend a client, the CCA's complete omission of evidence of Comer's possible prejudice and questionable character for truthfulness in analyzing whether Comer acted "reasonabl[y]" at the time of Skinner's trial, casts serious doubt on the soundness of the CCA's holding.

Students from Northwestern University investigated Skinner's case in 2000 and publicized the facts about Comer's prior relationship with Skinner and Comer's suspension from the bar.[102] Additionally, the students publicized the fact that Busby's uncle—who is believed to be the murderer—had an incestuous relationship with the victim and had stalked her the night of her murder.[103] Despite strong evidence pointing to the uncle's culpability and Comer's knowledge during the trial of evidence proving the uncle's incest and stalking of the victim, Comer chose to not request DNA testing of any evidence, including the rape kit.[104] After the Northwestern University investigation caused national media focus on the case, the State agreed to test some of the evidence, including blood from a notebook, bloodstained gauze, and hair found in Busby's hands.[105] The results from the gauze "reflected the profile of an unknown male individual" and blood on a cassette tape revealed the profile of two unknown people.[106] The CCA refused—despite the results of the 2000 DNA results and the facts that Comer prosecuted Skinner twice, ignored evidence that implicated Busby's uncle, and refused to request that any of the evidence be tested—to allow testing of evidence that might reveal the identity of the true murderer. By ignoring the evidence of Comer's questionable character and previous adversarial relationship with Skinner and the fact that a key witness recanted her testimony, the CCA has created a nearly impossible burden on a defendant to make a particularized showing of lack of fault when a trial attorney failed to or chose to not request DNA testing during the trial.

b. DNA Not Previously Tested? Movant Must Explain Why (Three Motions Denied)

As a corollary of the requirement that a movant must show that testing was not done through no fault of his own, if the biological evidence was not previously tested, a movant must also prove that the testing was not done because of one of two reasons: (1) DNA testing was "not available"[107] or (2) DNA testing "was available, but not technologically capable of providing probative results."[108] When the evidence was not previously tested, the CCA requires a movant to show "*why* the biological evidence was not previously tested . . . ."[109] Additionally, "[t]he standard is not whether new technology would yield more probative results, but whether then-existing technology was capable of yielding any probative results at all."[110]

4. If Previously Conducted, a Movant Must Prove Why Newer Testing Ought to Be Conducted (Three Motions Denied)

If the biological evidence has been previously tested, a movant may request testing utilizing newer testing techniques only if the newer testing techniques "provide a reasonable likelihood of results that are more accurate and probative than the results of the previous test. . . ."[111] The CCA has interpreted this requirement to mean the following: "[I]f no results were in fact obtained through the old testing and the likelihood of obtaining a result is significantly enhanced by the newer 'clean up' techniques, we think that appellant has satisfied article 64(b)(2)."[112] The movant must state in his motion that the newer techniques will result in more "accurate and probative" results.[113] The Dallas appellate court set an even higher bar, denying testing because the movant failed to provide any evidence that the results would not be any different using a different testing method.[114] This holding seems to imply that a movant must supply some type of evidence, perhaps expert testimony, to establish that the new results would be more accurate and probative than the previous results.

In *Swearingen*, the appellant requested that blood found under the victim's fingernails be tested using the new STR or mini-STR testing.[115] This blood had already been tested by DPS during the original trial using PCR testing and both Swearingen and the victim were "excluded as contributors of the flakes."[116] Swearingen averred that if more advanced test results were submitted to the Combined DNA Index System (CODIS) database, there would be a greater chance of obtaining a match than with the older, less discerning results (which did not result in a CODIS match).[117] The CCA denied Swearingen's request that the flakes be tested using newer techniques because he failed to show "a reasonable likelihood that results would be more accurate or probative."[118] The CCA seemed to focus more on the fact that the older results excluded Swearingen and the victim, rather than on the fact that newer testing and more accurate results might result in a CODIS match to the actual murderer.[119] The reasoning used to justify this denial of Swearingen's request belies the purpose of the DNA statute and ignores one of the major principles of our criminal justice system: to make every possible effort to catch the guilty.

5. Identity Must Have Been or Be an Issue (Eleven Motions Denied)

Article 64.03(a)(1)(B) allows for DNA testing only if "identity was or is an issue in the case. . . ."[120] Even in a case where the victim knew her attacker and identified him at trial as the person who robbed and sexually assaulted her, DNA evidence can prove exculpatory and testing should be allowed in cases where there is a lone attacker.[121] The defendant must "bring forth an appellate record affirmatively demonstrating that identity was an issue during trial."[122] A court will deny testing if timing of the assault is the only issue.[123] Additionally, a court will deny testing if the court has previously held that identity was not an issue and the appellant fails to provide any additional factors that would make identity an issue.[124]

Five additional cases, where testing was denied because identity was held to not be an issue, seem rightly decided. For example, in *In re White*, the court held that identity was not an issue because the police saw appellant getting out of the same car that held the victim and that testing of a shirt to show absence of blood on it would only serve to impeach the complaining witness, not prove that identity was an issue.[125] In *Manning v. State*, subsequent testing was denied because previous testing showed that the "DNA profile was consistent with Manning's profile....[a] one in 116 quintillion" probability.[126] In *Spurlock v. State*, the court denied testing because even if another person's DNA was found, the defendant's stepdaughter had accused him of sexually assaulting her for seven years and therefore identity was not at issue.[127] In two cases the courts held that DNA testing could not be used to prove an affirmative defense where identity was not an issue.[128] These five cases seem consistent with the intent of the statute: post-conviction DNA testing is permitted under the statute because we want to establish the true identity of the assailant, not to allow for repeat testing when inculpatory DNA results have already been obtained, when testing is sought solely for impeachment or to establish affirmative defenses, or when DNA testing will not negate a victim's testimony.

In three cases, however, identity does seem to be an issue and testing ought to have been allowed. In *Cuellar v. State*, the appellant maintained that the victim "'wanted to have sex with [appellant]; however, [appellant] refused [and] claimed that the victim willingly had sex with his co-defendant."[129] If the results of the DNA test proved that Cuellar's co-defendant had sex with the victim, this fact would seem to cast doubt on the identity of the assailant and could be considered exculpatory evidence or impeachment evidence against Cuellar's co-defendant. Additionally, this holding seems to go against the holding in *Blacklock*: if there is a lone attacker, testing should be done.[130]

In *Cloud v. State*, a semen stain that was found on one of the victim's underwear was tested, and it did not belong to the defendant.[131] Appellant requested testing of hair that was found on one of the girl's underwear.[132] If the hair were tested (and the semen stain retested using more probative results) and the results were submitted to CODIS, there is a possibility that a match might be found; or, alternatively, the test might prove that the hair belongs to Cloud. Either way, in light of the exculpatory result the DNA testing of the semen stain, the court should have allowed testing of the hair. Ideally the court should have determined the identity of the person who left the semen stain by retesting the stain, testing the hair, and submitting both results to CODIS.

In the third case that contradicts legislative intent, *Conlin v. State*, DPS conducted testing of a stain. [133] Conlin "could not be excluded as a contributor to the stain," and, after the results were entered into the CODIS database, a match was found with a "convicted offender" in West Virginia.[134] The opinion does not state whether the offender was in Texas at the time of the assault and could have committed the assault. Conlin questioned whether the CODIS results were incorrect, and another person was responsible.[135] Again, where a test is inconclusive, the state ought to retest the evidence and resubmit the results to CODIS. Current and accurate test results are the only way our justice system can ensure that the truly guilty, and not the actually innocent, are punished.

6. Exculpatory Results: A Movant Need Only Establish a "Preponderance of the Evidence" (Twenty-three Motions Denied)

Article 64.03(a)(2)(A) states that "[a] convicting court may order DNA testing under this chapter only if . . . the convicted person establishes by a preponderance of the evidence that . . . the person would not have been convicted if exculpatory results had been obtained through DNA testing . . . ."[136] One court interpreted the statute thus: "[I]t is not [the court's] task to determine the likelihood that DNA testing will obtain results that are exculpatory" but rather to determine whether a defendant "would have been convicted in the event that the results *are* exculpatory."[137] A movant has met the statutory burden when "substantial corroboration of the appellant's exculpatory account would have a strong tendency to engender a reasonable doubt in an average juror's mind."[138]

In one line of cases, the appellate courts have held that the presence of another's DNA would not exculpate the defendant's guilt. In *Prible v. State*, the CCA noted that even if additional DNA testing found the presence of another person's DNA, the DNA results would not be exculpatory in the face of "the additional evidence presented at trial" and would not meet the statutory requirement that the results would establish "by preponderance of the evidence that Appellant would not have been convicted if the jury had heard that DNA from a third-party was present."[139] Likewise, in *Jacobs v. State*, the presence of another person's hair would only serve to "'merely muddy the waters,'" but would not, on its own, exonerate the defendant.[140] In a case where a victim was raped by multiple men, "a negative result . . . would not conclusively exonerate Appellant."[141] In *Sepeda v. State*, the court interpreted the statute to mean that "[e]ven if the evidence was favorable to appellant (meaning that appellant's DNA was not obtained in the fingernail scrapings), that *alone* falls far short of creating a reasonable inference that someone else killed the decedent . . . ."[142] In another case the court denied testing because "the mere touching of an object is not certain to leave testable biological material on the object."[143] In *Yarbrough v. State*, the court denied testing because even if the DNA of appellant's co-defendant were found on the deceased's clothing, this potentially exculpatory finding "would only muddy the waters and would not establish by a preponderance of the evidence that Yarbrough would not have been convicted."[144] While these opinions are compliant with the intent of the statute, co-conspirators might be identified and convicted if the evidence were tested. Moreover, if all the biological evidence in these cases was tested and the results submitted CODIS, we might catch the perpetrators in unsolved cases.

In a second line of cases, the appellate courts have found that DNA testing results would not prove exculpatory because of the amount of competing inculpatory* evidence. For example, in *Swearingen*, the CCA noted that even if the court were to grant all the requested testing, Swearingen "[could not] show by a preponderance of the evidence, or that there is a 51% chance, that he would not have been convicted."[145] A person has not met the exculpatory results requirement if "the record contains other substantial evidence of guilt independent of that for which the movant seeks DNA testing."[146] Some of the "substantial evidence" referenced by the CCA does not appear to be credible. For example, the CCA cited snitch testimony, a type of evidence that has historically proven to be highly unreliable, of other inmates who claimed that Swearingen admitted to killing the victim.[147]

Moreover, in *Swearingen* the CCA failed to consider other exculpatory evidence. First, the former Harris County Medical Examiner Joye Carter recanted her earlier testimony and admitted that the victim's body was most likely disposed of well after Swearingen was in jail on other charges.[148] Second, a retired forensic pathologist who reviewed the evidence in the case noted that "no rational and intellectually honest person c[ould] look at the evidence and conclude Larry Swearingen is guilty of this horrible crime."[149] A court ought not to be allowed to pick and choose the evidence it relies upon in determining whether to grant a motion. If a court is not willing to consider all the evidence, how can it arrive at a just decision?

Other cases do seem rightly decided in light of the great amount of inculpatory evidence. For example, in *Coronado v. State*, the court held that testing of hair found on the victim would not prove exculpatory because "[a]ppellant was seen at the park by a police officer who noted that appellant had grass in his pubic hair and grass hanging from his

* Refers to evidence which tends to refute a justification or excuse for a defendant's actions and which will tend to show the defendant is guilty or has the required criminal intent.

penis."[150] In *Harris v. State*, the court denied testing because "'without more, the presence of another person's DNA at the crime scene would not constitute affirmative evidence of the appellant's innocence.'"[151]

Appellate courts have also found that movants failed to establish by a preponderance of the evidence that they would not have been convicted for several other reasons: lack of evidence,[152] lack of DNA would not disprove culpability,[153] presence of DNA would not disprove elements of the crime,[154] and using DNA testing to prove perjury would not establish exculpatory results.[155] In two cases the appellate courts denied testing based on the lack of exculpatory results without explaining why those results would not be exculpatory.[156]

7. Convicted Person Requirement (One Motion Denied)

Article 64.01(a) allows for a "convicted person" to "submit to the convicting court a motion for forensic DNA testing."[157] In order to have standing, the movant must have been convicted of the crime for which he wishes to have evidence tested.[158] One denial of post-conviction DNA testing was affirmed because the movant had received deferred adjudication and was, therefore, not technically convicted of the crime.[159]

8. Affidavit Requirement: Testing Denied If Movant Fails to Include a Sworn Affidavit (Two Motions Denied)

Article 64.01(a) requires that a motion "be accompanied by an affidavit, sworn to by the convicted person, containing statements of fact in support of the motion."[160] Therefore, if a movant fails to include an affidavit or sworn statement, a court will deny his motion.[161] Appellate courts have twice upheld denials of DNA testing based on this type of noncompliance with Chapter 64's requirements .[162]

9. Reason for Denial Not Given (Four Motions Denied)

The statute does not require that a trial court "make written findings when denying a defendant's motion for forensic testing."[163] In four opinions the courts' denials of DNA testing did not state a specific reasons for the denials.[164]

C. Appointment of Counsel

Because appointment of counsel has no bearing on whether a court will ultimately grant testing, the cases regarding appointment of counsel have been grouped separately. Article 64.01(c) states: "a person is entitled to counsel during a proceeding under this chapter." The convicting court "shall appoint counsel for the convicted person" when three requirements are met:

1. the person informs the court that the person wishes to submit a motion under this chapter,
2. the court finds reasonable grounds for a motion to be filed, and
3. the court determines that the person is indigent.[165]

The reasonable grounds requirement is the only one that courts have used in the last two years to deny appointment of counsel.

1. "Reasonable Grounds" Requirement (Four Requests Denied)

The reasonable grounds requirement was added in 2003 after "counties and judges" reported being "'flooded' with letters from inmates asking for DNA testing" and the requests "provide[d] no information as to whether post-conviction DNA [testing] would be appropriate."[166] From 2001 to 2003 a judge was required to appoint an attorney upon submission of a motion for testing.[167] The addition of the reasonable grounds requirement was intended to "weed out frivolous claims [such as possession of drug or theft] while still ensuring a person with a valid claim access to testing."[168] The Legislature did intend a liberal standard when appointing counsel: When in doubt, a judge would err on the side of caution and appoint a lawyer in case the convicted person had a valid claim.[169]

From January 2008 to March 2010, appellate courts have denied appointment of counsel four times, each for the same reason: lack of reasonable grounds. Courts have found lack of reasonable grounds for appointing counsel in the following scenarios: when the evidence has been destroyed[170]; the movant fails to "identify [in his motion] any evidence containing biological material;"[171] "there is no evidence that can be submitted for DNA testing or if 'no viable argument for testing can be made;'"[172] or when "[t]he presence of another person's DNA at a crime scene will not, without more, constitute affirmative evidence of appellant's innocence."[173]

2. Counsel Appointed (Two Requests Granted)

From January 2008 to March 2010, appellate courts appointed counsel twice. In appointing counsel in *In re Padilla*, the court held that counsel should be appointed even though the victim knew the appellant, following the holding in *Blacklock* where the CCA held that testing should not be precluded even when the victim knows the defendant.[174] "Significantly," the State "conceded" that Padilla was entitled to appointment of counsel in light of *Blacklock*.[175] In *Franklin*, the appellate court reversed the trial court's refusal to appoint counsel, noting that the facts of the case presented reasonable grounds.[176]

D. Non-Statutory-Based Problems and Issues

No statute can completely ameliorate shoddy representation or a court that tarries in issuing an opinion. There are four cases where an appellate court had to deal with these issues.

1. Attorney Failing to Represent Client (One Petition Denied)

In *In re Marshall*, the appellant filed a petition for writ of mandamus because he had not heard from his attorney Jerome Godinich in the nine months since the attorney's appointment.[177] The court denied the petition because no evidence showed that the trial court had held a hearing regarding Godinich's representation.[178] While it is heartening to know that a court appointed an attorney, the appointment of an ineffectual attorney who fails to contact a defendant for almost a year is certainly not the type of counsel our Legislature envisioned when implementing Chapter 64.[179]

2. Courts Failing to Rule on Motions (Two Writs Granted; One Writ Denied)

In three cases, appellate courts ruled on motions to compel a trial court to act. In *In re Lockett*, the court conditionally granted the writ to compel the trial court to respond to Lockett's motions for testing and appointment of counsel.[180] The appellate court held that because seven months had passed, the trial court had abused its discretion by "failing to timely rule on [Lockett]'s motion for DNA testing."[181] Likewise, in *In re McGary*, the court granted the petition for writ of mandamus against the trial court for failing to issue a ruling after a hearing had been held ten months earlier and McGary's counsel had made three inquiries to the trial court about issuing the ruling.[182] Conversely, in *In re Ryan*, even though the defendant claimed that the court had not ruled on a motion for testing and appointment of counsel filed six months prior, the court denied the petition because the defendant failed to prove that he brought the motions to the trial court's attention.[183]

E. Testing Approved (Five Motions Approved)

From January 2008 to March 2010, appellate courts approved five motions for post-conviction DNA testing.

In *Ex parte Chabot*, DNA testing conducted in 2007 proved that the only witness in the case, Pabst, Chabot's co-conspirator, had perjured himself by testifying that Chabot had sexually assaulted the victim before murdering her.[184] In fact, Pabst was the only person whose DNA was found in vaginal samples.[185] On December 9, 2009, as a result of these findings, the CCA vacated Chabot's conviction for a 1986 murder and his life sentence.[186] According to Chabot's appellate lawyer, Bruce Anton, the court denied Chabot's requests for DNA testing prior to the passage of the DNA statute in 2001. [187] After the DNA statute was passed, Chabot's request for testing was finally allowed.[188] Mr. Anton believes that the DNA statute was crucial to Chabot's success in obtaining testing of the DNA.[189]

In *In re Morton*, the Williamson County District Attorney, John Bradley, denied testing of a bloody bandana that was found near the home the murder victim shared with her husband, who was convicted of her murder.[190] The appellate court reversed the trial court's denial of testing of the bandana.[191] In ordering the bandana to be tested, the court noted that post-trial testing of a bed sheet showed that the accused had not, as the State contended at trial, masturbated on the sheet after killing his wife.[192] The appellate court held that "when a defendant obtains exculpatory results as a result of court-ordered DNA testing, those exculpatory results may be considered when conducting a Chapter 64 analysis with respect to subsequent requests for DNA testing of other evidence in the case."[193] The court noted that if the bandana were to contain the deceased's as well as that of a third-party's DNA, the results would be exculpatory.[194] The court also noted that a similar murder had occurred six years earlier in the Mortons' neighborhood, a few years before the Mortons had moved to the neighborhood.[195]

In *Routier v. State*, the CCA approved testing of a blood stain on a tube sock, flakes from the garage door of the house in which the defendant's two sons were murdered, blood on a nightgown, a pubic hair, and a facial hair.[196] All of these items had been tested previously, but the testing did not yield any results.[197] The CCA applied a two-step test in determining whether to approve testing. First, Routier was able to show that newer DNA testing techniques would provide more accurate and probative results than previously utilized tests.[198] Second, the CCA ruled that if the new test results proved the presence of a stranger, this exculpatory evidence would "more likely than not have caused the jury to harbor a reasonable doubt as to the appellant's guilt and decline to convict her."[199]

In *Esparza v. State*, the CCA actually reversed the lower court's ruling and ordered testing of the rape kit and victim's clothing.[200] Although two witnesses identified the appellant as the rapist, this eyewitness identification:

> is of no consequence in considering whether Esparza has established that, by a preponderance of the evidence, exculpatory DNA tests would prove his innocence. In sexual assault cases like this, any overwhelming eye-witness identification and strong circumstantial evidence . . . supporting guilt is inconsequential when assessing whether a convicted person has sufficiently alleged that exculpatory DNA evidence would prove his innocent under Article 64.03(a)(2)(A).[201]

This holding is noteworthy because the CCA ordered testing despite the great weight of inculpatory evidence.

In *State v. Labonte*, the appellate court upheld the trial court's order to test evidence.[202] Gabriel Sexton was present with two young women the night they were murdered.[203] Sexton claimed that a car drove up, he ran away, and when he returned the girls were badly injured.[204] Instead of going for help he stole the girls' cell phones, a watch, and cigarettes.[205] Sexton did not call the police because he was "'already in enough trouble.'"[206] After the police learned that Sexton had been with the girls the night of the murder, he told "several false stories."[207] Lonnie Labonte knew one of the victims, and he and Melissa Brannon were charged with murdering the two girls.[208] Brannon was promised immunity from a possible forty-year sentence in return for her testimony stating that Labonte murdered the girls.[209] Although no physical evidence connected Labonte to the crime scene, a crime scene investigator for Montgomery County testified at the trial that one of two tests of stains in Labonte's truck tested positive for blood.[210] The investigator also testified that the stains appeared to be blood spatter, even though a DPS chemist could not confirm that the stains were blood.[211] While the appellate court held that Brannon's post-trial recantation could not be considered, the court also held that if the stains from Labonte's truck were not blood and the jury had not heard the county investigator's testimony that blood was present on Labonte's truck, then "there [wa]s a 51% chance that the jury would have found a reasonable doubt of appellee's guilt."[212]

These five cases are examples of how the Texas post-conviction DNA testing statute has afforded defendants the opportunity to prove their innocence. In order to ensure that all convicted persons with statutorily-compliant requests are allowed access to testing, the Legislature ought enact the following amendments: (1) clarify the method to establish that biological material exists; (2) clarify who has the burden of proof in establishing that evidence in a testable condition exists and has been maintained in a proper chain of custody; and (3) ensure that a court cannot deny testing because DNA testing has not been previously conducted. While the 2009 proposed amendment would solve the third issue, the first two issues must also be addressed.[213] If these statutory changes are implemented, Texas will make great progress in ensuring justice is not denied, both for individuals who have been wrongfully, and tragically, convicted, and for society, whose members will feel safer knowing the truly guilty are punished for the crimes they commit.

III. 2009 Proposed Amendment to Chapter 64: Movant Would No Longer Be Required to Explain Why DNA Testing Was Not Previously Conducted

The 2009 proposed amendment would have deleted part of article 64.01(b)(1) of the current statute, which requires a defendant to explain why DNA testing had not been previously done if he requests testing on untested biological material.[214] This proposed change to the statute would have increased a convicted person's access to testing. Unfortunately, the Legislature was not able to vote on the amendment because of wrangling on an unrelated bill. Hopefully, this amendment will be resubmitted in 2011 and finally become law.

Under the 2009 amendment, article 64.01(b)(1) would no longer require a convicted person to explain why testing was not previously conducted on evidence containing biological material.[215]

The new section would only require the defendant to establish that the evidence had not been previously subjected to DNA testing.[216] The deletion of the requirement to explain why testing had not previously been done would prevent "an unsympathetic judge" from denying a motion "even where material went untested due to failure on the part of the defense attorney rather than defendant."[217] The Legislature recognized that "[a]llowing convicted persons to move for the DNA testing of untested biological material, regardless of the reason it had not been tested, would help secure the release of wrongfully convicted persons and help ensure that justice was done."[218]

According to testimony given during the House hearings, the change was made because of cases like Ricardo Rachell's, a Houston man who was wrongfully convicted and incarcerated for over six years before DNA testing exonerated him.[219] In Rachell's case, "[n]either the D.A. nor the court-appointed defense attorney requested testing despite the fact that biological evidence existed. If not for a sympathetic judge, Mr. Rachell's post-conviction request for DNA testing could [have been] denied because the evidence existed at trial but was not tested."[220] The bill would have helped to ensure that if exculpatory DNA existed, testing would not be denied solely on the basis that it had not been tested previously.[221]

Deleting the fault provision would also help the six convicted persons whose cases were detailed in Part II.B.3.a: Johnson, Cooper, Faison, Robinson, Skinner, and Routier.[222] Deleting the requirement of having to explain why the evidence was not previously tested would help two other convicted persons: Garcia and Swearingen.[223] If the 2009 amendment were passed, these eight convicted persons and countless other prisoners could finally be able to have evidence tested and possibly be exonerated just as Ricardo Rachell was freed after being wrongfully convicted.

IV. Recommendations for Additional Statutory Reform

A. Legislature Must Clarify Method of Identifying Biological Material So Movant Is Not Caught in Statutory *Catch-22*

As described above in Part II.B.1, how can a convicted person prove that evidence containing biological material exists before said evidence is tested to determine if biological material exists? The CCA created this *Catch-22* interpretation of Chapter 64 in its opinion in *Swearingen*.[224] In order to eradicate this *Catch-22*, the Legislature must answer the CCA's request to clarify the method by which evidence is determined to contain biological material.

One remedy might be to provide a definition of "biological evidence." The Justice Project's Model DNA statute contains the following definition of "biological evidence":

> When used in this Act, "biological evidence" means the contents of a sexual assault examination kit; and/or any item that could contain blood, semen, hair, saliva, skin tissue, or other identifiable biological material from a victim of the offense that was the subject of the criminal investigation or may reasonably be used to incriminate or exculpate any person for the offense. This definition applies whether that material is catalogued separately (*e.g.*, on a slide, swab, or in a test tube) or is present on other evidence (including, but not limited to, clothing, ligatures, bedding or other household material, drinking cups, cigarettes, etc.).[225]

While this addition does not supply a method for determining whether biological material exists, the addition of this definition would provide the CCA with clarification as to the types of evidence on which the Legislature seeks to allow DNA testing.

B. Legislature Must Clarify That State Has Burden of Proof in Establishing Existence of Testable Evidence and Proper Chain of Custody

The Legislature must clarify the burden of proof under section 64.02(a) so that no court can claim that ambiguity exists as to the burden of proof and erroneously force a convicted person to prove that evidence exists and has been maintained in a proper chain of custody. Rather, the Legislature must make clear that the State has the burden of either proving that the evidence no longer exists in a testable condition or that the evidence has not been maintained in a proper chain of custody.

The construction of the statute further bolsters the argument that the State has the burden to establish that the evidence is in a testable condition and has been in a proper chain of custody. The beginning of section 64.02(a)(1)(A) states relief will be granted "if the *court* so finds . . . ."[226] In contrast, section 64.03(a)(2), which deals with proving that a convicted person would not have been convicted with exculpatory DNA results, states that relief will be granted if "the *convicted person* establishes . . . ."[227] Thus, the plain reading of the statute places the onus on the court to determine that the evidence exists in a testable condition and has been kept in a proper chain of custody. Until the CCA rules or the Legislature clarifies who has the burden of proof in establishing that evidence is in a condition to be tested and has been maintained in a proper chain of custody, movants in certain courts, such as the Fourteenth Court of Appeals and at least one Harris County criminal court, face an almost impossible burden of proof in satisfying the requirements imposed by these the courts' erroneous interpretation of Chapter 64.

There is also a compelling public policy argument in favor of conclusively codifying that the state has the burden of establishing the existence of the evidence and proper chain of custody of biological evidence. When the state has the burden of looking for evidence, evidence that was thought to be lost may be found. This very scenario has occurred at least three times in the last seven years.

In San Antonio evidence was discovered twenty years after the crime, despite the State's belief that the evidence had been destroyed.[228]

The police officer assigned to the "cold case," went to the Criminal Investigation Laboratory and spoke with the Chief Medical Examiner, who located the "missing" evidence in the Medical Examiner's Office.[229] The discovery of the missing rape kit resulted in the conviction of the killer twenty-two years after the rape and murder of Rachel Kosub.[230]

In Houston, a request was originally denied because no evidence was believed to exist.[231] The trial judge ordered another search be conducted after sworn statements indicated no evidence existed.[232] The second search revealed that evidence did in fact exist.[233] Although "conventional [DNA] testing" did not garner results, Burke's attorney believes that "more complex and expensive mitochondrial DNA* tests" might produce results.[234] Burke is still waiting for permission and funding to have the mitochondrial DNA testing performed.[235]

In Harris County, because of the efforts of the District Attorney's Post-Conviction Review Section, evidence was located and tested, resulting in the exoneration of Michael Anthony Green.[236] Green's attorney "credited attorneys and investigators" in the D.A.'s Post-Conviction Review Section for locating in a warehouse the clothing worn by the victim.[237] The Harris County First Assistant District Attorney believes the State's efforts led to the locating and testing of the evidence that ultimately freed Green after twenty-seven years of incarceration.[238]

Much like the examples of the State's numerous good faith efforts to locate missing evidence or ascertain that it had been destroyed as discussed above in Part II.B.2.b, if the State were consistently required to search for evidence and attest to whether it exists in a testable condition and has been subjected to a proper chain of custody, society as a whole benefits. We may have more situations where lost evidence is found and can be tested, as with Burke; where the guilty are convicted, as with Dossett; or where the innocent are freed, as with Michael Anthony

---

* Mitochondrial DNA analysis (mtDNA) can be used to examine the DNA from samples that cannot be analyzed by other types of tests such as STR (short tandem repeat), PCR (polymerase chain reaction), or RFLP (restriction fragment length polymorphism). Nuclear DNA must be extracted from samples for testing by RFLP, PCR, and STR. However, mtDNA analysis uses DNA extracted from another cellular organelle called a mitochondrion. Older biological samples that lack nucleated cellular material, such as hair, bones, and teeth, cannot be analyzed with standard tests, but they can be analyzed with mtDNA.

Green. At the very least, defendants and society would be assured that every effort was made to find the evidence that might ultimately have exonerated the wrongly incarcerated and implicated the guilty.

V. CONCLUSION

This paper has focused on one component of the criminal justice process: post-conviction DNA testing. Chapter 64 has provided convicted persons access to testing: to-date, forty-two people have been found actually innocent of crimes for which they were wrongfully convicted.[239]

Some weaknesses in the statute have allowed courts to strictly or even incorrectly interpret the statute and deny access to testing for appellants who seem to have compelling cases. In these cases specifically, there are three situations in which courts have erroneously denied testing by utilizing three particular sections of the statute: where the defendant is unable to prove before testing that biological material exists; where courts have placed on the defendant the burden to prove both that evidence exists in a testable condition and that the evidence has been maintained in a proper chain of custody; and where courts have denied testing because a convicted person has failed to adequately explain why DNA testing was not previously done.

The 2009 proposed change to the DNA statute would fix the third problem. Additional changes to the statute—in order to clarify the method for determining the existence of biological material and to clarify that the State has the burden to establish the existence of testable evidence that has been maintained in a proper chain of custody—would make the statute even stronger, thus ensuring that more wrongfully convicted persons have the chance to test evidence.

All Texans involved in the criminal justice system—the judiciary, the State, and the Legislature—owe their constituents and society a criminal justice system where justice is served: where the actually innocent have the means by which to prove their innocence. By creating a stronger post-conviction DNA testing statute, our Legislature will ensure that justice is not denied.

ENDNOTES

1. Dist. Attorney's Office for the Third Judicial Dist. v. Osborne, 129 S. Ct. 2308, 2312 (2009).

2. Jeff Carlton, *Innocence Group Taking DNA Case Reviews Statewide*, AP ALERT – POLITICAL, June 4, 2009. As of February 20, 2010, forty-one people had been exonerated through DNA testing. Added to this list are Jerry Lee Evens and Ernest Sonnier, THE JUSTICE PROJECT, CONVICTING THE INNOCENT: THE LATEST TEXAS EXONERATIONS, http.//www.thejusticeproject.org/blog/texas/convicting-the-innocent-the-latest-texas-exonerations (last visited Feb. 20, 1010). The author had to update this number while revising this paper. On July 30, 2010, Michael Anthony Greene was released from prison after being exonerated. Brian Rogers, *DNA Clears Man 27 Years After Rape Conviction*, HOUS. CHRON, July 28, 2010 [hereinafter *DNA Clears Man*], *available at* http://www.chron.com/disp/story.mpl/metropolitan/7128807.html. Mr. Greene was incarcerated longer than any of the other forty-one exonerees, spending twenty-seven years in prison. *Id.*

3. Senate Journal, 81st Legislature—Regular Session, Proceedings 15-16, Eighth Day, Feb. 4, 2009, *available at* http://www.journals.senate.state.tx.us/sjrnl/81r/html/81RSJ02-04-F.HTM.

4. *Id.* Cole's innocence was proved seven years after his death. *Id.*

5. *Id.*

6. Task Force on Indigent Defense, Timothy Cole Advisory Panel on Wrongful Convictions, www.courts.state.tx.us/tfid/tcap.asp (last visited Feb. 1, 2010).

7. *See* Part III for an analysis of the proposed post-conviction DNA testing statute.

8. *See* S.B. 3, 77th Leg. (Tex. 2001).

9. *See* TEX. CODE CRIM. PROC. ANN. arts. 64.01-.05 (Vernon 2007).

10. As of February 10, 2010, there were 467 state and federal opinions that resulted with the Westlaw search "64 /p post /p conviction /p DNA."

11. S.B. 3, 77th Leg. (Tex. 2001) (Bill Analysis). *See* Appendix A for the text of the current statute.

12. *Id.*

13. *See* TEX. CODE CRIM. PROC. ANN. art. 38.43 (Vernon 2007). Article 38.43 requires the State, or a clerk or officer in charge of the evidence in a criminal case resulting in a conviction to preserve evidence. *Id.* The State may destroy evidence in cases where the conviction is longer than ten years in length, if the defendant receives notice of the destruction order and no objection is received within 90 days. The statute allows for counties with populations under 100,000 to send the evidence to the Department of Public Safety (DPS) for storage. *Id.*

14. *See* arts. 64.01-64.05. In 2007 the Legislature made two changes to the statute. First, the statue "broaden[ed] the circumstances under which the court may order that forensic DNA testing be conducted in a laboratory other than a Department of Public Safety Laboratory." H.B. 681, 80 Leg. (Tex. 2007) (Bill Summary). A court may order testing even if the State, or any other party, objects and the State will pay for the private testing "if good cause is shown." *Id.* A court may order testing even if one of the parties objects, and the State is required to pay for such testing "if good cause is shown." *Id.* Second, the statute as amended imposed a time requirement of forty-five days on judges to appoint counsel after a finding that reasonable grounds exist for such an appointment. *Id.*

15. H.B. 1011, 78th Leg. (Tex. 2003) (Bill Summary). The three other changes were: a guardian is authorized to submit motions on behalf of a defendant and may be represented by counsel if provided to the convicted person; the court may "modify or withdraw an execution date in a death penalty case if it determines that additional proceedings are necessary for

a forensic DNA testing motion"; and clarifies that a person convicted of murder and sentenced to death has the right to direct appeal to the Court of Criminal Appeals. *Id. See* Appendix B for the text of the proposed amendment.

16. *Id. See* part II.C for further discussion of the judicial interpretation of this section. The bill analysis is important because it conveys a sense of trust for judges and a common sense approach to allowing DNA testing that, as this author's analysis will show, is not always practiced by the Texas judiciary. The bill analysis states:

    Judges would not find it difficult to decide if reasonable grounds existed for motions to be filed. Even if the convicted person sends the court a postcard with little information, the judge can make an appropriate decision based on the type and age of the case, among other factors, For example, certain types of cases, such as possession of a controlled substance or theft, would not lend themselves to DNA testing, and some cases are so old that no biological material exists to be tested. These factors would facilitate easy decisions by judges. *When in doubt, a judge would err on the side of caution and appoint a lawyer in case the convicted person had a valid claim. Id.* (emphasis added).

17. *Id. See* Part II.B.6 for further discussion of the judicial interpretation of this section. Article 64.03(a)(2) currently reads:

    A convicting court may order forensic DNA testing under this chapter only if: (2) the convicted person establishes by a preponderance of the evidence that: (A) ~~a reasonable probability exists that~~ the person would not have been ~~prosecuted or~~ convicted if exculpatory results had been obtained through DNA testing . . . .

    art. 63.03(a)(2). The strikethrough indicates the text deleted by the 2003 amendment. H.B. 1011, 78th Leg. (Tex. 2003 Bill Summary).

18. H.B. 1011, 78th Leg. (Tex. 2003) (Bill Analysis) (citing Kutzner v. State, 75 S.W.3d 427 (Tex. Crim. App. 2002)).

In *Kutzner*, the Texas Court of Criminal Appeals (CCA) held that a movant must show that a "reasonable probability" exists "that exculpatory DNA tests would prove that person's innocence before obtaining a court order for DNA testing." *Id.*

19. *Id.*

20. *Id.*

21. This paper was written for a seminar at the University of Houston Law Center. Due to time constraints, opinions predating this period were not examined.

22. As of March 16, 2010, there were 104 Texas state and federal opinions within the Westlaw search rubric "64 /p conviction /p DNA" with the date restriction "after 12/2007." *See* Appendix C for a list of these cases. This number includes ninety-four state opinions and ten federal opinions. *Id.*

23. These weaknesses are examined in part II.B.1, 2, and 3(a) and (c) respectively.

24. In the cases where the court denied the motion for more than one statutory-based reason, the case is mentioned in those respective sections if the court's opinion clarifies how the judiciary is interpreting Chapter 64.

25. *Ex Parte* Twiss, No. WR-69619-04, 2009 WL 623988, at *1 (Tex. Crim. App. Mar. 11, 2009 (denying claim because Chapter 11.07 writ of habeas corpus not available for a Chapter 64 motion); *Ex parte* Thompson, No. WR-50417-03, 2009 WL 330162, at *1 (Tex. Crim. App. Feb. 11, 2009).

26. Salinas v. State, No. 01-06-00831-CR, 2009 WL 1331966, at *1 (Tex. App.—Houston [1st Dist.] May 14, 2009, no pet.) (mem. op., not designated for publication) (where Harris County District Attorney's office and defendant had voluntarily agreed to retest DNA evidence, court lacked jurisdiction to rule on defendant's motion for re-testing because testing was not ordered under Chapter 64); Leal v. State, No. 04-08-00818-CR, 2008 WL 5377753, at *1 (Tex. App.—San Antonio Dec. 23, 2008) (mem. op., not

designated for publication), *aff'd on other grounds,* 303 S.W.3d 292, 302 (Tex. Crim. App. 2009) (appeals from trial court in death penalty cases are appealed directly to Court of Criminal Appeals); Seitz v. State, No. 05-07-01389-CR, 2008 WL 217596, at *1 (Tex. App.—Dallas Jan. 28, 2008, no pet.) (mem. op., not designated for publication) (appellate court lacked jurisdiction to rule on denial of appointment until trial court ruled on motion for testing).

27. Reyes v. Quarterman, Civil Action No. G-99-0037, 2008 WL 4415122, at *1 (S.D. Tex. Sept. 24, 2008) (holding that habeas claim regarding denial of request of expert to analyze inculpatory DNA results was time barred); Ellis v. Quarterman, Civil Action No. H-07-2768, 2008 WL 2963467, at *1 (S.D. Tex. July 30, 2008) (holding that habeas appeal was time barred even where DNA testing was done, three people contributed to DNA sample, and appellant could not be excluded); *In re* Shepard, No. 03-07-00528-CR, 2008 WL 678383, at *1 (Tex. App.—Austin Mar. 12, 2008, no pet.) (mem. op., not designated for publication) (denying motion because brief overdue); Barnes v. State, No. 14-08-00304-CR, 2008 WL 1991777, at *1 (Tex. App.—Houston [14th Dist.] May 8, 2008, no pet.) (mem op., not designated for publication) (refusing to rule on request for appointment of counsel because appeal was filed late).

28. *In re* Pollard, No. 98-08-382 CV, 2008 WL 4587874, at *1 (Tex. App.—Beaumont Oct. 16, 2008, no pet.) (mem. op.) (dismissing appeal because Chapter 64 motion, rather than Chapter 11 motion, was filed for "fingerprint tests, shot pattern tests, distance tests and GSR tests" when there was no biological evidence to be tested).

29. Sanchez v. Thaler, No. 07-10812, 2010 WL 608913, at *1 (5th Cir. Feb. 12, 2010) (discussing whether state Chapter 64 motion tolled limitations for a petition in federal court); Ard v. Thaler, No. 3:07-CV-1127-D, 2009 WL 4249133, at *1 (N.D. Tex. Nov. 24, 2009) (granting habeas application for reasons other than Chapter 64 claim); *Ex parte* Chi, 256

S.W.3d 702, 710 (Tex. Crim. App. 2008) (noting holding in another case that "claims challenging the adequacy of counsel in Chapter 64 hearings for post-conviction DNA testing are not cognizable under Article 11.07"); *Ex parte* Alba, 256 S.W.3d 682 (Tex. Crim. App. 2008) (using statute as an example of when direct appeal is available); *In re* Kitt, No. 01-08-00450-CR, 2008 WL 5102533, at *1 (Tex. App.—Houston [1st Dist.] Dec. 4, 2008, no pet.) (mem. op., not designated for publication) (denying petition for writ of mandamus because petition did not meet requirements of Texas Rules of Appellate Procedure, including required elements such as designation of parties, table of contents, and index of authorities); *In re* Scott, No. 06-08-00096-CV, 2008 WL 4329214, at *1 (Tex. App.—Texarkana Sept. 24, 2008, no pet.) (mem. op.) (denying petition for mandamus relief because defendant's petition did not make clear if trial court had actually ruled on motion for post-conviction testing).

30. Christ v. State, No. 14-08-00902-CR, 2009 WL 5227884, at *1 (Tex. App.—Houston [14th Dist.] Sept. 1, 2009, no pet.) (mem. op., not designated for publication) (denying challenge alleging that requirements of the statute violate due process rights); Lara v. State, Nos. 14-08-00150-CR, 14-08-00152-CR, 2008 WL 4585246, at *1 (Tex. App.—Houston [14th Dist.] Oct. 16, 2008, no pet.) (mem. op., not designated for publication) (holding that the trial court did not violate Lara's rights by conducting the hearing in his absence).

31. Rodriguez v. State, No. 08-07-00248-CR, 2009 WL 1547741, at *1 (Tex. App.—El Paso June 3, 2009, pet. ref'd) (not designated for publication).

32. *In re* Wright, No. 05-08-000728-CV, 2008 WL 376162, at *1 (Tex. App.—Dallas Feb. 13, 2008, no pet.) (mem. op.).

33. Skinner v. Switzer, No. 2:09-CV-0281, 2010 WL 273143, at *1 (N.D. Tex. Jan, 20, 2010; Burke v. Harris County District Attorney, Civil Action No. H-08-1968, 2008 WL 4533929, at *1 (S.D. Tex. Oct. 9, 2008) (dismissing § 1983 claim for failure to state a claim for which relief can be granted).

Subsequently, new evidence unrelated to Burke's § 1983 claim was discovered after the trial court ordered another search for testable evidence. *See* part IV.B for a discussion of how the evidence was discovered in Burke's case.

34. Burrell v. Director, TDCJ-CID, Civil Action No. 1:06-CV-390, 2008 WL 150489, at *2 (E.D. Tex. Jan. 14, 2008); *see also* Cash v. Director, TDCJ-CID, Civil Action No. 5:07cv6, 2008 WL 4104490, at *1 (E.D. Tex. Aug. 29, 2008) (denying habeas relief because denial of DNA testing is state issue and "does not provide a basis for federal habeas relief."); Turner v. Quarterman, Civil Action No. 3:06-CV-0709-D, 2008 WL 2941124, at *1-3 (N.D. Tex. July 30, 2008) (noting that defendant failed to "cite authority supporting his proposition that the state courts' administration of the postconviction DNA proceedings or his right to competent counsel in those proceedings, arising solely under Texas law, violates clearly established Supreme Court law").

35. Brisco v. State, No. 05-07-01507, 2009 WL 1058730 (Tex. App.—Dallas Apr. 21, 2009, pet. ref'd) (mem. op., not designated for publication) (holding that statute does not require trial court to hold hearing; defendant only appealed failure of trial court to hold hearing, not whether identity or exculpatory results was an issue); Becerra v. State, No. 14-07-00774-CR, 2008 WL 5220482, at *1 (Tex. App.—Houston [14th Dist.] Dec. 11, 2008, no pet.) (mem. op., not designated for publication) (overruling movant's claim that a movant must be present at a hearing on a Chapter 64 motion) (mem. op., not designated for publication). Apparently DNA testing had already been done in *Becerra*. *Becerra*, 2008 WL 5220482, at *1 ("The State responded with an affidavit, demonstrating the DNA results were unfavorable to appellant.").

36. Randle v. State, No. 05-07-00849-CR, 2008 WL 933424, at *1 (Tex. App.—Dallas Apr. 8, 2008, no pet.) (mem. op., not designated for publication) (remanding denial of appointment of counsel because at least one report did not "appear to relate

to [appellant's] offense" and State requested appellate court to vacate and remand trial court's denial of counsel).

37. *In re* Gutierrez v. State, No. AP-76186, 2009 WL 4936399, at *1 (Tex. Crim. App. Dec. 16, 2009) (remanding to trial court for additional briefing on the following issue: "[w]hether an order denying appointed counsel under Article 64.01(c) is an immediately appealable order").

38. art. 64.01(a).

39. Routier v. State, 273 S.W.3d 272, 249-50 (Tex. Crim. App. 2008) (citing art. 64.01(a) as the reason for denying testing a tube sock for saliva where neither Routier nor the State had tested the sock for saliva at the time of the trial).

40. *See* Stevens v. State, No. 2-08-408-CR, 2009 WL 485714, at *1 (Tex. App.—Fort Worth Feb. 26, 2009, no pet.) (mem. op., not designated for publication) (because complaining witness waited a month to make accusations, the police department could not collect any biological evidence, and, therefore, no DNA existed to be tested).

41. Swearingen v. State, 303 S.W.3d 728, 729 (Tex. Crim. App. 2010). *See* Boykin v. State, 818 S.W.2d 782, 785 (Tex. Crim. App. 1991). In *Boykin*, the CCA gave a detailed and cogent explanation of acceptable judicial interpretation of statutes: Texas courts are required by the Texas Constitution to "faithfully follow" the intent of the Texas Legislature and follow the plain meaning of the statute. *Id.* Only when the "application of a statute's plain language would lead to absurd consequences that the Legislature could not possibly have intended" should Texas court disregard the literal application of the statutory language. *Id.*

42. *Swearingen*, 303 S.W.3d at 729.

43. *Id.* at 732-33 (noting an indication of favorable results of touch DNA testing in the infamous child-murder case of Jon Benet Ramsey).

44. *Id.* at 733-34. ("[T]he record was devoid of any concrete evidence that biological material existed on the evidence sought to be tested.").

45. *Id.* at 732.

46. *Id.* (citing Routier v. State, 273 S.W.3d 272, 256 (Tex. Crim. App. 2008)) ("...the appellant fails to meet her threshold burden of showing that there is even any evidence containing biological material to be tested.")).

47. *Id.*

48. *Id.*; *see Routier*, 273 S.W.3d at 256. Router presented no evidence to support her claim that either rape kit evidence was ever collected at the hospital the night of her children's murders or ever "maintained" after her examination. *Id.*

49. *Id.*

50. *Swearingen*, 303 S.W.3d at 732-33.

51. *Boykin*, 818 S.W.2d at 785 (emphasis in original).

52. *Id.* (emphasis in original).

53. S.B. 3, 77th Leg. (Tex. 2001) (Bill Analysis).

54. *Swearingen*, 303 S.W.3d at 732. The CCA did display more logical reasoning in its denial of testing of left- and right-hand scrapings, though this denial suffers from the same constitutionally impermissible reasoning as noted in the preceding paragraphs. The scrapings had already been tested by DPS and were found either to not contain human DNA or the material appeared to be sand or gravel or "'very tiny, bright red flakes.'" *Id.* at 733. At least this evidence had either actually been previously tested or had been examined to see if it were appropriate to test for the presence of biological materials. However, depending on which type of DNA testing was used on this material, newer and more probative tests might yield DNA results. Therefore, the CCA ought to have allowed this material to be tested anew with more discriminating and advanced DNA tests.

55. art. 64.01(b).

56. art. 64.02(a)(2)(A). *See, e.g.*, Alvarez v. State, No. 14-08-00792, 2009 WL 3109907, at *1 (Tex. App.—Houston [14th Dist.] Sept. 17, 2009, no pet.) (mem. op., not designated for publication) (where state procured affidavits from "the property and evidence records custodian for the Houston Police Department, the custodian for the crime lab, and the custodian for the latent print lab.").

57. art. 64.02(a)(2)(A).

58. Rodriguez v. State, No. 08-07-00248-CR, 2009 WL 3152471, at *1 (Tex. App.—El Paso Sept. 30, 2009, pet. ref'd) (not designated for publication) (denying motion for failure to follow the procedural requirements of either 64.01(a) or (b) because neither motion nor affidavit identified "the items to be tested" and did not "address whether the items were in the State's possession at the time of trial.").

59. Atkins v. State, 262 S.W.3d 413, 416-17 (Tex. App.—Houston [14th Dist.] 2008, no pet.). Atkins was given a life sentence upon his convictions for aggravated sexual assault and prohibited sexual conduct. *Id.* at 414. This opinion is curiously opaque because the court fails to mention whether any testable evidence ever existed or still exists. However, the court notes that:

    the *record* contains no indications that such evidence may have been taken from the scene of the crime or from appellant or the victim . . . A record before a court of appeals in this type of case [a request for DNA testing] will seldom, if ever, reflect whether biological evidence was taken or exists unless the appellant attaches an affidavit to his motion or unless the prosecutor reveals this sort of information in response to a motion for appointment of counsel . . . . A court of appeals record typically will contain only the motion and any secondary motions or other documents filed in connection with the motion and the court's order.

    Id. at 417 (emphasis in original); *see also In re* Ruffin, No. 03-08-00071-CR, 2008 WL 3166314, at *1 (Tex. App.—Austin Aug. 6, 2008, no pet.) (mem. op., not designated for publication) (denying motion for testing because Ruffin had not established that any "physical evidence relating to this case and containing biological material currently exists."). The opinion does not state if the attorney attempted to obtain any affidavits or ascertain whether or not any evidence ever did exist that might have contained biological evidence. *Id.* *Delacruz v. State* is another example of an opinion that is vague as to whether there ever was evidence to be tested. Nos. 14-08-00150-CR, 14-08-00152-CR, 2008 WL 4585246, at *1 (Tex. App.—Houston [14th Dist.] Oct. 16, 2008, no pet.) (mem. op., not designated for publication). The court states that Delacruz "failed to demonstrate that any biological evidence exists and is in a condition making DNA testing possible." *Id.* The opinion only notes that the State provided affidavits but does not specify to what the affidavits attested. *Id.*

60. *See, e.g.,* Lomax v. State, No. 14-07-00934-CR, 2008 WL 5085653, at *1 (Tex. App.—Houston [14th Dist.] Nov. 25, 2008, no pet.) (mem. op., not designated for publication) (denying request because defendant failed to specify which evidence he wanted tested, even though the State's brief states: "'Apparently, the appellant is suggesting that he was not intoxicated, the results of the blood test were inaccurate and he did not cause the accident . . . Clearly, if the appellant's DNA[] did not match the DNA in the blood sample taken at the hospital . . . there would be insufficient proof that the appellant was intoxicated, and he would not have been convicted").

61. *See* art. 38.43 (requiring that evidence not be destroyed unless notice is given to the trial attorney and defendant and no objection is received within ninety days).

62. *See* Hutson v. Thaler, Civil Action No. H-05-1163, 2010WL 272283, at *1 (S.D. Tex. Jan. 21, 2010) (state submitted affidavits from both Houston Police Department crime lab and property room and Harris County Clerk's Office stating they did not have custody of any evidence); Broussard v. State, No. 07-07-

0405, 2009 WL 290968, at *1 (Tex. App.—Amarillo Feb. 6, 2009, no pet.) (mem. op., not designated for publication) (state providing affidavits from Jefferson County Criminal D.A.'s office, a letter from Beaumont Police Department, and memo from Jefferson County Sheriff's Department Regional Crime Laboratory stating that no evidence existed in case); Allen v. State, No. 08-07-00301-CR, 2010 WL 696495 (Tex. App.—El Paso Feb. 26, 2010, no pet.) (not designated for publication) (state presenting witnesses from El Paso District Clerk's Office, DPS lab, El Paso County, and El Paso Police Department to testify that no evidence existed); Hunnicutt v. State, No. 05-07-01332-CR, 2008 WL 4743488, at *2 (Tex. App.—Dallas Oct. 30, 2008, no pet.) (mem. op., not designated for publication) (in responding to appellant's motion for DNA testing, state informed trial court that Dallas Police Department had destroyed evidence.); *Alvarez*, 2009 WL 3109907, at *1 (where state procured affidavits from "the property and evidence records custodian for the Houston Police Department, the custodian for the crime lab, and the custodian for the latent print lab" to substantiate that the State was not in possession of evidence containing biological material); Robinson v. State, No. 05-07-01585-CR, 2008WL 4725649, at *1 (Tex. App.—Dallas Oct. 29, 2008, no pet.) (mem. op., not designated for publication) (noting that the vaginal swab and smear were no longer "available for testing" in case involving an aggravated sexual assault of a child); Truman v. State, No. 14-08-00315, 2009 WL 396282, at *1-*3 (Tex. App.—Houston [14 Dist.] Feb. 19, 2009, no pet.) (mem. op., not designated for publication) (noting that the State, in its motion to deny testing, filed affidavits from the Harris County District Clerk's Office, HPD, and the Houston Crime Lab attesting that none of the agencies had any evidence in the case despite a witness testifying at trial that Truman's blood was "retrieved at the crime scene").

63. No. 05-07-00597-CR, 2008 WL 2454675, at *1 (Tex. App.—Dallas June 19, 2008, no pet.) (mem. op., not designated for publication).

64. *Id.*

65. *Id.*

66. *Id.*

67. *Id.*

68. No. 03-09-00212-CR, 2009 WL 3400993, at *1 (Tex. App.—Austin Oct. 21, 2009, no pet.) (mem. op., not designated for publication).

69. *Id.* Bowman had been convicted of aggravated sexual assault in 1983. *Id.*

70. *Id.*

71. *Id.* at *2 (noting that "[n]o law required law enforcement to retain such evidence until 2001, 17 years after Defendant's trial").

72. art. 64.03(a)(1)(A) (emphasis added).

73. No. PD-1039-08, 2009 WL 3042392, at *1 (Tex. Crim. App. 2009).

74. *Id.* (affirming the denial of testing because defendant failed to establish why testing was not previously done). The court of appeals had denied testing in part due to the failure of the affidavits to show a chain of custody. Garcia v. State, No. 01-05-00718-CR, 2008 WL 2466211, at *1 (Tex. App.—Houston [1st Dist.] June 19, 2008) (mem op., not designated for publication).

75. No. 14-09-00120-CR, 2010 WL 454935, at *1-*3 (Tex. App.—Houston [14th Dist.] Feb. 11, 2010, no pet.) (mem. op., not designated for publication) (conviction based on uncorroborated testimony of defendant's daughter that he touched her and then ejaculated on her and on results from testing of semen, where the results showed that DNA "was consistent with appellant's DNA type").

76. *Id.* at *3 (emphasis added) (referring to hairs that trial court had authorized to be tested in 2002 but no record of the testing can be found) .

77. *See Boykin*, 818 S.W.2d at 785 (holding that the judiciary is required to follow the plain meaning of a statute unless doing so would lead to absurd results).

78. *Durden*, 2010 WL 454935, at *3.

79. *See* Part IV.B for a discussion of possible statutory reforms regarding chain of custody.

80. 2008 WL 4585246, at *1. It bears noting that this opinion is a scant one page long and lacks any detail of the evidence or any effort by the state to locate the evidence. *Id.*

81. *Id.*

82. The trial court referred to is the174th District Court, Trial Court Cause No. 821151. No. 14-07-00975-CR, 2008 WL 2520791, at *1 (Tex. App.—Houston [14th Dist.] June 24, 2008, no pet.) (mem. op., not designated for publication).

83. *Id.*

84. *Id.*

85. art. 64.02(a)(2).

86. Sepeda v. State, 301 S.W.3d 372, 375 (Tex. App.—Amarillo 2009, pet. struck) (denying testing on grounds that identity was not an issue).

87. *Robinson*, 2008WL 4725649, at *1. In response, the State told the Dallas trial court that it had only a pubic hair, which the lab had determined, based on a microscopic test, belonged to the victim. *Id.* The court denied testing because Robinson failed to argue that the hair had not previously been subjected to DNA testing through no fault of his own. *Id.* at *2.

88. art. 64.01(b)(1)(B).

89. *Routier*, 273 S.W.3d at 247. The CCA used the fault provision in denying testing of never-previously-tested blood stains on a tube sock and testing of parts of a night shirt that had never been previously tested. *Id.* at 251-22, 254-55.

90. Johnson v. State, No. 14-08-00441-CR, 2009 WL 1493040, at *2 (Tex. App.—Houston [14th Dist.] May 28, 2009, no

pet.) (mem. op., not designated for publication) (denying motion that fingernail scrapings and blood be tested to determine identity of person who committed aggravated robbery because appellant failed to make a "'particularized showing' of the absence of fault in his motion." (quoting *Routier*, 273 S.W.3d at 24[7]); Faison v. State, No. 05-08-01311-CR, 2010 WL 851406, at *1 (Tex. App.—Dallas Mar. 12, 2010, no pet. h.) (not designated for publication) (denying motion because appellant failed to make "'a particularized showing of the absence of fault'" (quoting *Routier*, 273 S.W.3d at 247) where untested biological evidence existed); *Robinson*, 2008WL 4725649, at *2 (holding that even if appellant had raised issue of testing shirt prior to appeal, he did not make a "particularized showing of the absence of fault . . ." (quoting *Routier*, 273 S.W.3d at 247) because "[h]e d[id] not offer any specific evidence or explanation about why lack of DNA testing during his trial was not his fault"). *See infra* for an analysis of the Court's decision in Skinner v. State, 293 S.W.3d 196, 202 (Tex. Crim. App. 2009). *See also* State v. Cooper, No. 05-08-01642-CR, 2009 WL 2232456, at *1 (Tex. App.—Dallas July 28, 2009, no pet.) (mem. op., not designated for publication) (reversing trial court's order that testing of bed sheets and a comforter be done, where step-daughter recanted at time of trial, saying she'd fabricated story of aggravated sexual assault). Appellant asserted in his affidavit that he did not know the sheets and comforter might contain biological evidence, but the court held that appellant failed to present a particularized showing that lack of testing was not his fault. *Id.*

The 26-month period was from January 1, 2008 to March 16, 2010.

91. *Routier*, 273 S.W.3d at 247 ("It would relieve all post-conviction DNA movants from any obligation ever to seek DNA testing under technologies available at the time of trial . . .").

92. *Skinner*, 293 S.W.3d at 202.

93. *Routier*, 273 S.W.3d at 248.

94. *See Skinner*, 293 S.W.3d 196.

95. *Id.* at 197-98.

96. Brandi Grissom, *Case Open: The Investigation*, TEXAS TRIBUNE, Jan. 29, 2010, www.texastribune.org/stories/2010/jan/29/case-open/print/. Skinner commented, "I can't understand what purpose it serves for any . . . state to execute somebody who is innocent by not letting him prove it and then killing him . . . How unfair can you get? Does that sound right to you?" *Id.*; *see also* Order in Pending Case, Mar. 24, 2010, *available at* www.supremecourt.gov/orders/courtorders/032410zr.pdf (staying Mr. Skinner's March 24, 2010 execution date).

97. *Skinner*, 293 S.W.3d at 209 (quoting art. 64.01(b)(1)(B)).

98. *Id.* at 202-03.

99. *Id.* at 209. The neighbor later claimed she was coerced by police to give incriminating testimony. Grissom, *supra* note 96.

100. Grissom, *supra* note 96. Comer had prosecuted Skinner for car theft and assault. *Id.*

101. *Id.*

102. *Id.*

103. *Id.*

104. *Id.*

105. *Id.*

106. *Skinner*, 293 S.W.3d at 199.

107. art. 64.01(b)(1)(A)(i).

108. art. 64.01(b)(1)(A)(ii).

109. *Garcia*, 2009 WL 3042392, at *1 (emphasis in original) (denying request for DNA testing, in part, because appellant never explained why no testing had been done). The court of appeals denied Garcia's motion for the same reason. *See Garcia*, 2008 WL 2466211, at *1.

110. *Swearingen*, 303 S.W.3d at 734 (denying testing of left- and right-hand scrapings because technology that existed at time of trial could have yielded results).

111. art. 64.01(b)(2).

112. Routier, 273 S.W.3d at 251 (approving testing of previously tested blood stain on a tube sock).

113. Marks v. State, No. 2-09-144-CR, 2010 WL 598459, at *1 (Tex. App.—Fort Worth Feb. 18, 2010, no pet. h.) (mem. op., not designated for publication) (denying motion because Marks did not allege that a private lab would use "newer testing techniques that provide a reasonable likelihood of results that are more accurate and probative than the results of the previous test," where DNA had been tested twice (the second time after "questions arose about the practices at the Fort Worth Police Department Forensic Science Laboratory") and the results were "inculpatory").

114. Garrett v. State, No. 05-07-00131-CR, 2008 WL 2840688, at *2 (Tex.App.—Dallas July 24, 2008, no pet.) (mem. op., not designated for publication) (denying motion because movant failed to show how "[n]ewer techniques such as Polymerase Chain Reaction (PCR) replication, short tandem repeat (STR) testing, and mitochondrial DNA analysis" would allow DNA to be tested from a degraded sample when the original testing using RFLP "'inculpated [appellant] at a probability of one in 5.5 billion,'" even though one of six probes did not quantitatively match appellant).

115. *Swearingen*, 303 S.W.3d at 735.

116. *Id.*

117. *Id.* at 736.

118. *Id.* at 735. *But see Routier*, 273 S.W.3d at 255-54 (approving new testing using STR test because "the newer technology is reasonably likely to turn up evidence of an unknown intruder's DNA that the technology extant in 1996 may not have"). Even the Supreme Court has acknowledged the dramatic scientific advances that make it possible to identify DNA matches "with

near certainty." *See Osborne*, 129 S.Ct. at 2316 ("Modern DNA testing can provide powerful new evidence unlike anything known before . . . . [Scientific advancements have] culminate[ed] in STR technology. It is now often possible to determine whether a biological tissue matches a suspect with near certainty.").

119. *See also* Part III (examining the 2009 proposal to require registration of unidentified DNA test results on the CODIS database).

120. art. 64.03(a)(1)(B).

121. Blacklock v. State, 235 S.W.3d 231, 238 (Tex. Crim. App. 2007) (noting that DNA testing done during trial of semen was inconclusive "on the issue of identity").

122. *Truman*, 2009 WL 396282, at *3. The opinion focuses mostly on the fact that no evidence exists to be tested. *Id.* at *1-*3. Then, at the very end of the opinion, the court notes that Truman never alleged that identity was an issue and thus denies the motion for failing to allege that identity was an issue. *Id.* at *4.

123. Smith v. State, No. 01-06-00416-CR, 2009 WL 3248206, at *1-*2 (Tex. App.—Houston [1st Dist.] Oct. 8, 2009, no pet.) (mem. op., not designated for publication) (denying testing where appellant admitted that he abused corpse after victim had already died and appellant was only trying to prove when he attempted to have sexual intercourse—pre- or post-death).

124. Sutton v. State, No. 04-08-00867-CR, 2009 WL 1329835, at *2 (Tex. App.—San Antonio May 13, 2009, pet. ref'd) (mem. op., not designated for publication) (noting its previous holding in Sutton v. State, No. 04-05-00453-CR, 2006 WL 927330, at *1 (Tex. App.—San Antonio Apr. 12, 2006)). The court does not provide any details about the crime and why identity was or is not an issue. *Id.* at *1-*2. In the previous opinion, the court denied testing because no evidence existed—the State submitted affidavits stating that evidence had not been

retained in the case—and identity was not an issue. *Sutton*, 2006 WL 927330, at *1

125. No. 03-08-00796-CR, 2009 WL 3319859, at *1 (Tex. App.—Austin Oct. 15, 2009, no pet.) (mem. op., not designated for publication).
126. No. 05-07-00363-CR, 2008 WL 2719935 (Tex. App.—Dallas July 14, 2008, pet. ref'd) (mem. op., not designated for publication) (counsel was appointed and testing done).
127. No. 2-08-339-CR, 2009 WL 1564967, at *1 (Tex. App.—Fort Worth June 4, 2009, no pet.) (mem. op., not designated for publication).
128. Birdwell v. State, 276 S.W.3d 642, 646 (Tex. App.—Waco 2008, pet. struck) (denying testing because issue at trial was not who stabbed the victim, "but *why* Birdwell stabbed her," where Birdwell claimed he killed the victim by mistake, thinking she was an intruder) (emphasis in the original); Lyon v. State, 274 S.W.3d 767, 767-70 (Tex. App.—San Antonio 2008, pet. ref'd) (denying testing because defendant wanted to use the results to establish not the identity of the assailant but affirmative defense of self-defense rather than the identity of the assailant).
129. No. 14-07-00255-CR, 2008 WL 4308408, at *1 (Tex. App.—Houston [14th Dist.] Aug. 28, 2008, no pet.) (mem. op.).
130. *See* Blacklock v. State, 235 S.W.3d at 238.
131. Nos. 05-07-01414-CR, 05-07-01415-CR, 2008 WL 3020817, at *1 (Tex. App.—Dallas Aug. 6, 2008, no pet.) (not designated for publication) (defendant was convicted after two girls who spent the night with his daughter at his house testified that appellant inserted his finger vaginally into both the girls).
132. *Id.*
133. No. 09-07-344 CR, 2007 WL 5101236, at *1 (Tex. App.—Beaumont Apr. 16, 2008, no pet.) (mem. op., not designated for publication).
134. *Id.* at *2.

135. *Id.*

136. art. 64.03(a)(2)(A). Also, testing is not ordered if DNA testing would prove exculpatory for only one of two aggravating factors in a capital murder case. Leal v. State, 303 S.W.3d 292, 302 (Tex. Crim. App. 2009).

137. *In re* Morton, 2010 WL 45866, at *5 (Tex. App.—Austin Jan. 8, 2010, no pet.) (emphasis in original).

138. Routier, 273 S.W.3d at 258 (ordering testing of five of nine items). The CCA ruled that testing should be ordered where evidence that bolstered Routier's claim that there was an intruder would "more likely than not have caused the jury to harbor a reasonable doubt as to the appellant's guilt and decline to convict her." *Id.* at 259.

139. 245 S.W.3d 466, 470 (Tex. Crim. App. 2008) (where testing done of DNA in victim's mouth established a probability of 1 in 26 billion that DNA belonged to appellant). *See also* Greenland v. State, No. 01-06-00109-CR, 2009 WL 5174239, at *5 (Tex. App.—Houston [1st Dist.] Dec. 31, 2009, no pet.) (mem. op., not designated for publication) (denying testing because Greenland failed to "show that he 'would not have been convicted if exculpatory results had been obtained through DNA testing'" (quoting art. 64.03(a)(2)(A))). Interestingly, the court still found "reasonable grounds" and had appointed counsel even where many inculpatory facts existed: the defendant and two or three other suspects had kidnapped the complainant, hit him with a gun, and terrorized him. *Id.* at *2. Moreover, the court did not detail what "additional evidence presented at trial" would have so diminished the value of the DNA results (quoting *Prible*, 245 S.W.3d at 470). *Id.*

140. 294 S.W.3d 192, 196-97 (Tex. App.—Texarkana 2009, pet. ref'd). *See also In re* Biegel, No. 03-07-00274, 2008 WL 341552, at *1 (Tex. App.—Austin 2008, no pet.) (mem. op., not designated for publication) (noting that even if the DNA testing showed the presence of his girlfriend's father at the crime scene, "this would merely confirm that the stepfather

was part of the conspiracy; it would not exculpate" the defendant); Willis v. State, No. 2-06-091-CR, 2008 WL 2780666, at *1 (Tex. App.—Fort Worth July 17, 2008, pet. ref'd) (mem. op., not designated for publication) (where presence of a third-party would not prove that Willis did not murder his stepfather).

141. Harrison v. State, No. 14-07-00287-CR, 2008 WL 220711, at *3 (Tex. App.—Houston [14th Dist.] Jan 29, 2008, pet. struck) (mem. op., not designated for publication) (noting that a negative DNA test would not exculpate appellant in light of the great weight of inculpatory evidence including defendant's guilty plea, the testimony of the other two assailants that appellant raped victim, and fact that the victim identified defendant in a line-up).

142. 301 S.W.3d at 375.

143. *In re* Crayton, No. 03-09-00099-CR, 2009 WL 3486365, at *1 (Tex. App.—Austin Oct. 27, 2009, no pet.) (mem. op.) (holding that neither the absence of appellant's DNA nor the presence of another person's DNA would prove exculpatory).

144. 258 S.W.3d 205, 207 (Tex. App.—Waco 2008, no pet.).

145. Swearingen, 303 S.W.3d at 735.

146. *Id.* In crafting its denial, the CCA cites *Skinner* noting that "[a]nother requirement is the 'different outcome' showing, which is satisfied when the 'convicted person establishes by a preponderance of the evidence that . . . the person would not have been convicted if exculpatory results had been obtained through DNA testing.'" *Id.* at 736 (citing *Skinner*, 293 S.W.3d at 200).

147. *Id.* at 737. For a discussion of the unreliability of snitch testimony see Keith A. Findley, *Toward a New Paradigm of Criminal Justice: How the Innocence Movement Merges Crime Control and Due Process*, 41 Tex. Tech L. Rev. 133, 169 (2009) ("One of the most notoriously unreliable forms of

evidence used in criminal cases is the testimony of jailhouse informants or snitches.").

148. Lisa Falkenberg, *Time is Running Out for Inmate*, Hous. Chron., Jan. 21, 2009, *available at* http://www.chron.com/disp/story.mpl/metropolitan/falkenberg/6223834.html.

149. Editorial, Room for Doubt: Convicted Murderer's Execution Should Be Stayed Pending Reconsideration of Evidence, Hous. Chron., Jan. 22, 2009, *available at* http://www.chron.com/disp/story.mpl/editorial/6226203.html (quoting Dr. Glenn Larkin).

150. Coronado v. State, No. 01-08-00101-CR, 2009 WL 3152118, at *1 (Tex. App.—Houston [1st Dist.] Oct. 1, 2009, no pet.) (mem. op., not designated for publication). *See also* King v. State, No. 05-07-00036-CR, 2008 WL 2877752, at *1 (Tex. App.—Dallas July 28, 2008, no pet.) (mem. op., not designated for publication) (where non-victim DNA matched the defendant and not the other two suspects). *See also* Campos v. State, No. 01-08-00032-CR, 2008 WL 5102463, at *1 (Tex. App.—Houston [1st Dist.] Dec. 4, 2008, no pet.) (mem. op., not designated for publication) (where victim and Campos had spent evening drinking together, murder weapon was found in the kitchen sink of Campos's family home, and Campos fled the scene).

151. No. 01-08-00144-CR, 2008 WL 5651469, at *3 (Tex. App.—Houston [1st Dist.] Feb. 19, 2009, no pet.) (mem. op., not designated for publication) (quoting Bell v. State, 90 S.W.3d 301, 306 (Tex. Crim. App. 2002)) (noting that inculpatory evidence included a history of domestic violence, the fact that the victim was in the process of divorcing the defendant, and witnesses who saw an African-American male (the defendant was African-American) load a large bundle into a vehicle and an arm fall out of the bundle while he was loading it into the vehicle; the witnesses wrote down the license plate number, which matched that of the defendant).

152. *In re* Gonzales, No. 03-07-00649-CR, 2009 WL 2195421, at *1 (Tex. App.—Austin July 24, 2009, no pet.) (mem. op., not

designated for publication) (in explaining its denial of testing, noted that Gonzales testified that he was unable to rape the victim because he failed to "'get hard'" and had admitted to attacking the victim with an accomplice); Lacy v. State, No. 2-08-318-CR, 2009 WL 885938, at *1 (Tex. App.—Fort Worth Apr. 2, 2009, no pet.) (mem. op., not designated for publication) (holding that Lacy failed to meet burden of proof that DNA testing result would prove to be exculpatory in stabbing of victim at dry cleaners; fingernails, blood, and pulled scalp hair would not prove exculpatory because absence of Lacy's DNA under victim's fingernails would not prove that he did not stab the victim and where there was eyewitness identification of Lacy and three witnesses testified that he admitted to killing someone).

153. King v. State, No. 13.0700096-CR, 2008 WL 4724435, at *1 (Tex. App.—Corpus Christi July 29, 2008, pet. ref'd) (mem. op., not designated for publication) (denying request of DNA testing of defendant's shirt to prove that it did not have victim's blood on it); Graves v. State, No. 14-06-00794-CR, 2008 WL 442592, at *2 (Tex. App.—Houston [14th Dist.] Feb. 19, 2008, no pet.) (mem. op., not designated for publication) (holding that even if another's DNA were found on a marijuana cigarette, and not Graves' DNA, appellant "still ha[d] not shown by a preponderance of the evidence that he would not have been convicted if exculpatory results had been obtained through DNA testing…"). In *Graves*, the court noted that the cigarette could belong to Graves even if he never touched it. *Graves*, 2008 WL 442592, at *2 .

154. *In re* Anderson, No. 03-07-00655-CR, 2008 WL 2777424, at *2 (Tex. App.—Austin July 18, 2008, pet. dism'd) (mem. op., not designated for publication) (denying testing because even if complainant's DNA was found on property, this would not "establish the manner by which the defendant took possession of the victim's property"). The movant claims she found the property and did not steal it. *Id.*

155. *In re* Kennard, No. 03-07-00308-CR, 2008 WL 899606, at *1 (Tex. App.—Austin Apr. 3, 2008, no pet.) (mem. op., not designated for publication) (holding that impeaching victim by showing presence of sperm other than her boyfriend's would not prove that Kennard did not rape the victim).

156. McConnell v. State, No. 05-07-00675-CR, 2008 WL 3412201, at *1 (Tex. App.—Dallas Aug. 13, 2008, no pet.) (mem. op., not designated for publication) (only noting that a bloody t-shirt and vest exist to be tested but providing no details as to why testing these items would not establish that defendant would not have been convicted); *see also* Picone v. State, No. 01-08-00226-CR, 2009 WL 1886181, at *1, (Tex. App.—Houston [1st Dist.] July 2, 2009, no pet.) (mem. op., not designated for publication). In *Picone*, the court merely stated that "that the applicant fail[ed] to establish by a preponderance of the evidence that he would not have been convicted if exculpatory results had been obtained through DNA testing of the remaining biological evidence . . ." *Picone*, 2009 WL 1886181, at *1. No specific details were given about the case. *Id.*

157. art. 64.01(a).

158. *See* State v. Young, 242 S.W.3d 926, 928 (Tex. App.—Dallas 2008, no pet.) (holding that defendant did not have standing to request DNA testing because he had received deferred adjudication for aggravated sexual assault and was, therefore, not convicted as required under the statute).

159. *Id.*

160. Art. 64.01(a).

161. *See Biegel*, 2008 WL 341552, at *1 (denying the motion even though appellant claimed he was framed by his girlfriend, that her father was the actual murderer, and that DNA testing of items at the murder scene would prove the father's presence at the killing, in part because appellant failed to submit an affidavit and his motion was not sworn); *Marks*, 2010 WL 598459, at *1 (denying motion because appellant did not

include affidavits or "affirm that all factual allegations in the motion were true").

162. Id.

163. Dixon v. State, 242 S.W.3d 929, 933 (Tex. App.—Dallas 2008, no pet.) (denying motion without stating a specific reason). Initially, the trial court had granted Dixon's motion for testing. *Id.* at 931. Four years later, in response to the State's motion to deny testing, the trial judge denied Dixon's motion for testing. *Id.* No information is given as to whether any testable evidence exists. *Id.* at 931-33. However, one could infer that some testable evidence still exists because the initial order granted testing

164. *Dixon*, 242 S.W.3d at 929; Hamilton v. State, No. 05-06-01273-CR, 2008 WL 217564, at *1 (Tex. App.—Dallas Jan. 28, 2008, no pet.) (mem. op., not designated for publication) (noting only that former counsel had filed an *Anders* brief); Fugon v. State, No. 01-08-00577-CR, 2009WL 1958742, at *1 (Tex. App.—Houston [1st Dist.] July 9, 2009, no pet.) (mem. op., not designated for publication) (merely noting that Fugon's former attorney mentioned in his *Anders* brief that "the record presents no reversible error"); Minnfee v. Simms, No. 03-07-00374-CV, 2008 WL 678554, at *2 (Tex. App.—Austin Mar. 13, 2008, no pet.) (mem. op.) (denying request for DNA testing without stating a reason and upholding trial court's designation of Minnfee as a vexatious litigant). *See* Testimony of Brandon Moon, who was exonerated, testifying in 2007 that he was almost branded a vexatious litigant. Hearings on SB 1864 Before the House Jurisprudence Committee, 81st Leg., R.S., House Criminal Jurisprudence Committee Video and Archives, Mar. 31, 2009, http://www.senate.state.tx.us/avarchive/?mo=03&yr=2009&lim=0 [hereinafter House Hearings].

In Hamilton and Fugon's cases, the attorneys filed *Anders* briefs. *Hamilton*, 2008 WL 217564, at *1; *Fugon*, 2009 WL 1958742, at *1. An attorney files an *Anders* brief when he or she believes that an appeal is "wholly frivolous and without merit."

Hamilton, 2008 WL 217564, at *1. As the court explained, "[t]he [*Anders*] brief presents a professional evaluation of the record showing why, in effect, there are no arguable grounds to advance." *Id.* After an attorney withdraws, an appellant retains the right to file a *pro se* response. *Id.*

165. art. 64.01(c).

166. H.B. 1011, 78th Leg. (Tex. 2003) (Bill Analysis).

167. *Id.*

168. Id.

169. *Id. See also* note 16 and accompanying text.

170. *Bowman*, 2009 WL 3400993, at *2.

171. Barnes v. State, No. 14-08-00930-CR, 2009 WL 3817888, at *1 (Tex. App.—Houston [14th Dist.] Nov. 17, 2009, no pet.) (mem. op., not designated for publication) (denying appointment of counsel because appellant failed to establish reasonable grounds where motion requesting DNA testing of an Uzi machine gun and ammunition failed to identify any evidence containing biological material); *see also Atkins*, 262 S.W.3d at 416-17 (declining to define "'reasonable grounds' because appellant ha[d] failed to allege even that DNA was taken and exists" and trial record did not indicate "that such evidence may have been taken from the scene of the crime or from appellant or the victim").

172. *Gonzales*, 2009 WL 2195421, at *4 (holding that reasonable grounds exist "'when the facts stated in the request for counsel or otherwise known to the trial court reasonably suggest that a plausible argument for testing can be made'" (quoting *In re* Franklin, No. 03-07-00563-CR, 2008 WL 2468712, at *1 (Tex. App.—Austin June 19, 2008, no pet.) (mem.op., not designated for publication)). Gonzales was convicted of aggravated sexual assault after admitting to attacking the victim. *Id.* at *1. The court, in explaining its denial of testing, noted that Gonzales testified that he was unable to rape the victim because he failed to "'get hard'" and had admitted to attacking the victim with an accomplice. *Id.*

173. Wicker v. State, No. 05-07-00163-CR, 2008 WL 2440270, at *2 (Tex. App.—Dallas June 18, 2008, no pet.) (mem. op., not designated for publication) (holding that testing of pubic hairs found on the victim which crime lab found were dissimilar to appellant's would "merely muddy the waters").

174. *In re* Padilla, No. 03-07-00712-CR, 2008 WL 2468735, at *1 (Tex. App.—Austin June 18, 2008, no pet.) (memo op., not designated for publication) (citing *Blacklock*, 235 S.W.3d at 233).

175. *Id.*

176. *Franklin*, 2008 WL 2468712, at *2 (appointing counsel to assist on motion to test hair that was in deceased's hand). The court noted that even though there had been a history of domestic violence and Franklin had admitted to strangling his wife, proof that the hair belonged to someone other than the victim or Franklin might exculpate Franklin; therefore, reasonable grounds existed to appoint counsel. *Id.* at *2-*3.

177. No. 14-09-00796-CR, 2010 WL 27054, at *1 (Tex. App.—Houston [14th Dist.] Jan. 7, 2010, no pet.) (mem. op., not designated for publication).

178. *Id.* at *2.

179. *See* Lise Olsen, *Lawyers' Late Filing Can Be Deadly*, HOUS. CHRON., Mar. 22, 2009, *available at* http://www.chron.com/disp/story.mpl/metropolitan/6328865.html (describing how Godinich filed late in three death penalty cases, costing the men their right to appeal); Lise Olsen, *Lawyers Face Few Penalties*, HOUS. CHRON., Apr. 20, 2009 (noting that the Fifth Circuit "chastised" Godinich for missing a deadline for a client on death row).

180. *In re* Lockett, No. 2-08-452-CV, 2009 WL 1740145, at *1 (Tex. App.—Fort Worth June 16, 2009, no pet.) (mem. op., not designated for publication).

181. *Id.* "Chapter 64 does not impose a deadline on a trial court to rule on a motion for DNA testing, but that does not mean

the trial court has unfettered discretion to postpone a ruling indefinitely." *Id.*

182. No. 06-08-000200-CR, 2008 WL 4812594, at *1 (Tex. App.—Texarkana Nov. 6, 2008, no pet.) (mem. op., not designated for publication).

183. *In re* Ryan, No. 07-09-0183-CV, 2009 WL 1940911, at *2 (Tex. App.—Amarillo July 7, 2009, no pet.) (mem. op.).

184. 300 S.W.3d 768, 769 (Tex. Crim. App. 2009).

185. *Id.* at 770.

186. *Id.*

187. Telephone interview with Bruce Anton, Partner, Sorrels, Udashen & Anton, Apr. 28, 2010.

188. *Id.*

189. *Id.* The State wants to try Chabot again, but currently no new proceedings have been initiated. *Id.*

190. 2010 WL 45866, at *1; *see* Rick Casey, *Court Dings Forensic Panel Chief*, Hous. Chron., Jan. 14, 2010, *available at* http://www.chron.com/disp/story.mpl/metropolitan/casey/6816502.html (noting that Bradley is "the controversial new head of the Texas Forensic Science Commission").

191. *Morton*, 2010 WL 45866, at *1.

192. *Id.* at *5. Morton was convicted in 1987 of the murder, and the subsequent testing of the bed sheet was conducted in 1991. *Id.* at *1, *5.

193. *Id.*

194. *Id.*

195. *Id.* at *9. Similar to the method used to kill the defendant's late wife, the earlier murder victim was bludgeoned to death and furniture was piled over her body. *Id.*

196. *Routier*, 273 S.W.3d at 257-59.

197. *Id.*

198. *Id.* at 259.

199. *Id.*
200. Esparza v. State, 282 S.W.3d 913 (Tex. Crim. App. 2009). Esparza was convicted of aggravated sexual assault and sentenced to life imprisonment. *Id.* at 913.
201. *Id.* at 922 (listing the inculpatory evidence that the victim and witness identified and tied Esparza to the crime scene: "e.g., Esparza's business card, light-blue, four door car, age, and the fire-works on the floor-board"). This holding could be interpreted as creating a separate standard for sexual assault cases: exculpatory DNA evidence seems to weigh against extensive inculpatory evidence.
202. State v. Labonte, No. 14-08-00340-CR, 2009 WL 62932, at *1 (Tex. App.—Houston [14th Dist.] Jan. 13, 2009, no pet.) (mem. op.).
203. *Id.*
204. *Id.*
205. *Id.*
206. *Id.*
207. *Id.* at 2.
208. *Id.* Telephone records established that Labonte knew one of the girls. *Id.*
209. *Id.* at *2-*4 (noting that "no match was made between appellee and the hair, fibers, or footprints left at the scene").
210. *Id.*at *3.
211. *Id.*
212. *Id.* at *5-*6.
213. *See generally* Part III *infra* (discussing the 2009 proposed amendment); Part IV (noting that additional statutory changes are in order to achieve the first two clarifications).
214. S.B. 1864, 81st Leg., Reg. Sess. (Tex. 2009) (Bill Analysis); *see* Appendix B for the text of the proposed amendment.

    Moreover, the amendment would have added a new section, which would have required unidentified DNA profiles to be submitted to the CODIS database for possible matches to unsolved crimes. S.B. 1864, 81st Leg., Reg. Sess. (Tex. 2009) (Bill Analysis). The convicting court, after completion of the testing, would have "order[ed] any unidentified DNA profiles to be compared with the DNA profiles in the CODIS DNA database established by the Federal Bureau of Investigation" and held a hearing on the comparison of results. *Id.* The purpose of this change was to "identify perpetrators more quickly and bring them to justice." *Id.* This addition to the statute would also help to ensure that the database contains as many samples as possible, thus increasing the possibility of more matches in the future.

215. *Id.* Although these sections were broken into two categories in Parts II, II.B.3.a and b, respectively, the proposal is examined in a single section here for ease and clarity.

216. Section 64.01(b)(1)(A) would have been completely deleted. S.B. 1864, 81st Leg., Reg. Sess. (Tex. 2009) (text of bill). Article 64.01(b)(1) would have read:

The motion may request forensic DNA testing only of evidence described by Subsection (a) that was secured in relation to the offense that is the basis of the challenged conviction and was in the possession of the state during the trial of the offense, but: (1) was not previously subjected to DNA testing

(A) because DNA testing was

(i) not available, or

(ii) available, but not technologically capable of providing results, or

(B) through no fault of the convicted person, for reasons that are of a nature such that the interests of justice require DNA testing; or . . .

Id. Section 64.01(b)(2) would have remained unchanged and would still have required a convicted person to prove that newer techniques would result in more "accurate and probative" results on previously tested biological material. *See id.*

217. S.B. 1864, 81st Leg., Reg. Sess. (Tex. 2009) (Bill Analysis).
218. *Id.*
219. *See* House Hearings, *supra* note 164; *see also* Lise Olson, *Man Freed by DNA Wonders What to Do Next*, HOUS. CHRON., Dec. 14, 2008.
220. House Hearings, *supra* note 164, at 1:39:22.
221. *Id.*
222. For Skinner, the amendment would allow the evidence that has not been tested (namely the rape kit, the jacket with blood and hair on it, and the towel) to be tested, or at least require the court to find another reason not to test this evidence.
223. *See* Part II.B.3.b, *supra*.
224. *See* Part II.B.3.b, *supra* for a discussion of the holding in *Swearingen*. *Swearingen*, 303 S.W.3d 728.
225. THE JUSTICE PROJECT, IMPROVING ACCESS TO POST-CONVICTION DNA TESTING: A POLICY REVIEW 17, http://www.thejusticeproject.org/wp-content/uploads/post-convictiondna-fin.pdf (last visited Aug. 5, 2010).
226. Art 64.02(a)(1)(A) (emphasis added).
227. Art. 64.03(a)(2) (emphasis added).
228. *See Sutton*, 2009 WL 1329835, at *2 (denying testing on grounds that identity was not an issue) (citing Dossett v. State, 216 S.W. 3d 7, 15-16 (Tex. App.—San Antonio 2006, pet. ref'd) (sexual assault kit discovered in 2003 in medical examiner's freezer instead of the Criminal Investigation Laboratory where the state mistakenly believed the evidence was last located)).
229. Dossett, 216 S.W.3d at 15-16. The improbability of the events leading to the fortuitous discovery of the evidence bears reprinting:
    In 2002, Detective George Saidler, who was assigned to the SAPD "cold case" squad, began reviewing and re-investigating the Kosub case. In 2003, over the span of several months, Detective Saidler inquired at the Bexar County Criminal

Investigation Laboratory ("CIL") [The CIL was the new name of the crime lab, which had split off from the Medical Examiner's office and had become a separate entity under a new director; however, the CIL was still located in the same medical center building as the ME's office. The Toxicology Department remained part of the ME's office.] about the Kosub sexual assault kit. When he was informed that the kit could not be found at the CIL, Saidler went to the Medical Examiner's offices where, by chance, he ran into the Chief Medical Examiner, Dr. Vincent DiMaio, who had been there since 1981. Upon being asked about the Kosub kit, Dr. DiMaio easily located the kit in the Toxicology Department's freezer. . . . The kit was submitted to the CIL for DNA testing on April 17, 2003. The 20-year old samples in the kit were degraded, with mold, fungus, and bacteria present. However, sufficient genetic material was present to create a DNA profile and DNA analysis was completed on the swabs. Male DNA present on the vaginal swab "matched" Dossett's DNA-99.9% of all other individuals were excluded as the donor. Dossett was indicted for Kosub's murder twenty years after it occurred.

Id. In fact, in 1995, at the prompting of the victim's daughter, the San Antonio Police Department (SAPD) had tried to locate the evidence and was told by the Bexar County crime lab that the evidence could not be located. *Id.* at 14.

230. *Man Gets 40-year Sentence for 1983 Slaying*, San Antonio Express-News, Jan. 20, 2008. The SAPD cold case section submitted evidence collected from the victim's body, and the DNA test result matched Dossett's DNA profile in the "state's registered sex offender database." *Id.*

231. Lise Olsen, *DNA No Help in Old Case*, Hous. Chron., Sept. 22, 2009; *see also Burke*, 2008 WL 4533929 (denying a §1983 claim in part because no evidence had been tested that proved Burke's innocence). Burke was released on parole in 1999 after serving over eighteen years for rape and subsequently requested DNA testing in 2000. Lise Olsen, *10 Years Out of Cell, He's Still Not Free: Convicted of Child Rape in '81, Former Inmate*

Wants DNA to Clear His Name, Hous. Chron., May 4, 2009. The victim spotted Burke on the street a full year after the rape. *Id.* At some point, the victim had been Burke's waitress on several occasions. *Id.* An expert testified that Burke was the victim of mistaken identification—that trauma caused the victim to confuse a café patron with her true attacker. *Id.*

232. Lise Olsen, *DNA No Help in Old Case*, Hous. Chron., Sept. 22, 2009. Judge Randy Roll ordered the additional search, which resulted in the evidence being located. *Id.* The rape kit has not been located and is believed to have been destroyed. *Id.*

233. *Id.* The subsequent search, ordered by Judge Roll, resulted in the discovery of slides containing hair. *Id.*

234. *Id.* The news story does not specify the exact type of DNA testing used. *Id.*

235. *Id.* The state does not perform the "more complex and expensive" mitochondrial DNA testing. *Id.*

236. DNA Clears Man, *supra* note 2.

237. *Id.*

238. *Id.* First Assistant District Attorney Jim Leitner commented, "The evidence in this case had been sitting in the District Clerk's Office for 27 years, and no one had taken the initiative to do anything with it in the past . . . . The difference now is that you've got the Post Conviction Review Section looking into it—and that made all the difference in the case of Mr. Green." *Id.*

239. *See* note 2 and accompanying text.

Appendix A

Texas' Post-Conviction DNA Testing Statute

Motion for Forensic DNA Testing.

Art. 64.01. Motion

(a) A convicted person may submit to the convicting court a motion for forensic DNA testing of evidence containing biological material. The motion must be accompanied by an affidavit, sworn to by the convicted person, containing statements of fact in support of the motion.

(b) The motion may request forensic DNA testing only of evidence described by Subsection (a) that was secured in relation to the offense that is the basis of the challenged conviction and was in the possession of the state during the trial of the offense, but:

(1) was not previously subjected to DNA testing:

(A) because DNA testing was:

(i) not available; or

(ii) available, but not technologically capable of providing probative results; or

(B) through no fault of the convicted person, for reasons that are of a nature such that the interests of justice require DNA testing; or

(2) although previously subjected to DNA testing, can be subjected to testing with newer testing techniques that provide a reasonable likelihood of results that are more accurate and probative than the results of the previous test.

(c) A convicted person is entitled to counsel during a proceeding under this chapter. The convicting court shall appoint counsel for the convicted person if the person informs the court that the person wishes to submit a motion under this chapter, the court finds reasonable grounds for a motion to be filed, and the court determines that the person is indigent. Counsel must be appointed under this subsection not later than the 45th day after the date the court finds reasonable grounds or the date the court determines that the person is indigent, whichever is later. Compensation of counsel is provided in the same manner as is required by:

(1) Article 11.071 for the representation of a petitioner convicted of a capital felony; and
(2) Chapter 26 for the representation in a habeas corpus hearing of an indigent defendant convicted of a felony other than a capital felony.

Art. 64.011. Guardians and Other Representatives

(a) In this chapter, "guardian of a convicted person" means a person who is the legal guardian of the convicted person, whether the legal relationship between the guardian and convicted person exists because of the age of the convicted person or because of the physical or mental incompetency of the convicted person.

(b) A guardian of a convicted person may submit motions for the convicted person under this chapter and is entitled to counsel otherwise provided to a convicted person under this chapter.

Art. 64.02. Notice to State; Response

(a) On receipt of the motion, the convicting court shall:
(1) provide the attorney representing the state with a copy of the motion; and
(2) require the attorney representing the state to take one of the following actions in response to the motion not later than the 60th day after the date the motion is served on the attorney representing the state:
(A) deliver the evidence to the court, along with a description of the condition of the evidence; or
(B) explain in writing to the court why the state cannot deliver the evidence to the court.

(b) The convicting court may proceed under Article 64.03 after the response period described by Subsection (a)(2) has expired, regardless of whether the attorney representing the state submitted a response under that subsection.

Art. 64.03. Requirements; Testing

(a) A convicting court may order forensic DNA testing under this chapter only if:

(1) the court finds that:

(A) the evidence:

(i) still exists and is in a condition making DNA testing possible; and

(ii) has been subjected to a chain of custody sufficient to establish that it has not been substituted, tampered with, replaced, or altered in any material respect; and

(B) identity was or is an issue in the case; and

(2) the convicted person establishes by a preponderance of the evidence that:

(A) the person would not have been convicted if exculpatory results had been obtained through DNA testing; and

(B) the request for the proposed DNA testing is not made to unreasonably delay the execution of sentence or administration of justice.

(b) A convicted person who pleaded guilty or nolo contendere or, whether before or after conviction, made a confession or similar admission in the case may submit a motion under this chapter, and the convicting court is prohibited from finding that identity was not an issue in the case solely on the basis of that plea, confession, or admission, as applicable.

(c) If the convicting court finds in the affirmative the issues listed in Subsection (a)(1) and the convicted person meets the requirements of Subsection (a)(2), the court shall order that the requested forensic DNA testing be conducted. The court may order the test to be conducted by:

(1) the Department of Public Safety;

(2) a laboratory operating under a contract with the department; or

(3) on the request of the convicted person, another laboratory if that laboratory is accredited under Section 411.0205, Government Code.

(d) If the convicting court orders that the forensic DNA testing be conducted by a laboratory other than a Department of Public Safety laboratory or a laboratory under contract with the department, the State of Texas is not liable for the cost of testing under this subsection unless good cause for payment of that cost has been shown. A political subdivision of the state is not liable for the cost of testing under this subsection, regardless of whether good cause for payment of that cost has been shown. If the court orders that the testing be conducted by a laboratory described by this subsection, the court shall include in the order requirements that:

(1) the DNA testing be conducted in a timely and efficient manner under reasonable conditions designed to protect the integrity of the evidence and the testing process;

(2) the DNA testing employ a scientific method sufficiently reliable and relevant to be admissible under Rule 702, Texas Rules of Evidence; and

(3) on completion of the DNA testing, the results of the testing and all data related to the testing required for an evaluation of the test results be immediately filed with the court and copies of the results and data be served on the convicted person and the attorney representing the state.

(e) The convicting court, not later than the 30th day after the conclusion of a proceeding under this chapter, shall forward the results to the Department of Public Safety.

Art. 64.04. Finding

After examining the results of testing under Article 64.03, the convicting court shall hold a hearing and make a finding as to whether, had the results been available during the trial of the offense, it is reasonably probable that the person would not have been convicted.

Art. 64.05. Appeals

An appeal under this chapter is to a court of appeals in the same manner as an appeal of any other criminal matter, except that if the convicted person was convicted in a capital case and was sentenced to death, the appeal is a direct appeal to the court of criminal appeals.

Appendix B

(Editor's Note: Strikethroughs indicate language in the current statute that would be deleted by enactment of this bill.)

By: Ellis S.B. No. 1864

A BILL TO BE ENTITLED

AN ACT

relating to postconviction forensic DNA analysis.

BE IT ENACTED BY THE LEGISLATURE OF THE STATE OF TEXAS:

SECTION 1. Subsection (b), Article 64.01, Code of Criminal Procedure, is amended to read as follows:

(b) The motion may request forensic DNA testing only of evidence described by Subsection (a) that was secured in relation to the offense that is the basis of the challenged conviction and was in the possession of the state during the trial of the offense, but:

(1) was not previously subjected to DNA testing[~~:~~

~~[(A) because DNA testing was:~~

~~[(i) not available; or~~

~~[(ii) available, but not technologically capable of providing probative results; or~~

[(B) through no fault of the convicted person, for reasons that are of a nature such that the interests of justice ~~require DNA testing~~]; or

(2) although previously subjected to DNA testing, can be subjected to testing with newer testing techniques that provide a reasonable likelihood of results that are more accurate and probative than the results of the previous test.

SECTION 2. Chapter 64, Code of Criminal Procedure, is amended by adding Article 64.035 to read as follows:

Art. 64.035. UNIDENTIFIED DNA PROFILES. On completion of the testing under Article 64.03, the convicting court shall order any unidentified DNA profile to be compared with the DNA profiles in the CODIS DNA database established by the Federal Bureau of Investigation.

SECTION 3. Article 64.04, Code of Criminal Procedure, is amended to read as follows:

Art. 64.04. FINDING. After examining the results of testing under Article 64.03 and any comparison of a DNA profile under Article 64.035, the convicting court shall hold a hearing and make a finding as to whether, had the results been available during the trial of the offense, it is reasonably probable that the person would not have been convicted.

SECTION 4. The change in law made by this Act applies to a motion for forensic DNA testing filed on or after the effective date of this Act. A motion for forensic DNA testing filed before the effective date of this Act is covered by the law in effect at the time the motion was filed, and the former law is continued in effect for that purpose.

SECTION 5. This Act takes effect September 1, 2009.

Appendix C

List of 75 Cases Regarding Chapter 64, Post-Conviction DNA Testing (in alphabetical order), Status of Representation Indicated

1. Allen v. State, No. 08-07-00301-CR, 2010 WL 696495 (Tex. App.—El Paso 2010, no pet.) (not designated for publication), pro se
2. Alvarez v. State, No. 14-08-00792, 2009 WL 3109907 (Tex. App.—Houston [14th Dist.] Sept. 17, 2009, no pet.) (mem. op., not designated for publication), representation status not indicated
3. In re Anderson, No. 03-07-00655-CR, 2008 WL 2777424 (Tex. App.—Austin July 18, 2008, pet. dism'd) (mem. op., not designated for publication), pro se
4. Atkins v. State, 262 S.W.3d 413 (Tex. App.—Houston [14th Dist.] 2008, no pet.), pro se
5. Barnes v. State, No. 14-08-00930-CR, 2009 WL 3817888 (Tex. App.—Houston [14th Dist.] Nov. 17, 2009, no pet.) (mem. op., not designated for publication), Patrick McCann
6. In re Biegel, No. 03-07-00274-CR, 2008 WL 341552 (Tex. App.—Austin Feb. 8, 2008, no pet.) (mem. op., not designated for publication), pro se
7. Birdwell v. State, 276 S.W.3d 642 (Tex. App.—Waco 2008, pet. struck), pro se
8. In re Bowman, No. 03-09-00212-CR, 2009 WL 3400993 (Tex. App.—Austin Oct. 21, 2009, no pet.) (mem. op., not designated for publication), pro se
9. Broussard v. State, No. 07-07-0405, 2009 WL 290968 (Tex. App.—Amarillo Feb. 6, 2009, no pet.) (mem. op., not designated for publication), Douglas M. Barlow

10. Campos v. State, No. 01-08-00032-CR, 2008 WL 5102463 (Tex. App.—Houston [1st Dist.] Dec. 4, 2008, no pet.) (mem. op., not designated for publication), pro se
11. Ex parte Chabot, 300 S.W.3d 768 (Tex. Crim. App. 2009), Bruce Anton
12. Cloud v. State, Nos. 05-07-01414-CR, 05-07-01415-CR, 2008 WL 3020817 (Tex. App.—Dallas Aug. 6, 2008, no pet.) (not designated for publication), pro se
13. Conlin v. State, No. 09-07-344 CR, 2007 WL 5101236 (Tex. App.—Beaumont Apr. 16, 2008, no pet.) (mem. op., not designated for publication), pro se
14. State v. Cooper, No. 05-08-01642-CR, 2009 WL 2232456 (Tex. App.—Dallas July 28, 2009, no pet.) (mem. op., not designated for publication), counsel status unknown
15. Coronado v. State, No. 01-08-00101-CR, 2009 WL 3152118 (Tex. App.—Houston [1st Dist.] Oct. 1, 2009, no pet.) (mem. op., not designated for publication), Clyde Williams
16. In re Crayton, No. 03-09-00099-CR, 2009 WL 3486365 (Tex. App.—Austin Oct. 27, 2009, no pet.) (mem.op.), pro se
17. Cuellar v. State, No. 14-07-00255-CR, 2008 WL 4308408 (Tex. App.—Houston [14th Dist.] Aug. 28, 2008, no pet.) (mem. op.), Stephen Morris
18. Delacruz v. State, Nos. 14-08-00150-CR, 14-08-00152-CR, 2008 WL 4585246 (Tex. App.—Houston [14th Dist.] Oct. 16, 2008, no pet.) (mem. op., not designated for publication), pro se
19. Dixon v. State, 242 S.W.3d 929 (Tex. App.—Dallas 2008, no pet), Robert Udashen
20. Durden v. State, No. 14-09-00120-CR, 2010 WL 454935 (Tex. App.—Houston [14th Dist.] Feb. 11, 2010, no pet.) (mem. op., not designated for publication), pro se

21. Esparza v. State, 282 S.W.3d 913 (Tex. Crim. App. 2009), pro se
22. Faison v. State, No. 05-08-01311-CR, 2010 WL 851406 (Tex.App.—Dallas Mar. 12, 2010, no pet. h.) (not designated for publication), Kathleen Walsh
23. In re Franklin, No. 03-07-00563-CR, 2008 WL 2468712 (Tex. App.—Austin June 19, 2008, no pet.) (mem.op., not designated for publication), pro se
24. Fugon v. State, No. 01-08-00577-CR, 2009WL 1958742 (Tex. App.—Houston [1st Dist.] July 9, 2009, no pet.) (mem. op., not designated for publication) , Bob Wicoff
25. Garcia v. State, No. PD-1039-08, 2009 WL 3042392 (Tex. Crim. App. Sept. 23, 2009), counsel statuts unknown
26. Garcia v. State, No. 01-05-00718-CR, 2008 WL 2466211 (Tex. App.—Houston [1st Dist.] June 19, 2008(mem op., not designated for publication), aff'd on other grounds Garcia, 2009 WL 3042392, Bob Wicoff
27. Garrett v. State, No. 05-07-00131-CR, 2008 WL 2840688 (Tex.App.—Dallas July 24, 2008, no pet.) (mem. op., not designated for publication), Gary Udashen
28. In re Gonzales, No. 03-07-00649-CR, 2009 WL 2195421 (Tex. App.—Austin July 24, 2009, no pet.) (mem. op., not designated for publication), pro se
29. Graves v. State, No. 14-06-00794-CR, 2008 WL 442592 (Tex. App.—Houston [14th Dist.] Feb. 19, 2008, no pet.) (mem. op., not designated for publication), pro se
30. Greenland v. State, No. 01-06-00109-CR, 2009 WL 5174239 (Tex. App.—Houston [1st Dist.] Dec. 31, 2009, no pet.) (mem. op., not designated for publication), Nicole Deborde
31. Hamilton v. State, No. 05-06-01273-CR, 2008 WL 217564 (Tex. App.—Dallas Jan. 28, 2008, no pet.) (mem. op., not designated for publication), Roger V. Dickey

32. Harris v. State, No. 01-08-00144-CR, 2008 WL 5651469 (Tex. App.—Houston [1st Dist.] Feb. 19, 2009, no pet.) (mem. op., not designated for publication), Rosa Eliades
33. Harrison v. State, No. 14-07-00287-CR, 2008 WL 220711 (Tex. App.—Houston [14th Dist.] Jan 29, 2008, pet. struck) (mem. op., not designated for publication), pro se
34. Hunnicutt v. State, No. 05-07-01332-CR, 2008 WL 4743488 (Tex. App.—Dallas Oct. 30, 2008, no pet.) (mem. op., not designated for publication), Bradley K. Lollar
35. Hurley v. State No. 05-07-00597-CR, 2008 WL 2454675 (Tex. App.—Dallas June 19, 2008, no pet.) (mem. op., not designated for publication), Robert Udashen
36. Hutson v. Thaler, Civil Action No. H-05-1163, 2010WL 272283 (S.D. Tex. Jan. 21, 2010), pro se
37. Jacobs v. State, 294 S.W.3d 192 (Tex. App.—Texarkana 2009, pet ref'd), Carlo D'Angelo
38. Johnson v. State, No. 14-08-00441-CR, 2009 WL 1493040 (Tex. App.—Houston [14th Dist.] May 28, 2009, no pet.) (mem. op., not designated for publication), counsel status unknown
39. In re Kennard, No. 03-07-00308-CR, 2008 WL 899606 (Tex. App.—Austin Apr. 3, 2008, no pet.) (mem. op., not designated for publication), Karyl Anderson Krug
40. King v. State, No. 05-07-00036-CR, 2008 WL 2877752 (Tex. App.—Dallas July 28, 2008, no pet.) (mem. op., not designated for publication), pro se
41. King v. State, No. 13.0700096-CR, 2008 WL 4724435 (Tex. App.—Corpus Christi July 29, 2008, pet. ref'd) (mem. op., not designated for publication), J. Sidney Crowley
42. State v. Labonte, No. 14-08-00340-CR, 2009 WL 62932 (Tex. App.—Houston [14th Dist.] Jan. 13, 2009, no pet.) (mem. op.), Robyn Nance and Jeff Blackburn

43. Lacy v. State, No. 2-08-318-CR, 2009 WL 885938 (Tex. App.—Fort Worth Apr. 2, 2009, no pet.) (mem. op., not designated for publication), Robert Ford
44. Leal v. State, 303 S.W.3d 292 (Tex. Crim. App. 2009), Mark Stevens and Sandra Babcock
45. In re Lockett, No. 2-08-452-CV, 2009 WL 1740145 (Tex. App.—Fort Worth June 16, 2009, no pet.) (mem. op., not designated for publication), pro se
46. Lomax v. State, No. 14-07-00934-CR, 2008 WL 5085653 (Tex. App.—Houston [14th Dist.] Nov. 25, 2008, no pet.) (mem. op., not designated for publication), Sharon E. Slopis
47. Lyon v. State, 274 S.W.3d 767 (Tex. App.—San Antonio 2008, pet. ref'd), John M. Economidy
48. Manning v. State, No. 05-07-00363-CR, 2008 WL 2719935 (Tex. App.—Dallas July 14, 2008, pet. ref'd) (mem. op., not designated for publication), Christian T. Souza
49. Marks v. State, No. 2-09-144-CR, 2010 WL 598459 (Tex. App.—Fort Worth Feb. 18, 2010, no pet. h.) (mem. op., not designated for publication), James W. Volberding
50. In re Marshall, No. 14-09-00796-CR, 2010 WL 27054 (Tex. App.—Houston [14th Dist.] Jan. 7, 2010, no pet.) (mem. op., not designated for publication), Jerome Godenich
51. McConnell v. State, No. 05-07-00675-CR, 2008 WL 3412201 (Tex. App.—Dallas Aug. 13, 2008, no pet.) (mem. op., not designated for publication), Kathleen A. Walsh
52. In re McGary, No. 06-08-000200-CR, 2008 WL 4812594 (Tex. App.—Texarkana Nov. 6, 2008, no pet.) (mem. op., not designated for publication), James W. Volberding
53. Minnfee v. Simms, No. 03-07-00374-CV, 2008 WL 678554 (Tex. App.—Austin Mar. 13, 2008, no pet.), pro se
54. In re Morton, 2010 WL 45866 (Tex. App.—Austin Jan. 8, 2010, no pet.) (emphasis in original)

55. In re Padilla, No. 03-07-00712-CR, 2008 WL 2468735 (Tex. App.—Austin June 18, 2008, no pet.) (memo op., not designated for publication), pro se
56. Picone v. State, No. 01-08-00226-CR, 2009 WL 1886181 (Tex. App.—Houston [1st Dist.] July 2, 2009, no pet.) (mem. op., not designated for publication), Danny Karl Easterling
57. Prible v. State, 245 S.W.3d 466 (Tex. Crim. App. 2008), Roland Brice Moore III
58. Robinson v. State, No. 05-07-01585-CR, 2008WL 4725649 (Tex. App.—Dallas Oct. 29, 2008, no pet.) (mem. op., not designated for publication), Kathleen A. Walsh
59. Rodriguez v. State, No. 08-07-00248-CR, 2009 WL 3152471 (Tex. App.—El Paso Sept. 30, 2009, pet. ref'd) (not designated for publication), pro se
60. Routier v. State, 273 S.W.3d 272 (Tex. Crim. App. 2008), J. Stephen Cooper, Richard A. Smith, and Richard Burr
61. In re Ruffin, No. 03-08-00071-CR, 2008 WL 3166314 (Tex. App.—Austin Aug. 6, 2008, no pet.) (mem. op., not designated for publication), pro se
62. In re Ryan, No. 07-09-0183-CV, 2009 WL 1940911 (Tex. App.—Amarillo July 7, 2009, no pet.) (mem. op.), pro se
63. Sepeda v. State, 301 S.W.3d 372 (Tex. App.—Amarillo 2009, pet. struck), Erika Copeland
64. Skinner v. State, 293 S.W.3d 196 (Tex. Crim. App. 2009), Robert C. Owen
65. Smith v. State, No. 01-06-00416-CR, 2009 WL 3248206 (Tex. App.—Houston [1st Dist.] Oct. 8, 2009, no pet.) (mem. op., not designated for publication), Winifred Akins
66. Spurlock v. State, No. 2-08-339-CR, 2009 WL 1564967 (Tex. App.—Fort Worth June 4, 2009, no pet.) (mem. op., not designated for publication), Pamela A. Walker

67. Stevens v. State, No. 2-08-408-CR, 2009 WL 485714 (Tex. App.—Fort Worth Feb. 26, 2009, no pet.) (mem. op., not designated for publication), Robert Ford
68. Sutton v. State, No. 04-08-00867-CR, 2009 WL 1329835 (Tex. App.—San Antonio May 13, 2009, pet. ref'd) (mem. op., not designated for publication), Angela J. Moore
69. Swearingen v. State, 303 S.W.3d 728 (Tex. Crim. App. 2010), Philip H. Hilder and James G. Rytting
70. Truman v. State, No. 14-08-00315, 2009 WL 396282 (Tex. App.—Houston [14 Dist.] Feb. 19, 2009, no pet.) (mem. op., not designated for publication), counsel status unknown
71. In re White, No. 03-08-00796-CR, 2009 WL 3319859 (Tex. App.—Austin Oct. 15, 2009, no pet.) (mem. op., not designated for publication), pro se
72. Wicker v. State, No. 05-07-00163-CR, 2008 WL 2440270 (Tex. App.—Dallas June 18, 2008, no pet.) (mem. op., not designated for publication), pro se
73. Willis v. State, No. 2-06-091-CR, 2008 WL 2780666 (Tex. App.—Fort Worth July 17, 2008, pet. ref'd) (mem. op., not designated for publication), Don Hase
74. Yarbrough v. State, 258 S.W.3d 205 (Tex. App.—Waco 2008, no pet.), Joseph L. Sheppard and Richard Alley
75. State v. Young, 242 S.W.3d 926 (Tex. App.—Dallas 2008, no pet.), Robert Udashen

List of 29 Cases Excluded from the Analysis of Appellate Court Opinions Regarding Chapter 64, Status of Representation Indicated

1. Ex parte Alba, 256 S.W.3d 682 (Tex. Crim. App. 2008), Anthony S. Houghton
2. Ard v. Thaler, No. 3:07-CV-1127-D, 2009 WL 4249133 (N.D. Tex. Nov. 24, 2009), counsel status unknown
3. Barnes v. State, No. 14-08-00304-CR, 2008 WL 1991777 (Tex. App.—Houston [14th Dist.] May 8, 2008, no pet.) (mem op., not designated for publication), counsel status unknown
4. Brisco v. State, No. 05-07-01507, 2009 WL 1058730 (Tex. App.—Dallas Apr. 21, 2009, pet. ref'd) (mem. op., not designated for publication), pro se
5. Becerra v. State, No. 14-07-00774-CR, 2008 WL 5220482 (Tex. App.—Houston [14th Dist.] Dec. 11, 2008) (mem. op., not designated for publication), Stephen Morris
6. Burke v. Harris County District Attorney, Civil Action No. H-08-1968, 2008 WL 4533929 (S.D. Tex. Oct. 9, 2008), pro se
7. Burrell v. Director, TDCJ-CID, Civil Action No. 1:06-CV-390, 2008 WL 150489 (E.D. Tex. Jan. 14, 2008), pro se
8. Cash v. Director, TDCJ-CID, Civil Action No. 5:07cv6, 2008 WL 4104490 (E.D. Tex. Aug. 29, 2008), pro se
9. Ex parte Chi, 256 S.W.3d 702 (Tex. Crim. App. 2008), Wes Ball and David R. Dow
10. Christ v. State, No. 14-08-00902-CR, 2009 WL 5227884 (Tex. App.—Houston [14th Dist.] Sept. 1, 2009, no pet.) (mem. op., not designated for publication), counsel status unknown
11. Ellis v. Quarterman, Civil Action No. H-07-2768, 2008 WL 2963467 (S.D. Tex. July 30, 2008), pro se
12. In re Gutierrez v. State, No. AP-76186, 2009 WL 49336399 (Tex. Crim. App. Dec. 16, 2009), counsel status not indicated

13. In re Kitt, No. 01-08-00450-CR, 2008 WL 5102533 (Tex. App.—Houston [1st Dist.] Dec. 4, 2008, no pet.) (mem. op., not designated for publication), pro se
14. Lara v. State, No. 14-07-00975-CR, 2008 WL 2520791 (Tex. App.—Houston [14th Dist. June 24, 2008, no pet.) (mem. op., not designated for publication), counsel status not indicated
15. Leal v. State, No. 04-08-00818-CR, 2008 WL 5377753 (Tex. App.—San Antonio Dec. 23, 2008) (mem. op., not designated for publication), aff'd on other grounds, 303 S.W.3d 292, 302 (Tex. Crim. App. 2009), Mark Stevens
16. In re Pollard, No. 98-08-382 CV, 2008 WL 4587874 (Tex. App.—Beaumont Oct. 16, 2008, no pet.) (mem. op.), pro se
17. Randle v. State, No. 05-07-00849-CR, 2008 WL 933424 (Tex. App.—Dallas Apr. 8, 2008, no pet.) (mem. op., not designated for publication), Kathleen A. Walsh
18. Reyes v. Quarterman, Civil Action No. G-99-0037, 2008 WL 4415122 (S.D. Tex. Sept. 24, 2008), Forrest D. Lumpkin
19. Rodriguez v. State, No. 08-07-00248-CR, 2009 WL 1547741 (Tex. App.—El Paso June 3, 2009, pet. ref'd) (not designated for publication), pro se
20. Salinas v. State, No. 01-06-00831-CR, 2009 WL 1331966 (Tex. App.—Houston [1st Dist.] May 14, 2009, no pet.) (mem. op., not designated for publication), Shawna L. Reagin
21. Sanchez v. Thaler, No. 07-10812, 2010 WL 608913 (5th Cir. Feb. 12, 2010), pro se
22. In re Scott, No. 06-08-00096-CV, 2008 WL 4329214 (Tex. App.—Texarkana Sept, 24, 2008, no pet.) (mem. op.), pro se

23. Seitz v. State, No. 05-07-01389-CR, 2008 WL 217596 (Tex. App.—Dallas Jan. 28, 2008, no pet.) (mem. op., not designated for publication), pro se
24. In re Shepard, No. 03-07-00528-CR, 2008 WL 678383 (Tex. App.—Austin Mar. 12, 2008, no pet.) (mem. op., not designated for publication), pro se
25. Skinner v. Switzer, No. 2:09-CV-0281, 2010 WL 273143 (N.D. Tex. Jan, 20, 2010, Robert Owen, Douglas Robinson, and Maria Cruz Melendez
26. Ex parte Thompson, No. WR-50417-03, 2009 WL 330162 (Tex. Crim. App. Feb. 11, 2009), counsel status unknown
27. Turner v. Quarterman, Civil Action No. 3:06-CV-0709-D, 2008 WL 2941124 (N.D. Tex. July 30, 2008), pro se
28. Ex Parte Twiss, No. WR-69619-04, 2009 WL 623988 (Tex. Crim. App. Mar. 11, 2009), counsel status not indicated
29. In re Wright, No. 05-08-000728-CV, 2008 WL 376162 (Tex. App.—Dallas Feb. 13, 2008, no pet.) (mem. op.), pro se

B. The Case for Innocence Commissions

1. Inadequacies of the Habeas Process

Why Innocent Texas Prisoners Cannot Expect Habeas Relief and How an Innocence Commission Can Help

Yesero T. Olowo-Okello*

I. Introduction

In a society committed to truth and justice the most important function of the criminal justice system is to separate the innocent from the guilty.[1] Sometimes, however, the system breaks down and the innocent are declared guilty. Few things are more heinous than the state sending an innocent person to prison. Gregory Taylor's story illustrates this point. Gregory Taylor was wrongfully convicted of murdering a prostitute based on a faulty investigation and unreliable testimony from witnesses.[2] Because Gregory Taylor's case did not involve DNA evidence, he could not conclusively prove that he did not commit the murder.[3] Sentenced to prison for sixteen years for a crime he did not commit, Gregory Taylor

* Yesoro Olowo-Okello is a 2011 J.D. Candidate, University of Houston Law Center. He currently is an intern at the Gulf Advocacy Regional Center in the area of criminal defense.

faced the real prospect of spending the rest of his life in prison because he had exhausted all of his appeals, including all available habeas corpus claims.[4] With all of his appeals exhausted, Gregory Taylor turned to the one place left that could prove his innocence, the North Carolina Innocence Commission. After a three-judge panel found Gregory Taylor innocence by "clear and convincing evidence," he was exonerated of the crime that he was wrongfully convicted of all those years ago.[5] Gregory Taylor is the first innocent person ever to be exonerated by the North Carolina Innocence Commission.[6] However, the outcome of Gregory Taylor's story would have been different had he been a Texas inmate because his chance to prove his innocence would have ended after his appeals. Despite the best efforts of those who have sworn to uphold and protect the integrity of the criminal justice system, the sad reality is that people are not infallible and mistakes are made with tragic results for all. The Texas criminal justice system is no exception.[7]

The current procedures that Texas has in place to detect wrongful convictions have not been adequate. Habeas corpus petitions, filed both in State and federal courts, are the last line of defense for those who are wrongfully convicted of crimes in Texas. However, habeas corpus is necessarily an ineffective tool for proving innocence. Innocent prisoners must overcome a myriad of procedural hurdles to obtain relief on a State or federal habeas petition. The Texas post-conviction system should be supplemented by the establishment of a Texas Innocence Commission.

A particular circumstance of habeas corpus that merits special recognition is that actually innocent prisoners may not be able to obtain relief because DNA is not available to prove their innocence. In the vast majority of cases biological evidence is not present.[8] Without DNA evidence, it is particularly difficult for an innocent prisoner to prove their innocence.[9] In non-DNA cases, an innocent prisoner must prove their innocence through newly discovered evidence, such as confessions by the actual criminal, statements by previously unknown witnesses, and recantations by trial witnesses[10] or finding critical physical evidence that was not available at trial.[11] Because newly discovered, non-scientific evidence is subjective; it does not command the same respect as newly discovered scientific evidence.[12] Where the wrongfully convicted person's case does not involve DNA, habeas relief is unlikely because of doubts on the reliability of the newly discovered evidence.

An innocent Texas prisoner that has a strong claim of innocence will face a variety of barriers in attempting to prove their innocence in a habeas corpus proceeding because such a petitioner must overcome strict deadlines, poor lawyering, a high burden of proof, restrictions on subsequent petitions, denial of counsel for subsequent petitions, and the circumstance that habeas goes back to the convicting court.

The Texas post-conviction system should be supplemented by establishing a separate forum for uncovering wrongful convictions. This article proposes the establishment of a Texas Innocence Commission, in the fashion of the North Carolina Actual Innocence Commission. Such a Commission would provide an independent investigation and review of claims of actual innocence that is simply unavailable within the traditional habeas process, even when innocent prisoners are involved.

Part II is an overview of both the Texas and federal habeas corpus systems and their inadequacies in vindicating the interests of factually innocent petitioners. Part III of this article explores a new method for investigating claims of factual innocence pioneered by North Carolina in the form of an Innocence Commission. Part IV recommends a similar model for adoption by Texas that reflects the unique interest and attributes of the State.

II. A Two Layered System of Post-Conviction Relief

Texas currently employs habeas corpus as the only post-conviction process by which inmates may challenge their convictions after direct appeals have been exhausted.[13] A prisoner filing a habeas corpus petition in Texas must first file the petition in State court and, thereafter, the petition may be filed in federal court. Habeas corpus proceedings in both jurisdictions have common procedures and ostensibly have the same goal of protecting against unlawful imprisonment.[14]

The Supreme Court has admonished that the writ of habeas corpus* is a fundamental tool for protecting the freedom of individuals from

* A legal action through which a prisoner can be released from unlawful detention.

capricious and lawless action in behalf of the state or by the state against individuals.[15] Habeas is guaranteed by the Texas and federal constitutions.[16] In general terms, the writ of habeas corpus is an order from one branch of government, the judiciary, ordering another branch, the executive, to bring before it the petitioner claiming false imprisonment.[17] Separate from the criminal trial and its direct appeals, a habeas corpus petition is a discrete civil proceeding that is considered a "collateral" attack or a "post-conviction" proceeding.[18] The writ of habeas corpus is not the avenue through which the petitioner continues the criminal case seeking to prove innocence.[19] Instead, the writ is an extraordinary remedy and only the confinement itself is examined to see if it accords with the constitutional rights afforded to the petitioner.[20] As a result of this limitation, the ability to raise claims in a writ of habeas is severely limited.[21]

The writ may only issue after the criminal justice system, with all of its procedural safeguards and appeals, has finally determined that the person is guilty of the crime and sentenced in accord with the law.[22] Ideally, petitioners would utilize the writ in the manner in which it was intended, and courts would seriously consider their claims. However, the reality is far different from this ideal. Whether by federal or state habeas, inmates filing habeas petitions face an up-hill battle against both federal and state judicial precedent, as well as statutes that are designed to curtail petitioner's ability to prevail on their claims. These restrictions on habeas corpus reflect the presumption petitioner's are in fact guilty, which works against innocent prisoners who find the courthouse doors shut.

A. First Layer: Habeas Corpus Inadequacies in Texas

An innocent inmate must first brave the post-conviction habeas procedures of the State of conviction before attempting the complicated federal writ.[23] In Texas, one might get the impression that inmates will have access to a speedy and effective review process. After all, the Texas Constitution explicitly states that the legislature should make every effort to ensure that the right of habeas corpus is an effective and speedy remedy.[24] Unlike the federal Constitution, which grants the right to the writ of habeas corpus only be implication,[25] the Texas Constitution explicitly grants the writ of habeas corpus ands states that it should never be suspended.[26]

There are two important procedural avenues in Texas for obtaining review of an inmate's writ of habeas corpus, depending on whether the case involves the death sentence or not.[27] The following sections will address the numerous challenges that all inmates face under these two procedural avenues and highlights the ways in which even innocent prisoners would find it difficult, if not impossible to obtain relief.

1. Judicial Conflict of Interest

A habeas corpus petition not involving the death penalty must be filed in accordance with Texas Code of Criminal Procedure 11.07.[28] An applicant for a writ of habeas corpus where no death penalty is involved must file his writ with the convicting court where his writ will be heard.[29] The convicting court decides whether there are challenged, previously unresolved facts material to the legality of the petitioner's imprisonment. If the court concludes that there are no such unresolved issues, then the case proceeds to the Court of Criminal Appeals for further review.[30] However, if the convicting court finds that there are unresolved issues, then it will enter an order to the state to reply to the issues that the court feels need to be resolved.[31] Upon receiving the prosecutor's response, the court must rule on the petition.[32]

As a practical matter, having the same court that determined the applicant's guilt decide the habeas corpus petition presents a type of conflict of interest in that it requires a judge to overturn a verdict rendered in her own prior court, which is unlikely. In contrast, when the North Carolina Assembly established its Actual Innocence Commission, it recognized the possibility of prejudice due to prior involvement and so prohibited any judge who had substantial prior involvement in the case from presiding over a claim of factual innocence.[33]

2. Filing Deadlines, Restrictions on Multiple Petitions, and Access to Effective Legal Representation

Actually innocent prisoners may not be in a position to present evidence of their innocence in their first petition as the evidence of innocence may not yet be available. After a final ruling on an initial petition, a petitioner may not file a subsequent habeas application unless one of two exceptions is met.[34] The first exception is that the issues have not and could not have been presented previously in a previous petition because the factual or legal basis for the claim was unavailable on the date the petitioner filed the first application.[35] The second exception to the subsequent petition rule requires that the petitioner show that but for a violation of the United States Constitution "no rational juror could have found the applicant guilty beyond a reasonable doubt."[36]

When a habeas petitioner is facing the death penalty another set of rules apply. Petitioners in habeas proceedings challenging death sentences have the right to competent counsel,[37] and also enjoy the right to have their attorneys conduct thorough investigations.[38] Tragically, despite these rights an innocent prisoner may be precluded from filing a petition because his lawyer misses the filing deadline, and these are strictly enforced.[39] A petition may be dismissed unless the petitioner can show good cause for the petition being late.[40]

An innocent inmate who has been sentenced to death and who has new evidence of innocence is not likely to obtain relief in a subsequent habeas petition for lack of representation. Rather than making the habeas corpus petition speedy and effectual, the legislature has actually hampered prisoners' access to this right. In his dissenting opinion in *Ex parte Davis*, Justice Clinton exposes this statutory shortcoming.[41] As Justice Clinton explains, the Texas Code of Criminal Procedure states that the Court of Criminal Appeals is forbidden from considering the merits of a claim if it is untimely brought or after a first timely application unless he can satisfy three exceptions.[42] He must show that either the factual or legal basis for his successive claim was not available at the time the application was filed;[43] that, by the preponderance of the evidence, but for a violation of the Constitution, no rational jury would have convicted him;[44] or that, by clear and convincing evidence, but for a violation of the Constitution no rational juror would have answered one or more of the special issues in such a way that the death penalty would be imposed.[45] However, the State does not have to provide an attorney to the petitioner filing a subsequent petition until *after* he has proved one of the three exceptions. No relief will be found in Supreme Court precedent because there is no federal constitutional right to counsel for petitioner in state post-conviction proceedings.[46] As a practical matter, without counsel, inmates are unlikely to be able to file a timely petition or to be able to establish an exception. Since the Court of Criminal Appeals is powerless to grant relief upon any untimely or unexcused claim of federal constitutional error that does not meet any of the three exceptions, petitioners do not have any viable means of recourse.[47]

3. Issue Preclusion Due to Poor Lawyering

The habeas petitioner faces daunting odds for other reasons as well. First, the Court of Criminal Appeals has stated that if an inmate has not raised an issue that should have been raised on direct appeal, then the claim cannot be raised in a habeas action, even if that claim was constitutional in nature.[48] As a result, there is a very real danger of default of a claim by an inmate who has an incompetent attorney.[49] Despite the fact that the claim of ineffective assistance of counsel exists as a derivative for claims that were defaulted during the original proceeding,[50] it is of slight comfort because it is difficult to conduct the investigation of attorney incompetence. On top of all this, the competency of a prior habeas counsel is not a recognized claim on habeas corpus review; the claim does not meet the requirements for a subsequent writ.[51]

4. Induced Waivers of Habeas Rights

The State can persuade an innocent person to waive his or her right to habeas corpus review in order to obtain the prosecutor's agreement to recommend a specific sentence to the judge.[52] The waiver is valid if voluntarily, knowingly, and intelligently made.[53] An innocent person may agree to waive his right to habeas corpus if the alternative sentencing is draconian enough. After the court announces the judgment and sentence, the waiver of habeas corpus is enforceable because it would presumably be made with knowledge of any errors made during trial.[54] As a result, it is usually at this point that the prosecutor seeks the wavier. The waiver will be enforced if the waived claim was based on facts of which the petitioner was aware that could have been discovered by due diligence with the assistance of counsel or of which petitioner should have been aware at the time of waiver.[55]

5. No Right to Challenge the Sufficiency of the Evidence

Since the writ of habeas corpus exists as a means to collaterally attack a final judgment, a sufficiency of the evidence claim is not available.[56] Because a court hearing a writ of habeas corpus may not assume the characteristics of a direct court, a petitioner may not challenge the sufficiency of the evidence used to convict him because this claim relates to guilt or innocence which must be decided at trial and on direct appeal.[57] As a result, an actually innocent petitioner may not claim that there was not enough evidence to convict him of the crime in a habeas proceeding.[58]

6. High Hurdle to Prevail on Claim Based on Newly Discovered Evidence

Texas courts acknowledge that imprisoning an innocent person offends due process.[59] They examine a habeas corpus petitioner's newly discovered evidence that may show actual innocence, the crime of conviction, even if this new evidence is beyond the record that was presented at trial.[60] However, the hurdle a petition must clear to prove innocence is exceedingly high.

When reviewing a habeas corpus petition that alleges newly discovered evidence, Texas courts must attempt to assess the likely impact of newly discovered evidence upon the persuasiveness of the State's case as a whole.[61] A petitioner looking for acquittal on a bare innocence claim must show that there is new confirmatory evidence[62] that unquestionably proves his innocence. The petitioner must prove by clear and convincing evidence that no reasonable jury could have convicted him in light of the new evidence.[63] This is done by evaluating the new evidence in light of the old evidence used to convict.[64] Of course, this presupposes that the evidence is admissible. If a petitioner obtains inadmissible evidence, then the court will not consider it.[65] For example, a petitioner could not use the results of polygraph examination to establish innocence because those are not admissible in Texas courts.[66] The fact that an innocent person pleaded guilty will work against a claim of innocence.[67] The courts do not ignore the reality that a person pleaded guilty and must analyze the reliability of the newly presented evidence in light of the guilty plea.[68]

Texas courts have put an exceedingly heavily burden on a petitioner who attempts to overturn a conviction in which no errors are alleged since society has an interest in obtaining a final resolution of criminal matters.[69] The petitioner has the burden because proof of guilt has been established.[70] Because appellate courts afford almost complete deference to trial courts in matters of habeas corpus, applying an abuse of discretion standard of review, it will be the rare case in which a trial court is overruled because the record does not contain evidence to support its decision.[71]

In conducting a review of a claim where testimony was vital to convict, the Court of Criminal Appeals has stated that recantations made by the crucial witness should be approached with caution and that a conviction should not be overturned without strong corroborating, independent evidence.[72] If a habeas petitioner presented evidence that merely attacked the veracity of the prosecution's main witness on an important matter at trial, this would not be enough to get relief.[73]

At least one appellate court has also ruled that an applicant has not exercised due diligence when he or she claims difficulty in obtaining documents; as a result this does not qualify for as newly discovered evidence.[74] This is significant for any innocent prisoner who may not be able to obtain important documents to establish innocence.

In summary, an innocent person is presumed innocent at trial until proven guilty.[75] However, once trial is over and the defendant has been found guilty in a fair proceeding, the presumption of innocence disappears.[76] Thereafter, in the eyes of the Texas courts, the petitioner is presumed guilty.[77] The innocent Texas prisoner will encounter significant, and often insurmountable, hurdles on the road to freedom.

B. Second Layer: Inadequacies of Federal Habeas Corpus

An actually innocent Texas inmate challenging his or her state court conviction may file a federal habeas petition after exhausting all state habeas remedies.[78] Like the Texas process, the petitioner filing a federal petition will encounter daunting road-blocks on the path to prove his or her innocence in the form of restrictive statutes and Supreme Court precedent. The following sections address the various challenges to obtaining habeas relief in federal courts.

1. Crushing Caseloads of Federal Courts

Explicit authority of federal courts to hear habeas petitions from state prisoners comes from Congressional statute, which provides that a petitioner may have his or her habeas corpus petition heard by the Supreme Court or any affiliate of it.[79] In practice, however, the Supreme Court itself grants few habeas petitions. The Supreme Court gets applications of over seven thousand general writs of certiorari* per year and grants around one hundred writs with plenary review and fifty to sixty without it.[80]

The Supreme Court is not alone in the amount of cases that it receives every year. The Court of Appeals for the Fifth Circuit is similarly burdened by large amounts of cases. In 2009, the Fifth Circuit commenced 7,415 cases in 2009.[81] Texas district courts are in no better position to hear cases by habeas inmates. The Western District alone had 10,547 cases filed in 2008.[82] In 2008, the Eastern District had 3,498 cases filed with it.[83] Similarly, the Northern District received 5,076 petitions.[84] By far the most filings received were in the Southern District, which was burdened with 14,512 cases.[85] Taken together, all of these filings by various parties make it exceedingly difficult for the Texas District Courts to carefully scrutinize habeas petitions because these Courts are pressured by other types of cases.

---

* An order issued by the Supreme Court of the United States to a lower court which indicates that the Court has decided to review the lower court's judgment for legal error.

2. Restrictive Legislation: United States Code Sections 2241 and 2254

A petitioner using habeas corpus must also contend with Congressional statutes that severely restrict habeas corpus. Sections 2241 and 2254 of Title 28 of the United States Code place severe restrictions on a prisoner's ability to file a writ of habeas corpus.[86] Federal law does not guarantee the right of access to the federal courts by a state petitioner in a habeas proceeding.[87] The petitioner must first meet three requirements under the statute.[88] First, the petitioner must have exhausted his or her remedies that exist in the state courts where the conviction was obtained.[89] Second, the petitioner must establish that the state in which he or she is held has a lack of available corrective process.[90] Third, the petitioner must prove that there are circumstances which would make the already established state corrective process unreliable to preserve the rights of the petitioner.[91] For example, even if a petitioner shows a clear violation of constitutional law by the state holding him, the federal courts are bound to reject the writ if the exhaustion requirement has not been met.[92] Clearly, the exhaustion requirement has not been met if there is an available procedure that is presently open to the petitioner within state law that may be used to address the issue.[93]

Once a petitioner qualifies to file a petition, Section 2254 (d) sets a high burden of proof on an applicant to prevail on the claim.[94] The petitioner would have to prove either that the state court decision on the merits involved an unreasonable application of clearly established federal law,[95] or that the conviction was based on an unreasonable determination of the facts in light of the evidence presented during the State trial.[96] Further, the Supreme Court has declared that the "unreasonable application" clause means that a state conviction cannot be overturned by a federal court simply because the state incorrectly applied federal law in its decision; instead, the use of federal law must be unreasonable.[97] As one can well imagine, it will be the rare case in which a State court applies explicit federal law in an unreasonable manner.

A situation where a court applied explicit federal law in an unreasonable manner is found in *Williams v. Taylor*. In that case the Virginia Supreme Court's decision was contrary to and involved an unreasonable application of federal law as applied to a *Strickland* claim* of ineffective-assistance of counsel.[98] The Virginia Supreme Court's analysis of prejudice was unreasonable in one respect because it misapplied the *Strickland* test for determining if a lawyer's assistance was effective within meaning of the Constitution.[99] In making its outcome determinative analysis, the Virginia Supreme Court's decision turned on a mistaken view that mere difference in outcome is not enough to show constitutionally ineffective assistance of counsel.[100] That mistaken analysis was not only "contrary to," but also, as far as the Virginia Supreme Court relied on the inapplicable exception recognized in *Lockhart*, "an unreasonable application of" explicit federal law as found by the Supreme Court.[101]

Further burdening the petitioner is the fact a State court judgment is presumed correct, and this assumption must be overcome by clear and convincing evidence on any factual issue determined by the State court.[102] If the petitioner fails to demonstrate that factual determination made by the State court was incorrect, then no evidentiary hearing on the claim may be heard unless it satisfies two very narrow exceptions.[103] First, "the claim relied on must be a new rule of constitutional law, made retroactive to cases on collateral review by the Supreme Court, that was previously unavailable, and the facts in the case adequately show by clear and convincing evidence that but for the constitutional error, no sensible juror would have found the applicant guilty.[104] Second, the petitioner may be able to prove that the claim relies on a factual predicate that could not have been previously discovered through use of due diligence, and the facts in the case are adequate to show by clear and convincing evidence that but for the constitutional error, no sensible juror would have found the applicant guilty.[105]

An innocent prisoner may have the necessary evidence to prove his innocence, but be unable to get relief. Federal habeas law, under Section 2254, was intended to restrict inmates' ability to use the writ of habeas corpus, as reflected in the report of the influential judicial committee known as the Powell Committee.[106] The Powell Committee thought that the previous habeas corpus regime was flawed because it was full of needless postponements and duplications due to a lack of coordination between the federal and state criminal justice systems.[107] This resulted

* † A claim challenging a conviction on the basis that defense counsel performance constituted "ineffective assistance" in violation of the Sixth Amendment's right to effective counsel as defined in *Strickland v. Washington*, 466 U.S. 668 (1984).

in numerous inmates shuttling back and forth between both systems before having used all available state remedies, as well as inmates who filed excessive, last minute motions for stays of execution.[108] The Powell Committee proved to be influential in the creation of the Antiterrorism and Effective Death Penalty Act passed by Congress because several of its recommendations were adopted in House Resolution 729 involving the Effective Death Penalty Act of 1995.[109]

Prior to enactment of Section 2254, there had been no statute of limitations period, enabling inmates to file multiple writs at any point during incarceration.[110] Section 2254 adopted a one year statute of limitations period,[111] so an innocent prisoner finds himself in a race against time to gather all the necessary information to prove his innocence. Waiting to present the evidence in another habeas petition is a foolish gamble in light of the myriad of tough restrictions now placed on subsequent petitions. With the adoption of sections 2254 and 2241, the petitioner must now mount daunting barriers in order to prevail in a habeas corpus petition. Thus, an inmate will find little, if any relief, by seeking refuge in these statutes.

3. Supreme Court Precedent

In addition to the complicated statutes that apply to habeas corpus, there is a large body of case law that goes firmly against applicants in their efforts to get a writ of habeas corpus. Supreme Court precedents in this area make clear that the federal courts should show extreme deference to the final rulings of State courts, even when those rulings involve questions of federal law that are raised for the first time on appeal.[112] In order to give State courts a fair opportunity to rule on a federal constitutional claim, the Supreme Court has mandated that a prisoner must raise that claim in State court to give it a chance to correct the error.[113] Accordingly, a petitioner is not permitted to bring up, for the first time, a federal constitutional claim that could have been brought in state court on the first try.[114] The Supreme Court strives to avoid confrontation between federal and state courts, and emphasizes the doctrine of comity, which requires that state courts respect and enforce federal law.[115] The Supreme Court's decisions aim to minimize the drain from federal collateral litigation on limited federal judicial resources.[116] Time and again, the Court has emphasized that habeas corpus is an extraordinary remedy that should only issue as a last resort and will not be allowed as a direct appeal.[117]

Of real significance in federal habeas proceedings involving petitioners claiming innocence, though, is the Supreme Court case of *Herrera v. Collins*.[118] In *Herrera*, an inmate was convicted of murder in Texas.[119] The inmate petitioned the Supreme Court for a writ of habeas corpus claiming to be actually innocent of the crime he was convicted for committing based on newly discovered evidence.[120] The Supreme Court faced the issue whether, standing alone, a claim of actual innocence based on newly discovered evidence was a recognized federal habeas corpus ground of review.[121] The Supreme Court emphatically answered the question negatively.[122] The Court ruled that claims of actual innocence by a petitioner alleging newly discovered evidence has never been a sufficient reason for federal habeas relief without an independent constitutional violation also arising in the underlying state criminal prosecution.[123] Thus, in the habeas context, federal courts are more focused on constitutional rights, regardless of factual innocence.[124] The Court in *Herrera* justified its decision by stating that federal habeas is not a chance for a new trial to correct errors of fact, but exists only to correct wrongful imprisonment in violation of the Constitution.[125]

Innocence is only relevant in the habeas context under the miscarriage of justice exception outlined in *Sawyer v. Whitley*.[126] In *Sawyer v. Whitley*, the Supreme Court explained that if any state raises the defense of abuse of the writ of habeas corpus, a federal court still has discretion to hear, on the merits, a petitioner's claim as long as an adequate showing of actual innocence provided.[127] Under the miscarriage of justice exception, factual innocence is only relevant as a gate keeping mechanism to let the federal court consider other constitutional claims that would be barred.[128]

The Supreme Court is reluctant to allow federal courts to second-guess state convictions by allowing claims of actual innocence.[129] In *Herrera*, Justice Blackmun dissented, opining that the cruel and unusual punishment clause of the Eighth Amendment and the due process clause in the Fourteenth Amendment provided a pathway for claims of actual innocence in habeas corpus proceedings.[130] He stated that even a prisoner who appeared to have had a constitutionally perfect trial has a powerful and legitimate interest in being released if he is innocent of the crime for which he has been imprisoned.[131]

If an actually innocent person were to plead guilty to the charges due to the pressures of plea negotiations, Supreme Court precedent would strictly limit his or her ability to challenge the plea.[132] It is generally not possible to overturn on collateral attack a voluntary and intelligent guilty plea made by a petitioner who was advised by adequate counsel.[133] Even if the petitioner is challenging the voluntariness and intelligence of his or her guilty plea in the federal courts, the claim may be deemed as defaulted if not raised first under the State's direct appeals process.[134] Generally, federal court appear to be more concerned with preserving the integrity of a final state court judgment than with probing errors, perhaps out of concern that public confidence in criminal trials will be undermined.[135] Furthermore, federal courts are concerned with being swamped by habeas petitions based on invalid pleas, the most common means of disposition of criminal charges.[136] In the name of deference to State court authority, federal courts have all but abdicated the responsibility to collaterally review State court judgments. In summary, the post-conviction procedures that are currently in place are not sufficient to help an actually innocent prisoner. The petitioner starts with the disadvantage of being presumed guilty. Texas gives a habeas petitioner the right to bring an actual innocence claim and to prove it through newly discovered evidence, but the statute puts an exceedingly heavy burden on the petitioner. The petitioner is in even more dire straits in a death penalty case because he must prove good cause without counsel. Federal courts will not even acknowledge an innocent petitioner's claim of factual innocence based on newly discovered evidence. The petitioner must contend with legislatively created habeas statutes which reflect the judgment that all habeas claims should be swiftly decided, generally against the petitioners.

Greater protection is needed for those prisoners claiming complete factual innocence of their charged crime. New procedures are needed to provide greater protection to this special class of habeas corpus petitioners. An Innocence Commission would provide the needed protection.

III. Innocence Examined: The North Carolina Actual Innocence Commission

In order to supplement and protect the rights granted by the Constitution to the prisoner claiming innocence, the establishment of an Innocence Commission is necessary. Texas has had more of its convictions overturned by DNA testing than any other state.[137] More disturbing still is the fact that nine people came close to being executed by Texas for crimes that they did not commit and have been released from death row.[138] These wrongful convictions have cost Texas more than $17 million in civil settlements and statutory compensation to victims.[139] Because the specter of the death penalty looms in the background, Texas owes it to those who claim innocence to provide them the opportunity to prove their innocence in a forum specially-designed to address these issues: an Innocence Commission.

The North Carolina legislature realized the importance of speedy post-conviction review of plausible claims of factual innocence.[140] The legislature also discerned that complete and timely inquires into claims of factual innocence would strengthen public confidence in the justice system.[141] It concluded that factual claims of innocence could be most effectively evaluated by an independent board and so created the North Carolina Actual Innocence Commission.[142]

A. Structure and Composition of the Innocence Commission

The structure of the North Carolina Actual Commission has no parallel in the United States because it is the first body of its kind created in the country. The enabling statute creating the Innocence Commission states that the body will be an independent commission under the Judicial Department for administrative purposes.[143] The Commission was put under the authority of the Administrative Office of the Courts because the North Carolina Legislature intended that organization to provide administrative assistance when needed.[144] However, the Administrative Office of the Courts has no power over the Commission's budget.[145]

The Commission consists of eight voting members with various backgrounds that relate to each part of the criminal justice system so as to bring a wide range of perspectives to the board.[146] Those committee members are:

- a superior court judge[147]
- a prosecutor[148]
- a victim advocate[149]
- a defense attorney[150]
- a public member who is not an attorney or employee of the Judicial Department[151]
- a sheriff currently in office at the time of appointment[152]
- two remaining seats filled by the State Supreme Court Chief Justice.[153]

The statute assigns to the Chief Judge of the Court of Appeals the responsibility of selecting the people who will fill the seats held by the superior court judge, the prosecutor, and the victim advocate.[154] Once an appointee has his or her first three-year term, the Chief Justice or Chief Judge who did not make the previous appointment will make the next one.[155] After this, the power to appoint committee members will alternate between the Chief Justice and Chief Judge, save for the discretionary power to select members reserved to the Chief Justice in subdivision (7).[156] The General Assembly also had in mind that the person with authority to appoint members to the Commission should make a good faith effort to appoint members with different perspectives and backgrounds,[157] including geographical location, gender, and race.[158] The diversity of the Commission's membership lends greater legitimacy to its decisions.

Members on the Commission serve for three years.[159] Members cannot serve more than two consecutive three-year terms.[160] With the exception of the sheriff, if a member is serving because of elective or appointive office, then that member may serve on the board only as long as that member holds office.[161] An important power that the Chief Justice holds is the power to remove any member for cause.[162] If a member of the Commission becomes unable to fulfill his or her duties for the full term, the open seat on the Commission will be filled in the manner provided for the position.[163] Commission members receive no salary, but the members are entitled to necessary subsistence and travel expenses.[164] The superior court judge who presides over the Commission has the duty to call the Commission into session at least once every six months.[165]

The Commission must keep the Assembly and the State Judicial Council appraised of its current activities by submitting reports which would include the Commission's budgetary requests.[166] The reports made by the Commission may recommend any legislative changes that the Commissioners feel are needed in connection with its activities.[167]

B. Investigating Claims of Factual Innocence

During the investigation stage, the Commission has real power to carry out its mission.[168] Among the powers given the Commission is the power to issue process to compel attendance of witnesses and the production of evidence, administer oaths, petition the jurisdiction for enforcement of process issued or for other needed relief, and to create its own procedures.[169] Most importantly, the Commission's Chair is entrusted with the duty to hear all changes contesting lack of authority in her judicial capacity, including in camera review.[170] The Director or her designee may serve subpoenas* or other process issued by the Commission throughout North Carolina in the same and effect as an officer of the court.[171] To back up its subpoena power, the Commission has at its disposal the North Carolina laws dealing with discovery and disclosure when the formal inquiry is begun. These are enforceable as if the applicant were currently being tried for the charge for which he or she is claiming innocence.[172]

The Commission has powers similar to a trial court to order witnesses to testify or to produce other evidence. Witnesses testify under oath subject to prosecution for perjury.[173] A witness may claim a privilege against self-incrimination, and the Commission may order the testimony or production of other information if it is found that the witness's testimony is indispensible to reach the right determination.[174] Of course, the chair cannot order testimony if "that would incriminate

---

* A writ by a government agency, most often a court, that has authority to compel testimony by a witness or production of evidence under a penalty for failure.

the witness in the prosecution of any other offense for which the witness is granted immunity under this subsection."[175] If the testimony would be self-incriminating to the witness, the chair may issue an order for compelled testimony but must also grant the witness use-immunity in exchange. However, before this order can be issued, the prosecutor has a right to make the case against a grant of immunity.[176]

The formal procedure for investigating claims proceeds in four stages: the review stage, the investigation stage, the formal inquiry stage, and the hearing stage. A person claiming actual innocence can bring his or her claim to the Commission, or any person may do so on the person's behalf.[177] The petition must meet several criteria: (1) the conviction must have been in North Carolina;[178] (2) the conviction must have been for a felony;[179] (3) the petitioner must be alive;[180] and (4) the applicant must be claiming complete factual innocence for any criminal responsibility of the crime.[181] Claims of reduced culpability or secondary involvement will not qualify.[182] Priority is given to cases in which the applicant is imprisoned only for the crime in which he or she claims complete innocence.[183] A person may still bring a claim if he or she has been convicted of another crime for which he or she does not claim innocence. If, however, an applicant has pleaded guilty to the charged crime, the claim may still be heard if, at the time of plea, credible and verifiable evidence of innocence was not reasonably available to the pleader or scientific testing on evidence was not yet complete.[184] The fifth criterion is that trustworthy evidence of innocence must exist.[185] Sixth, the trustworthy evidence of innocence must be verifiable.[186] Seventh, a post-conviction court must not have previously heard the claim,[187] specifically the evidence cannot have been ruled upon by the judge or it will not be considered.[188] This is equally true for evidence heard by the jury.[189] Finally, an agreement waiving procedural safeguards and privileges must be signed by the petitioner.[190] Only if all of these conditions are met will the investigation commence.

The first stage, which is review, is mainly controlled by the Director of the Commission. This stage involves preliminary review of a case and not a detailed investigation.[191] In this stage court opinions and other records are gathered, and timelines are created.[192] In the event a claim is rejected, the Commission keeps the file for a maximum of three years after which a basic claim summary is kept that includes the name of the applicant, date of application, people involved in the review, and the reason for rejection.[193] During the second investigative stage, the staff interviews witnesses and conducts field work.[194]

Complete discretion to accept or reject a claim is vested in the Commission, and it may informally screen and dismiss a case if it so decides,[195] especially if a claim is found not to meet the requirements for review by the Commission.[196] Also, the Commission must dismiss a case if the applicant does not cooperate or is deemed to be uncooperative.[197] Discretion rests with the Director or her deputy to make the decision to reject a case, call it for further review, or send it to formal inquiry.[198] Once the Director or her designee has determined that the claim meets the criteria, the case may be sent into the formal inquiry phase.[199] Even if a claim is rejected, an applicant may reapply, but before the case is accepted for review again, there must be new evidence not seen before.[200]

Following the investigation stage, a formal inquiry may be commenced. At the formal inquiry stage the applicant must agree to waive certain rights. No formal inquiry into a claim may begin until the Director or her designee receives the signed document from the applicant agreeing to waive procedural safeguards and privileges, to cooperate with the Commission, and to give full disclosure relating to all inquiry requirements of the Commission.[201] However, the waiver is applicable only to matters relating to the claim of innocence.[202] Prior to signing the waiver, the petitioner has the right to discuss the ramifications with his or her lawyer.[203] In the event that the petitioner cannot afford to appoint a lawyer, the Commission will appoint one for the purpose of advising on the agreement.[204]

It is during the formal inquiry that the victim is alerted to the fact that the Commission is determining the guilt or innocence of the person convicted of the crime. The victim is made to feel like an active participant because the Director of the Commission is required to use all possible due diligence when notifying the victim to explain any matter dealing with the inquiry process that is not clear.[205] A victim of the crime is not ignored—the victim may present his or her views and concerns regarding the Commission's investigation.[206]

At the beginning of the investigation, the Director or her staff is required to create a procedure that is unique to each case and keep detailed records until the completion.[207] Throughout the formal inquiry, Commissioners are required to make regular reports to the Director, who is responsible for coordinating all investigations.[208] Any formal requests, like subpoenas, court orders, and DNA testing, must be approved by the judge who chairs the Commission.[209] If it is determined that it no longer meets the requirements for review, a case will be dismissed prior to hearing by the Commission, with the consent of the Director.[210]

C. Judging Claims of Factual Innocence

After the investigation is concluded and evidence is compiled, the claim is presented to the full eight-member body of the Commission.[211] Whether the hearing will be open to the public or held behind closed doors is for the Commission to decide.[212] Even if a hearing is closed to the general public, a victim and/or relative of the victim are allowed to be present, except during Commission deliberations.[213] The Commission Chair, however, may exclude a victim or relative if it is determined that the victim's presence will disrupt proceedings. Regardless, of whether the victim or relative is permitted to attend, the Director or his or her deputy must inform the interested party of the decision made by the Commission.[214]

Before a formal hearing begins, every Commissioner must check to see if he or she was in any way involved with the case.[215] If there was prior involvement on the part of the Commissioner, then he or she is required to abstain from the proceedings.[216] In the event that a Commissioner becomes influenced by some other outside event that so biases his or her view of the case, then that member must abstain from the proceedings.[217] Independent investigation by Commission members is strictly prohibited by established rules,[218] but it is contemplated that information about cases be made known to members prior to the hearing.[219] Determination of whether formal recusal is appropriate is made by the chair.[220] In the event that a Commissioner is unable to attend a hearing or has abstained, the Commissioner's alternate will fill in.[221]

All deliberations made by the Commission are recorded and written down, including votes by Commission members.[222] These recordings may only be made public when the Commission votes in favor of judicial review, but if it votes against judicial review, the records remain undisclosed.[223]

At the actual hearing, the Director or her deputy is responsible for presenting all of the relevant evidence.[224] It is contemplated that the evidence heard at the hearing will take many forms beyond affidavits, including testimony, presentation of physical evidence, expert testimony, laboratory reports, medical evidence and documents.[225] If live testimony is needed, then the chair may administer the oath to the witness.[226] The Director or her deputy must examine the live witness, but the Commission members are permitted to ask further questions to clarify matters.[227] The Commission members deliberate using the written reports that contain relevant evidence that they received before the hearing.[228] When all the evidence has been presented, the Commissioners vote together behind closed doors,[229] on whether enough adequate evidence of factual innocence has been presented to justify judicial review.[230] In voting, the Commission members are guided by whether there is "sufficient evidence of factual innocence to merit judicial review."[231]

The last stage in the process of finding for innocence is the post-conviction panel of judges. If the Commission votes in favor of judicial review, finding that there is serious doubt about a person's guilt, the chair requests the Chief Justice to form the three-judge panel to hear the case.[232]

The state is represented at the hearing and will argue its side to the panel.[233] The applicant may choose to be represented by his own counsel, opt for self-representation, or request a court-appointed attorney.[234] Whichever method of representation is chosen, the applicant has the right to be present during the hearing.[235] At the actual hearing, the Director will be present to answer questions and give an outline of the case.[236] The hearing itself is evidentiary in nature, and the judges have the right to order witnesses to testify, including the applicant.[237] All of the judges must be convinced that there is clear and convincing evidence of a person's innocence and must vote in favor of release to clear the applicant's name.[238] Once the judges make their final decision, no appeal is available to either side.[239] However, if the claim is rejected, the applicant will still retain his right to other post-conviction relief.[240]

D. Benefits to Law Enforcement in Discovering Evidence of Guilt

Another duty of the Commission is the obligation to disclose inculpatory material information found at any point in the process. The Commission has the obligation to report to the district attorney evidence that supports an applicant's guilt if it was not available at the time of conviction.[241] This reporting obligation also applies to evidence of other crimes committed by the applicant,[242] as well as evidence of more serious crimes committed by the applicant than the crime of conviction,[243] and evidence of another person's involvement.[244]

Similarly, if the Commission finds favorable evidence, it will be released to the applicant or the attorney, even if the applicant loses.[245] Additionally, evidence of criminal or professional misconduct, or evidence of abuse of power that is uncovered during investigations is reported to the agency that is affected.[246]

IV. A New Tool for Separating the Innocent from the Guilty: The Texas Innocence Commission

Texas legislators must understand that its citizens have invested them with a great responsibility to separate the guilty from the innocent so as to protect the innocent. Too many times Texas has wronged innocent people by convicting them, stigmatizing them as criminal in the eyes of society. Texas can assure its citizens that it is not being negligent in its punishment of prisoners by building in safeguards to protect the innocent. The proposal that follows is a recommendation based mainly on the North Carolina model, but incorporating changes that better suit Texas.

There may be some fundamental misunderstandings of the role that an Innocence Commission would play in the justice system. Three criticisms come readily to mind. First, some may argue that the Commission is just another trial or chance for a criminal to escape his or her rightful punishment. Second, some may claim that this is just another bureaucracy that that will divert much needed funds from other worthy projects. Third, alarmists may contend that a Commission will help hardened criminals get another chance at proving their innocence.

First, the Innocence Commission is not another trial. Instead, the Commission would conduct an investigation to determine if there is any new evidence of complete factual innocence that is verifiable and that was not available in the original trial because it was not known to the applicant at the time and could not have been known through reasonable investigative efforts. Only then will there be deliberations on whether this new information is sufficient for a judicial panel to find the applicant innocent.

Second, the Innocence Commission would be composed of professionals who would only be compensated for reasonable expenses related to travel based on the activities of the Commission. Commission members would not be given a regular salary as state employees are given. Thus, there would be no cost to Texas beyond the necessary travel expenses related to Commission work. Because the members would not receive a fixed salary, the Commission would not meet throughout the year because its members would be employed elsewhere. The Commission would meet for no more than three months every year.

Third, an Innocence Commission does not help criminals; it sifts through evidence to find those people who are innocent. Innocent prisoners are *victims* of the criminal justice system and worthy of our utmost concern. Only those claiming complete innocence make it past the preliminary screening stage. Indeed, rather than hindering the justice system, a fully operational Commission would enhance prosecutions. Like the North Carolina model, a Texas Innocence Commission would be bound to report evidence of other crimes committed by the applicant or another person's involvement with a crime.[247] If the applicant is exonerated, and the true assailant is found, that would be reported as well.[248] In this way, the Commission would increase public confidence in the criminal justice system and enhance public safety as well.

A. Powers of the Commission

In order to make the Texas Innocence Commission an effective body, it is necessary to give it panoply of powers, so that it may carry out its investigative mission. The two most important powers to give to the Commission would be the subpoena power and the power to exonerate innocent people. Just as the North Carolina Innocence Commission has the power to subpoena important witnesses or documents that relate to the materiality of an applicant's factual innocence,[249] the Texas Innocence Commission should have this same power. Subpoena power would be appropriate because the Commission chair would be a judge who would exercise his or her judicial discretion to determine if it is necessary to subpoena a witness or documents. The Commission would have the power to subpoena throughout the state if the Commission chair decides this is necessary. The second important power given would be the power of exoneration. Similar to the North Carolina model, a Texas panel of judges would consist of three members and should have the power to exonerate a convicted person upon referral from the Commission.[250] Like the North Carolina model, a unanimous vote by all three members of the judge panel should be necessary.

B. Procedures

The Texas Innocence Commission would be governed by a set of procedures that it would be compelled to follow. There would be procedures for electing members to the Commission and for investigating claims of factual innocence. In any established Texas Innocence Commission there would be four parts that would comprise the entire investigative process. The first part would be a preliminary screening of claims received. The second part would be the actual investigation of the claims. The third part would be Commission members deciding on whether there is enough evidence to recommend a judicial hearing on the claim. The fourth part would be a panel of judges deciding on whether the person is in fact innocent.

Procedures for selecting members will be straightforward. The Commission would represent the entire State of Texas. The Commission would consist of eight members as the North Carolina Commission does.[251] In membership composition, any Texas Innocence Commission would be like that of North Carolina.[252] Membership would include:

- an appellate court judge
- a prosecutor

- a victim advocate
- a defense attorney
- a public member who is not an attorney or employee of the Judicial Department
- a sheriff currently in office at the time of appointment
- two remaining seats filled by Chief Justice of the Court of Criminal Appeals.

The same diverse perspectives that North Carolina seeks to attain through the composition of its Commission's membership should also apply to a Texas Commission.[253] The goals of geographical, gender, and racial diversity would also apply. In contrast to the North Carolina Innocence Commission where there is no time requirement of practicing law to be appointed to that body, in order to be selected to the Texas Commission, it should be necessary to be a practicing criminal attorney for at least ten years.[254] Members would be selected by a majority vote of the Court of Criminal Appeals. Every Commissioner would serve a five-year term. Even though North Carolina only has a three-year term, a five-year term would be desirable because it would give members more time to adjust to the job. At no time will any selected Commissioner preside over a case in which he or she has been personally involved at any stage during the original proceeding. This requirement is similar to the North Carolina counterpart and is crucial to eliminate any possible bias regarding the original trial.[255]

In the preliminary stage of the investigation, the Commission members and their staff would screen applicants' petitions, as the North Carolina Commission does.[256] Petitions would have to meet the same requirements criteria for claims of factual innocence applicable in North Carolina.[257] Any petition not meeting these criteria would be dismissed. Most importantly, the petition must present new verifiable evidence apart from the evidence originally heard at trial.

In the second stage, the investigative stage, detectives take the lead. The detectives would be assisted by employees of the Commission in whatever capacity needed. During this stage, potential witnesses would be investigated, leads would be followed-up, and old investigations reviewed. The goal of the investigative stage will be to verify evidence of innocence. These investigations would probably focus on cases in which there is no DNA evidence, which are typically harder for people to prove their innocence. If any evidence is found of another person's involvement, or of a greater crime committed by the applicant or another crime, then the detective will report this to the prosecuting authority where the crime was committed.

In the third stage Commission members will receive the information from the investigations carried out. Commission members will review the information and decide if there is sufficient evidence of complete factual innocence to merit judicial review by the panel of judges. If the Commission members decide by a majority vote that there is sufficient evidence of factual innocence to put the conviction in serious doubt, then they will recommend that the case be sent for judicial review. If a majority vote is not obtained, then the case will be dismissed. This would be true regardless of whether the applicant pleaded guilty at the original trial.

The final stage would be the judicial review. As in the North Carolina model,[258] the panel would be composed of three judges who would receive the Commission report. The judges must determine by clear and convincing evidence that a person is in fact not guilty of the crime. During its deliberations, the judges may call witnesses and hear evidence. The judges would also have subpoena power. A Commission representative would be present to assist the panel. A unanimous vote by the judicial panel would be needed to overturn a conviction. Victims will have the right to be present to the same extent as in North Carolina.[259]

V. Conclusion

A Texas Innocence Commission would be of immense help as a supplement to the current post-conviction system to uncover cases of wrongful conviction. The current post-conviction habeas corpus system is inadequate to assist Texas in assisting petitioners, and a new complementary process in the form of an Innocence Commission should be established. Again, for anyone doubting the efficacy of any Innocence Commission, the case of Gregory Taylor should provide perspective.[260] The North Carolina Innocence Commission gave him back his life by obtaining his release and clearing his name.[261] Though Gregory Taylor managed to prove his innocence without DNA evidence against all the odds, this typically will not be case because wrongfully convicted inmates do not have the opportunity to prove their innocence before a body like the Innocence Commission. Instead the wrongfully convicted must depend on appeals and habeas corpus petitions that are difficult to prove without DNA evidence. Habeas corpus is no good for these inmates. Without an Innocence Commission, there is no other way to get non-DNA cases cleared. For innocent prisoners outside of North Carolina, there is little hope.

ENDNOTES

1. Herrera v. Collins, 506 U.S. 390, 398 (1993).
2. Robbie Brown, *Judges Free Inmate on Recommendation of Special Panel*, N.Y. TIMES, Feb. 18, 2010, at A14, *available at* http://www.nytimes.com/2010/02/18/us/18innocent.html.
3. *Id.*
4. *See* North Carolina v. Taylor, 533 S.E.2d 475 (N.C. 1999); Taylor v. Hamilton, 6 Fed. App'x 196 (4th Cir. N.C. 2001).
5. Brown, *supra* note 2, A14.
6. *Id.*
7. Texas has exonerated 40 innocent people. INNOCENCE PROJECT, INC., THE INNOCENCE PROJECT IN PRINT 15 (2010), http://www.innocenceproject.org/docs/ip_summer_10.pdf. Nationally, 250 innocent people have been exonerated through DNA testing alone. INNOCENCE PROJECT, INC., 250 EXONERATED TOO MANY WRONGFULLY CONVICTED 54, http://www.innocenceproject.org/docs/InnocenceProject_250.pdf. (last visited Jul. 29, 2009).
8. THE JUSTICE PROJECT, CONVICTING THE INNOCENT: TEXAS JUSTICE DERAILED 6 (2009), http://www.thejusticeproject.org/wp-content/uploads/convicting-the-innocent.pdf.
9. *Id.*

10. Daniel S. Medwed, *Up the River Without A Procedure: Innocent Prisoners and Newly Discovered Evidence Non-DNA Evidence in State Courts,* 47 Ariz. L. Rev. 655, 657-58 (2005).

11. Schlup v. Delo, 513 U.S. 298, 324 (1995) (superseded on other grounds by 28 U.S.C. § 2244 (a)-(d) (2006) & 28 U.S.C. § 2255 (e)-(h) (2006)).

12. *Id.*

13. Tex. Code Crim. Proc. Ann. Art. 11.07 (Vernon 2005 & Supp. 2009) (describing habeas corpus procedure after conviction without death penalty); art. 11.071 (Vernon 2005 & Supp. 2009) (describing habeas corpus procedure in death penalty cases). A third avenue exists for habeas corpus for persons under community supervision. art. 11.072 (Vernon 2005) (describing habeas corpus procedure in community supervision cases).

14. Boumediene v. Bush, 553 U.S. 723 (2008).

15. Harris v. Nelson, 394 U.S. 286, 291 (1969).

16. U.S. Const., art. I, § 9, cl. 2; Tex. Const. art. I, § 12.

17. West's Encyclopedia Of American Law, 169 (2d ed. 2004) [hereinafter West's Encyc.].

18. The Oxford Companion To American Law 349 (Kermit L. Hall et al. eds., 2002).

19. West's Encyc., *supra* note 17, at 171.

20. Kermit et al., *supra* note 18, at 349.

21. West's Encyc., *supra* note 17, at 171.
The writ is usually issued to the government official accused of depriving the person of his or her liberty. Tex. Code Crim. Proc. Ann. art. 11.02 (Vernon 2005).

22. West's Encyc., *supra* note 12, at 170. As a result of the unique nature of the writ of habeas corpus, the initial burden of proof is squarely on the petitioner to prove that he or she is being held in violation of the federal or state constitution. *Id.* Once this initial burden has been overcome by the petitioner,

the burden then shifts to the official, who is in charge of restraining the petitioner, to justify continued detention. *Id.*

Only the sentencing court where the prisoner is being housed against the law may hear the writ. *Id.* This same requirement applies to federal prisoners. *Id.* at 171. When a person is in custody under a judgment and sentence of a State court files a writ of habeas corpus in a state that has more than one federal district court, that person may file the writ of habeas corpus with the district court that covers the area where he is being held or in the district court where the state obtained the conviction. 28 U.S.C. § 2241 (d) (2006).

Similar to the federal system, in Texas the writ of habeas corpus is a command issued to an official by a court with jurisdiction to bring the inmate before it and justify the detention. Tex. Code Crim. Proc. Ann. art. 11.01. (Vernon 2005). Texas has taken a step further than the federal system in classifying its habeas proceedings as more criminal than civil in that such proceedings are grouped as criminal for jurisdictional purposes, and the Texas Rules of Civil Procedure do not ordinarily apply. *Ex parte* Rieck, 144 S.W.3d 510, 516 (Tex. Crim. App. 2004).

Instead the Texas legislature has deemed Article 11.07 habeas proceedings as criminal proceedings by statute. *Id.*

23. 28 U.S.C. § 2254 (b) (1) (A) (2006).
24. Tex. Const. art. I, § 12.
25. U.S. Const. art. I, § 9.
26. Tex. Const. art. I, § 12.
27. Tex. Code Crim. Proc. Ann. art. 11.07 (Vernon 2005 & Supp. 2009).
28. Tex. Code Crim. Proc. Ann art. 11.07 § 3 (Vernon 2005 & Supp. 2009).
29. *Id.* at (b).
30. *Id.*
31. *Id.* at (d).

While conducting the finding, the court may order the use of affidavits, depositions, interrogatories, additional forensic testing, and hearings. *Id.*

The court may also use personal recollection. *Id.*

Also the convicting court may appoint an attorney or a magistrate judge to hear the evidence and make findings of fact. *Id.*

32. *Id.* at (c).
The failure of the court to act within the allotted twenty days will constitute a finding that there are controverted, previously unresolved facts material to the legality of the applicant's confinement. *Id.*

33. N.C. Gen. Stat. § 15A-1469 (a) (2009).

34. Tex. Code Crim. Proc. Ann. art. 11.07 § 4 (a) (Vernon 2005 & Supp. 2009).

35. *Id.* at (a) (1).
For a legal basis claim to be unavailable, it must be found that the Supreme Court, a court of appeals of the United States, or an appellate court of Texas would not have recognized the legal basis of the claim nor could the legal basis of the claim have been reasonably devised from a final decision from any one of those courts on or before the date of the first petition. *Id.* at (b).

For a factual basis of a claim to be unavailable, it must be found that the petitioner through the exercise of reasonable diligence could not have found the factual basis of the claim on or before the date of the first petition. *Id.* at (c).

36. *Id.* at (a) (2).
The burden of proof is by a preponderance of the evidence. *Id.*

The Court of Criminal Appeals may deny relief on the findings and conclusions of the hearing judge, or hear the case as though it were originally in that court on appeal. Tex. Code Crim. Proc. Ann. art. 11.07 § 5.

37. Tex. Code Crim. Proc. Ann art. 11.071 § 2 (a) (Vernon 2005 & Supp. 2009).

38. *Id.* at § 3.

39. *Id.* at § 4; Lise Olson, *Death Row Lawyers Get Paid While Messing Up*, HOUSTON CHRONICLE, Apr. 20, 2010, http://www.chron.com/disp/story.mpl/metropolitan/6381687.html (discussing how several attorneys routinely miss deadlines in death row cases).; Lise Olson, *Lawyer's Late Filings Can be Deadly For Inmates*, HOUSTON CHRONICLE, Mar. 22, 2009, http://www.chron.com/disp/story.mpl/metropolitan/6328865.html (discussing how nine inmates have lost the right to final appeals before execution because of missed deadlines by their lawyers).

40. TEX. CODE CRIM. PROC. ANN art. 11.071 § 4A (b) (1) (Vernon 2005 & Supp. 2009). Texas Code of Criminal Procedure 11.071 has a set of requirements for subsequent applicants of habeas corpus. *Compare* TEX. CODE CRIM. PROC. ANN. art. 11.071(Vernon 2005 & Supp. 2009), *with* TEX. CODE CRIM. PROC. ANN. art. 11.07 (Vernon 2005 & Supp. 2009).

41. *Ex parte* Davis, 947 S.W.2d 216, 237 (Tex. Crim. App. 1996).

42. *Id.*; TEX. CODE CRIM. PROC. ANN art. 11.071 § 5 (a) (1)-(3) (Vernon 2005 & Supp. 2009).

43. TEX. CODE CRIM. PROC. ANN art. 11.071 § 5 (a) (1) (Vernon 2005 & Supp. 2009); *Ex parte* Davis, 947 S.W.2d at 237.

44. TEX. CODE CRIM. PROC. ANN art. 11.071 § 5 (a) (2) (Vernon 2005 & Supp. 2009); *Ex parte* Davis, 947 S.W.2d at 237.

45. TEX. CODE CRIM. PROC. ANN art. 11.071 § 5 (a) (3) (Vernon 2005 & Supp. 2009); *Ex parte* Davis, 947 S.W.2d at 237.

46. Murray v. Giarratano, 492 U.S. 1, 7 (1989).

47. *Ex parte* Davis, 947 S.W.2d 216, 237 (Tex. Crim. App. 1996).

48. *Ex parte* Townsend, 137 S.W.3d 79, 81 (Tex. Crim. App. 2004).

49. *Id.*

50. *Ex parte* Graves, 70 S.W.3d 103, 117 (Tex. Crim. App. 2002).
51. *Id.* at 105.
52. *See* Blanco v. State, 18 S.W.3d 218, 220 (Tex. Crim. App. 2000).
53. *Ex parte* Reedy, 282 S.W.3d 492, 495-96 (Tex. Crim. App. 2009).
54. *Id.* at 496-497.
55. *Id.* at 503-04.
56. *Ex parte* Grigsby, 137 S.W.3d 673, 674 (Tex. Crim. App. 2004).
57. *See Ex parte* Williams, 703 S.W.2d 674, 677 (Tex. Crim. App. 1986).
58. *Grigsby*, 137 S.W.3d at 674.
59. *Ex parte* Tuley, 109 S.W.3d 388, 390 (Tex. Crim. App. 2002).
60. *Compare Ex parte* Elizondo, 947 S.W.2d 202, 206 (Tex. Crim. App. 1996) *with Herrera*, 506 U.S. at 400.
61. *Elizondo*, 947 S.W.2d at 206.
62. *Schlup*, 513 U.S. at 324. Affirmative evidence may include trustworthy witness recantations, exculpatory scientific evidence, trustworthy eyewitness accounts, and critical physical evidence, however, because such evidence is rarely available in the majority of cases, such claims invariably fail. *Id.*
63. *Tuley*, 109 S.W.3d at 390.
64. *Id.*
65. *Id.*
66. Tennard v. State, 802 S.W.2d 678, 683 (Tex. Crim. App. 1990).
67. *Id.*
68. *Id.* at 392-93.

69. *Elizondo*, 947 S.W.2d at 208.

70. *Id.* at 207.

71. Guzman v. State, 955 S.W.2d 85, 89 (Tex. Crim. App. 1997).

72. *Ex parte* Brown, 205 S.W.3d 538, 549 (Tex. Crim. App. 2006).

73. *See Ex parte* Franklin, 72 S.W.3d 671, 678 (Tex. Crim. App. 2002).

74. State v. Nkwocha, 31 S.W.3d 817, 821 (Tex. App. 2000).

75. *Herrera*, 506 U.S. at 398.

76. *Id.* at 399.

77. *Id.* at 399-400.

78. 28 U.S.C. § 2254 (b) (1) (A) (2006).

79. 28 U.S.C. § 2241 (a) (2006). By implication of the United States Constitution, found in Article One, Section 9, clause 2, a Texas prisoner has the right to petition for a writ of habeas corpus with federal courts to challenge his or her continued imprisonment. U.S. Const. art. I, § 9, cl. 2.

80. Asian American Justice Center: Advancing Equality 3, http://www.napalc.org/files/supremecourt_faq.pdf.

81. *Judicial Workload Statistics: United States Court of Appeals for Fifth Circuit* at 5, available at http://www.ca5.uscourts.gov/clerk/docs/arstats.pdf.

82. U.S. District Court-Judicial Caseload Profile, http://www.uscourts.gov/cgi-bin/cmsd2008.pl.

83. *Id.*

84. *Id.*

85. *Id.*

86. 28 U.S.C. § 2241(c).; 28 U.S.C. § 2254 (b)-(d).
In section 2254, Congress made clear that U.S. Code Section 2241(c) (3) was the only way a federal court could obtain

jurisdiction over a state petitioner in a habeas proceeding. 28 U.S.C. § 2241 (a).; 28 U.S.C. § 2254 (a).

87. 28 U.S.C. § 2241 (c).; 28 U.S.C. § 2254 (b)-(d).

88. 28 U.S.C. § 2254.

89. *Id.* at (b) (1) (A).

90. *Id.* at (b) (1) (B) (i).

91. *Id.* at (b) (1) (B) (ii).

92. Duckworth v. Serrano, 454 U.S. 1 (1980) (superseded on other grounds by 28 U.S.C. § 2254 (b) (2) (2006)).

93. 28 U.S.C. § 2254 (c).
A petitioner cannot argue that the State has waived the exhaustion requirement or is estopped from relying on the requirement until the convicting State, through its prosecutor, explicitly waives the requirement. 28 USCS § 2254(b) (3) (giving the convicting state a chance to assert a defense).

94. 28 U.S.C. 2254 (d).

95. *Id.* at (d) (1).

96. *Id.* at (d) (2).

97. Williams v. Taylor, 529 U.S. 362, 411 (2000).

98. *Id.* at 391.

99. *Id.* at 397.

100. *Id.*

101. *Id.*

102. 28 U.S.C. § 2254 (e) (1).

103. *Id.* at (e) (2) (A).

104. *Id.* at (e) (2) (A) (i) (B).

105. *Id.* at (e) (2) (A) (ii) (B).

106. Judicial Conference of the United States Ad Hoc Committee on Federal Habeas Corpus in Capital Cases, Committee Report and Proposal 1(1989), *reprinted in* 135 Cong. Rec. 24, 694 (1989) [hereinafter *Committee Report*].

107. *Id.* at 2.
108. *Id.* at 3.
109. *See* 141 Cong. Rec. 4120-4121 (1995).
110. Mayle v. Felix, 545 U.S. 644, 654 (U.S. 2005).
111. 28 U.S.C. § 2244 (d) (1). The claim could be considered again but only if it is shown that the claim is based on a new constitutional rule, made to apply to previous cases on collateral review by the Supreme Court, that was not available before; or the factual basis for the claim could not have been discovered before with the use of due diligence; and the facts on which the claim is based, if proven and viewed in light of the evidence as whole, would be enough to prove by clear and convincing evidence that, but for constitutional error, no reasonable juror would have found the petitioner guilty of the crime. *Id.* at (b) (2).
112. *See, e.g.*, Duncan v. Henry, 513 U.S. 364, 365-66 (1995).
113. *Id.*
114. *Id.*
115. O'Sullivan v. Boerckel, 526 U.S. 838, 844-45 (1999).
116. McCleskey v. Zant, 499 U.S. 467, 491 (1991) (superseded on other grounds by 28 U.S.C. § 2244 (a)-(d) (2006) & 28 U.S.C. § 2255 (e)-(h) (2006)).
117. Reed v. Farley, 512 U.S. 339 (1994).
118. *Herrera*, 506 U.S. 390.
119. *Id.* at 393.
120. *Id.* at 396-97.
121. *Id.*
122. *Herrera*, 506 U.S. at 400.
123. *Id.*
124. Moore v. Dempsey, 261 U.S. 86, 88 (1923). Facts establishing guilt cannot be re-examined by federal courts.; *Ex parte* Terry, 128 U.S. 289, 305 (1888).

125. *Herrera*, 506 U.S. at 400.

126. Sawyer v. Whitley, 505 U.S. 333 (1992).

127. *Id.* at 339.

128. *Herrera,* 506 U.S. at 404.

129. *Id.* at 401. (Blackmun, J., dissenting).

130. *Id.* at 431-36.

131. *Id.* at 438. In his dissenting opinion, Justice Blackmun contended that the reasoning extended to substantive claims of actual innocence and that this should be recognized as a claim of federal habeas corpus. *Id.* at 439. Justice Blackmun summarized the majority's position as previously requiring a petitioner who claims to be held in violation of the Constitution to show actual innocence and now requiring a petitioner who is actually innocent to show a constitutional violation to receive aid. *Id.* He surmised that the only principle that could resolve the two positions of the majority was the principle that habeas corpus aid should be refused if at all feasible. *Id.*

132. Bousley v. United States, 523 U.S. 614, 621 (1998).

133. *Id.*

134. *Id.*

135. United States v. Timmreck, 441 U.S. 780, 784 (1979).

136. *Id.*

137. Innocence Project, Inc., *supra* note 7, at 15 (number of convictions overturned by DNA testing stands at 40).

138. *Id.*

139. *Id.*

140. 2006-184 N.C. Adv. Legis. Serv. 1. (LexisNexis).

141. *Id.*

142. *Id.*

143. N.C. Gen. Stat. § 15A-1462 (a) (2009).

144. *Id.* at (b).

145. *Id.*
146. N.C. Gen. Stat. § 15A-1463 (a) (2009).
147. *Id.* at (a) (1).
148. *Id.* at (a) (2).
149. *Id.* at (a) (3).
150. *Id.* at (a) (4).
151. *Id.* at (a) (5).
152. *Id.* at (a) (6).
153. *Id.* at (a) (7).
154. *Id.* at (a).
155. *Id.*
156. *Id.* Whoever holds the authority to appoint members to the board is also required to appoint alternate Commission members for the members who are elected officials in order to account for conflicts of interest, unavailability or other disqualifications that are unique to the case under investigation. *Id.* at (b). Although not primary members of the Commission, the alternates are required to have the same qualifications as the main members. *Id.*
157. *Id.*
158. *Id.*
159. *Id.*
160. *Id.*
161. *Id.* at (b).
162. *Id.*
163. *Id.*
164. *Id.*
165. *Id.* at (c). The Chair has the discretion to choose the meeting place and time. The Commission is delegated the responsibility of creating the rules on notice of meetings. In order to carry on business of the Commission, a majority of the members

must be present to constitute a quorum. Voting on all matters before the Commission is by majority vote. *Id.*

166. N.C. Gen. Stat. § 15A-1475 (2009).
167. *Id.*
168. N.C. Gen. Stat. § 15A-1467 (d) (2009).
169. *Id.*
170. *Id.*
171. *Id.* at (e).
172. *Id.* at (f).
173. N.C. Gen. Stat. § 15A-1468 (a) (1) (2009).
174. N.C. Gen. Stat. § 15A-1467 (f) (2009).
175. *Id.*
    The order will also prohibit a prosecutor from using the testimony, or any evidence from it, for prosecution for perjury. *Id.* at § 15A-1468 (a) (1).
176. *Id.*
177. *Id.* at §15A-1467 (a).
178. *Id.* at §15A-1460 (1).
179. *Id.*
180. *Id.* at §15A-1467 (a).
181. *Id.* at § 15A-1460 (1).; North Carolina Innocence Inquiry Commission Rules and Procedures, App. A, http://www.innocencecommission-nc.gov/rulesandprocedures.htm#_ftnref2 (last visited August 1, 2010).
182. North Carolina Innocence Inquiry Commission Rules and Procedures, *supra* note 171, at App. A.
183. N.C. Gen. Stat. § 15A-1466 (2) (2009).
184. North Carolina Innocence Inquiry Commission Rules and Procedures, *supra* note 181, at Art. 2 (b).
185. N.C. Gen. Stat. § 15A-1460 (1) (2009).
186. *Id.*

187. *Id.*

188. North Carolina Innocence Inquiry Commission Rules and Procedures, *supra* note 181 at App. A.

189. *Id.*

190. N.C. Gen. Stat. § 15A-1467 (2009).

191. North Carolina Innocence Inquiry Commission, http://www.innocencecommission-nc.gov/statistics.htm (last visited August 1, 2010).

192. *Id.* The Director and her deputy are in charge of creating procedures for reviewing and gathering information on an innocence claim. N.C. Gen. Stat. § 15A-1465 (a) (2009). The Director or his or her designee is obligated by law to create and maintain a tracking system that records the name of the petitioner and the ultimate resolution of their claim. § 15A-1465 (a); North Carolina Innocence Inquiry Commission Rules and Procedures, *supra* note 171, at Art. 4 (A).

193. North Carolina Innocence Inquiry Commission Rules and Procedures, *supra* note 181, at Art. 4 (B) (1).

194. North Carolina Innocence Inquiry Commission Rules and Procedures, *supra* note 181.

195. §15A-1467 (a). As it is clear from the purpose statement, the Assembly was aware that it was creating an extraordinary procedure to investigate claims of factual innocence and one extraordinary consequence of using the Commission is that the applicants willingly surrender any procedural safeguards and privileges. N.C. GEN. STAT. § 15A-1461 (2009).

196. North Carolina Innocence Inquiry Commission Rules and Procedures, *supra* note 181, at Art. 4 (D).

197. N.C. Gen. Stat.§ 15A-1467 (g) (2009).

198. North Carolina Innocence Inquiry Commission Rules and Procedures, *supra* note 181, at Art. 4 (F).

199. N.C. Gen. Stat. § 15A-1467 (a) (2009); North Carolina Innocence Inquiry Commission Rules and Procedures, *supra* note 181, at Art. 4 (G).

200. North Carolina Innocence Inquiry Commission Rules and Procedures, *supra* note 181, at Art. 4 (H).

201. N.C. Gen. Stat. § 15A-1467 (b) (2009).

202. *Id.*

203. *Id.*

204. *Id.*

205. *Id.* at (c).

206. *Id.*

207. North Carolina Innocence Inquiry Commission Rules and Procedures, *supra* note 181, at Art. 5 (E).

208. N.C. Gen. Stat. § 15A-1465 (a) (2009).

209. North Carolina Innocence Inquiry Commission Rules and Procedures, *supra* note 181, at Art. 5 (K).

210. N.C. Gen. Stat. § 15A-1467 (a) (2009); North Carolina Innocence Inquiry Commission Rules and Procedures, *supra* note 171, at Art. 5 (L).

211. North Carolina Innocence Inquiry Commission Rules and Procedures, *supra* note 181, at Art. 6.

212. N.C. Gen. Stat. § 15A-1468 (a) (2009).
A victim or the victim's relative may attend a hearing if they give ten days notice to the Commission of their intention to be present. North Carolina Innocence Inquiry Commission Rules and Procedures, *supra* note 181, at Art. 6 (E) (1).

213. *Id.* at (b); North Carolina Innocence Inquiry Commission Rules and Procedures, *supra* note 181, at Art. 6 (E).

214. N.C. Gen. Stat. § 15A-1468 (e) (2009).

215. North Carolina Innocence Inquiry Commission Rules and Procedures, *supra* note 181, at Art. 6 (B).

216. *Id.*

217. *Id.*

218. *Id.* at (B) (3).

219. *Id.* at (B) (2).
220. *Id.* at (B) (1).
221. N.C. Gen. Stat. § 15A-1463 (b) (2009).
222. *Id.* at §§ 15A-1468 (e) & 15A-1468 (b); North Carolina Innocence Inquiry Commission Rules and Procedures, *supra* note 181, at Art. 6 (F).
223. N.C. Gen. Stat. § 15A-1468 (e) (2009).; North Carolina Innocence Inquiry Commission Rules and Procedures, *supra* note 181, at Art. 6 (F).
224. North Carolina Innocence Inquiry Commission Rules and Procedures, *supra* note 181, at Art. 6 (G).
    Each Commissioner receives evidence at the same time from the Director. *Id.* at (G) (1).
225. *Id.* at (G) (2).
226. *Id.* at (G) (2) (a).
227. *Id.*
228. *Id.* at (G) (3).
229. North Carolina Innocence Inquiry Commission Rules and Procedures, *supra* note 181, at Art. 6 (H) (1).
230. N.C. Gen. Stat. § 15A-1468 (c) (2009).; North Carolina Innocence Inquiry Commission Rules and Procedures, *supra* note 181, at Art. 6 (H) (1).
231. § 15A-1468.
    Whether a petitioner pleaded guilty is crucial because if the petitioner has not pleaded guilty, only five Commission votes are needed to advance the case to judicial review. *Id.* at (c). If the case involves a guilty plea, then it will take all eight members to find there is sufficient evidence of factual innocence for referral to the judicial panel. *Id.* If the Commission needs more time, it may vote to continue the hearing and request additional information. North Carolina Innocence Inquiry Commission Rules and Procedures, *supra* note 171, at Art. 6 (I). If there is a lack of votes in favor of advancement for judicial review, then the Commission will write its opinion

with supporting findings of fact, and file those documents. N.C. Gen. Stat. § 15A-1468 (c) (2009).

232. *Id.* at § 15A-1469 (a). The panel may not include any judge who had substantial prior involvement in the case. The panel will look over evidence that was relevant to the Commission's finding. *Id.* The senior resident superior court judge in the original jurisdiction of the case is in charge of the order setting the hearing for a special session of superior court. *Id.* The government must respond to the Commission's opinion within sixty days of the order setting the hearing. *Id.* at (b).

233. *Id.* at (c).

234. *Id.* at (e).

235. *Id.* at (d).

236. North Carolina Innocence Inquiry Commission Rules and Procedures, *supra* note 181, at Art. 7 (F).

237. N.C. Gen. Stat. § 15A-1469 (d) (2009).
Interruption of the hearing may occur if the senior judge on the panel decides it is necessary to have a conference. *Id.* at (g).

238. *Id.* at (h).

239. *Id.* at f§ 15A-1470 (a) (2009).

240. *Id.* at (b).

241. North Carolina Innocence Inquiry Commission Rules and Procedures, *supra* note 181, at Art. 9 (A).

242. *Id.* at (A) (1).

243. *Id.* at (A) (2).

244. *Id.* at (A) (3).

245. N.C. Gen. Stat. § 15A-1468 (d) (2009).

246. *Id.*

247. *See supra* notes 241-44 and accompanying text.

248. *See supra* notes 244 and accompanying text.

249. *See supra* notes 168-69 and accompanying text.

250. *See supra* notes 232, 238 and accompanying text.

251. *See supra* note 146 and accompanying text.

252. *See supra* notes 147-153 and accompanying text.

253. *See supra* notes 157-58 and accompanying text.

254. See *supra* notes 146-153 and accompanying text.

255. *See supra* notes 215-17 and accompanying text

256. *See supra* notes 191-93 and accompanying text.

257. *See supra* notes 179-190 and accompanying text.
If a petition is dismissed because no new evidence is placed forward, the applicant will have the chance at a later date to present any new evidence that is found.

258. *See supra* note 232 and accompanying text.

259. *See supra* notes 205-06, 213-14 and accompanying text.

260. *See supra* notes 2-5 and accompanying text.

261. *See supra* note 6 and accompanying text.

2. Comparative Models

POST-CONVICTION ACTUAL INNOCENCE REVIEWS IN THE UNITED KINGDOM AND CANADA

EMILY EARTHMAN ZIEMBA*

I. INTRODUCTION

In 2003, Houstonian Ricardo Rachell was convicted of sexual assault of a child and sentenced to forty years in prison.[1] He was convicted primarily upon evidence of eyewitness identification by the eight-year-old victim.[2] The victim had testified that in 2002 a stranger offered him money for help with chores before taking the victim to another location and molesting him. After the trial and sentencing, some may have considered the conviction as justice done, but Rachell maintained his innocence.[3] After reading articles in the *Houston Chronicle* about other victims assaulted after being offered money for chores, Rachell wrote letters to lawyers for both the prosecution and the defense, as well as the judge, urging them to investigate.[4] As it turned out, DNA evidence had been gathered from the original crime scene in 2002 but never

* Emily Earthman Ziemba received her law degree from the University of Houston Law Center in 2010. She is employed as an attorney with the United States government.

tested.[5] Subsequent testing proved that Rachell did not commit the crime.[6] Five years after being convicted, Rachell's plea for exoneration was finally realized. He was released from prison after DNA evidence exonerated him.[7]

Since 1994, forty people have been exonerated in Texas by post-conviction testing of DNA evidence.[8] Unfortunately, unlike Rachell, many people have no real recourse when they have been wrongly convicted, either during direct appeal, habeas corpus proceedings, or executive clemency.[*] As discussed below in Part IV, receiving a new trial in Texas because of newly discovered evidence is exceedingly difficult.[9] Furthermore, in death penalty cases, writs of habeas corpus rarely provide effective relief.[10] Moreover, executive clemency in Texas is also very difficult to receive.[11] Accordingly, a state-wide, systematic way to review convictions after an inmate has completed his appeals would be an important step to ensuring that wrongfully convicted persons have an effective means of appealing their convictions. In considering a system of post-conviction review, Texas has much to learn from the state-sponsored post-conviction review organizations of Canada and the United Kingdom.

A preliminary note is appropriate before the discussion begins. There are competing views as to what exactly a "wrongful conviction" really means. One school of thought, made up of layperson and journalists, means actual, factual innocence – people like Ricardo Rachell – who did not actually commit the underlying crime.[12] The other meaning, used mostly by courts and lawyers, is that of legal innocence – the defendant's trial was not fair, and that a conviction should not have resulted, regardless of whether the defendant actually committed the crime.[13] DNA exonerations mean actual innocence. Due process violations mean legal innocence. Although the controversy in Texas mainly concerns actual innocence, both are included in today's discussion because the British system accounts for both legal and actual innocence, while the Canadian system tends toward factual innocence.[14]

* In the criminal justice system, this refers to an act by an executive member of government of extending mercy to a convicted individual. In the United States, clemency is granted by a governor for state crimes and by a president for federal crimes. Clemency can take one of three forms: a reprieve, a commutation of sentence, or a pardon.

Both the United Kingdom and Canada have systems that review convictions. Before 1995, the United Kingdom had long maintained a practice of having the Home Secretary (a rough equivalent of the United States Attorney General) send cases back to the highest appellate court. This practice has recently been transferred to a commission of eleven members. On the other hand, in Canada, the Minister of Justice may, after consultation with a group of investigators, send a conviction back to the courts.

In Part II, this article begins with a brief overview of the Criminal Cases Review Commission, the convictions review group in the United Kingdom, followed by a closer look at certain features that could be applied to a Texas system of post-conviction review. Part III provides a brief overview of the Canadian Criminal Convictions Review Group, similarly followed by an analysis of features relevant to Texas. Finally, Part IV addresses in more depth the need for a post-conviction review system in Texas and proposes recommendations in creating such a system.

II. The United Kingdom – Criminal Cases Review Commission (CCRC)

Inquiries into possible miscarriages of justice are handled in Great Britain by the Criminal Cases Review Commission ("CCRC," or "Commission").[15] The following is a discussion of why the CCRC came about and how the CCRC works. First, the origins of the CCRC are described, including how post-conviction review was conducted before the CCRC and the outcry over wrongful convictions that led to its formation. Next follows a discussion of how the CCRC processes an application, including the legal standards applied by the CCRC and the Court of Appeal to quash a conviction. Finally, notable aspects which reflect the CCRC's independence from and accountability to the rest of British government are analyzed and critiqued, with an eye to applying those aspects to a Texas commission.

A. Origins of the CCRC

The CCRC was created in order to foster independence in post-conviction review from the police and judiciary. The idea of forming the CCRC took hold in the mid-1990's in the wake of public outcry over several wrongful conviction cases where local police botched investigations.[16] Before the CCRC was created, post-conviction review was handled by the same government body that oversaw the police investigations into the crimes. As a result, the CCRC is now a separate government body that can bypass local police in conducting investigations.

1. Post-Conviction Review Before the Formation of the CCRC

Before the CCRC was formed, the power to refer cases to the Court of Appeal for suspected miscarriages of justice rested in the hands of the Home Office,[17] specifically, the Criminal Cases Unit (CCU, or C3 as it was commonly known).[18] However, the Home Office was, and still is, the same government body responsible for conducting the criminal investigations in the first place; it oversees the police.[19] Consequently, the C3 was criticized for showing too much deference to the court and referring too few cases, eventually leading to the creation of an independent review body.[20]

In the late 1980s, two cases are credited with exposing the problems with having the Home Office be in charge of both the initial investigation and reference.[21] The "Birmingham Six" and the "Maguire Seven" cases arose from a rash of bombings by the IRA.[22] After the defendants in these cases had been convicted, it became apparent during appellate litigation that police had withheld certain material evidence,[23] and that investigators failed to perform certain forensic tests,[24] which might have cleared the suspects. Consequently, a Royal Commission on Criminal Justice, known as the Runciman Commission, named after the chairman, was established to investigate and propose reforms.[25]

2. The Runciman Commission

One of the Runciman Commission's main criticisms of post-conviction review was the conflict of interest posed by having the Home Secretary call into question a conviction the same department investigated and prosecuted.[26] It further found that, although statute was not so stringent, in practice Home Secretaries only sent a conviction back to the Court of Appeal if there was newly discovered evidence.[27] Thus, the proposed reforms included ending the Home Office's responsibility of referring cases to the Court of Appeal and establishing the CCRC as an authority independent of the Home Office.[28] To further establish independence from the judiciary, the Runciman Commission recommended that the head of the CCRC not be a member of the judiciary.[29] Thereafter, Parliament passed the Criminal Appeal Act of 1995 which, in part, created the CCRC.[30]

B. The Role of the CCRC in a Conviction

Today, the CCRC is an independent commission composed of no fewer than eleven commissioners[31] who, after an investigation has taken place, may send (or "refer") a case back to the Court of Appeal.[32] The following is an overview of what role the CCRC plays in a conviction, and how a conviction is overturned in the British courts. First, the process is briefly and generally described. Next, the legal standards of review for rejecting cases or sending cases back to the courts are discussed. Finally, the legal standard for overturning a conviction in the courts is discussed.

1. Process by which the CCRC Reviews an Application

When a person believes he has been wrongfully convicted of a crime, he may apply for the CCRC to review his conviction.[33] Upon receiving an application, the CCRC first reviews it for eligibility.[34] The most important factor determining eligibility is whether the applicant's appeals have been exhausted, either by review by the British Court of Appeal or by denial of leave to appeal.[35] By statute, an applicant must show that he has exhausted his legal remedies, unless "exceptional circumstances" are present.[36] In its application form, the CCRC describes "exceptional circumstances" as "scientific knowledge that casts doubt on expert evidence given at . . . trial" or that an inmate could not appeal because it could not get access to information possessed by the government.[37] Most of the cases weeded out for ineligibility are done so because of failure to exhaust legal remedies without the presence of "exceptional circumstances."[38]

Next, staff members determine whether the conviction has a "real possibility" of being overturned by a court.[39] The staff member's decision is passed on to a Commissioner for review. In reviewing a case that has a "real possibility" of being overturned, a Commissioner may decide he or she needs more information to make the determination whether to send the case back to the courts. If so, a Commissioner may appoint an officer to conduct an investigation of the facts.[40] The investigation may be conducted either by police or by the CCRC itself,[41] although the CCRC strives to do most of its investigations itself.[42]

Next, the Commissioner makes the decision whether to send the case back to the appeals court. The decision *not* to refer is called "not minded to refer"[43]; those decisions are made by a single Commissioner and are accompanied by a list of reasons.[44] An applicant may reply to the reasons within twenty-eight days; however, judicial review of a "not minded to refer" decision is generally not available except in situations where the CCRC abuses its power.[45] If an applicant is still unsatisfied with the CCRC's decision not to refer the case, he or she may apply to the CCRC again, but the new application must be based on entirely new information.[46]

The decision to send a case back to the appeals court is made by a panel of three Commissioners using the "real possibility" standard, which will be discussed immediately below.[47] If a case is referred to the Court of Appeal, the CCRC relinquishes jurisdiction, and the case proceeds as if it were a normal British Court of Appeal case.[48]

2. How a Conviction Is Overturned by CCRC Review

Two standards of review are relevant for a conviction to be overturned in addition to the preliminary standard used by CCRC staff to screen applications. The first standard is what must be met in order for the CCRC to believe an inmate was wrongfully convicted in order to send it back to the court system. The second standard is that which the courts use to actually find that a defendant has been wrongfully convicted and to reverse the conviction.

a. The Standard of Referral from the Commission

In most cases, the CCRC may refer a case to the Court of Appeal[49] when "there is a real possibility that the conviction, verdict, finding or sentence would not be upheld were the reference to be made."[50] The Court of Appeal has defined a "real possibility" that the conviction would not be upheld as "more than an outside chance or a bare possibility, but which may be less than a probability or a likelihood or a racing certainty" that the conviction is "unsafe."[51] A determination by the Commissioners to refer is made based on "an argument, or evidence, not raised in the proceedings" or an "exceptional circumstance."[52] In addition to the examples of given by the CCRC in its application form,[53] one commentator has defined "exceptional circumstances" to include instances when evidence was available at the time of the proceedings but was not used due to attorney incompetence or failed trial strategy.[54]

b. The Standard for Quashing a Conviction on Appeal

Once a reference is made back to the courts, the case proceeds like a normal appeal. As a preliminary matter, it should be noted that unlike American appeals courts, the Court of Appeal may consider new evidence in making its decision.[55] Indeed, a British appeals court *must* receive new evidence if:

- it appears to the court that the evidence may afford any ground for allowing the appeal;
- the evidence would have been admissible in the proceedings from which the appeal lies on an issue;
- which is the subject of the appeal; and
- there is a reasonable explanation for the failure to adduce* the evidence in those proceedings.[56]

This is especially significant because, as discussed below,[57] the CCRC has broad powers of investigation.[58] For example, it may order witnesses to be interviewed, or documents to be turned over, or new forensic

* To produce or offer evidence.

tests to be performed.[59] Therefore, armed with new evidence, an inmate could convince an appeals court to quash his conviction rather than ordering a new trial.

The standard of review for quashing a conviction in Britain is whether the conviction is considered "unsafe;"[60] that is, whether there exists "lurking doubt" with regard to the conviction. The standard for quashing a conviction is the same standard the British Court of Appeal applies when it decides to take a case, and it is fraught with subjectivity. For example, the Criminal Appeal Act of 1995 provides that "the Court of Appeal . . . shall allow an appeal against conviction if they think that the conviction is unsafe."[61] This includes not only errors in law or procedure,[62] but also general uneasiness about the jury's verdict: "an 'unsafe' conviction is one in which the court entertains a 'lurking doubt' that the defendant was rightly convicted, i.e., one in which the court is not 'sure' that the defendant was 'rightly convicted.'"[63] In turn, the "lurking doubt" standard is itself subjective.[64] Indeed, lurking doubt may be based on the "general feel of the case as the court experiences it."[65] Enough has been written to criticize the murkiness of this standard, and it is not recommended for adoption in Texas.

Post-conviction review in Britain begins with an application to the CCRC, continues with screening process and initial determination of whether there is a real possibility the conviction will be overturned, continues with a possible referral to the appeals court, and concludes with a British court's determination whether a conviction is unsafe. What follows next is a discussion of certain features of the British post-conviction review process that are noted for their focus on independence and accountability.

C. Twin Goals of Independence and Accountability – Consideration and Critique of CCRC Features Applicable to Texas

In its struggle against wrongful convictions, the British government made several improvements to increase post-conviction review's credibility with the public. These improvements focus on increasing the independence of the Commission and accountability to Parliament.

After discussing the improvements, their real-world effect on the CCRC is critiqued.

1. Independence and Accountability of the Commission

This analysis and critique focuses on two features reflecting independence: the appointment of commissioners unaffiliated with the Government and the ability of the CCRC to control its investigations. The independence of the Commissioners is seen both in a healthy mix of laypersons and criminal law experts as well as in the Commission's statutorily mandated independence from the Crown or any other government agency.

a. Independence of the Makeup of the Commission Itself

The first way the CCRC is independent is in the makeup of the commission itself. The statute creating the CCRC calls for the appointment of at least eleven Commissioners.[66] Its independence from the criminal justice establishment is reflected in its mix of experts and laypersons. For example, at least one-third of the Commissioners must be lawyers,[67] and two-thirds must be knowledgeable in the criminal justice systems of England and Northern Ireland.[68] Furthermore, the Commissioners serve either full-time or part time for a period of five years.[69] A Commissioner may be reappointed once, and may resign at any time.[70] Furthermore, a Commissioner may be relieved of duty under certain circumstances.[71] Finally, the appointment of Commissioners must conform with standards for other civil servants in the United Kingdom.[72] Conformity with these objective standards prohibits the choosing of a Commissioner because of partisan influences.[73]

Another notable aspect of the CCRC's independence is its statutorily mandated distance from the Crown.[74] The Commissioners "shall not be regarded as the servant or agent of the Crown or as enjoying any status, immunity or privilege of the Crown; and the Commission's property shall not be regarded as property of, or held on behalf of, the Crown."[75] In other words, the CCRC was designed to be "'independent both of the Government and its courts.'"[76] This is important because the Home Office, which was responsible for overseeing police investigations, is no longer in charge of post-conviction review.

b. Independence in the Commission's Power to Investigate

With regard to the second measure of independence, if the CCRC requires police assistance in investigation, the CCRC has the power to choose who does the investigating.[77] Specifically, the CCRC may require the appointment of local police forces to conduct investigations,[78] as opposed to a police force independent and special to the CCRC, which was suggested during Parliamentary debate.[79] However, if the CCRC does not want the local police force re-investigating a crime, the statute allows the CCRC to "direct that a police force . . . shall not be appointed [to investigate]."[80] This power creates independence in the CCRC because otherwise, the same police department would be required to re-investigate a case it had initially investigated.[81] Thus, the problem with the former method of reviewing convictions, which put the power within the purview of the governmental body responsible for the initial investigation, has been avoided.[82]

c. Accountability in Reporting Requirements

The Runciman Commission wished to make the new group accountable to parliament by requiring annual reports.[83] The recommendation is included in the Schedule to the Criminal Appeal Act of 1995.[84] According to the schedule, the CCRC must send to the Secretary of State an annual report on their activities.[85] The annual report also requires a statement of accounting by the CCRC, which is subject to auditing by the Comptroller and Auditor General.[86] The Home Secretary submits the report to Parliament, and the report is then published.[87]

The annual reporting requirements demonstrate the British Government's concern with accountability in three ways. First, requiring the CCRC to provide a report to the Home Office allows the Prime Minister's government a way to measure and evaluate the activities of the CCRC. That is, an annual report informs the Home Office of the CCRC's activities, and thus the Prime Minister. Secondly, it informs Parliament, which is superior in power to both the executive and judiciary branches of British government.[88] Thirdly, it attributes transparency to the CCRC, so that the public is better informed of its actions and decisions to refer cases to the appeals courts.

The creation of the CCRC with a conscious eye towards independence and accountability helps not only the CCRC's public image, but it also helps the branches of government work together in reviewing wrongful convictions. By creating an independent organization, the problem of post-conviction review merely "rubber stamping" the original police investigation has been avoided.[89] Lastly, the rigorous annual reporting requirement provides accountability and transparency to not only the rest of government but also the public.

2. Questioning the CCRC's Independence and Accountability

The CCRC's conscious eye towards independence and accountability does not quiet all criticisms, however. Critics have questioned whether, as it exists today, the CCRC is independent enough in its appointments, specifically as to who has the power to appoint the Commissioners. By statute each commissioner is "appointed by Her Majesty on the recommendation of the Prime Minister."[90] Some critics thought that the Lord Chancellor, a member of Parliament, should appoint the members instead,[91] or that Parliament should have oversight over whom the Prime Minister chooses, so that certain groups of people would not be excluded, and so that Parliament could have more control over the Commission.[92] However, in the final statute, these opinions were rejected, although criticism of the role of the Prime Minister in choosing commissioners remains.[93]

The criticisms of the independence of the Commission are without much merit. First, the implementation of term limits[94] prevents a Prime Minister from permanently installing commission members who serve his or her agenda. Second, the Queen may remove a commissioner for cause, such as dereliction of duty or commission of a criminal offense in his own right.[95] Third is perhaps the most institutionally sound reason. The appointments of CCRC commissioners are required to conform to the Code of Practice for the Office of the Commissioner of Public Appointments.[96] What this means is that the practice of appointing public positions by ministers, such as the Prime Minister, is heavily regulated, and the regulations apply to the CCRC. The regulations refer to a rule that must be followed by all ministers, specifically, that they "have a duty to ensure that influence over public appointments is not abused for partisan purposes."[97] In other words, partisan politics should have no role in CCRC commissioner appointments.

Lastly, there is criticism as to whether the United Kingdom's system of post-conviction review works at all. Indeed, some have called for adopting of an additional model, that of the "innocence commissions" found in the United States and other countries.[98] There are fears that the British system of post-conviction review focuses too much on due process denials, and not enough on actual innocence.[99] This is because, as the critics say, the CCRC staff and members are not paid enough to conduct thorough investigations, and inmates often need assistance to explain why they require post-conviction review, assistance which they often cannot get without an organization like the innocence projects.[100] Indeed, if Texas adopts a "hybrid" system of post-conviction review, as discussed below, it will be heeding these criticisms of the CCRC and, as a result, will be one step ahead of the British system.[101]

Certain features of the CCRC, such as the method by which Commissioners are appointed, give it institutional independence from the rest of the government, and reporting requirements which make it accountable to the rest of government and to the British people, were created intentionally to dispel any appearance that post-conviction review is somehow biased or suffers from tunnel vision. We now turn to how another country deals with wrongful convictions through a post-conviction review system—Canada.

III. Canada's Dual Approach – the Minister of Justice and the Criminal Conviction Review Group

Similar to the United Kingdom, inmates who believe they were wrongfully convicted in Canada may apply for post-conviction review. The most significant difference between the Canadian and British systems of post-appellate conviction review is that in Canada, the decision to send a case back to court lies with the Minister of Justice; while in the United Kingdom, the decision is made by an eleven-member Commission.[102] The power concentrated in the Minister of Justice is fully acknowledged as an offshoot of the Royal Prerogative of Mercy.[103] On the other hand, the British CCRC fully disclaims any such royal prerogative of mercy by noting that it is independent of the Crown.[104]

In Canada the Minister of Justice makes post-appeal determinations of possible miscarriages of justice. The Minister of Justice also fulfills the role of the Attorney General of Canada.[105] However, a separate body, the Criminal Conviction Review Group ("Group"), investigates each case and makes recommendations to the Minister. Since 2002, when certain reforms were enacted that created today's system of post-conviction review, the Canadian system has completed a total of eighty-three applications, referring twelve to the court system via the Minister of Justice, and dismissing ten.[106] The rest were dismissed because there was no basis for investigation.[107]

What follows is a discussion of how and why the current model of post-conviction review exists in Canada, offering comparisons and contrasts to the British system along the way. Like the discussion of the British CCRC, the description of the Canadian model begins with how it came about, explores how it works, including the roles of the Group and the Minister of Justice, and concludes with analysis and critique of certain features that might be applicable to Texas.

A. Origins of the Canadian System of Post-Conviction Review

The Minister's power to intervene after the appeals process has been part of the Canadian criminal code since 1892,[108] and the Group was established in 1968.[109] In 2002 certain reforms were enacted, resulting in the current process of application and review.[110] The Minister of Justice has the power either to order a new trial or to refer a case to the appropriate court of appeals if the "Minister is satisfied that there is a reasonable basis to conclude that a miscarriage of justice likely occurred."[111]

B. How Canadian Post-Conviction Review Works

Although the British and Canadian government bodies reflect similar concerns of independence and efficiency, in fact, they exhibit very different ways of handling the wrongful convictions problem. The most important differences in Canada are the legal standards used in screening the application, and the use of a governmental minister, as well as government employees within the minister's department, to review a conviction.

1. Submission of the Application

Similar to the United Kingdom's CCRC, the post-review conviction process begins with the submission of an application by anyone incarcerated in Canada,[112] and like the CCRC, the first stage is a preliminary review for eligibility. However, the similarities end there. On one hand, CCRC applicants can apply even if they have not exhausted all their appeals under the "exceptional circumstances" exception to the exhaustion requirement.[113] On the other hand, Canadian applicants *must* have exhausted all of their legal remedies to be considered eligible.[114] Furthermore, unlike the CCRC, where applicants merely need to show that there is a "real possibility" that their conviction could be overturned, Canadian applicants must show the availability of "new and significant" information in their case.[115] New and significant information is information that was not available during the trial and appeals process *and* that could have affected the outcome of the case.[116] If the applicant fails to show the existence of such information, the application will be rejected, but the applicant has one year to return with new and significant information.[117]

2. The Role of the Review Group in Ministerial Review

If an application exhibits "new and significant information," it moves to the second stage, investigation. At this stage an application is examined more thoroughly by a staff lawyer of the Criminal Conviction Review

Group. The Group is an office within the Canadian Department of Justice.[118] It examines the application's "new and significant information" for reliability and relevance.[119] The Group's staff has the power to subpoena documents or testimony, and may have scientific tests performed.[120] Because the Group is located within the Canadian Department of Justice, potential conflicts may arise when reviewing a conviction prosecuted by the Department of Justice, such as federal drug crimes.[121] When such a conflict arises, as discussed further below, an outside lawyer may examine the application.[122]

The fruits of the investigation are then compiled in an investigation report. The report is sent to the applicant, and the applicant may provide comments.[123] Once the comments are received, the Group staff member prepares a legal memorandum and then forwards that, along with the investigation report, to the Minister of Justice's office to await the Minister's decision.[124]

3. The Role of the Minister of Justice

The Minister of Justice may send a case back to the courts if he believes a "miscarriage of justice" has occurred. In order to make the decision, the Minister relies on the analysis and investigatory support of the Group, as well as guidance from the Canadian courts and a "special advisor."

a. Standard for Determining Miscarriage of Justice

By statute, the Minister may order a new trial or send it back to the court of appeals if he "is satisfied that there is a reasonable basis to conclude that a miscarriage of justice likely occurred."[125] In practice, the Group's lawyers make this determination by drafting recommendations and memoranda and sending them to the Minister's office.[126] Nevertheless, if the Minister concurs with the Group that the legal standard is met and the applicant has submitted "new and significant" information, a case may be referred back to the court system.[127]

b. Advisory Roles to the Minister of Justice

Although the Minister of Justice personally reviews application materials and Group's recommendations to decide whether to send a case back to the court system, the system provides for two other sources of advice. First is the role of the Special Advisor, and the second is the ability to receive guidance from Canadian courts on a question of law.

First, in addition to the analysis and recommendation of the Group, the Minister may receive guidance from a Special Advisor.[128] The Special Advisor is an independent role that gives an outside voice to the convictions review process.[129] He is not a member of the Canadian civil service. For example, the current Special Advisor is a retired judge.[130] Not only does the Special Advisor weigh in on whether to grant the application, but he may also make recommendations during other stages of the review, such as whether the application should pass from the preliminary review to investigation.[131]

Second, the Minister may receive guidance from a Canadian provincial appeals court on a question of law.[132] This may also be done at any time during the application process, and it is similar to the American concept of a federal court certifying a question of state law to a state supreme court.[133]

Just as in the United Kingdom, if a person in Canada believes he has been wrongfully convicted, he can apply for post-conviction review. Unlike in the United Kingdom, however, post-conviction review is handled by a single minister, after receiving recommendations from the Criminal Convictions Review Group, a Special Advisor, and possibly a provincial appeals court. Furthermore, an inmate must prove there is new evidence, and his case is evaluated under a different standard. Next we take a closer look at certain aspects of the Canadian system that could be applied to a Texas system of post-conviction review.

C. Twin Goals of Independence and Accountability – Consideration and Critique of Canadian Review Features Applicable to Texas

Parts of the Canadian model deserve a closer look, especially in considering an application to Texas. First, despite having only one person make the final decision to revisit a conviction, the system is mindful of how to ensure independence and accountability. The Minister of Justice may receive guidance and input from the Group's staff, Canadian courts and an independent advisor. Furthermore, the Canadian system is subject to rigorous public reporting requirements, which holds it accountable to both Parliament and the electorate. In this way, if Texas decides to follow the Canadian model, it should incorporate Canada's safeguards.

1. The Struggle for Independence and Accountability in the Canadian Model

Before the current reforms were enacted in 2002, there was a loud call for Canada to establish an independent commission, such as the CCRC.[134] For example, a Canadian organization called AIDWYC recommended an independent tribunal investigate cases that were potentially politically embarrassing if the Minister handled them.[135] Disregarding politics, the reasoning went, the organization could more easily review convictions for the indigent, and would "remove all political considerations from the review of the applications submitted to it."[136] Moreover, with Ministerial review, there was the appearance of a conflict of interest: just as the Home Secretary was responsible before 1995 for reviewing convictions in the United Kingdom, which were based on investigations conducted by his own department, the Minister of Justice was responsible for reviewing convictions in Canada.[137]

In 2002 the government rejected the call for an independent commission, leaving the Minister of Justice in charge of reviewing convictions.[138] The reasons Parliament gave were threefold. First, the Canadian Minister of Justice "was not subject to the same perceived conflict of interest as was the British Home Secretary."[139] This is because the Canadian Minister of Justice, in his capacity as Canadian Attorney General, only prosecutes federal crimes, while the majority of applications for post-conviction review are from provincially prosecuted crimes.[140] Second, the British CCRC was falling behind on its case load,[141] which was presumed to be due to the large size of the Commission; therefore, the Canadians concluded that having one minister make all the decisions would be more efficient. Third, Parliament found that "ministerial accountability trumps the principle of independence in providing a remedy for the few exceptional cases of miscarriage of justice."[142]

These reasons are not overwhelmingly persuasive to everyone. For the most part, having the Minister of Justice second-guess his decisions as Attorney General is counterintuitive. Although the Group must appoint non-Justice Department lawyers to investigate applications for federal offenses,[143] any bias, whether real or perceived, remains. Indeed, it has been noted that whether or not the Group's lawyers working on the case are impartial is unimportant; rather, the appearance that justice has been served impartially is what matters.[144]

2. Features Providing Independence and Accountability

Three features of the current Canadian model counter the claims that post-conviction review power in one Minister is not independent and accountable enough. These features are the structure of the Group, the role of the Special Advisor to the Minister, and the reporting requirements.

The first feature relates to the parallel-jurisdiction system used by Canada, which is slightly similar to that of the United States.[145] As noted above, Canadian post-conviction review is available for all convictions, not simply federal ones. As a result, much of the caseload is provincial conviction.[146] In other words, there is little chance of a real conflict of interest because the Group's staff lawyers and the Minister of Justice are not second-guessing their own prosecutions. Moreover, whenever a case arrives that was prosecuted on behalf of the Attorney General of Canada, such as in federal drug prosecutions or criminal prosecutions in certain territories,[147] the Group may appoint outside counsel to conduct the review and investigation.[148] Outside counsel is required when there is an explicit conflict of interest; however, the Minister makes the final decision on all cases, no matter who does the investigatory legwork.[149]

Furthermore, the location of the Group's lawyers within in the Canadian Department of Justice was designed to increase the appearance of independence. When the Group was created, its members were placed not in the litigation section of the Department of Justice, but in the section handling policy initiatives.[150] This decision to separate the Group's lawyers from the litigators within the Department contributes to the public appearance of independence of the review Group, even though both the litigation sections and the policy sections are under the umbrella of the Minister of Justice.

The second way the Canadian model achieves independence is by means of the Special Advisor. Statute has created a Special Advisor to help the Minister of Justice decide whether to refer cases back to court.[151] The Special Advisor is important because by law, he or she must "ensure[] that the review of all applications is complete, fair, and transparent."[152] Unlike the Group's staff and the Minister of Justice, the current Special Advisor is not an employee of the Canadian Department of Justice, nor is he even a public servant.[153] Rather, the Special Advisor is appointed by a special order known as an "Order-in-Council," which must come from outside the Department of Justice.[154] The current Special Advisor is Bernard Grenier, a retired judge from the Court of Quebec, who has assisted the Minister since 2003.[155]

The third feature that furthers the goal of accountability is its rigorous reporting requirements. By statute, the Minister of Justice must submit an annual report to parliament detailing its activities.[156] The regulations specify what the report must include. The annual report must include statistical information, such as how many applications were made to the Minister, how many applications were incomplete, how many applications were at the preliminary assessment stage, how many applications are undergoing investigation, and the number of decisions the Minister has made.[157] The annual reports are listed on the Canadian Department of Justice website, ensuring access to the Canadian population.[158]

As a result, the Canadian system of ministerial review has taken important steps to increase the appearance and reality of independence and impartiality, rather than accede to calls for an independent agency. The use of an independent special advisor to the Minister of Justice, the use of outside investigative counsel, the segregation of the review Group from the prosecution unit of the Canadian Department of Justice, and finally the annual reporting requirement, help compensate for the lack of an independent commission in the model of the British CCRC. If Texas decides to follow Canada's model, it would be well advised to adopt these safeguards.

IV. Applying the British and Canadian Models to Texas

If Texas forms a system for post-conviction review, the British and Canadian models provide guidance and useful features. This section recommends following the British model in that any review should be done by a commission that is independent of the rest of Texas government. However, should Texas align itself with a Canadian model, that is, concentrating power within a government official, certain steps can be taken to ensure that any system review is sufficiently independent and accountable.

A. The State of Wrongful Convictions in Texas

As stated in the Introduction, forty people in Texas have been exonerated on post-conviction DNA evidence.[159] How has the Texas system failed, allowing innocent people to be wrongfully convicted? The answer to this question is the same answer to a related question: why does Texas need an institutionalized system for post-conviction review? There are four main areas of insufficiency in Texas: motions for new trial, direct appellate review, habeas relief, and executive clemency.

Texas law authorizes a new trial when "material evidence favorable to the accused has been discovered since trial."[160] However, motions for new trial based on newly discovered evidence are generally disfavored by Texas courts, and are viewed with great caution.[161] The burden is great. In order to even have a hearing for a motion for new trial, an inmate must attach an affidavit that "rais[es] matters not determinable from the record, upon which the accused could be entitled to relief."[162] Although such an affidavit need not establish a prima facie[*] case, it must reflect that reasonable grounds exist for holding that a new trial is necessary.[163] As a result, if an inmate is unable to conduct investigations (or afford to pay someone else to do so), it is nearly impossible to request a new trial based on new evidence.

---

* A prima facie case refers to a party's burden to allege facts adequate to prove the underlying conduct supporting the claim and thereby prevail.

Furthermore, the Texas appellate system also makes it very difficult to uncover new evidence. Like other American courts, Texas appellate courts cannot consider new evidence.[164] As a result, new information cannot be considered. This is in contrast to British courts, where appeals can contain new information that may be considered by the reviewing court.[165] Accordingly, the appeal of wrongful convictions due to new evidence, such as DNA, are impossible to redress using the normal appeals process.

Furthermore, for inmates sentenced to death, filing habeas petitions in Texas and federal courts offer little redress. It has been said that collateral review through habeas proceedings is considered a "central part of the review process for prisoners sentenced to death."[166] Moreover, unlike direct appeal, habeas proceedings allow for an inmate to introduce new evidence.[167] The inmate's lawyer at the habeas stage is responsible for investigating the existence of new evidence, as well as introducing new evidence in a way that will overcome the high burden of habeas proceedings.[168] However, in reality, this is rarely easily done, because with the setting of an execution date, habeas petitions are often hastily prepared, with inadequate time to conduct a thorough investigation.[169] Furthermore, even if an inmate prepares a well-executed petition, courts are hesitant to grant the writ because they tend to rely on other considerations, such as the principle of finality and the availability (however remote) of executive clemency.[170]

Executive clemency is also rare to come by for an inmate who believes he has been wrongfully convicted. First of all, in order for the Governor to exercise clemency, there must be a recommendation from the Texas Board of Pardons and Paroles.[171] But before an inmate can even petition for clemency, he must conduct an investigation to gather exculpatory evidence. As we have seen, this is a virtual impossibility for inmates lacking financial resources.

Accordingly, along with the sheer number of inmates exonerated by DNA evidence, the insufficiency of new trial motions, direct appeal, collateral attack on an inmate's conviction and clemency show that the need for a state-sponsored post-conviction review group in Texas is strong.

B. The Structure of Texas Post-Conviction Review Should Reflect Independence and Accountability

With the need for post-conviction review established, what follows is a description of what a review group should look like, based on the features of the Canadian and British models discussed above. First, it is argued that a group of people, rather than a single commissioner, be established. Moreover, the group should be independent, not within a branch of government. However, even if Texas decides to pursue a process similar to Canada's ministerial review, there are safeguards available to promote independence and accountability.

1. The Texas System Should Be a Commission

In forming a post-conviction review group in Texas, it should truly be a *commission* of several people, not merely one person. In this way Texas should follow the United Kingdom's CCRC, rather than Canada's system where the Minister of Justice has full power. As discussed above, the Minister of Justice makes the final decision on whether to send a criminal conviction back to the courts, with input from an office within the Department of Justice and an independent Special Advisor. This system appears to work well in Canada,[172] which received only twenty-five applications last year.[173] Unfortunately, such a system would not work in Texas.

First, there is no "royal prerogative of mercy" in Texas, because Texas is not a constitutional monarchy. As mentioned above, the Minister of Justice in Canada has the power to review convictions because it is an extension of the royal prerogative of mercy. Unlike Canada, in Texas the power that most resembles the royal prerogative of mercy is merely the pardon power of the governor.[174] However, as discussed above, the governor may grant pardons only on the written recommendation and advice of the Texas Board of Pardons and Paroles.[175] As such, Texas does not already have in place a system for one person revisiting convictions.

The second reason why power cannot be concentrated in simply one person is the workload. Texas housed over 172,000 prisoners in 2008, or about 640 per 100,000 Texans.[176] By contrast, in the years 2007 to 2008, Canada's rate of incarceration was only 108 per 100,000.[177] Strictly mathematically speaking, then, Texas would receive at least six times the caseload as Canada. Assuming a figure such as the Texas Attorney General had the power to order case reviews, it is difficult to imagine that a small group of lawyers working for one person could handle the expected caseload. This would be untenable for a state office to handle.

However, a "hybrid" system of review could alleviate the workload pressure on the Texas Attorney General and his staff. If innocence groups already established in Texas, such as the Texas Innocence Network and the Innocence Project of Texas, handle the initial stages of screening and investigation, the Texas Attorney General's office would not be as burdened. Indeed, if independent organizations conduct investigations (as they are already doing),[178] and send legal memoranda and recommendations to the Attorney General's office, all the Attorney General and his staff need to do is make the decision and issue an order.

The third consideration behind the adoption of a commission is the need for political independence. If the power to order reviews of cases were concentrated in one person, that person would likely have been placed in that role by partisan action, that is, by political appointment.[179] Political concerns may arise (which will be discussed immediately below) from a commissioner's decision that would reflect poorly on figure that appointed the commissioner. On the other hand, if a group makes a politically unpopular decision, especially a group with staggered terms whose members were not all appointed by one person, political blame is less likely to fall back on the appointing official. Accordingly, a model based on several commissioners, as in the CCRC, is the better route to take, rather than a model where the case review power is concentrated in one person.

2. The Texas Commission Should Be Bipartisan or Nonpartisan

An important feature of a Texas post-conviction review system is a mixed political makeup. Although the British model of the CCRC provides guidance, the commission could also follow some of the steps of another Texas governmental body, the Texas Ethics Commission.

The CCRC stresses its political independence, which any Texas commission should likewise do. For example, by statute the CCRC is an independent body, which can "not be regarded as the servant or agent of the Crown."[180] Furthermore, the CCRC proclaims itself to be "completely independent and impartial and do not represent the prosecution or the defence."[181] Although the British Minister of Justice sets the terms and conditions of each Commissioner's employment,[182] it is a far cry from charging the Home Office, which investigates criminal cases,[183] with the responsibility for ordering review of those same cases.

Political party bias in overturning convictions does not appear to be as necessary in the United Kingdom and in Canada as it does within the United States. Even though criminal justice is ostensibly politically neutral,[184] it continues to be fraught with political considerations. For example, the United States Sentencing Commission ("USSC"), which is responsible for promulgating the United States Sentencing Guidelines, contains strict statutory restrictions on who may be appointed and which parties the members come from.[185] Accordingly, just as United States Congress saw a need to mix temper political bias in the USSC, Texas equally has a need to formulate an innocence commission free from partisan bias.

We could look to the Texas Ethics Commission for guidelines. Members of the Texas Ethics Commission are chosen in an elaborate manner by the governor, lieutenant governor, and the Speaker of the Texas House of Representatives.[186] Even the nominees for the Commission must come from both sides of the aisle.[187] The complicated manner in which the Texas Ethics Commission is appointed reflects its role: to enforce the laws governing campaign finance, contributions to legislators, the actions of lobbyists, and state agencies.[188] Although a Texas post-conviction review commission need not be appointed in such a complicated manner as the Texas Ethics Commission, it may still serve as a model. A mixed composition of political parties in a Texas innocence commission would reflect the goal of independent, nonpartisan review of criminal convictions.

If the State decides to pursue a "hybrid" system, the appearance and reality of political neutrality could still be achieved, at least in part. If the initial screening and investigation is done with resources and funding from non-profit organizations, no tax dollars are directly used.[189] As a result, little pressure is put on the budget of the Attorney General's office to dictate how the cases should be screened and investigated and, as a result, no political pressure on the investigating organizations' recommendations can be foreseen. However, because the Attorney General is itself an elected, partisan role,[190] an absolutely politics-free hybrid system is an impossibility.

3. Commission Should Be an Independent Agency, Not Contained Within Any Branch of Government

Where to place a post-conviction review commission within the structure of Texas government makes a difference. The United Kingdom and Canada provide two different examples of where the power can be located. First, the CCRC is completely independent and not within any other agency.[191] Indeed, the British enabling statute insists that the "Commission shall not be regarded as the servant or agent of the Crown, or as enjoying any status, immunity or privilege of the Crown."[192] Furthermore, the CCRC is geographically separated from central British government because its headquarters are in Birmingham, not London.[193] So, there are bureaucratic as well as geographic boundaries separating the CCRC and the rest of the government.

On the other hand, in Canada almost the entire power to review cases is located within the Canadian Department of Justice. The Minister of Justice is the one who makes the decisions to review cases,[194] even though the minister oversees the federal prosecutions in the country. Furthermore, members of the Minister's advisory group are also employees of the Canadian Department of Justice.[195] Also, both the Minister of Justice and the Group are located in Ottawa, the capital of Canada.[196]

If a Texas innocence commission wishes to give a strong impression that the commission is independent, it should not locate its office within a branch of Texas government, either the judiciary or the executive. A further sense of independence could also be achieved by locating the commission's headquarters outside of Austin, perhaps in another area with a high inmate population. Or, perhaps Dallas is the most appropriate location because Dallas County has had more wrongful convictions reversed than any other county in the United States.[197]

On the other hand, a hybrid system could achieve at least partial independence from the Texas executive and judiciary. Locating the work of investigation and screening within non-profits and schools across Texas would take post-conviction review out of the hands of the government and into the hands of nonpolitical entities. This would increase public perception of the independence of such a review system.

4. A Hybrid System Should Include Canadian Features that Promote Its Independence

If Texas chooses a hybrid system, one which uses the existing network of nonprofits and schools to investigate claims of innocence, but locates the decisional power to send cases back to the courts within the Attorney General's office, there are additional steps that should be taken to promote the appearance of independence. Canada's measures are instructive.

First, there is the appearance of conflict of interest between the Texas Attorney General's prosecuting power and the contemplated power of post-conviction review. The Canadian system recognized this conflict, especially since the Canadian Department of Justice is responsible for prosecuting federal crimes as well as sending cases back to the courts based on miscarriages of justice.[198] Canada's solution to this is to require the appointment of outside counsel to investigate and make recommendations on applications where the underlying conviction was prosecuted by the Canadian Department of Justice.[199]

The same problem that Canada has could arise in Texas. In addition to prosecuting non-violent crimes such as public corruption and election fraud, the Texas Attorney General's Office also provides support to state and federal authorities prosecuting violent crimes.[200] Although county and district attorneys in Texas have jurisdiction to prosecute violent crimes, they may request the assistance of the Attorney General's office, or may take referrals from local prosecutors.[201] Thus, if a conviction is prosecuted by the Texas Attorney General, and the inmate files an application for post-conviction review, a decision by the Attorney

General whether to send the case back to the courts could create a conflict of interest.

The conflict of interest can be sidestepped in part by the "hybrid" system of using outside lawyers and investigators to screen and investigate applications as seen by using the innocence projects. Indeed, one commentator advocates that the United Kingdom also adopt a system innocence projects in addition to the CCRC, albeit for other reasons.[202]

Accordingly, a rough model of the British system is recommended for Texas post-conviction review. Even if Texas decides to follow Canada and place power of post-conviction review in one person, the use of a hybrid system would mirror the safeguards Canada has put in place with its system.

C. The Procedures of the Commission Should Reflect Effectiveness and Accountability

Regardless of which model Texas adopts, there are certain features that a post-conviction review system must have to ensure effectiveness and accountability. First, the standard of eligibility for review should be clear and, because DNA exonerations are the main reason behind having a system, the inmate should show the existence of newly discovered evidence. Furthermore, the commission should adopt regular and accessible reporting requirements to ensure accountability to the Legislature and the public.

1. Eligibility Standard Should Be Clear

In order to handle a large amount of applications that would no doubt be sent to any Texas post-conviction review group, screening applications for eligibility must play a large role. The British and the Canadian models have effective methods of screening cases for eligibility of review, to which a Texas innocence commission could look for guidance.

As stated in Part III above, applications for review are sent to the CCRC and are immediately reviewed by staff members to ensure that either the inmate has exhausted his appeals or that "exceptional circumstances" are present.[203] Similarly, Canada's screening process is similar to the United Kingdom's, but its legal standard for eligibility is even clearer. In addition to making sure the applicant has exhausted all his appeals, the Canadian Group's staffers must make sure that the applicant demonstrates "new and significant information."[204] Then, if the applicant does demonstrate new and significant information, staff lawyers examine it for relevance, and may order scientific tests.[205] This standard is arguably better than the British standard because there is no exception to the exhaustion requirement for "exceptional circumstances." As noted above, there is no official guidance as to what the term "exceptional circumstances" means; rather, it is looked at on a case-by-case basis.[206] Furthermore, this standard would further the goal of a Texas system in the first place—to make it easier for cases of potential DNA exonerees to be considered.

However, one word of caution is needed with regard to a "new and significant information" standard for screening applications. As noted above,[207] Texas already allows new trials when a defendant proves that "material evidence favorable to the accused has been discovered since trial."[208] However, as also noted above, such a motion is disfavored and relief is rarely granted.[209] As a result, in order for the hybrid system to be able to investigate claims, the standard for introducing new evidence should not adopt the case law surrounding the new trial standard,[210] but rather should adopt a standard low enough to permit investigation.

2. Reporting Should Be Regular and Accessible to the Public

The Canadian model provides a good example of reporting for Texas to follow. As noted above,[211] statistics are used by overseeing governmental bodies to evaluate the efficacy of a post-conviction review system. Furthermore, statistics provide accountability to the public, especially when they are available to the public on the Internet. As a result, Texas would be advised to require yearly reporting and publish those reports as well.

One consequence of reporting to the public is not contemplated by the British and Canadian systems—the effect of reporting on the composition of Texas government. For example, if the number of cases sent back to the court system by a Texas review group is perceived by the public or the media to be "too large," it might possibly reflect poorly on the judiciary in Texas and create fodder for the next judicial elections.[212] Alternatively, if the power to refer cases back to court is vested in an executive such as the Attorney General, and that number is perceived to be "too large" or "too small," these reports could also become another point of contention in an election, possibly affecting its outcome.

Regardless, little can be lost by requiring an annual report, and much accountability to the public and to the rest of government can be gained. The reporting requirement, along with the a clear standard of eligibility that requires new evidence, are features that should be included in any system of post-conviction review that Texas adopts, regardless of the form of review Texas chooses.

V. Conclusion

Because the problem of wrongful convictions appears to have no solutions within the court system, Texas must create a system of post-conviction review. Such a system would take applications, investigate and consider newly discovered evidence, and have the power to send cases back to the courts for new trials.

Texas has at its disposal the post-conviction review systems of the United Kingdom and Canada. The United Kingdom has a multi-member commission (the CCRC), and Canada has a single-member system of ministerial review. Although it is recommended that Texas adopt the multi-member, bureaucratically independent model, there are safeguards that Texas can implement to ensure at least partial independence and accountability of any post-conviction review system. Furthermore, any system Texas chooses should ensure there is a clear standard for review and that there is adequate reporting to ensure effectiveness and accountability. If Texas adopts these measures, or other similar ones, hopefully the tragic stories of wrongful convictions such as that of Ricardo Rachell will become things of the past.

ENDNOTES

1. Roma Khanna & Carolyn Feibel, *Unanswered Questions: Attacks on Kids Continued after Rachell Was Jailed*, HOUSTON CHRON., Dec. 18, 2008, at 1.
2. Roma Khanna, *Study: Witness Errors Cause Most Wrongful Convictions*, HOUSTON CHRON., Mar. 26, 2009, at 1.
3. *Id.*
4. Roma Khanna, Lise Olsen & Dane Schiller, *Freed by DNA to Life as an Innocent Man*, HOUSTON CHRON., Dec. 13, 2008, at 1.
5. *Id.*
6. *Id.*
7. *Id.*
8. Innocence Project of Texas, Texas Exonerations, http://www.innocenceprojectoftexas.org/index.php?action=at-a-glance (last visited July 30, 2010).
9. *See infra* notes 160-63 and accompanying text.
10. *See infra* notes 166-70 and accompanying text.
11. *See infra* notes 170-71 and accompanying text.
12. *See* RICHARD NOBLES & DAVID SCHIFF, UNDERSTANDING MISCARRIAGES OF JUSTICE 16-17 (2000) (characterizing actual innocence as "a concern with truth").
13. *Id.* (characterizing this definition as "a concern with due process").
14. *See* Criminal Cases Review Commission, Can We Help? http://www.ccrc.gov.uk/canwe/canwe_27.htm (last visited May 2, 2010) (noting that British review of wrongful convictions extends not only to inmates who feel they were "wrongfully convicted," but also to those who feel they were "unfairly sentenced"); Ernest A. Young, *Institutional Settlement in a Globalizing Judicial System*, 521 DUKE L.J. 1143, 1182-83

n.174 (2005) (characterizing Canadian post-conviction review as concerned only with actual innocence).

15. About Us, http://www.ccrc.gov.uk/about.htm (last visited May 2, 2010). Since its inception in 1997, the CCRC has reviewed 11,871 cases and referred 454 cases to the British Court of Appeal. Criminal Cases Review Commission, Case Statistics, http://www.ccrc.gov.uk/cases/case_44.htm (last visited May 2, 2010) (statistics compiled as of Mar. 31, 2010). Of the cases heard by the Court of Appeal, 293 convictions have been quashed. *Id.* For convictions in Scotland, there is a separate Scottish Criminal Cases Review Commission, which was established in 1999. Scottish Criminal Cases Review Commission, About the Commission, http://www.sccrc.org.uk/home.aspx (last visited May 2, 2010). The Scottish Commission is not discussed here.

16. Lissa Griffin, *Correcting Injustice: Studying how the United Kingdom and the United States Review Claims of Innocence*, 41 U. Tol. L. Rev. 107, 111 (2009).

17. *See* Criminal Appeal Act, 1995, c. 35, § 3 (Eng.) (abolishing from the Home Secretary the power to refer).

18. Richard Nobles & David Schiff, *The Criminal Cases Review Commission: Establishing a Workable Relationship with the Court of Appeal*, Crim. L. Rev. 2005, 173, 173.

19. *See, e.g.*, Home Office, About Us, http://www.homeoffice.gov.uk/about-us/index.html ("The Home Office is the lead government department for immigration and passports, drugs policy, counter-terrorism and police.").

20. Nobles & Schiff, *supra* note 18, at 173.

21. *See* Nobles & Schiff, *supra* note 12, at 189 (framing the creation of the CCRC in the aftermath of the Birmingham Six and Maguire Seven appeals).

22. *Id.*

23. *Id.* at 192.

24. *Id.* at 196.

25. *Id.* at 171.

26. David Horan, *The Innocence Commission: An Independent Review Board for Wrongful Convictions*, 20 N. Ill. U. L. Rev. 91, 126-27 (2000).

27. *Id.* at 127.

28. Nobles & Schiff, *supra* note 12, at 172; Horan, *supra* note 26, at 128.

29. Horan, *supra* note 26, at 131.

30. Criminal Appeal Act, 1995, c. 35, § 8 (Eng.).

31. *Id.*; *but see* Criminal Cases Review Commission, Commissioners, http://www.ccrc.gov.uk/about/about_29.htm (last visited Aug. 1, 2010) (listing only ten commissioners).

32. Criminal Appeal Act, 1995, c. 35, § 13 (Eng.).

33. The application is available at http://www.ccrc.gov.uk/documents/application.pdf. It is noted for its ease of use and clarity of language, and this approach is recommended for Texas. *See* Criminal Cases Review Commission Application at 1.

34. Lissa Griffin, *The Correction of Wrongful Convictions: A Comparative Perspective*, 16 Am. U. Int'l L. Rev. 1241, 1279 (2001).

35. Criminal Appeal Act, 1995, c. 35, § 13 (Eng.).

36. *Id.*; *see* Stephanie Roberts & Lynne Weathered, *Assisting the Factually Innocent: the Contradictions and Compatibility of Innocence Projects and the Criminal Cases Review Commission*, 29 Oxford J. Legal Studies 43, 48 (2009).

37. Criminal Cases Review Commission Application at pt. 4. Other "exceptional circumstances" include the fact that a co-defendant's case has already been referred to an appeals court for reasons affecting the inmate's case, or that an inmate was prevented from appealing by "serious threats" against the inmate or his family. *Id.*

38. Griffin, *supra* note 34, at 1279.

39. *Id.*
40. *Id.*
41. *Id.*
42. Griffin, *supra* note 16, at 113.
43. Griffin, *supra* note 34, at 1280.
44. *Id.*
45. *Id.* The standard of review is whether the decision was "perverse or absurd." *Id.*
46. Criminal Cases Review Commission, FAQ, http://www.ccrc.gov.uk/about/about_faq.asp (last visited May 2, 2010).
47. *See, e.g.*, Horan, *supra* note 26, at 150.
48. Criminal Appeal Act, 1995, c. 35, § 14 (Eng.).
49. The CCRC may also refer certain cases to another court known as the Crown Court. Criminal Appeal Act, 1995, c. 35, § 11 (Eng.). Cases falling under this category are convictions emanating from a magistrates' court, *id.* § 11(1), and applications from the magistrates' court tend to be rare. *See* Kevin Kerrigan, *Miscarriage of Justice in the Magistrates' Court: The Forgotten Power of the Criminal Cases Review Commission*, CRIM. L. REV. 2006, 124, 127 (noting that the percentage of applications from a magistrates' court conviction is 6%).
50. Criminal Appeal Act, 1995, c. 35, § 13 (Eng.).
51. R. v. CCRC *ex parte* Pearson, [2000] 1 Crim. App. 141, 149 (Q.B. 1999).
52. Criminal Appeal Act, 1995, c. 35, § 13.
53. Criminal Cases Review Commission Application, pt. 4.
54. Griffin, *supra* note 16, at 112; *see supra* notes 36-38 and accompanying text.
55. Griffin, *supra* note 34, at 1269.
56. Criminal Appeal Act, 1995, c. 35, § 23(2) (Eng.).
57. *See infra* notes 77-82 and accompanying text.

58. Criminal Cases Review Commission, How We Review Your Case, http://www.ccrc.gov.uk/canwe/canwe_33.htm (last visited May 2, 2010).
59. *See, e.g.*, Criminal Appeal Act, 1995, c. 35 § 17 (Eng.) (outlining broad powers of obtaining documents).
60. Criminal Appeal Act 1995, c. 35, § 2 (Eng.).
61. *Id.*
62. *See* J.R. Spencer, *Quashing Convictions for Procedural Irregularities*, CRIM. L. R. 2007, Nov., 835, 835 (discussing an attempt to limit appeals to those cases where the defendant was factually innocent because the standard encompasses due process).
63. Griffin, *supra* note 34, at 1269 (quoting R. v. Cooper, [1969] 1 Q.B. 267 (Eng. C.A. 1969)).
64. R. v. Cooper, [1969] 1 Q.B. 267, 271 (Eng. C.A. 1969); *see* L.H. Leigh, *Lurking Doubt and the Safety of Convictions*, CRIM. L. REV. 2006, 809, 810 (describing the subjective "feel" of a certain case which gave rise to the term "lurking doubt").
65. R. v. Cooper, 1 Q.B. at 271.
66. Criminal Appeal Act, 1995, c. 35, § 8(3) (Eng.).
67. *Id.* § 8(5).
68. *Id.* § 8(6).
69. *Id.* sched. 1, paras. (2) & (3).
70. *Id.* sched. 1, paras. (5) & (6).
71. *Id.* sched. 1, para (7).
72. COMMISSIONER FOR PUBLIC APPOINTMENTS, CODE OF PRACTICE FOR MINISTERIAL APPOINTMENTS TO PUBLIC BODIES 37 (2009), *available at* https://www.publicappointmentscommissioner.org/web-app/plugins/spaw2/uploads/files/Code%20of%20Practice%20August%202009.pdf (last visited Mar. 24, 2010).
73. *Id.* ("Ministers have a duty to ensure that influence over public appointments is not abused for partisan purposes").

74. Criminal Appeal Act, 1995, c. 35, § 8(2) (Eng.).
75. *Id.* However, it should be noted that the Home Secretary retains the power to recommend the exercise of the sovereign's royal prerogative of mercy. *See* Criminal Appeal Act 1995, c. 35, § 16(1) (Eng.). Indeed, the statute authorizes the CCRC to consider and give its opinion on whether to exercise such power. *Id.* However, it bears repeating that the CCRC's actions in referring cases back to the Court of Appeal do not constitute the royal prerogative of mercy. *But see infra* note 103 and accompanying text (discussing Canada's review system as an extension of the royal prerogative of mercy).
76. Horan, *supra* note 26, at 140 (quoting the Home Secretary during Parliamentary debate).
77. Criminal Appeal Act, 1995, c. 35, § 19(6) (Eng.).
78. *Id.* § 19(1).
79. Horan, *supra* note 26, at 142 & n.261.
80. Criminal Appeal Act, 1995, c. 35, § 19(6) (Eng.).
81. Horan, *supra* note 26, at 142.
82. Griffin, *supra* note 34, at 1279.
83. Horan, *supra* note 26, at 131.
84. Criminal Appeal Act, 1995, c. 35, sched. 1, para. 8(1).
85. *Id.*
86. *Id.* para. 8(4).
87. *Id.* para. 8(3).
88. *See, e.g.*, UK Government, Overview of the UK System of Government, http://www.direct.gov.uk/en/Governmentcitizensandrights/UKgovernment/Centralgovernmentandthemonarchy/DG_073438 (last visited May 2, 2010).
89. Horan, *supra* note 26, at 175.
90. Criminal Appeal Act, 1995, c. 35, § 8(4) (Eng.).
91. Horan, *supra* note 26, at 143, 145.

92. *Id.* at 143.

93. *Id.* at 145.

94. Criminal Appeal Act, 1995, c. 35, schedule 1, para. (5) (Eng.).

95. *Id.* sched. 1, para. (7).

96. CCRC, About Us, http://www.ccrc.gov.uk/about.htm (last visited May 2, 2010).

97. COMM'R FOR PUBLIC APPOINTMENTS, *supra* note 72, at 37.

98. Roberts & Weathered, *supra* note 36, at 45.

99. *Id.* at 51.

100. *Id.* at 60-62.

101. *See infra* notes 176-78 and accompanying text.

102. About Us, http://www.ccrc.gov.uk/about.htm.

103. DEP'T OF JUSTICE (Can.), ANNUAL REPORT 2009, *available at* http://www.justice.gc.ca/eng/pi/ccr-rc/rep09-rap09/p2.html; *see generally* Gary T. Trotter, *Justice, Politics and the Royal Prerogative of Mercy: Examining the Self-Defence Review*, 26 QUEEN'S L.J. 339 (2001).

104. Criminal Appeal Act, 1995, § 8(2) (Eng.) ("The Commission shall not be regarded as the servant or agent of the Crown or as enjoying any status, immunity or privilege of the Crown; and the Commission's property shall not be regarded as property of, or held on behalf of, the Crown.").

105. *See, e.g.*, The Honourable Robert Douglas Nicholson, http://www.justice.gc.ca/eng/mag-mpg/index.html (last visited May 2, 2010).

106. DEP'T OF JUSTICE (Can.), ANNUAL REPORT 2008, *available at* http://www.justice.gc.ca/eng/pi/ccr-rc/rep08-rap08/02.html.

107. *Id.*

108. Patrician Braiden & Joan Brockman, *Remedying Wrongful Convictions Through Applications to the Minister of Justice*

Under Section 690 of the Criminal Code, 17 WINDSOR Y.B. OF ACCESS TO JUSTICE 3, 5 (1999).

109. DEP'T OF JUSTICE (Can.), ANNUAL REPORT 2008, http://www.justice.gc.ca/eng/pi/ccr-rc/rep08-rap08/02.html.

110. *Id.*

111. Criminal Law Amendment Act, 2002 S.C., ch. 13, *codified at* Criminal Code, R.S.C. § 696.3(3) (Can.).

112. DEP'T OF JUSTICE (Can.), ANNUAL REPORT 2009, http://www.justice.gc.ca/eng/pi/ccr-rc/rep09-rap09/p2.html.

113. Criminal Appeal Act, 1995, c. 35 § 13(2) (Eng.).

114. DEP'T OF JUSTICE (Can.), ANNUAL REPORT 2009, http://www.justice.gc.ca/eng/pi/ccr-rc/rep09-rap09/p2.html.

115. Applying for a Conviction Review, http://canada.justice.gc.ca/eng/pi/ccr-rc/app-dem/proc.html (last visited May 2, 2010).

116. *Id.* "New and significant information" must not be confused or compared with the Texas new-trial requirement of "material evidence favorable to the accused . . . discovered since trial." TEX. CODE CRIM. P. § 40.001. *See infra* notes 207-10 and accompanying text.

117. *Id.*

118. *See, e.g.*, Bruce A. Green & Ellen Yaroshefsky, *Prosecutorial Discretion and Post-Conviction Evidence of Innocence*, 6 OHIO ST. J. CRIM. L. 467, 491 (2009).

119. Applying for a Conviction Review, http://canada.justice.gc.ca/eng/pi/ccr-rc/app-dem/proc.html.

120. *Id.*; *see* Peter H. Howden, *Judging Errors of Judgment: Accountability, Independence & Vulnerability in a Post-Conviction Review Process*, 21 WINDSOR Y.B. ACCESS TO JUST. 569, 572 (2002).

121. James G. Bell & Kimberley A. Clow, *Student Attitudes Toward the Post-Conviction Review Process in Canada*, 2007 J. INST. JUST. INT'L STUD. 90, 94.

122. Applying for a Conviction Review, http://canada.justice.gc.ca/eng/pi/ccr-rc/app-dem/proc.html.
123. *Id.*
124. *Id.*
125. Criminal Law Amendment Act, 2002 S.C. ch. 13, *codified at* Criminal Code, R.S.C. § 696.3(3) (Can.).
126. *See* Green & Yaroshefsky, *supra* note 118, at 491-92.
127. *Id.* at 492.
128. Dep't of Justice (Can.), Annual Report 2009, http://canada.justice.gc.ca/eng/pi/ccr-rc/rep09-rap09/p2.html.
129. *Id.*
130. *Id.*
131. *Id.*
132. Criminal Law Amendment Act, 2002 S.C. ch. 13, *codified at* Criminal Code R.S.C. § 696.3(2) (Can.). This is worded in the statute as "refer[ring]." *Id.*
133. *See, e.g.*, Tex. Const. art. V, § 3-c(a) ("The supreme court and the court of criminal appeals have jurisdiction to answer questions of state law certified from a federal appellate court.").
134. *See, e.g.*, Horan, *supra* note 26, at 185 (calling for an "independent tribunal").
135. *Id.*
136. *Id.*
137. *Id.*
138. *See, e.g.*, Criminal Law Amendment Act, 2002 S.C. ch. 13, *codified at* Criminal Code R.S.C. § 696.2(1) (Can.).
139. Howden, *supra* note 120, at 572 (quoting parliamentary debate).
140. *Id.* at 586.
141. *Id.* at 572.

142. *Id.*
143. Applying for a Conviction Review, http://canada.justice.gc.ca/eng/pi/ccr-rc/app-dem/proc.html.
144. Bell & Clow, *supra* note 121, at 94.
145. Canada has a parallel system of provincial courts and a system of federal courts. *See, e.g.*, Department of Justice Canada, Canada's Court System, http://canada.justice.gc.ca/eng/dept-min/pub/ccs-ajc/page3.html (last visited May 2, 2010). However, unlike the American system, both tracks of courts fall under the Supreme Court of Canada. *Id.*
146. *See* Howden, *supra* note 120, at 586.
147. *Id.*
148. Applying for a Conviction Review, http://canada.justice.gc.ca/eng/pi/ccr-rc/app-dem/proc.html.
149. *Id.*
150. Trotter, *supra* note 103, at 355 n.58.
151. Applying for a Conviction Review, http://canada.justice.gc.ca/eng/pi/ccr-rc/app-dem/proc.html.
152. *Id.*
153. *Id.*
154. *Id.*
155. *Id.*
156. Criminal Law Amendment Act, 2002 S.C. ch. 13, *codified at* Criminal Code R.S.C. § 696.5 (Can.).
157. Regulations Respecting Applications for Ministerial Review - Miscarriages of Justice § 7 SOR/2002-416 (Can.).
158. *See* Criminal Conviction Review, http://www.justice.gc.ca/eng/pi/ccr-rc/index.html.
159. *See* Part I, *supra*.
160. Tex. Code Crim. P. § 40.001.
161. Drew v. State, 74 S.W.2d 207, 226 (Tex. Crim. App. 1987).

162. Wallace v. State, 106 S.W.3d 103, 108 (Tex. Crim. App. 2003).

163. *Id.* (citations and quotations omitted).

164. *See, e.g.*, Hannah Robertson Miller, *"A Meaningless Ritual": How the Lack of a Postconviction Competency Standard Deprives the Mentally Ill of Effective Habeas Review in Texas*, 87 TEX. L. REV. 267, 280 (2008).

165. Griffin, *supra* note 34, at 1269.

166. Miller, *supra* note 163, at 281.

167. *Id.* at 280 & n.84. *But see* Kelli Hinson, *Post-Conviction Determination of Innocence for Death Row Inmates*, 48 S.M.U. L. REV. 231, 232 (1994) (noting that traditionally habeas corpus was not seen as the favored avenue to discover new evidence).

168. *Id.* at 280.

169. *See* Carol S. Steiker & Jordan M. Steiker, *A Tale of Two Nations: Implementation of the Death Penalty in "Executing" Versus "Symbolic" States in the United States*, 84 TEX. L. REV. 1869, 1883-84 (2006).

170. Horan, *supra* note 26, at 111 (discussing the wrongful reliance of courts upon executive clemency); Daryl E. Harris, *By Any Means Necessary: Evaluating the Effectiveness of Texas' DNA Testing Law in the Adjudication of Free-Standing Claims of Actual Innocence*, 6 SCHOLAR 121, 128-29 (2003) (noting courts' reliance on the principle of finality).

171. *See* TEX. CONST. art. IV § 11(b) (discussing how a pardon is recommended to the governor by the Texas Board of Pardons and Paroles); Horan, *supra* note 26, at 111 (discussing the wrongful reliance of courts upon executive clemency).

172. *But see* Roberts & Weathered, *supra* note 36, at 44 (mentioning the success of a University-based innocence project in Canada).

173. Dep't of Justice (Can.), Annual Report 2009, http://canada.justice.gc.ca/eng/pi/ccr-rc/rep09-rap09/p5.html (noting statistical information).

174. Tex. Const. art. IV § 11(b) (giving the governor the power to grant pardons).

175. *Id.*

176. Texas Department of Criminal Justice, Statistical Report: Fiscal Year 2008 1 (2009); Texas Department of State Health Services, Estimated Texas Population by Area, 2008, http://www.dshs.state.tx.us/chs/popdat/st2008.shtm.

177. Public Safety Canada Portfolio Corrections Statistics Committee, Corrections and Conditional Release Statistical Overview 5 (2008).

178. *See, e.g.*, Innocence Project of Texas, About Us, http://ipoftexas.org/about-us/ (last visited Apr. 30, 2010); Texas Innocence Network, http://www.texasinnocencenetwork.com/index.cfm (last visited Apr. 30, 2010).

179. As applied to Texas, the most logical person to make a political appointment would be the governor or the attorney general.

180. Criminal Appeal Act, 1995, c. 35 § 8(2) (Eng.).

181. CCRC, About Us, http://www.ccrc.gov.uk/about.htm (last visited May 2, 2010).

182. Roberts & Weathered, *supra* note 36, at 48.

183. *See, e.g.*, Home Office, About Us, http://www.homeoffice.gov.uk/about-us/index.html ("The Home Office is the lead government department for immigration and passports, drugs policy, counter-terrorism and police.").

184. *See, e.g.*, 5 U.S.C. § 3331 (2006) (reciting the oath of office required of all Executive department employees).

185. The statute governing the USSC mandates that in a commission of seven voting members, no more than four members may be of the same political party. 28 U.S.C. § 991(a) (2000). Furthermore, as part of the judicial branch of government, the USSC must have at least three federal judges

as members. *Id.* Federal judges have essentially lifetime tenure in order to resist the influence of short-term political gain. U.S. Const. art. III § 1 (noting that the tenure for federal judges is "good Behaviour"); Maria Simon, *Bribery and Other Not So "Good Behavior": Criminal Prosecution as a Supplement to Impeachment of Federal Judges*, 94 Colum. L. Rev. 1617, 1655 (1994).

186. Tex. Const. art. III § 24a(a)(1).

187. *Id.*

188. *See* Mark Desnoyer, *In Through the Out-Door: Conflicts of Interest in Private-to-Public Service, Revolving Door Statutes, and Ethical Considerations*, 5 Tex. Tech J. Admin. L. 113, 120 (2004); Tex. Gov't Code § 571.061 (enumerating areas of enforcement by the Texas Ethics Commission).

189. *See, e.g.*, Texas Innocence Network, About Us, http://www.texasinnocencenetwork.com/About-Us.cfm (noting the independent, non-profit status of the organization); Innocence Project of Texas, FAQ, http://ipoftexas.org/faq/ (same).

190. *See, e.g.*, Tex. Const. art. 4, § 2.

191. CCRC, About Us, http://www.ccrc.gov.uk/about.htm.

192. Criminal Appeal Act, 1995, c. 35, § 8(2) (Eng.).

193. CCRC, About Us, http://www.ccrc.gov.uk/about.htm.

194. Criminal Law Amendment Act, 2002 S.C. ch. 13, *codified at* Criminal Code R.S.C. § 696.3(3) (Can.).

195. Trotter, *supra* note 103, at 355.58.

196. Canadian Department of Justice, Addressing Possible Miscarriages of Justice, Annual Report, http://www.justice.gc.ca/eng/pi/ccr-rc/rep08-rap08/02.html (2008).

197. Britton Douglas, *"That's What She Said": Why Limiting the Use of Uncorroborated Eyewitness Identification Testimony Could Prevent Wrongful Convictions*, 41 Tex. Tech L. Rev. 561, 564 (2009).

198. *See supra* notes 146-47 and accompanying text.

199. *See supra* notes 147-48 and accompanying text.

200. Texas Attorney General, Criminal Investigations, http://www.oag.state.tx.us/criminal/investigation.shtml (last visited May 2, 2010).

201. Texas Attorney General, Criminal Prosecutions, http://www.oag.state.tx.us/criminal/prosecution.shtml (last visited May 2, 2010).

202. Roberts & Weathered, *supra* note 36, at 59-62.

203. Griffin, *supra* note 34, at 1279.

204. Applying for a Conviction Review, http://canada.justice.gc.ca/eng/pi/ccr-rc/app-dem/proc.html.

205. *Id.*

206. *See supra* notes 37-38 and accompanying text.

207. *See supra* note 161 and accompanying text.

208. Tex. Code Crim. Proc. Ann. § 40.001 (Vernon 2006).

209. *See supra* note 162 and accompanying text.

210. *See, e.g.*, Keeter v. State, 24 S.W.3d 31, 36-37 (Tex. Crim. App. 2002).

211. *See supra* notes 156-58 and accompanying text.

212. Whether it is a real reflection of poor performance by the judiciary absolutely cannot be determined by the amount of convictions returned to the courts. As discussed above, the need for post-conviction review is caused by the failings of the entire legal system, not because of any political bent of any certain judges.

VI. Conclusion

Webster's Dictionary defines "justice" as the "assignment of merited rewards or punishments." But what should we think when innocent citizens are erroneously identified as criminals and punished for crimes they did not commit? Why should we, as a society, care when innocent citizens are wrongfully convicted?

Two stories stand out. Both of the innocent men were law-abiding military veterans who were attending college when they were misidentified as criminals. Both men, Timothy Cole and Anthony Robinson, were wrongfully convicted. Tragically, Cole died in prison before the true perpetrator was identified. The Texas Legislature later named an advisory panel in honor of Cole. Robinson was a bit more "lucky": he was freed from prison and subsequently proved his innocence. After his exoneration, Robinson graduated from law school and now serves on the board of directors of a Texas-based innocence organization. American society should care about wrongful convictions because, like Cole and Robinson, our children, siblings, friends, and coworkers also might be wrongly accused of crimes.

The articles in this anthology reveal that simple remedial measures would decrease the incidence of misidentification of suspects and the subsequent conviction of innocent citizens. Police departments should change their investigative practices with respect to interrogations, eyewitness identifications and the use of jailhouse informants so as to conform to the protocols advocated in this book. Basic procedural improvements could lessen the incidence of coerced confessions and eyewitness misidentification. Additionally, prosecutors and defense attorneys can provide reciprocal discovery so that both sides can properly investigate cases before trial. Broad reciprocal discover practice better enables lawyers to uncover the cases of the wrongly accused criminal justice system, long before they are convicted and punished. These measures are just a few of the reforms our criminal system needs to implement in order to lessen the likelihood that an innocent citizen is wrongfully accused and then convicted of a crime.

Other articles in this anthology address the procedures used to investigate possible cases of wrongful conviction, such as the availability of DNA testing and the use of innocence commissions. As the number of exonerations grows, there is further realization of the vast number of cases yet to be investigated. In cases in which DNA testing is available, procedural hurdles for obtaining testing would best be minimized. No better means of clearing a person's name exists, and it smacks of vindictiveness to deny an inmate testing for petty reasons. Jurisdictions might also explore the use of official, government Innocence Commissions as instituted in North Carolina and in other countries. The commissions offer many benefits unavailable to university-based innocence projects or individual defense attorneys.

One may wonder why police, attorneys, and judges have not already implemented these better practices. In fact, some have changed their practices, but most have not. Possible answers include inertia—the attitude that "we've always done things this way," or institutional pride—"we don't want outsiders telling us how to do our jobs." To some degree those attitudes persist, but much progress is taking place with the cooperation of the law enforcement establishment. Comprehensive innocence legislation in states like Ohio and New Jersey give other states much to emulate, and many have adopted smaller pieces of innocence legislation. In Texas the comprehensive work of the Timothy Cole Advisory Panel on Wrongful Convictions, which included prosecution and police representatives, has provided the legislature with many important reform recommendations. Prosecutors in Dallas and Houston now have conviction integrity units devoted to investigating claims of wrongful convictions. Perhaps the most important new development is the growing involvement law enforcement in addressing the causes of wrongful convictions. No one favors punishing the innocent and leaving criminals at large. The time has come for any remaining institutional pride to be put aside and for all participants in the criminal justice system to unite behind reform proposals. Innocent people should no longer be the victims of ineffective, inaccurate, and outmoded practices.

Righteousness demands that every morally conscientious person should favor a criminal justice system designed to be accurate and fair. Only when these criteria become our guiding principles can we hope to achieve justice in the age of innocence.